Italian and Italian American Studies
Stanislao G. Pugliese
Hofstra University
Series Editor

This publishing initiative seeks to bring the latest scholarship in Italian and Italian American history, literature, cinema, and cultural studies to a large audience of specialists, general readers, and students. I&IAS will feature works on modern Italy (Renaissance to the present) and Italian American culture and society by established scholars as well as new voices in the academy. This endeavor will help to shape the evolving fields of Italian and Italian American Studies by reemphasizing the connection between the two. The following editorial board consists of esteemed senior scholars who act as advisors to the series editor.

REBECCA WEST
University of Chicago

JOSEPHINE GATTUSO HENDIN
New York University

FRED GARDAPHÉ
Queens College, CUNY

PHILIP V. CANNISTRARO†
Queens College and the Graduate School, CUNY

ALESSANDRO PORTELLI
Università di Roma "La Sapienza"

Queer Italia: Same-Sex Desire in Italian Literature and Film
edited by Gary P. Cestaro, July 2004

Frank Sinatra: History, Identity, and Italian American Culture
edited by Stanislao G. Pugliese, October 2004

The Legacy of Primo Levi
edited by Stanislao G. Pugliese, December 2004

Italian Colonialism
edited by Ruth Ben-Ghiat and Mia Fuller, July 2005

Mussolini's Rome: Rebuilding the Eternal City
Borden W. Painter Jr., July 2005

Representing Sacco and Vanzetti
edited by Jerome H. Delamater and Mary Anne Trasciatti, September 2005

Carlo Tresca: Portrait of a Rebel
Nunzio Pernicone, October 2005

Italy in the Age of Pinocchio: Children and Danger in the Liberal Era
Carl Ipsen, April 2006

The Empire of Stereotypes: Germaine de Staël and the Idea of Italy
Robert Casillo, May 2006

Race and the Nation in Liberal Italy, 1861–1911: Meridionalism, Empire, and Diaspora
Aliza S. Wong, October 2006

Women in Italy, 1945–1960: An Interdisciplinary Study
    edited by Penelope Morris, October 2006

Debating Divorce in Italy: Marriage and the Making of Modern Italians, 1860–1974
    Mark Seymour, December 2006

A New Guide to Italian Cinema
    Carlo Celli and Marga Cottino-Jones, January 2007

Human Nature in Rural Tuscany: An Early Modern History
    Gregory Hanlon, March 2007

The Missing Italian Nuremberg: Cultural Amnesia and Postwar Politics
    Michele Battini, September 2007

Assassinations and Murder in Modern Italy: Transformations in Society and Culture
    edited by Stephen Gundle and Lucia Rinaldi, October 2007

Piero Gobetti and the Politics of Liberal Revolution
    James Martin, December 2008

Primo Levi and Humanism after Auschwitz: Posthumanist Reflections
    Jonathan Druker, June 2009

Oral History, Oral Culture, and Italian Americans
    edited by Luisa Del Giudice, November 2009

Italy's Divided Memory
    John Foot, January 2010

Women, Desire, and Power in Italian Cinema
    Marga Cottino-Jones, March 2010

The Failure of Italian Nationhood: The Geopolitics of a Troubled Identity
    Manlio Graziano, September 2010

Women and the Great War: Femininity under Fire in Italy
    Allison Scardino Belzer, October 2010

Italian Jews from Emancipation to the Racial Laws
    Cristina M. Bettin, November 2010

Anti-Italianism: Essays on a Prejudice
    edited by William J. Connell and Fred Gardaphé, January 2011

Murder and Media in the New Rome: The Fadda Affair
    Thomas Simpson, January 2011

Mohamed Fekini and the Fight to Free Libya
    Angelo Del Boca; translated by Antony Shugaar, January 2011

City and Nation in the Italian Unification: The National Festivals of Dante Alighieri
    Mahnaz Yousefzadeh, April 2011

The Legacy of the Italian Resistance
    Philip Cooke, May 2011

New Reflections on Primo Levi: Before and After Auschwitz
    edited by Risa Sodi and Millicent Marcus, July 2011

Italy on the Pacific: San Francisco's Italian Americans
    Sebastian Fichera, December 2011

Memory and Massacre: Revisiting Sant'Anna di Stazzema
    Paolo Pezzino, translated by Noor Giovanni Mazhar, February 2012

In the Society of Fascists: Acclamation, Acquiescence, and Agency in Mussolini's Italy
    edited by Giulia Albanese and Roberta Pergher, September 2012

Carlo Levi's Visual Poetics: The Painter as Writer
    Giovanna Faleschini Lerner, October 2012

Postcolonial Italy: The Colonial Past in Contemporary Culture
    Edited by Cristina Lombardi-Diop and Caterina Romeo, January 2012

Women, Terrorism and Trauma in Italian Culture: The Double Wound
    Ruth Glynn, February 2013

The Italian Army in Slovenia: Strategies of Antipartisan Repression, 1941–1943
    Amedeo Osti Guerrazzi, translated by Elizabeth Burke and Anthony Majanlahti, July 2013

Italy and the Mediterranean: Words, Sounds, and Images of the Post-Cold War Era
    Norma Bouchard and Valerio Ferme, September 2013

Italian Women Filmmakers and the Gendered Screen
    Edited by Maristella Cantini, December 2013

Forging Shoah Memories: Italian Women Writers, Jewish Identity, and the Holocaust
    Stefania Lucamante, June 2014

Italian Birds of Passage: The Diaspora of Neapolitan Musicians in New York
    Simona Frasca, September 2014

Berlusconism and Italy: A Historical Interpretation
    Giovanni Orsina, September 2014

George L. Mosse's Italy: Interpretation, Reception, and Intellectual Heritage
    Edited by Lorenzo Benadusi and Giorgio Caravale, September 2014

Thinking Italian Animals: Human and Posthuman in Modern Italian Literature and Film
    Edited by Deborah Amberson and Elena Past, September 2014

Thinking Italian Animals

Thinking Italian Animals

Human and Posthuman in Modern Italian Literature and Film

Edited by Deborah Amberson and Elena Past

THINKING ITALIAN ANIMALS
Copyright © Deborah Amberson and Elena Past, 2014.

Iovino, Serenella. "Storie dell'altro mondo. Calvino post-umano." *MLN* 129.1 (2014): 118–38. © 2014 Johns Hopkins University Press. Translated, revised, and reprinted with permission of Johns Hopkins University Press. Softcover reprint of the hardcover 1st edition 2014 978-1-137-45475-1

All rights reserved.

First published in 2014 by PALGRAVE MACMILLAN® in the United States—a division of St. Martin's Press LLC, 175 Fifth Avenue, New York, NY 10010.

Where this book is distributed in the UK, Europe and the rest of the world, this is by Palgrave Macmillan, a division of Macmillan Publishers Limited, registered in England, company number 785998, of Houndmills, Basingstoke, Hampshire RG21 6XS.

Palgrave Macmillan is the global academic imprint of the above companies and has companies and representatives throughout the world.

Palgrave® and Macmillan® are registered trademarks in the United States, the United Kingdom, Europe and other countries.

ISBN 978-1-349-49801-7   ISBN 978-1-137-45477-5 (eBook)
DOI 10.1057/9781137454775

Library of Congress Cataloging-in-Publication Data

   Thinking Italian animals : human and posthuman in modern Italian literature and film / edited by Deborah Amberson and Elena Past.
   pages cm
   Includes bibliographical references and index.
                                         1. Italian literature—History and criticism. 2. Motion pictures—Italy—History. 3. Animals in literature. 4. Animals in motion pictures. 5. Human beings in literature. 6. Human beings in motion pictures. 7. Ecocriticism—Italy. I. Amberson, Deborah, editor. II. Past, Elena, editor.

PQ4053.A55T48 2014
850.9'362—dc23   2014011514

A catalogue record of the book is available from the British Library.

Design by Scribe Inc.

First edition: September 2014

10 9 8 7 6 5 4 3 2 1

Contents

Acknowledgments	xi
Foreword: Mimesis: The Heterospecific as Ontopoietic Epiphany *Roberto Marchesini*	xiii
Introduction: Thinking Italian Animals *Deborah Amberson and Elena Past*	1

Part 1 Ontologies and Thresholds

1 Confronting the Specter of Animality: Tozzi and the Uncanny Animal of Modernism *Deborah Amberson*	21
2 Cesare Pavese, Posthumanism, and the Maternal Symbolic *Elizabeth Leake*	39
3 Montale's Animals: Rhetorical Props or Metaphysical Kin? *Gregory Pell*	57
4 The Word Made Animal Flesh: Tommaso Landolfi's Bestiary *Simone Castaldi*	75
5 Animal Metaphors, Biopolitics, and the Animal Question: Mario Luzi, Giorgio Agamben, and the Human–Animal Divide *Matteo Gilebbi*	93

Part 2 Biopolitics and Historical Crisis

6 Creatureliness and Posthumanism in Liliana Cavani's *The Night Porter* and Pier Paolo Pasolini's *Salò* *Alexandra Hills*	111
7 Elsa Morante at the Biopolitical Turn: Becoming-Woman, Becoming-Animal, Becoming-Imperceptible *Giuseppina Mecchia*	129

8   Foreshadowing the Posthuman: Hybridization,
    Apocalypse, and Renewal in Paolo Volponi   145
    Daniele Fioretti

9   The Postapocalyptic Cookbook: Animality,
    Posthumanism, and Meat in Laura Pugno and Wu Ming   159
    Valentina Fulginiti

Part 3   Ecologies and Hybridizations

10 The Monstrous Meal: Flesh Consumption
    and Resistance in the European Gothic   179
    David Del Principe

11 *Contemporaneità* and Ecological
    Thinking in Carlo Levi's Writing   197
    Giovanna Faleschini Lerner

12 Hybriditales: Posthumanizing Calvino   215
    Serenella Iovino

13 (Re)membering Kinship: Living with Goats in
    The Wind Blows Round and *Le quattro volte*   233
    Elena Past

Contributors   251

Index   255

Acknowledgments

We thank our contributors for their immense patience and generosity during the editing process and for all that they and their insightful essays taught us. A special thank you to philosopher Roberto Marchesini for contributing the thought-provoking foreword that opens our volume. We also thank Eleonora Adorni and Marchesini's other collaborators at the Scuola d'Interazione Uomo-Animale (SIUA) for their commitment to this project. We dedicate this volume to our families and companions, human and nonhuman.

Foreword

Mimesis

The Heterospecific as Ontopoietic Epiphany

Roberto Marchesini
Translated by Elena Past with the collaboration of Deborah Amberson

The ability/tendency to enter into synthesis with external reality seems to be a founding characteristic of the human being. The human incorporates otherness through mimesis, portraying this otherness in representations centered on his or her own body. Flesh becomes the first layer on which to write this making oneself other: painting the body, tattooing or scarifying it, transforming it into a sculpture, using it as a base on which to layer feathers or skins, moving it kinesthetically and rhythmically, or configuring it through gestures and facial expressions. The first form of art is therefore body art—more a way to experiment with the world of the other and to know oneself through the other than a way to show off: a way to exhibit the ability to metamorphose. Here, perhaps, we find in nuce the Baumgartian concept of art as a form (albeit imperfect) of knowledge,[1] since it is in the relationship with the other that the self becomes aware of the actual and virtual predicates of being. The embodied work, then, reveals itself to us as art that, through mimesis, is not a flat, passive adaptation to reality but a *mise en scène*: an interpretation of a reality that has been represented and transvalued.

For Plato, this second copy of the world becomes another phase in the degradation of the Idea by way of an analogical process—a photocopy of the photocopy—but for Aristotle, mimesis is above all knowledge, and it finds its foundation in human nature. For the Stagirite, "imitation is innate from man's infancy, and he distinguishes himself from other animals because he is more inclined to imitate" (Aristotle qtd. in Bertoli 232). Here we find two traits of mimesis: (1) the marked correspondence with human nature, from which, among other consequences, the hedonistic, curative, cathartic, and ecstatic effect of mimesis emerges, and (2) the epistemological aspect, connected on the one hand with the promotion of the marvelous, the driving force of knowledge, and on the other with its didactic role in showing what is verisimilar and necessary. We are thus confronted with an interpretation of mimesis that is anthropological (imitation as education) but also, as we would say today, ethological: imitation as part of human nature. Not by chance, in the *Poetics* Aristotle traces the pleasure caused by a work of art to an epistemic principle: "[T]o learn is an enormous pleasure not just for philosophers, but also for everyone else" (Aristotle qtd. in Bertoli 232).

Reinterpreting Mimesis

Mimesis, an aspect that characterizes the human being as a hybrid, opens us to readings of anthropopoiesis[2] (the human self-making shaped within the cultural sphere) that contest the idea of the emergence of identity as a self-referential process. The liminal interface of the human being not only is passively permeable by external influences but in fact constructs its morphodynamic condition using systems predisposed for referential acquisition. A plant fulfills its condition thermodynamically in nonequilibrium through its leaf structure, which, like photovoltaic cells, captures the flux of solar energy allowing for the maintenance of an orderly structure (we recognize here the postulates of Rudolf Clausius). In the same way, human identity, in all its complexity, is an unstable structure in marked nonequilibrium that can maintain itself only by acquiring information from the outside. Mimesis, thus, is our leaf structure. Some scholars, including Ugo Fabietti and Francesco Remotti, have underlined the dialogic significance of the emergence of identity in different cultures, emphasizing the structures of intercultural relations that, as bridges, allow for the continual mestizoization of different competences. If we consider complexity in terms of thermodynamic needs, mestizoization not only is clearly inevitable but also represents the very condition that allows complexity to emerge. Cultural identity is possible only through structures of mestizoization that capture external information in an active way.[3]

The ontogenetic process, too, requires a mimetic interpretation, one capable of surpassing both the self-referential formulation of the a priori educational model's concept of development and the concept of stimulation or external determination of the associative vision (the tabula rasa) of the behavioralist model.[4] Jean Piaget (Piaget and Inhelder) places imitation at the root of the evolutionary process, in a path that leads from relational mimesis (imitation in the presence of the thing to be imitated) to representational mimesis, by way of the phenomenon of deferment. The reference to a model is a leitmotiv in the interpretation of evolutionary processes evident in nearly all psychological schools: from the concept of the "secure base" in John Bowlby (1989) to the zone of proximal development in Lev Vygotsky (1973); from the function of "modeling" in Albert Bandura (1969) to imprinting in Konrad Lorenz (1989). Certainly today neurobiology (e.g., research on mirror neurons) has shown how mimetic activity develops (at least as an ability), especially in primates.[5] The permanent connection between observed act and thought act gives us all the more reason to read the ontogenetic process as a structuring of the evolutionary order (the phylogenetic legacy), according to the directions for growth offered by the external world. In this way, at the end of the ontopoietic process, identity reflects external reality by way of its own evolutionary legacy: each arboreal essence reflects the environment in which it grows, but it does so by way of the particular evolutionary organization of its own species.

Mimesis is thus the result of a dialogical process; it is an interpretation that anticipates the representation of the other through the evolutionary organization proper to identity. Thus it can never be regarded as a passive, generic assumption of the form of the other. In mimesis, we recognize (1) a projective process, since it is by way of one's own, internal, informational organization that otherness is reflected, and (2) an eccentrative process [*processo eccentrativo*], because through otherness one gains access to a new existential dimension, a form of being that changes in both an ontological and an epistemological sense. Otherness thus introjected does not limit itself to strengthening the inherent predicates of identity but rather redefines the dynamics of the system and the predicative domain—in other words, it modifies the predicates themselves.[6] Thus crumbles the pretense of considering the heteroreference to be juxtapositive and potentiating (in other words, the false opinion that holds identity assumption to be sedimentary-superstructural, and therefore deducible from the system at any moment or not able to change its internal qualities). With it crumbles the paradigm of the purity of identity. The ontopoietic process is always a hybridizing process that introduces new predicates. There remain two important questions to resolve: (1) if beyond mimetic capacity, there also exists mimetic propensity, or whether we can hypothesize a motivational foundation that brings the human to mimesis; (2) if, in the species-specific perimeter, there exists a Rubicon that cannot be crossed.

René Girard affirms that man's actions are determined by his desire to emulate; he thus defines a real desire/need for mimesis as the basis not just of learning processes but also of those frustrative drifts [*derive frustrative*] that can have problematic results, like the Oedipus complex and feelings of jealousy. Essentially, where a motivational languor exists[7] (translatable as a propensity to seek gratification through particular behavioral repertoires), it is not enough to refer to a simple ability. That is because what is compelling is the need, which indicates levels of expressive probability, frustrative vulnerabilities, an active search for a being to imitate. And what if mimesis were the result of a motivational convergence? We could identify the propensity to explore, to gather objects [*propensione sillegica*], and to compete as important vocational motors that make mimesis not simply a human ability but also a form of gratification. This could reconcile the Aristotelian notion of the imitative nature of the human being with Girard's notion of an intrinsic emulative desire in human action. Marcel Jousse underlines the child's natural and spontaneous tendency to represent the beings-events [*enti-eventi*] with which he comes into contact in movements and gestures, in a game that dramatizes the real and in a language that is above all a gesture. The display of this behavior in spontaneous play begins to confirm one or more innate motivational sources in the mimetic act.

If we assume a propensity to mimesis, there follows the Girardian idea of derived risks, like envy, but also the liberating use of dramatization, which can open a person's emotional flow either in an ecstatic sense (dragging the soul out of the self, following the Aristotelian vision) or in a palliative sense, projecting the frustration and individuation (shaping and making recognizable) of the source of suffering. Otherness, emulated, assumes the curative-cathartic meaning, made evident by Girard, that can lead to the topos of the scapegoat. The emulative propensity becomes a pressing need, a sense of impotence, an internal pang that can either become a malicious gaze or transform itself into empathetic participation. At times, the gap separating these two possibilities is extremely narrow. In her essay "Envy," Elena Pulcini recalls a Baconian statement that sees, in the state of proximity, the place where comparison becomes harsher. She rightly relates envy to comparison (1) "when it happens in a sector about which we care a lot, to which we give great value," and (2) when there is "the realistic possibility of competing with someone" (*L'invidia* 14). On the other hand the encounter can happen (1) within an elective proximity, if the need to prevail over the other with respect to the shared qualities is central, a need ascribable to a competitive logic and a frustrative risk, or (2) within a relational proximity, if what prevails is the encounter, the connection, the interaction, and admiration of diversity, ascribable to the desire for the other's predicate, valued because there is no overlap. If in the first case Girard is right when he underlines the triangular outcome of mimesis based on mediation—the model that surpasses us in the elective predicate—in the second case things become more complex.

Only initially does the relational encounter happen between two entities, because, in fact, the encounter adds two new mediative beings: (1) the introjection of the other as a new structural dimension of internal predicates and (2) the making-eccentric into the other, the transmutation from a simple phenomenon into an epiphany, the heralding of a new possible dimension. That is to say, we recognize an other that is no longer just a phenomenal entity but becomes an epiphenomenon, heralding an ontological dimension possible for the subject that welcomes it. As I have said, it is not mere imitation but rather inspiration: through mimesis, the subject is thunderstruck by otherness that is presented not as a phenomenon—or as a being-event that, although relevant, remains extraneous to the subject—but rather as an epiphany,[8] an appearance of the subject, and yet a subject irremediably changed by hybridization with the other. In mimesis the subject thus discovers a new existential dimension able to create an irreversible transformation.

At this point, in the guise of an epiphany, otherness is (1) introjected, or rather welcomed in a nonjuxtaposing way, since it is assumed in terms of a new organization of identity, and (2) eccentrative, capable of taking the subject to a centrifugal ontological plane with respect to his or her former state. In this sense mimesis, an ascent to a new existential dimension, has nothing to do with the malevolent gaze of someone who wants to annihilate otherness. If it is true that it comes from emulation and comparison, it is also true that it has more to do with interaction than with commensurability. The closer the other is to us in terms of relation or projection, the less overlap there is with respect to our predicates; the more intimacy, in terms of space and time shared, the greater the astonishment aroused; and the more unsettling the encounter and frequent the occasions for comparison, then the more probable is mimesis.

The Rubicon: Between Human and Nonhuman

The question that we must now consider is whether it is still tenable to define an insurmountable boundary [*limes*] that encloses ontopoiesis, and more generally anthropopoiesis, within an intraspecific mimetic space. In other words, does it make sense to assume an uncrossable Rubicon that can take on only interhuman mimetic references, or is it more consistent to admit that human mimesis does not recognize limits?[9] In this regard Jousse affirms that one of the fundamental characteristics of the child is the art of "playing at everything": to enact, mimetically, with his body, the characteristics of the reality with which he comes into contact. Making oneself into a nonhuman other, implicit in "playing at everything," reveals another opening toward the nonhuman as a propensity to play (a propensity that is gratifying and evolutionary) and underlines how the epistemic function follows a path that is more dialogical-projective than reifying. But in that case the term *other* refers not just to our fellow humans but to nonhuman reality—to everything, in fact. The reluctance of many philosophers and anthropologists to accept this occurrence serves as a litmus test that reveals the revolutionary significance of such an admission.

If we assume a real mimesis with nonhuman others, and not a simple instrumental use—performative or technical—of the Epimethean palette,[10] we in fact find ourselves recognizing in nonhumans a cofactoriality in the construction of the ontopoietic dimension: a dialogical-referential role and not simply an illustrative or phenomenal one. Animality, as a paradigm of the nonhuman, would suddenly be transferred from the phylogenetic dimension (the common Darwinian heritage of origins) to the cultural or anthropopoietic one, stripping the human of the pretense of ontological autonomy that is the core and the foundation of humanistic thought. The self-centered foundation, the idea that culture, the anthropopoietic dimension of the human, pertains entirely to the human being, is the load-bearing wall of the entire house of cards that is humanism. Without it, everything falls. Yet in the nonhuman universe reigns a sense of marvel and upheaval that can inspire sentiments of the beautiful and of the sublime, to recall the analysis of Edmund Burke.[11] If mimesis is relation, even before it is the dramatic representation of the other, the nonhuman can elicit a sense of order and harmony when in its phenomenal form; it can also evoke anxiety and instability when it appears as an epiphany, or when it announces unusual dimensions.

There is ample evidence of this hybridization with the heterospecific[12]—for example, the technical solutions developed by man, dance and martial arts, music and prosody, cosmetics and fashion, expressions of identity in costumes and heraldry, symbolic and semiotic structure, divination and the sketching [*tratteggio*] of divinity, taxonomic categories and the zodiac. These would all require a zooanthropological reading of cultures and cultural phenomena. These reasons push me to affirm that in crossing the interspecies Rubicon we have proven and can prove mimesis. But we would be wrong to consider artistic phenomena as a mere representation of the nonhuman in an anthropomorphic key, a postulate that would bring us to a pre-Romantic reading of creative expression and aesthetic evaluation as the imitation of nature, through the lens of classical objectivism.

Mimesis is rather the imitation of the natural process, or of a morphodynamic event, that causes a new ontic plane to emerge and cannot be subsumed in the beings that determined it. A few examples are in order. The tendency to represent both the form and the movement of the other, through movements of the body in the postural stasis of yoga or in the kinetic movement of dance or kung fu, determines on the one hand the incorporation of the heterospecific and on the other the anthropomorphic interpretation of it. In mimesis we thus witness a process of threshold [*soglia*],[13] the hospitality of otherness, and not a simple homologous representation of the phenomenon. A process of threshold indicates a double event of hospitality: (1) one that is centripetal, reorganizing one's own predicates in welcoming otherness, inevitably modifying the internal dynamic of the system and creating new varieties (hosting the other), and (2) another that is centrifugal, an eccentrative process of the hybrid being, conducted outside of one's ontic space in order to participate in new dimensions of being (being hosted by the other).

The Jousseau idea of assimilation is not sufficient to understand the concept of centripetal hospitality, because it tends to read introjection in an absorbing [*fagocitico*] or appositive way, in the two humanistic meanings of (1) complementative [*complementativo*] or exonerative (Gehlenian in origin) or (2) potentiative [*potenziativo*] of the predicates inherent in sociobiology. Hosting otherness means modifying the overall dynamics of the system and allowing new qualities to emerge. In the mimetic act, the human being modifies his ontopoietic space under the chiseling of otherness, which frees some predicates from their function, virtualizing them or stating them according to different coordinates. It shifts the constraints of the system and allows new, unforeseen predicates to emerge, changing the internal constituents and information that shape identity. The otherness that is assumed, in other words, enters into the system and changes it at all levels, not only in its phenomenal expression, but also in its teleodynamic one.[14] The grey crowned crane's courting ritual assumes, in the Maasai dance, a social significance, just as the predatory art of the spider acquires other functions in the technique of weaving. The hybridizer, like a virus, enters the cell that hosts it and changes its functions, creating a new metabolome.

There is thus good reason to linger on the phenomenal aspect of otherness, which can appear to simply express the technical provisions of the performing [*performazione*], or "how to reach a certain objective"—in this case, "flying," considered an objective already inherent in man, prior to mimesis. But such lingering does not help us fully understand the eccentrative coordinates implicit in this becoming other. Observing flight in the mimetic act implies an inspiritive [*ispirativo*] process, the emergence of a new objective (being able to fly) whose presence does not precede the act: mimesis cannot thus be reduced to the simple technical clarification of the means of reaching a goal; rather, it is the construction of a new existential dimension, a different plane of being, in teleodynamic terms as well. Considering the flight of a bird, mimesis reads not simply the phenomenon as such but also the "ontologic intentionality" of the phenomenon (the referential being for ontopoiesis = saying something about being) with respect to the observer. In other words, if it is true that the flight of a bird has the characteristics of a phenomenon—which can be admired or studied in its aerodynamic or divinatory characteristics—we can talk about mimesis in the full sense of the word (and not just an observation) when the observer does not see the flight of the bird as such but sees in that flight his own possible existential dimension. This is what I call the "epiphanic function of otherness": when the flight of a bird transcends the phenomenal aspect and says something that goes beyond the extraneousness of the phenomenon, taking on an inspiritive role of ontopoietic order.

Imitated otherness is thus not a mere reproposing but an interpretation, because the human being, in representing this otherness, stages not the phenomenon itself but the sought-after existential dimension (in this example, being able to fly). Otherness is neither the phenomenon nor the recognition of something that pertains to the not-self. Otherness emerges in activating the process of hospitality, or when the other is recognized as a being with-self, significant for a dialogic event. Only after this step does otherness manifest itself, no longer in the guise of the other-of-self but as a dialogic counterpart: at this point, the mimetic process can take place, not exclusively as representing or reproposing otherness, but even before, as a discovery of the epiphanic sides of the other. In the moment when the detached observer of an extraneous phenomenon (other-of-self) recognizes a state of conviviality with the other and makes him with-self, all the while maintaining the awareness of a different predication, he can at last find an other and not simply a phenomenon, not an extraneousness. Thus we can say that an other is a nonextraneous other, an other who sits at the table with me, an other with whom to dialogue.

We would be wrong to consider otherness in the two terms of other-of-self and of phenomenal entity. Otherness does not precede the relationship of threshold, the place that makes the natures of Hestia (welcoming) and Hermes (pilgrimage) converge. In the moment in which the agapic situation of the with-self is recognized, the bird-in-flight becomes a companion who can show another dimension of being and figure this dimension as a possible and thus translatable condition. The phenomenon becomes epiphany, annunciation, and no longer shows itself in the form of a bird that flies but of a with-self-in-flight. In mimesis thus converge a welcoming of transferal [*traslato*] and projection into the foretold dimension. The threshold relationship is thus an irresistible invitation extended by the other, a sort of ecstasy of one's own habit-familiarity. This sublimation can be understood in the sense of rising up obliquely [*limus*] toward the other (obliqueness can be explained by having, in the beings in dialogue, two contrasting vectors) and likewise in the sense of entering another dimension [*limen*] in a quantum or nongradual (solid-gaseous) way, requiring from the subject a form of abandonment.

Only in emerging from its statute of otherness is the other able to offer a referential structure that can say something that concerns us. This meaning paradoxically was encrypted from the moment the phenomenon was proclaimed, because of its clear extraneousness and thus its intrinsic nontranslatability. The other as companion, absorbing and attracting in a different dimension of being, enacts an inversion of the process, making the subject in a certain sense extraneous to himself. The relationship of threshold materializes (1) by way of invasion—that is, by a centripetal hospitality where the self makes itself Hestia and domesticates [*focalarizza*] otherness, transforming itself into an impersonal form moved by an other, delirious in being possessed—and (2) by way of eccentration or in centrifugal hospitality, characterized by an extraneousness based on the suspension of the *I*, seeing oneself in an oneiric or indirect way, through a distancing that allows reflexivity.

The relationship of the threshold determines the participation of the subject in otherness, the embodiment of otherness in self, which only in these conditions can become an epiphany. Consequently, it ushers in (1) a sense of expropriation of the self or of suspension of control over contingent circumstances, which lose familiarity; (2) a sense of amazement with respect to the unpredictable and excessive nature of the new dimension; (3) a sense of loss, which is marvel [*thaumazein*] but also trauma, horror, and thrill [*deinos*]; (4) a sense of inadequacy, of obeisance, dread, and trepidation, the fear of not being capable, inability to maintain the gaze, of proximity and of unreachability; and (5) an inspiration, lived as an extraneous breath, submersion in otherness that, in showing us its other dimension, allows us to enter into the condition itself, beyond the appearance of the phenomenon, rendering this last space inhabitable. Otherness allows us to experience a presence that redefines all the coordinates of the past and can project a new future: it is in this sharing that mimesis can represent a meaning.[15] All the mysteries of being able to fly are revealed to the human: all the possibilities and fascination inherent in this existential dimension, the sublime beauty of being in an aerial dimension.[16] Acquiring the technique of flight is a later moment, the consequence of a *quesito* (how to fly?) born in its turn of a desire (I want to be able to fly). It is evident that in order to desire something, one must have already been initiated into that dimension; for this reason, mimesis is a true act of initiation. Otherness revealed in an epiphany realizes this process of suspension and falling into the unknown, which disorients and attracts; it gives a sense of vanity-lack and on the contrary causes the assumptions of *hybris* to emerge. It dismisses the *I* but at the same time elevates it, making the process of mimesis or incorporation possible, inevitably diachronic. In this lies the recursiveness of the sublime, restoring what Baldine Saint Girons made evident: "[T]he main difficulty of a philosophy of the sublime depends on the circular causality that implements it" (13). This is because every hybridization makes the system more hybridizable, as I underlined in *Post-human*.

Mimesis as Knowledge and Hybridization

At this point two questions arise: (1) whether it is still possible to endorse the Baumgartian view of art as an imperfect form of knowledge and aesthetics as a science of sensible knowledge; (2) whether the idea of the artistic process as autonomous—in other words, the solipsistic creativity of the artist as formulated by post-Sophist humanist thought—is endorsable. If mimesis is no longer a simple imitation of an extraneous other but rather dialogue with an other, it is evident that the artist who pursues it combines (1) the predicates of the crazed person, in terms of obsession, excitement, frenzy, incontinence, enthusiasm, instability, possession, abnormality, and expressive degeneracy [*degenerenza*], which together give evidence of a being moved by a viral presence that stirs within his identity, and (2) the predicates of the ecstatic person, in terms of reflection, reference, intentionality, eccentration, loss, anxiety, nonequilibrium, and survival, which together indicate a being carried beyond the limits of identity. This is what I have defined as centripetal and centrifugal hospitality, where the sense of possession and eccentration represent an artistic sensibility more than a true process in the shamanic sense of the term. Furthermore, in this way it is possible to explain the attributes that Aristotle recognized in mimesis, like care and catharsis, and the role that mimesis has always had in mysticism and more generally in the religious sphere.

With respect to the first question, both possession and eccentration reveal the central themes of epistemological reflection: (a) the definition of the epistemic framework proper to the human ontic, and thus the modalities of aggregation and interpretation of the context, beginning with the virtual of the real; (b) the causal (and thus specifying) explanation of the a priori epistemic framework proper to the human ontic; and (c) the definition of the structures and the counterintuitive coordinates that allow us to assign a particular domain of validity to the human epistemic. It is possible to assign to point "b" a merely phylogenetic meaning—we aggregate from reality the beings/events that were relevant to our replicative ability. Yet an evolutionary explanation is not viable for understanding (1) the definition of an epistemic identity in its characteristic and specific traits, or the recognizability indicated in point "a," or (2) the suspension of that identity, the so-called naïve physics, and the appearance of a true epistemology by way of the activation of structures and coordinates of counterintuition, the emergence of what we indicated with point "c."

The definition of an epistemic identity (point "a") arises when this identity differentiates itself from an other: when a possession or an eccentration allows us to distance ourselves from its expression. It is in fact possible to delimit one's own epistemic identity only if an external referent is accessible, just as in order to see oneself, a mirror is necessary. Nonhuman otherness represents the most immediate mirror for recognizing human identity in its ontic profile and assigning it a valid epistemic domain. At the same time, it is by way of hybridization with nonhuman others that it is possible to construct other epistemes that can furnish new aggregations/interpretations of reality. In this regard, mimesis underlies the epistemological process and in fact renders possible an epistemology in the fullest sense of the term through (1) the problematization of the species-specific episteme in the double sense of individuation (delimiting and definition) and definition of a domain and (2) the arising of counterintuitive thought,[17] or an epistemic approach that transcends epistemic identity and makes possible new aggregations/interpretations within the virtuality of the real. From this we can deduce that art is not an imperfect form of knowledge but, on the contrary, the expression of that which renders knowledge possible. Art is the basis of knowledge.

Knowledge anticipates being able to use a foundation of stability/familiarity to project oneself into an unknown dimension, which in turn can construct a new "plane of reality"—to quote Speusippus as recorded by Aristotle[18]—and so to begin a new adventure. Leaning out into an unknown dimension remains dizzying, and one cannot make the transition without the assistance of an other: to construct this dialectic, the hybridizing process, which can open new epistemic dimensions, is indispensable. In art, we recognize such a conjunctive process in the relationship between the beautiful (stability) and the sublime (unknown). Knowledge is thus the moment when "conventional beauty" [*bellezza aderente*], the familiar, stable order, can make itself available because of its capacity to reflect on the being (to recover/recognize it) from an eccentrated perspective. It is also the moment when, in eccentration, one can produce that state of suspension that makes the real fluid, subject to new aggregations. The epistemological emergence thus happens in delimiting the anthropocentric episteme, thanks to the expropriation of the *I*.

Only by defining a domain of validity for the ontic is it possible to establish the premises for ontopoietics: mimesis's eccentration is fundamental to such a sublimating suspension. As Saint Girons makes evident, "with the sublime emerges a form of reality that calls us into question, shocking us [. . .] [T]he plot of coexistence is undone, the mirror of representation breaks into pieces, we are spellbound, that is to say, in the trap of our amazement" (i). Mirage, delirium, dizziness, sense of lack, the shipwreck of Leopardi in "The Infinite" ("*L'infinito*"), but otherwise enthusiasm, amazement, Panic participation, and synesthesia, from which comes the "sweet shipwreck" [*naufragare dolce*].[19] The sense of eccentration is likewise Fellinian melancholy, anticipation and suspension in the auroral magic of the appearance, and also twilight nostalgia. Eccentration removes the spatio-temporal referents of being, almost a conceptual oxymoron, by which the artist in mimesis is present through absence, renouncing gravitation itself and accepting expropriation. This introduces us to the second question, of whether the idea of a solipsistic creativity of autonomous origin (present in the humanist concept of mimesis) is acceptable. In this tradition, the artist is represented as a sort of demiurge capable of conceiving of his work autonomously, filling a disorganized space—a kind of *chora*—with his creativity. The origin of the artistic composition can come from the contemplation of nature; an inspired feeling; the world of ideas; the adoption of the point of view of another but in the context of the human universe; the connection (in intimacy) that causes the good and the true to converge; or freedom as a spontaneous impulse to the ethical imperative.[20] Yet in no way is the role of an immanent nonhuman other recognized. The devaluation of nonhuman animals, both in their instrumentalization (the reified animal) and in their projection (the animal *minus habens*), makes it difficult to recognize the role of otherness in the heterospecific. Generally, the animal other is assimilated in the concept of "animality" as a category opposed to elevation, a regressive pole. Both the Pichian concept of the "brute" and the Gehlenian one of "rank" anchor the heterospecific in a telluric dimension that establishes the counterterm to the process of elevation. If sublimation is conceived as languor toward the *apeiron*, transgression of limits, conjugation with the infinite, on the contrary the heterospecific represents the nomothetic, that which is finished and rigidly controlled by *ananke*, the principle of lack of freedom that is synonymous with relief or capacity to emerge from the background of *natura naturans*. The creative tightrope walk of the human being is thus positioned in the gray zone, which scholars of chaos theory call the "edge of chaos," a concept that brings together and separates the quiet order of Leopardi's "solitary hill" [*ermo colle*] from the magmatic evanescence of the infinite. In this interpretation the heterospecific, solidly animal, plays the role of that which restrains and impedes the flight toward the *apeiron* or else is the abyss that continually risks making us fall regressively into our feral nature [*ferinità*].

This vision represented the fulcrum of humanist thought, although with some contradictions. An example of this is the specular nature of the two conditions, often defined with the predicate of indistinctness applied to nature (seen as unpredictable, chthonic, horrible) and to the hyperuranium (read as evanescent, magmatic, disorienting). Humanism made the human being into its distinguishing figure, underlining his role as protagonist, able to aggregate worlds from the chaos of the indistinct, to make concrete a *hic et nunc* from atemporality, and thus to be not entirely shipwrecked in the infinite. Through a subtle dialectic between *apeiron* and *ananke*, the human being takes the guise of creator—a category that does not exist in nature, which is generative and not creative. But this humanist reading of mimesis makes the artist a virtuoso of solipsism, one who plays at everything, anthropomorphizing the nonhuman and thus subsuming every other entity. Measuring stick and container, this Vitruvian entity, which transforms the inevitably anthropocentered ontic into an anthropocentric ideology, equally celebrates autonomy and coextensiveness with the world, yet admits only an internal dialectic.

Posthuman Poetics

The humanistic sublime is a gaze upward that claims to ignore the contributions of every immanent other (translated as a counterterm and not as a form of support for the human tightrope walk), and thus eccentration is confused with purifying emancipation (in the sense of disjoining and distancing). Yet in the encounter with technological multiplicity, distilled from that thought, the premises for the suspension of anthropocentric solipsism are created. In the splendor of the *belle époque*, the mirror was overturned, decreeing the decline of humanism. Never again as in that moment has the salvific myth of technopoiesis been celebrated. Yet the exposure of the machinic cannot be simply a paean but solicits a comparison, causes a lack to emerge, and inaugurates a social dynamic that requires new rooting and new forms of aggregation of systemics. Electric light and speed solidify the sublimate in the arteries of the here and now, carrying it into the cinema and the bars just as in the factories". The sublime moves into less icy and ethereal terrain, rarefies the heroic and solipsistic impulse that characterized the nineteenth century, and celebrates totality, anonymity, and transience. The progressive disappearance of humanistic foundations, the feebleness of a form of thought that seems ever weaker, lays the ground for a major philosophical transition that rediscovers the significance of the other and exposes the groundlessness of a self-centered foundation of the human.

Among the shards of his existence, man searches for structures that can continue to connect him to the world, but in this way he seems to rediscover the mystery of his carnality and his animality. The sublime assumes ancestral form, which from the depths of the unconscious or psychic illness reemerges to bring about those suspensions of the *I*, in terms of order and rationality, that some decades before had characterized the encounter with infinite space.[21] In the Leopardian sublime, we discover a breath of comfort in an ethereal dimension, where the relationship between proximity and distance is centered on earth and sky. Today, the territories of inspiration seem to have been displaced to other regions, more subterranean and rhizomatic, more able to infiltrate and include themselves, fractal-like, in the self. The pluriverse of the *bíos* offers new, amazing conjunctions, and *thaumazein* and *deinos* take on carnal aspects. The sublime unravels in the ambiguous fascination of common ancestry; new physiognomic diagnostics; the atelier of eugenics; the Lagers that institutionalize the practice of vivisection; and the renewal of the ancient myth of Golem. The flesh emerges, exposed to search by machines that are ever more invasive and that, upending the telescope, transform the romantic finitude of the creature—in opposition to the immensity of sidereal space—into infinite and virtual morphopoetics. The flesh catalyzes the attention of the artist, who, transforming the body into a new palette, realizes a sort of "sarcomimesis" and discovers, with the same trepidation, the magma of hybrid possibilities. We find ourselves facing no longer a celebration of the beauty of the body but rather the encounter with the sublime in the body; it is no longer a given form but rather a virtuality that awaits mimesis in order to take shape.

If we examine the poetics of different authors and works—the somatic traces of colorful bodies in Salvador Dalì, Leni Riefenstahl's *Olympia* (1938), the theater of Antonin Artaud, Fritz Lang's *Metropolis* (1927), to name a few—we realize that the laboratory of mimesis in the first decades of the twentieth century experienced a severe shift from the hyperuranium to geographies of the body. We would be wrong, though, to consider this inversion of direction as an even more individualistic and solipsistic introflection. When in the 1960s these experiences mature into body art, the metamorphosis of this body, which makes itself sublime, becomes clear:

the body is no longer a tyrannized space of identity but a place of expression of otherness. We are entering that magical dimension that, annihilating every form of theatrics in the landscape, renders the body a unique convivial space—for example, in films like *Hawks and Sparrows* (*Uccellacci e uccellini*, 1966) by Pier Paolo Pasolini or Federico Fellini's *8½* (1963).

The dissolution of the territory through the fractal-like invasion of the human in every context and in the speed of transit—themes focalized by scholars like Marc Augé and Paul Virilio, and in Italy by Eleonora Fiorani[22]—make the body into a sort of forestage able to inaugurate new protagonists in the form of external actors. From a territory, the body metamorphoses into a landscape, through the organizing action of a new Neolithic, roused by otherness. Unique and indivisible identity, no longer the measuring stick for the world, wanes when it discovers that it is measured from the outside. The others transform it into a kaleidoscope, multiple and changeable (to cite Francesca Alfano Miglietti's image),[23] in which we discover the need for heteroreferential cofactoriality.

The body becomes inflected [*declinabile*], a space created in the welcoming act; from "representing the real," mimesis becomes a "making possible—actualizing the real." It can at last be recognized as the very act appointed to bring forth form from the virtual. We thus enter, although tiptoeing and with scant awareness, into a posthuman poetic—which upends the terms of classical aesthetics—where the role of the protagonist is delegated ever more to others. It is posthumanist and not antihumanist because it interprets this shift as a result of the humanist parabola. If the Copernican revolution created the premises for a sense of loss and for a closed encounter with nature, a feeling that reinforced the anthropocentric anchoring, the modern era nevertheless multiplied the references within the human continent, preparing the polycentric and pluriversal culture observed by Tzvetan Todorov in his *Discovery of America*.[24] Even Darwinism has been subverted in an emancipative sense—the evolution of man as an elevation of a natural condition—with the anthropocentric results visible in concepts of both incompleteness and fullness. Nevertheless, theories of common ancestry, adaptive specialization, and the plurality of the human family profoundly modified the portrayal of our presence on the planet.

In other words, the corrosive seeds that showed the self-constituted groundlessness of the human tightrope walk were planted within humanism itself. And the artists of the second half of the twentieth century were the first to show an inversion of the tendency, staging the human in new dramatic forms based on nonhuman otherness. Italo Calvino's *Cosmicomics* (*Le Cosmicomiche*, 1978 [1965]), the zoomorphic imagination of Tommaso Landolfi and Dino Buzzati, and *The Parafossil* (*Il parafossile*, 1967) by Giorgio Celli are just a few examples of this changing sensibility. The fragment "Sibelius Valzer" in the animated film *Allegro non troppo* (1976) by Bruno Bozzetto is interesting in this regard, showing us the memories of a cat who walks among the ruins of what used to be his house.

It is impossible not to grasp the poignant and revolutionary effect that makes the form of the house—a warm and emotionally charged space— take shape through the eyes of the cat. Paolo Volponi's *The Irritable Planet* (*Il pianeta irritabile*, 1994 [1978]) is from this period, and it represents a break with the previous work of Calvino and Pasolini (I am thinking of the unfinished work *Petrolio*, published posthumously in 1992) because it underlines a rethinking of the pact between the human and the nonhuman with respect to an apparent anthropocentric dystopia.

With an audacious shift of course, the artists of the second half of the twentieth century turn to the heterospecific pluriverse as a new dimension of the sublime, at once able to fascinate and disconcert, to exhibit an excess able to retaliate for the vacuousness of the only human, to be a revelation and at the same time to say something that man seems to have lost. The perception of an endangered biodiversity emphasizes its magnitude, and the artist above all lives and expresses fascination. But this fascination is not expressed through the topos of nostalgia, of a lost nature that must be found, of a golden age sublimated in the haze of prehistory, of innocence uncontaminated by superstructures. Rather, it finds a new infinity in which to shipwreck. The heterospecific is figured as one who has seen things that humans cannot even imagine. In the 1980s, we enter an age strongly characterized by animal thought. In Italy, these years see the flourishing of a poetic oriented at the sublime of contaminated nature, of a nonhuman who makes his way in the interstices of a forestage that transforms *Dasein* into a threshold of conjunction between theriomorph and technomorph. The *doppelganger* is no longer a shadow or a zombie who, walking beside us, merely appears but rather a hybrid able to incarnate an even more profound being, like the replicant Roy Batty in Ridley Scott's *Blade Runner* (1982).[25]

And thus the heterospecific can show the potential and the epiphanic character it has always had in human culture, as an epistemic intermediary and poetic engine, able to open new existential horizons to the human because it can establish a relationship with man and not just serve as a phenomenon to admire or imitate. Artists like Orlan, Daniel Lee, and Matthew Barney bring to light the apparent paradox of becoming human through zoomimesis, showing us morphopoetic works that lend evidence of the vulnerability, the transitory nature, the imbalance, the openness, the being an "open site," and the lack of a predetermined ontological direction: the most authentic predicates of the human condition. And in Italy such experiments find synthesis in the "theriomorphic manifesto," which declares the hybrid nature of art, along with the cofactoriality of the heterospecific in artistic expression. Within this multiform laboratory, at the end of the 1990s, we find authors like Karin Andersen,[26] who works to blur the boundary between human and nonhuman in a logic of overcoming the nature–culture dichotomy, and Massimo Deganutti,[27] who criticizes speciesism and creates space for a poetics we can call authentically "postspecies."

In conclusion, the posthumanist aesthetic that arises in Italy stems from a philosophical and poetic approach that is significantly different from the paradigm in other countries (I am thinking of the work of authors like Peter Sloterdijk or Francis Fukuyama). In Italy, what is central to the discussion is not so much the posthuman perspective of the hybrid man or man strengthened by technology but rather the critique of the humanistic interpretation of the human condition: the autonomy and autopoiesis of becoming human that characterized humanism.[28] In this sense, the heterospecific assumes a privileged role—not, of course, an exclusive one—because it represents the elective alterity [*alterità elettiva*] with which we have always compared ourselves. Postulating a dialogic role for the heterospecific, we recognize its epiphanic significance, an inescapable property to go beyond the phenomenal, becoming the herald of new existential dimensions. The heterospecific thus becomes a being able to disclose contents and contradictions by way of its absence, like in the novel *The Lament of the Linnet* (*Il cardillo addolorato*, 1997 [1993]) by Anna Maria Ortese, or in Fellinian epiphanies such as the appearance of the bull in the fog in *Amarcord* (1973) or the manta at the end of *La dolce vita* (1960). The animal epiphany no longer adopts the guise of an omen, a litmus test of a world partially accessible to the human, but rather becomes an active presence able to break open the human system and introduce new, restructuring seeds.

Notes

1. In Baumgarten's work, a concept of the aesthetic as a gnoseological moment is already present, a moment in which knowledge is given through a relational experience with the external world. For Baumgarten, knowledge, far from being explained in rational terms, is the result of a sensory knowledge revealed through art and beauty. These are thus not autonomous areas of experience but an important moment in the act of knowing.
2. The concept of anthropopoiesis is a pivotal element of the thought of Italian anthropologists Francesco Remotti (who coined the term in the 1990s) and Ugo Fabietti. Literally the "construction of man," the anthropopoietic process delineates the mechanisms of constructing identity proper to man (anthropos) by way of an introjection and reshaping of the examples offered by the external world (other forms of humanity, animals, nature). Anthropopoiesis can thus be defined as an open site, a continual state of becoming. Mimesis fully responds to this process: observing the outside-of-myself through

the lens of imitation, I can appropriate (introjecting and shaping them) new "forms of humanity."
3. Aside from the genetic connotations to which it could incorrectly be linked, the term "mestizoization" [*meticciamento*] (like "creolization," "synchretism," etc.) is a strong suit of contemporary anthropology, describing a possible result of the process of acculturation. In *Mestizo Logics* (*Logiche Meticce*), however, Jean-Loup Amselle is critical of the term, since using it thus presupposes that "pure" identities existed and still exist, identities which, interweaving themselves, give rise to mestizoization: a sort of multicultural logic that is the other face of classificatory logic. My use of the term, though taken from the anthropological tradition, is traceable to a wider logic that transcends ethnic and cultural difference, a "contamination" that is interspecific (human/heterospecific, human/machine) from the beginning, not subject to the construction of pure and autonomous "identities."
4. Relevant on this topic are Konrad Lorenz's theses in the essay *The Other Face of the Mirror* (*L'altra faccia dello specchio*, 1974), a book that partially reclaims inductivism, attributing to it not so much an ontogenetic but rather an evolutionary expression. Lorenz demonstrates that our way of approaching the world—in other words, both the sum of possible experiences, from a sensorial and cognitive point of view, and the type of conjectures formulated about phenomena—is not absolute. It is not a prescientific form (a priori expectations freed from the object of knowledge, as Kant suggested) nor a form of complete openness to the world (i.e., in a perspective of pure inductivism). But neither is it removed from the influence of the world, as detractors of objectivity would have it. Knowledge, understood as an investigative potentiality of reality, assumes local, circumstantial characteristics, because it is a legacy of the phylogenetic process. In other words, the anthropomorphic episteme is no more than one of the many expressions of a relation to the world.
5. With the discovery of mirror neurons in Broca's area and in the inferior parietal cortex, the team at the University of Parma led by Giacomo Rizzolatti opened fertile ground for reflection on the relationship between neurobiology and culture. The "neurons of culture," as Rizzolatti terms them, are activated when an observed action induces the activation of the same nervous circuit that controls its execution in the observer: it induces, that is, the simulation of that very action. We can intuit the importance of mimetic observation in processes of knowledge and for culture. Vittorio Gallese, neurophysiologist and part of the team that discovered mirror neurons, observed,

> [W]hat happens in our brain when we observe communicative gestures of a person speaking, of a monkey communicating by

lipsmacking (a rhythmic opening of the lips, an affiliated gesture that indicates to his conspecific the absence of aggressive intentions), a dog that barks? [...] When we see a man speak, we observe a bilateral activation of the pre-motor system that includes Broca's area; when we see the monkey, we observe a pre-motor bilateral activation with reduced intensity; finally, when we see the dog bark there is a complete absence of motor activation. The results of this experiment tell us [...] that motor resonance is not necessary to understand what we see: I know perfectly well that there is a dog barking, but the nature of my comprehension of the barking dog is very different from the nature of my understanding that a man is talking. (200)

Mimesis thus presupposes an intentional knowledge that is not just imitation (a man that reproduces the barking of a dog) but the introjection of a specific comprehension created in part by my feeling in "assonance" (for reasons that are species/cultural/social specific, etc.) with my external referent.

6. In other contexts (Marchesini "Ruolo delle alterità"; *Il tramonto dell'uomo*; "Riflessioni per una filosofia postumanista") I have underlined how alterity, introjected, acts as a virus capable of inserting in the human system new codes for genetic replication and is not simply a potentiator of preexisting abilities. See in particular *Il tramonto dell'uomo* (9).
7. The motivational horizon is in fact always internal to the subject: it is that which sustains forms of choice. By way of the motivational lens, the world becomes interlocutive and transactional, irreducible to the merely pragmatic role proper to its negation. Languor opens the door to the identity of the subject and initiates him in the rite of contamination: excess transforms the transreality of the subject into heteroreference. Languor presents itself as an inexpressible condition of precariousness in its own state and of ecstasy or highly imaginative openness in totality.
8. I have written elsewhere (Marchesini and Tonutti) of the epiphanic/phenomenal character of alterity. The relational appeal does not just indicate a stupefying or narcotic effect but, vice versa, implies a deep contributing factor to human identity. The most important contribution regards the decentering effect that determines the human being in general and the subject in episodic occurrence. In other words, in the encounter with the heterospecific and in the appearance of the epiphany of otherness, a flux of crises begins: man is pushed on a path of distancing from his phylogenetic center. Making oneself animal, emerging from the dialogic fascination of the heterospecific, in the epiphany of otherness, initiates the cultural phenomenon and the transformation of the ontological dimension of the human being.

9. Speaking of the autonomistic view of Alfred Kroeber, for whom in animals there is only a weak, rudimentary, immature form of culture, Francesco Remotti defines the "Rubicon model," an explanatory model postulated to sanction an irremediable gap (from a qualitative point of view) between humans and animals. The Italian anthropologist Sabrina Tonutti, taking up that passage, writes, "[T]he animal world, notwithstanding its enormous internal variety and its irreducibility to a single figure, is thus compressed into a role of antithetical counterpart in the definition of culture of alterity, functional for the selection of a specifically human identity" (33). The Rubicon model has thus been an "anthropological machine" (Agamben) in that disjunctive construction between the human and the rest of the living world into which today, in man's exploitation of heterospecifics, we find ourselves to have fallen again.

10. On various occasions I have discussed how the myth of Prometheus, which sees the Greek god as the dispenser of fire and *technē* (culture) to man, should be overturned, looking instead at his brother Epimetheus, who, forgetting man while bestowing animals with natural gifts, condemned us to biological incompleteness. In the interaction with the other there emerges a lack that permitted man to distance himself from his species-specific dimension toward new existential possibilities. If our species in its phylogenetic character expresses the Promethean force of openness to the outside, the human dimension, as a result of hybridization, is Epimethean, or traceable to nonhuman contents on which the human is based. This means that the nonhuman has not only an economic, ecological, instrumental, or aesthetic value but also an ontological value for the human.

11. "The sublime is the echo of a great soul" (33), wrote Pseudo-Longinus in the first century AD in one of the most important texts on the aesthetics of the sublime, *On the Sublime*. This category has been amply surveyed by many thinkers starting in antiquity: in the medieval and classical periods the sublime represented "a more precious style than the high style" (Carrera 205), while in modernity there was a transition from the literal to the natural. Thus the sublime—from Edmund Burke to Giacomo Leopardi, by way of Immanuel Kant—came to define something able to provoke ideas of fear and pain. For Kant, "sublime is not so much that which seems surprising in the natural world, but rather the ability that man has to contemplate. Neither nature or the infinite are in and of themselves sublime, but rather the particular conflicts that they trigger in the perceiving subject" (Carrera 206). Sublime is thus that which is born in the intimacy of the subject in the face of vague and unknown images that, escaping the imagination's restraint, provoke in him fear and dread and a sense of abandonment.

12. In the book *Animal Appeal: Uno studio sul teriomorfismo* (Marchesini and Andersen), the fascination that the heterospecific has always inspired in man is central. A kind of enchantment caused man to make animal codes his own in order to re-present them, in hybrid guise, in representation. In fact, "through the theriomorph, man continues to supply himself or to contaminate himself, simultaneously reducing the divide between himself and the animal and between himself and God, or the image that he has of the divinity. This means that the cultural opportunities of man are in no way freed from the presence of the animal: a world stripped of animals would inevitably be suffocating [*anossico*] for the culture of man" (21).
13. I look at the concept of threshold not as an insurmountable limit [*limes*] that separates two self-referential dimensions. Rather, as I have expressed elsewhere, "perceiving a threshold signifies recognizing an other, knowing in that moment, that the Hermes that resides in each one of us has to ask 'permission' of Hestia, goddess of the threshold, point of conjugation and of division between two worlds, the navel that indicates a symbiotic communion but also diversity. Recognizing a threshold is thus the condition of dialogue, of commerce, the exchange of difference, reciprocal respect" (*Concetto* 11).
14. I take this concept from anthropologist Terrence Deacon's *Incomplete Nature: How Mind Emerged from Matter*, where Deacon describes a teleodynamic system as "a dynamical form of organization that promotes its own persistence and maintenance by modifying this dynamics to more effectively utilize supportive extrinsic conditions" (270). For Deacon, every complex organism is dissipative, or tries, in an energetically wasteful fashion, to oppose the second principle of thermodynamics, which says that each system tends, over time, to reach a balance from a phase of entropy. In this way, it becomes a teleodynamic system, or a system with the goal of conservation.
15. The anthropologist Christoph Wulf discussed the social aspects of mimesis in *Mimesis: Art and Its Models*—"[T]he mimetic processes influence the relationship of man with nature, with society, and with others" (47)—highlighting that this phenomenon is an unavoidable assumption of sociability itself, a social mimesis.
16. The expressive style of the heterospecific, revealed through mimesis, becomes a *habitus* or existential model, uniting bodily anatomy, functionality of equipment, and behavior, so that each aspect is related to the others as if they were gears in a machine. The flight of the heterospecific thus permits one to move beyond the traits of another possible dimension to elements of beauty and the sublime, languor and surrender, inducing a redefinition in/of the subject.
17. In this regard, Gaston Bachelard's concept of the "epistemological obstacle" is useful, as is Lewis Wolpert's notion of science as counterintuitive. For Bachelard the "epistemological error" is not a true

error but rather a structure of knowledge that characterizes the movement of scientific thought. The scientist deforms reality that he analyzes through his own interests; subjective involvement thus spoils, obstructs, the scientific spirit. Wolpert affirms that science, rather than explaining the "nonfamiliar" to render it in *familiar* terms, often uses an inverse process, explaining the familiar in nonfamiliar terms.

18. In the *Metaphysics*, Aristotle in fact writes, "[S]ome hold that nothing exists beyond the sensible, while others hold that there are various eternal realities endowed with a higher grade of being, like Plato, who proposes three planes of reality [. . .] Speusippus, instead, proposes various planes of reality starting from the One, and proposes principles for each of these, one of numbers and one of different sizes, and then a principle of the animal; he thus extends the numbers of the planes of reality" (Aristotle qtd. in Berti 14).

19. Useful here are the concepts of "vague" [*vago*] and "indefinite" [*indefinito*] as they emerge in "*L'infinito*," where the hedge that "excludes the edge of the horizon / from much of the gaze" can inspire vague and indefinite ideas (the infinite) about what is hidden beyond. For Leopardi such images are a source of pleasure and, as such, of compensation for a life that otherwise would be "mud," as he writes elsewhere. Such images, to Leopardi's minute scrutiny, permit the soul to open itself to the undefined in a tension that is already pleasure. The concept of the "sublime" as presented in Leopardi's work (of which "*L'infinito*" is the highest expression) is without a doubt central to this essay's argument. Beyond Leopardi's hedge, "where my heart is almost frightened," there is darkness, the unknown, the infinite forces of nature that leave the poet in a state of enervated happiness, after having been ricocheted from perception to imagination. The sublime is thus that sensation of pleasurable abandonment (almost ecstasy) experienced when we are unable to grasp with reason. On this topic, see Carrera, *La distanza del cielo*.

20. On this topic, Giulio Preti wrote in the introduction to Schelling's *Figurative Arts and Nature* (*Le arti figurative e la natura*) how German Romanticism saw aesthetics as "an encounter, in the intimacy of the internal conscience, of the beautiful, the good, and the true," a sort of *Kalokagathia*, so the external is simply a phenomenal expression of the internal (12).

21. The "baboon grandfather," as Zola described him, assumes the shape of the troublesome lodger, legacy of a past from which we want to be freed, but equally able to emerge from the dark depths of the human being. Consider also the criminal anthropology launched by Cesare Lombroso, but also decadent poetry.

22. I recall here Augé's disquisition on the nonplace (which he in part takes from Michel de Certeau's *The Practice of Everyday Life*

[*L'invenzione del quotidiano*, 2001]) as spaces characterized by surmodernity, where a process of depersonalization of space is in force. These are nonrelational spaces, nonhistorical and non-identity-based, which Augé counterposes to anthropological spaces. The philosopher and urbanist Paul Virilio has dedicated much time to relationships between space, power, speed, and technology; the degraded urban environment is a space linked to unemployment and to the economic, social, and global instability of the environment. Fiorani makes evident the different forms of anthropological change that we are witnessing today, arguing that the ecological crisis is perhaps one of the most evident, with its loss of landscape, together with the loss of our bodies and our senses.

23. Miglietti speaks of *mutant identities* [*identità mutanti*] to indicate bodies that emerge from a network of contamination that passes from the body's flesh, to a flesh/technology contamination, to machines, and that often finds expression in an art that migrates from messages to devices.
24. Todorov and Mikhail Bakhtin have also underlined that the human is not the keeper of sovereign power regarding his own identity. Instead, identity derives from a process with many centers—polycentric—that finds its being and its becoming in its dependence on the outside.
25. In *Blade Runner*, Roy Batty affirms, "I have seen things that *you humans* can't even imagine," an affirmation charged with potential because it highlights an eccentrative significance that uproots the human from his autonomous, autopoietic domain to restore him to a stage where both humans and nonhuman others take part in the performance.
26. For an idea of Andersen's artistic production, see http://www.karinandersen.com.
27. Deganutti's *Post-Species Manifesto* is available at http://www.massimodegas.com/index.php?post-specie-art#eng.
28. The focal point of posthumanist thought—and, in my opinion, the only practicable path in the future—is based on the ability to recognize the conjunctive significance of technology and the importance of the other, of the heteroreferent, in order to concretely recognize the inflection of the human being. Technological development is doubly tied to the safeguarding of the nonhuman basin, because it is the other pole that allows the cultural flame to spark.

Works Cited

Agamben, Giorgio. *L'aperto. L'uomo e l'animale.* Turin: Bollati Boringhieri, 2002.

Alfano Miglietti, Francesca. *Identità mutanti. Dalla piega alla piaga: Esseri delle contaminazioni contemporanee.* Genoa: Costa e Nolan, 1997.

Amselle, Jean-Loup. *Logiche meticce.* Turin: Bollati Boringhieri, 1999.

Aristotle. *Metafisica.* Milan: Rusconi, 1997.

Augé, Marc. *Nonluoghi: Introduzione e una antropologia della surmodernità.* Milan: Elèuthera, 1993.

Bachelard, Gaston. *La formazione dello spirito scientifico: Contributo a una psicoanalisi della conoscenza oggettiva.* Milan: Raffaello Cortina, 1995.

Bakhtin, Mikhail. *Dostoevskij: Poetica e stilistica.* Turin: Einaudi, 1968.

Bandura, Albert. *Social Learning and Personality Development.* London: Holt, Rinehart and Winston, 1969.

Baumgarten, Alexander Gottlieb. *Aesthetica.* Hildesheim: Olms, 1986.

Berti, Enrico. *In principio era la meraviglia: Le grandi questioni della filosofia antica.* Bari: Laterza, 2007.

Bertoli, Enrico. *Sumphilosophein: La vita nell'Accademia di Platone.* Bari: Laterza, 2010.

Bowlby, John. *Una base sicura: Applicazioni cliniche della teoria dell'attaccamento.* Milan: Raffaello Cortina, 1989.

Burke, Edmund. *Inchiesta sul bello e il sublime.* Palermo: Aesthetica, 1985.

Calvino, Italo. *Le cosmicomiche.* Turin: Einaudi, 1978 (1965).

Carrera, Alessandro. *La distanza del cielo: Leopardi e lo spazio dell'ispirazione.* Milan: Medusa, 2011.

Celli, Giorgio. *Il parafossile.* Milan: Feltrinelli, 1967.

Deacon, Terrence William. *Incomplete Nature: How Mind Emerged from Matter.* New York: W. W. Norton, 2011.

De Certeau, Michel. *L'invenzione del quotidiano.* Rome: Lavoro, 2001.

Fabietti, Ugo. *Antropologia culturale: L'esperienza e l'interpretazione.* Bari: Laterza, 1999.

Fiorani, Eleonora. *Il naturale perduto.* Bari: Dedalo, 1989.

Fukuyama, Francis. *La fine della storia e l'ultimo uomo.* Milan: BUR, 2003.

Gallese, Vittorio. "Dai neuroni specchio alla consonanza intenzionale. Meccanismi neurofisiologici dell'intersoggettività." *Rivista di psicoanalisi* 50 (2007): 197–208.

Girard, René. *Anoressia e desiderio mimetico.* Turin: Lindau, 2009.

Jousse, Marcel. *Antropologia del gesto.* Rome: Edizioni Paoline, 1979.

Leopardi, Giacomo. *Tutte le opere di Giacomo Leopardi.* Vols. 1–5. Ed. Francesco Flora. Milan: Mondadori, 1945–67.

Lorenz, Konrad. *L'altra faccia dello specchio: Per una storia naturale della conoscenza.* Milan: Adelphi, 1974.

———. *L'anello di re Salomone.* Milan: Adelphi, 1989.

Marchesini, Roberto. *Il concetto di soglia.* Naples: Theoria, 1996.

———. *Post-human: Verso nuovi modelli di esistenza.* Turin: Bollati Boringhieri, 2002.

———. "Riflessioni per una filosofia postumanista." *Bioetica e Società* 1–2 (2012): 38–47.

———. "Ruolo delle alterità nella definizione dei predicati." In *Apocalisse e post-umano. Il crepuscolo della modernità*, ed. Pietro Barcellona, Fabio Ciaramelli, and Roberto Fai, 33–56. Bari: Dedalo, 2007.

———. *Il tramonto dell'uomo: La prospettiva post-umanista*. Bari: Dedalo, 2009.

Marchesini, Roberto, and Karin Andersen. *Animal Appeal: Uno studio sul teriomorfismo*. Bologna: Hybris, 2003.

Marchesini, Roberto, and Sabrina Tonutti. *Manuale di zooantropologia*. Rome: Meltemi, 1999.

Ortese, Anna Maria. *Il cardillo addolorato*. Milan: Adelphi, 1997 (1993).

Pasolini, Pier Paolo. *Petrolio*. Turin: Einaudi, 1992.

Preti, Giulio. "Introduzione." In *Le arti figurative e la natura*, by Friedrich Schelling, 7–38. Milan: Alessandro Minuziano Editore, 1945.

Piaget, Jean, and Barbel Inhelder. *La psicologia del bambino*. Turin: Einaudi, 1982.

Pseudo-Longinus. *Del sublime*. Milan: BUR, 2012.

Pulcini, Elena. *L'invidia: La passione triste*. Bologna: Il Mulino, 2011.

Remotti, Francesco. *Contro l'identità*. Bari: Laterza, 1999.

———. "Introduzione." In *Antropologia dei modelli culturali*, by Alfred Kroeber, 7–21. Bologna: Il Mulino, 1976.

Rizzolatti, Giacomo, and Corrado Sinigaglia. *Mirrors in the Brain: How Our Minds Share Actions and Emotions*. Oxford: Oxford UP, 2006.

Saint Girons, Baldine. *Fiat lux: Una filosofia del sublime*. Palermo: Aesthetica, 2003.

Sloterdijk, Peter. *Devi cambiare la tua vita: Sull'antropotecnica*. Milan: Raffaello Cortina, 2010.

Todorov, Tzvetan. *La conquista dell'America: Il problema dell'altro*. Turin: Einaudi, 1992.

Tonutti, Sabrina. "La cultura come dispositivo di differenziazione tra uomini e animali." In *Manuale di zooantropologia*, ed. Roberto Marchesini and Sabrina Tonutti, 9–85. Rome: Meltemi, 1999.

Virilio, Paul. *Città panico: L'altrove comincia qui*. Milan: Raffaello Cortina, 2004.

Volponi, Paolo. *Il pianeta irritabile*. Turin: Einaudi, 1994 (1978).

Vygotsky, Lev Semyonovich. *Immaginazione e creatività nell'età infantile*. Rome: Editori Riuniti, 1973.

Wolpert, Lewis. *La natura innaturale della scienza*. Bari: Dedalo, 1992.

Wulf, Christoph. *Mimesis: L'arte e i suoi modelli*. Milan: Mimesis, 1995.

Introduction

Thinking Italian Animals

Deborah Amberson and Elena Past

Meditating on the curious status of the Iguana who lives and works for a family of dissolute Portuguese noblemen, the protagonist Daddo in Anna Maria Ortese's novel *The Iguana* (*L'Iguana*, 1965) muses, consoling himself, that "only the greatest philosophers and most elevated scholars can begin (perhaps) to tell us where the animal ends and where the true human being commences; to say nothing, then, of the way such differentiations grow ever more tenuous with the flowering of civilization, and of how one is often uncertain as to which of the two castes is encroaching upon the other" (112). As his relationship to the Iguana transforms throughout the novel, Daddo's uncertainty in the face of the purported border dividing the human from the animal echoes a line of questioning that has been driving discussions across the humanities in the past decade.

Recent years have witnessed an upsurge of interest in the nonhuman animal within the humanities. One of the defining features of this academic attention to animality, evident in multiple conferences, symposia, volumes, special issues, and monographs, is its interdisciplinarity. Indeed, grappling with the nonhuman animal has prompted a dismantling of traditional disciplinary borders. Change has been particularly visible in literary and cinematic studies, where scholars have engaged in a sustained manner with philosophy, politics, ethology, psychology, anthropology, and evolutionary biology (to name just a few fields) as they consider the question of our relationship to animal others. Cary Wolfe's essay in the special *PMLA* issue dedicated to animal studies in 2009 argues that we are witnessing a "gradual opening up of a theoretical and critical space" for the topic, and that we are seeing its expansion in both North America and elsewhere ("Human" 565–66). If the topic is animating the world of scholarly inquiry, it is in part because, as Wolfe argues, animal studies "fundamentally challenges the schema of the knowing subject and its anthropocentric underpinnings sustained and reproduced in the current disciplinary protocols of cultural studies" (568–69). In addressing the question of just how this field should refer to itself, Wolfe considers "animal studies" and "human-animal studies" (another essay in the issue addresses "animality studies").[1] Moreover, Wolfe argues forcefully that, in order to address adequately the questions posed, we must "confront them on two levels: not just the level of content, thematics, and the object of knowledge (the animal studied by animal studies) but also the level of theoretical and methodological approach (*how* animal studies studies the animal)" (568).

Within this burgeoning and complex field of inquiry, in the context of these disciplinary and species border crossings, how and why might a volume such as this one justify a focus on a national literature, and in particular on modern Italian literature and film?[2] A possible account begins during the period of the *Risorgimento* that led to the eventual unification of Italy in 1861. Often at play in competing visions of a unified nation were Italy's relationship to the underrepresented and a desire on the part of the more progressive thinkers to extend legal rights across genders and social classes. The republican activist Giuseppe Mazzini radically advocated for participatory democracy, the rights of women, universal education, and the emancipation of Italian Jews as well as the global emancipation of slaves.[3] More pertinent for this study, in 1871, the year Rome became the capital of the newly formed Italy, the revolutionary hero Giuseppe Garibaldi advocated for the formation of a Piedmontese Animal Welfare Society and was its first honorary president (Della Seta 71–72).[4] This fledgling society would eventually become the National Society for the Protection of Animals.

Yet despite this rather pleasing coincidence, the actual political entity that emerged from the activism and idealism of the *Risorgimento* was far from consistent in its attention to matters of rights for human *or* nonhuman animals. In Italy, the egalitarian foundations were shaky from the beginning; the establishment of the Italian nation was rooted in the ideals of neither Mazzini nor Garibaldi but rather in the political pragmatism of Camillo Benso, Count of Cavour. The "idea of Italy" was founded on liberal traditions that affirmed the rights of the citizenry and challenged the conservatism of various Italian states and the hegemony of the Papal States. However, the reality of the newly formed Italian state was constructed on foundations of Piedmontese monarchic privilege. This inequity was quickly made manifest in the centralizing policy that became known as "Piedmontization," by means of which the administrative structures and legal institutions of the Northern monarchy were imposed on the other regions of the new Italy. Antonio Gramsci understands this policy as evidence of Piedmontese expansionism, writing that, for Cavourian liberals, unification was not a "national movement from below" but a "royal conquest" (57). In effect, the optimistic bubble of Italy's *Risorgimento* was quickly burst by the sweeping disappointments that followed unification, so much so that it has become a critical commonplace to underscore the chasm between a "legal Italy" and a "real Italy."[5]

Regardless of any progress made at the legislative level on behalf of nonhuman (or human) Italian animals, scholars have frequently pointed out the limits of rights-based approaches to animal studies and the humanist tendency to rely on "anthropological universals" (Wolfe, *Posthumanism* xvi).[6] As Wolfe has argued, "one of the hallmarks of humanism—and more specifically of the kind of humanism called liberalism—is precisely its penchant for the sort of 'pluralism' that extends the sphere of consideration (intellectual or ethical) to previously marginalized groups without in the least destabilizing or throwing into question the schema of the human who undertakes such pluralization" ("Human" 568).[7] The chance to move beyond the paradigm of humanist condescension and to engage meaningfully with animality, both human and nonhuman, is offered by what Rosi Braidotti has termed the "bioegalitarian turn" (526). The task, argues Braidotti, is to "relate to animals as animals ourselves" and "bypass the metaphysics of substance and its corollary, the dialectics of otherness" (526). Rising to this challenge demands a "radical repositioning" of and by the human subject, who must now embrace "open-ended, interrelational, multisexed, and transspecies flows of becoming" in order to "[explode] the skin of humanism" (527). An ethical impulse also underpins Jacques Derrida's well-known call to do what he claims that philosophy forgets—namely, to understand that the animal other we behold as humans also looks back at us (11).[8] If, then, Italy is worth serious and separate consideration in animal studies, it is not because of Garibaldi's well-meaning ideals or any legal protections enshrined in Italian unification—not, in short, because of the way the new nation was or was not legislating for animal rights. Instead, what matters is Italy's undeniable contribution to how we think our biological animality and our relationship to nonhuman animals.

Philosophical Animals

In so far as it is possible or even desirable to delineate a "national" thought, we might suggest that Italian philosophy has been thinking the human and, more specifically, the living or embodied human with marked intensity for many centuries.[9] This is, in essence, the argument Roberto Esposito makes in *Living Thought: The Origins and Actuality of Italian Philosophy*. Turning the potential institutional weakness of Italian philosophy into a strength, Esposito writes that Italy's enduring political fragmentation and its tardy national unification allowed for the emergence of a "prestatal" philosophical tradition outside of the centralizing or homogenizing influence of a nation or state (21). As such, Italian philosophy differs from other Western currents of thought in that it moves beyond the horizon of language to traverse the disciplinary and lexical boundaries of the strictly philosophical (5–12),[10] positioning itself across the spheres of politics, history, and life (22).[11] A propensity for "contamination" with the "nonphilosophical" (11) allows Italian thought to incorporate, as it were, the living or embodied human within its conceptual scaffolding.[12] As such, Italian thought stands as a tradition that, unlike much of Western philosophy from Descartes to Heidegger, does not seek to suppress the biological or "animal" part of man in its construction of human identity.

While Lorenzo Chiesa, whose editorial work in introducing Italian thought into English-speaking circles is extensive, is somewhat reluctant to embrace fully Esposito's claim that "the link between life and politics has always been the privileged target of Italian philosophy," he does echo in part Esposito's claim for a "living" philosophy when he "cautiously" suggests that Italian thought has "time and again been able to connect theory with praxis, as well as be truly open to other disciplines" ("Biopolitics" 2). For Chiesa, this disciplinary openness produces "unforeseeable short-circuits" ("Biopolitics" 2) that—as he writes in the introduction to *The Italian Difference: Between Nihilism and Biopolitics* written together with Alberto Toscano—link politics, metaphysics, culture, and the anecdotal (3). Moreover, these links emerge in the context of the politico-philosophical debate of the Italian Left, a debate characterized by a "peculiar admixture" of the "extremely parochial" and, in a formulation that echoes to some extent Esposito, the "intensely universal (the attempt to address Politics, Being, Humanity)" (Chiesa and Toscano 3). This discussion of the short circuits of Italian thought and its paradoxical marriage of the local and the universal emerges as Chiesa and Toscano broach Antonio Negri's energetic pamphlet, which opens the volume. Negri denounces the "weakness" of the bulk of twentieth-century Italian thought,[13] bemoaning its distance from a creative and active vision of philosophy, which he describes, after Gentile, as a "critical activity which allows one to grasp one's time and orientate oneself within it" (13). For Negri, three exceptional figures within twentieth-century Italian philosophy—Antonio Gramsci, Mario Tronti, and Luisa Muraro—manifest the creative activity of thought by engaging with a reality that encompasses the living human. Gramsci "reinvented Gentile" in an effort to reposition philosophy "in the life and struggles of ordinary people" and "turn actualism into the basis of a thinking and praxis of the future" (15–16). Tronti's workerism, impelled by an insistence on the active power of the working classes against the reactive forces of capital, was able to "plunge its hands into the real" (16). And finally, Luisa Muraro's "feminist thought of difference" (16) locates itself within the "biopolitical field of reproduction" (17). The horizon of the biopolitical allows Italian philosophy to propose a marriage of theory and praxis; for Negri, this is precisely what distinguishes those "adventures of bodies and minds" of the Italian 1968 from concurrent developments around the world (18).

Positing, then, an Italian philosophical difference that revolves around a continued and transdisciplinary attention to the realities of an embodied subject warrants a more sustained consideration of biopolitics and biopower. Though originating in France with Michel Foucault, biopolitics has come to characterize an Italian thought at the vanguard of a broad spectrum of today's philosophy. Giorgio Agamben is easily the most internationally well-known Italian representative of biopolitical thought, thanks at least in part to the early translation of his works into English. Famous for his public refusal to travel to the United States in 2004 because of the American policy of scanning the fingerprints and retinas of all visitors, the philosopher justified his decision by drawing attention to the "new and 'normal' relation between citizens and the State," which, with the aid of enhanced technologies, now encompasses the "routine inscription and registration of the most private and most incommunicable element of subjectivity—the biopolitical life of the body" ("Biopolitical Tattooing" 202). For Agamben, biopolitics, a condition wherein "power confronts nothing other than pure biological life without any mediation" (*Means without End* 40), reaches its most exceptional form in the Nazi concentration camps. Agamben's meditations on biopower grow from the category of "bare life," or a politicized version of biological life that falls between the categories of *zoē*, "the simple fact of living common to all living beings," and *bíos*, "the form or way of living proper to an individual or group" (*Homo Sacer* 1). In thinking the embodied life we share with the nonhuman animal, albeit mostly from the human side of the equation, Agamben's philosophy broaches the shifting boundaries between the construct of humanity and that of animality. Indeed, he concludes *The Open: Man and Animal* with an invitation to recast our understanding of humankind: "[M]an has always been the result of a simultaneous division and articulation of the animal and the human, in which one of the two terms of the operation was always what was at stake in it. To render inoperative the machine that governs our conception of man will therefore [...] show the central emptiness, the hiatus that—within man—separates man and animal, and to risk ourselves in this emptiness" (92).

If biopolitics, currently the most internationally prominent stream of Italian thought, thinks the animal bodies of humanity before power, other currents of thought move a little closer to the "bioegalitarian" thinking lauded by Braidotti. Her advocacy for a "neoliteral relation to animals, anomalies and inorganic others" (528) resonates with new, materialist evaluations of space, place, and being, a philosophical turn that restores the specificity of biological, geographical, and geological life to contemporary ontology. In this sense, the Italian peninsula as material, geographic space provides a basis for thinking the animal question, this time from an environmental or ecocritical perspective. Serenella Iovino has been a leading voice in this regard, as she advocates for a "non-anthropocentric humanism" that recognizes nature's "dignity and worth, as well as the dignity and the worth of every form of otherness" (48). This form of thinking "relates itself to different situations not in order to find alleged metaphysical truths but to affirm contextual values of utility, solidarity, and social responsibility" (48). Franco Cassano contextualizes his thinking and writing in the

Mediterranean region, theorizing philosophies of "slow thought" that suggest the peculiar relationship linking philosophy and material existence. For Cassano, the Mediterranean is an alternative geopolitical space where, historically speaking, "[h]uman nature is part of a greater nature: It shares solidarity with the land that hosts it, in acknowledgment of a communal and silent mother" (70). This "primordial and deep relationship with the earth" was shattered, he argues, by a Judeo-Christian tradition that favored the "opposition between man and world and between man and nature" over the Greek continuities between them (70). Cassano's vision of Mediterraneanism pulses with a posthumanist "impurity," as he claims that the long borders of the Mediterranean's shores resist fundamentalism: "The hybridization of cultures and peoples weakens all claims of exclusivity, purity, and integrity, as the Mediterranean knows well, having been fraught, from time immemorial, with intertwined stories, mestizos, migrations, and shelters. [...] On this sea between lands, the Other was never a huge distance away" (147).

Even as Cassano celebrates the potentials of Mediterraneanism, his work is motivated by an awareness of struggles between East and West, North and South, and by concerns about the empty promises and normative models of Western modernity. It thus remains aware, as Norma Bouchard and Valerio Ferme observe in their introduction to the English-language translation of Cassano's text, of the "tensions, inequalities, and the asymmetries of power among cultures" (xix). In Italy, where ecological crisis looms large (illegal disposal of toxic waste, illegal building on fragile coastal ecosystems, and intensive cementification are three frequently discussed problems), tensions and inequalities on the peninsula further motivate the dialogue about the human–animal divide and about the material stakes of renegotiating our relationship to the more-than-human world.

Although his work is not yet extensively translated into English, Roberto Marchesini, who wrote the Foreword to this volume, takes us significantly toward a truly "bioegalitarian" thinking. Arguing that humans must work to "anthropodecenter" themselves, Marchesini proposes that posthumanism must think our relationship to the world in terms of "conjugation" and "hybridization" (*Tramonto* 202, translation ours). Most significant, evidence of our hybridization with nonhuman others is rooted not solely in that biological life we share with nonhuman animals but also in the cultural sphere so frequently identified as the exclusive domain of humankind. Marchesini's work, which stands at the crossroads of cognitive science and critical ethology, natural sciences and the humanities, opens dialogues across dramatically different disciplines and species. As the "primary exponent of zooanthropology in Italy" (Bussolini 188), his work not only seeks to reconfigure the relationships between dogs and humans but also includes a vast range of publications on philosophies of the posthuman. Marchesini's work offers, most critically, a means to reconsider "culture," as he views cultural practices as hybrid forms that are proper to humans and nonhuman animals (Bussolini 58–62). In fact, human culture frequently originates in animal practice, argues Marchesini, offering examples such as the Maasai people, whose dance reproduces a courting ritual of the gray crowned crane, or weavers, whose craft imitates that of the spider.

Animals Literary and Cinematic

Why not suspend our inquiry here, with these meditations on philosophy and on human and nonhuman embodiment? If philosophy, and Italian philosophy in particular, addresses the animal question from such a broad range of perspectives, why should we extend our analysis into other creative fields of human endeavor? Perhaps the answer comes from the philosophers themselves. In a move that insists on the hybrid, conjoined, and transversal quality of knowledge and being, philosophy urges us to think other forms of thought: artistic forms of knowledge that rely on imagination, fantasy, and empathy, and that reconsider the past and anticipate potential futures. Derrida endorses poetic thought as necessary for an ethical consideration of animal alterity: "[T]hinking concerning the animals, if there is such a thing, derives from poetry. [...] It is what philosophy has, essentially, had to deprive itself of. It is the difference between philosophical knowledge and poetic thinking" (7). Georges Bataille also underscores the limits of conventional philosophical method in grasping an animal being conceived of as unfathomably other and argues that the only "correct" way to speak of a universe without man "can *overtly* only be poetic" (21).[14]

Italian thinkers have shown themselves to be attentive to the need to broaden our methodological horizons when confronting the interlocked questions of humans, animals, and ecosystem. Cassano explains, "When we think rigorously of a place as dense and complex as the Mediterranean, we do not close ourselves in a banal regional ethnocentrism, because inside that complex place, we discover the world. And today more than ever, the world requires that future chapters be written together, drawn from different forms of knowledge and wisdom" (153). Iovino is explicit in her endorsement of art as one of the "different forms of knowledge" called on by Cassano; for her, literature is "an educational and reflexive form" whose "representations of nature, of the non-human, of environmental conflicts [...] contain ethical directions and can help us orient our behavior toward responsibility for and inclusion of otherness" (42). In representing nonhuman animals, literature can offer visions of a "complexity of interdependent languages. [...] Here, stirring up and listening to different intentional orders means creating a horizontal dialectic between human and non-human worlds" (44). Attentive to the languages and landscapes of a more-than-human world, literature and cinema provide a space in which our mortal bodies, both human and nonhuman, might be redefined in ways that are not only conceptual but also ethical and practical.

Turning to the contents of this volume, we must consider what, specifically, this selection of essays on Italian literature and cinema can add to a thinking of animality, human and otherwise. Ranging from an essay rooted in late nineteenth-century literature to a study examining a 2010 film, the collection considers works from the period following Italy's unification, through fascism and World War II, into the postwar economic boom, ending with contemporary modernity. Although each essay speaks of different animals in literature and film, different genres, and different historical moments, the collection is crisscrossed by common theories and themes. Drawing on Italian philosophers (including Agamben, Cassano, Iovino, Marchesini, and Muraro) and on non-Italian discussions of animality and posthumanism (Deleuze, Derrida, Haraway, and Wolfe, among others), all the essays engage with the body's—and not just the human body's—material dimensions and drives and its transformations and limits. The essays propose innovative views on texts canonical and non, showing how the literary and cinematic imagination have broached the complexities of the post-Darwinian loss of human privilege, challenged anthropocentrism, charted the risks and limits of dividing the human from the animal, or envisioned both utopian and dystopian worlds in which that divide collapses or is cast in dramatically different terms. The tripartite organization we propose is but one of many potential pathways through the thinking collected in this volume, one of the ways in which the essays resonate with one another. The order stands outside of any chronology or periodization, instead tracing itineraries through the manifold rhizomatic conversations opened by the artists and thinkers addressed therein. It underscores broad theoretical and thematic tendencies, which we might encapsulate as follows: Ontologies and Thresholds; Biopolitics and Historical Crisis; Ecologies and Hybridizations.

Essays in Part 1 cast animality as a concern that is, broadly speaking, ontological. Partaking of the legacy of humanism, albeit a humanism radically reconfigured by the momentum of modernity, the authors and texts that feature in these essays broach the nonhuman other in order to pose questions about that which is deemed proper to humanity. Appearing in a variety of representational styles and tones, ranging from the grotesquely realistic to the purely fantastic or surreal, the animal presences allow this grouping of authors to explore human embodiment and the perceived thresholds that separate man from the nonhuman animal. Prompting reactions that include benevolence, fraternity, anxiety, repulsion, and violence, ontological kinship with the animal (desired or otherwise) becomes a means for interrogating the borders of the human, the limits of human language, the conflict between genders and the patriarchal suppression of the feminine, and the very shape of divinity.

Deborah Amberson's study of Federigo Tozzi (1883–1920) in Chapter 1 underscores the Tuscan author's attention to humanity's agricultural instrumentalization of nonhuman animals. In this context, the pain felt by the animals generates a kinship between them and Tozzi's young human protagonists—a kinship based on a shared capacity for suffering. However, this bond does not sit easily. The animal others become uncanny presences that prompt more repulsion and anxiety than compassion and benevolence in the young protagonists. Amberson explores this anguished relationship with the nonhuman other, arguing that Tozzi stages a post-Darwinian anxiety that sees man wrestle with the implications of his own biological animality.

Elizabeth Leake's consideration of the work of Cesare Pavese (1908–50) in Chapter 2, which opens the discourse of human gender onto pressing questions of speciesism, foregrounds a female body bound up with the world of the nonhuman animal and repeatedly subjected to male violence. At work is a male anxiety triggered by female sexuality, maternity, and, most specifically, the generative power of female biology. The destructive violence done unto Pavese's females reflects an attempt to erase the maternal function by relegating the female body to the sphere of the natural and, by virtue of a fantasy of male self-generation, to arrogate reproduction to the sphere of masculinity. As such, Leake reads Pavese's texts against that symbolic matricide necessary for the suppression of a biological prehistory—a violence also instrumental to the emergence of history and phallogocentric humanism.

Gregory Pell tracks the nonhuman animal through the poetic opus of Eugenio Montale (1896–1981) in Chapter 3, identifying a mindful poet who reconsiders his own uses and abuses, both biographical and poetic, of nonhuman beings in a manner that can at times suggest a posthumanist sensibility for animal otherness. Considerations of the instrumentalization of nonhuman animals, animal divinity, metempsychosis, and communication are played out in a poetic bestiary that features, among others, hedgehogs, bats, lobsters, spiders, and even the mythological unicorn. Drawing on a gallery of poetic images, Pell identifies a willful indeterminacy in Montale's sometimes playful, sometimes sober engagement with animality.

In Chapter 4, Simone Castaldi identifies in the work of Tommaso Landolfi (1908–79) and the menagerie of animals, fantastic and actual, that populate his fiction a destabilizing force that can mark a crisis or offer an opportunity for transformation. In his analysis, Castaldi addresses the role played by intertextuality in Landolfi's thinking and writing, connecting the author and his work with a range of influences and allusions including Gogol, Kafka, and Lautréamont. Landolfi's tales, he argues, manifest a blurring of the category of the human, a blurring that engenders a theriomorphosis or animalization not only of man and the objects that surround him but also of that which is conventionally deemed proper to humanity—namely, the sphere of language.

Matteo Gilebbi explicitly places the poetic in dialogue with the philosophical in Chapter 5 as he traces the evolution of the nonhuman animal in the poetry of Mario Luzi (1914–2005), in the light of Giorgio

Agamben's theoretical reflections on the so-called animal–human divide. Gilebbi addresses the particular force of the animal metaphor, tracking its transformation through Luzi's opus from a rhetorical figure to an animetaphor, a hybrid element capable of challenging human linguistic practices. Gilebbi compares Luzi's evolution with Agamben's thought, in a reading attentive not only to the points of convergence between these two figures but equally to their significant differences. Luzi, Gilebbi argues, anticipates posthumanist thought as he comes to advocate a type of biocentrism in which human, nonhuman, and the divine encounter beyond speciesist categorization.

Part 2, where ontological inquiries continue to resonate, features essays that contemplate the sociopolitical import of the animal question. In texts that identify a crisis of human history, from World War II and the Holocaust to fictional future postapocalyptic societies, essays in this part of the book chart the potentially crushing power of the anthropological machine. The implications of equating humans with their animal nature, of appropriating what Agamben calls "bare life," are chilling, and these essays explore the dark consequences that ensue when human bodies are degraded to nonindividuated masses of flesh. Nevertheless, contributions in this section search out lines of resistance and provide possible counterbalances to the persecutions of humans and animals when the human–animal divide is enforced.

In her work in Chapter 6 comparing Liliana Cavani's (b. 1933) *The Night Porter* and Pier Paolo Pasolini's (1922–75) *Salò*, Alexandra Hills argues that the films, which investigate humanity at its philosophical and physical limits, show that Nazism and consumerism (and the aberrant bodies they engendered) were the logical results of moral humanism and its cultural traditions. Calling on notions of the creaturely and the posthuman body, Hills establishes that Pasolini and Cavani trace bodies no longer able to elicit compassion or affective responses from others—bodies brutalized and made available for consumption in the grim aftermath of humanism.

Giuseppina Mecchia's reflection on novelist Elsa Morante (1912–85) in Chapter 7 argues that discourses regarding biopolitics and concerns about the human–animal divide, which circulated in philosophical circles from Foucault to Deleuze and Guattari to Agamben, are anticipated in Morante's fictional works. Against the political strictures of the Italian critical establishment, Morante, who was Agamben's lifelong friend, condemned the workings of biopolitical power in her novels and finds, in poetry, a Deleuzian line of flight for the affirmation of the life of animate and inanimate beings.

Daniele Fioretti's analysis in Chapter 8 argues, like Mecchia's, that the Italian literary imagination anticipated the biopolitical concerns of philosophers including Agamben, Derrida, and Foucault. Fioretti analyzes two novels by Paolo Volponi (1924–94) written in the 1970s, demonstrating that the author seeks to redefine the human by casting him in a new, hybridized relationship to the animal. Set in the context of historical preoccupations about the atomic bomb, *Corporeal* casts as protagonist a man who dreams of hybridizations across the species, inverts the paradigms of anthropocentrism, and immerses himself in a world of corporeal sensation. *The Irritable Planet* instead envisions a world after a nuclear catastrophe; the dwarf, elephant, goose, and monkey protagonists lead the way to a society in which the human is radically repositioned.

In her consideration of contemporary Italian dystopian fiction in Chapter 9, Valentina Fulginiti traces fears about the end of humanity and the animals and monsters who accompany and fuel this fear. In an analysis of *Sirens* by Laura Pugno (b. 1970) and *Free Karma Food* by Wu Ming 5 (b. 1964), Fulginiti shows how these works stage the collapse of the boundary between the human and the animal, in particular through alimentary regimes that condemn our current practices of consumption, showing them to be coextensive with cannibalism. Arguing for the convergence of notions of posthumanism and cannibalism, Fulginiti shows that both concepts lead us to understand that artificial boundaries between humanity and the nonhuman world exert a potentially deadly toll on humanity.

The final section, Part 3, is composed of essays in which urgent questions about the future of the planet emerge in dialogue with concerns about the relationship between human and nonhuman animals. This relation becomes a sign and symptom of broader environmental concerns, revealing a dangerous human tendency to anthropocentrism that risks undervaluing human entanglement in the material world and human dependence on natural resources. These essays consider the crucial contribution that literature and cinema can make to reimagining our positioning in the world and to extending our ethical frame of reference outward to encompass nonhuman concerns. They also warn of the ethical and material consequences of avoiding these questions.

In David Del Principe's analysis in Chapter 10, *Pinocchio* by Carlo Collodi (1826–90) and *Fosca* by Igino Ugo Tarchetti (1839–69) are read against the backdrop of Gothic literature and its historical anxieties regarding meat eating, the rise of the slaughterhouse, and Malthusian fears of population expansion. Del Principe's innovative "ecogothic" approach maps a continuity linking the transhuman bodies of Frankenstein, Count Dracula, Pinocchio, and Fosca and charts these characters' "herbivorous" protests against the colonizing impulses of the nation. Fosca's unwillingness to procreate and Pinocchio's nonhuman birth, coupled with both characters' reluctance to eat, threaten the carnivorism prescribed by modern industrial society and challenge the tenuous, purported borders between species.

Giovanna Faleschini Lerner's study of Carlo Levi (1902–75) in Chapter 11 theorizes the importance of the author and painter's concept of *contemporaneità*, or temporal coexistence, and shows its rootedness in a complex space between humanism and a broader, ecological thought. Levi's experience in political exile in Southern Italy, and his resulting relationship with peasant culture, led the author to reposition himself within what he came to see as an anthropocentric and alienated modernity. Faleschini Lerner argues that Levi's work as writer and painter brims with tensions between his sense of solidarity with a more-than-human world and his awareness of the irrevocably rational power of the language he uses to represent this world; his work thus anticipates the ecocritical and ethical focus of much contemporary scholarship.

Serenella Iovino's essay in Chapter 12 traces a universe of hybrid landscapes and creatures in the work of Italo Calvino (1923–85) through the posthumanist lens of "relational ontology." Examining vibrantly mutable figures including the *Cosmicomics*' narrator Qfwfq or the reflective Mr. Palomar, Iovino finds evidence of a universe of beings whose bodily boundaries are porous and materially and culturally intertwined. Rooted in the emergent field of material ecocriticism, Iovino's study positions Calvino at the complex heart of contemporary discourses of coevolution and hybridization. In his fiction, humans, far from being cordoned off from any concept of "nature" or the animal, take their place in the history of the emergence of matter. Literature, in this view, thus moves to open the human subject to the universe.

Continuing in the vein of material ecocriticism, Elena Past argues in Chapter 13 that *The Wind Blows Round* (dir. Giorgio Diritti, b. 1959) and *Le quattro volte* (dir. Michelangelo Frammartino, b. 1968) reflect the coevolution of mountain landscapes, human communities, and goats. Set in rugged landscapes at the extreme ends of Italy, these two films show the complexities of cohabitation as they follow the historical, social, and philosophical pathways of goatherds and goats over the steep slopes. The unnostalgic *The Wind Blows Round* warns of the ethical and environmental risks of losing the memory of our interlocking, interspecies past, while the meditative *Le quattro volte* shows the way to a collaborative, posthuman cinema.

Of course this collection of essays opens numerous other possible dialogues—dialogues that extend beyond the sections we have delineated and that reach, ever rhizomatically, into conceptual areas that our organizational structure has not underscored. For example, anxieties of consumption and concerns about cannibalism trace paths between Pinocchio, Fosca, and the mermaids of Laura Pugno's *Sirene*, creating a strangely compelling alliance of rebellious mermaids, puppets, and anorexics. The indivisible coupling of embodiment and suffering binds Tozzi's agrarian Tuscany to Cavani's post-Nazi Vienna. Cesare Pavese's world of gendered landscapes and self-generating male protagonists is contrasted by the minoritarian becomings of characters in Elsa Morante's novels, and in particular Manuele of *Aracoeli*, who becomes woman. Volponi's hybrid Gerolamo Aspri, who imagines himself becoming animal, plant, and microorganism, has much in common with Calvino's Mr. Palomar, as both characters open the borders of the human onto a universe of materially and ontologically connected beings. The dialogues could continue.

***

In a concluding chapter of *The Iguana*, the narrator addresses the reader, noting, "You, too, Reader, will have noticed how the facts of life that most approach sublimity tend to come to mean conclusions, or at best to pass unobserved, making way for trifles that literally leave the community breathless" (188). Sublimity notwithstanding, Ortese's gentle irony underscores the difficult task of closing an introduction on such a vast topic and allows us to acknowledge the many lacunae, perhaps inevitable, that recommend continued attention to nonhuman animals. There are countless creatures throughout Italian literature who have not made appearances in essays in this volume, beginning with the elusive Iguana at the incipit of this introduction. We might also invoke the beasts of burden—human and non—of Giovanni Verga's Sicily, the fantastic creatures of Dino Buzzati's literary imagination, Carlo Cassola's anxieties of human embodiment, Giorgio Celli's many cats, or Amara Lakhous's kidnapped dog in *Clash of Civilizations over an Elevator in Piazza Vittorio*. But as Cary Wolfe points out, writing about animals is akin to "herding cats" ("Human" 564): an endeavor that is chaotic and ultimately inexhaustible. This volume, with its cats, goats, mermaids, turtles, lobsters, and phallic potato dogs (among others), reflects just a few of the complicated ways in which nonhuman lives touch the lives of humans across Italian literature and film. As such, our work invites further efforts to hybridize, destabilize, and deanthropocenter the creaturely world around us.

Notes

1. Michael Lundblad sees "animal studies" as a form of advocacy concerned with the material conditions of nonhuman animals, and he argues that "animality studies" emphasizes our history of thinking nonhuman animals (496–98).
2. A number of works have undertaken to examine the animal question through the lens of national or area studies. See, for example, Janice Fiamengo, ed., *Other Selves: Animals in the Canadian Literary Imagination*; Wendy Woodward, *The Animal Gaze: Animal Subjectivities in Southern African Narratives*; and Jane Costlow and Amy Nelson, eds., *Other Animals: Beyond the Human in Russian Culture and History*.
3. For a thorough account of Mazzini's politics, see Giuseppe Mazzini, *A Cosmopolitanism of Nations: Giuseppe Mazzini's Writings on Democracy, Nation Building, and International Relations*, ed. Stefano Recchia and Nadia Urbinati; Massimo Scioscioli, *Giuseppe Mazzini:*

I princìpi e la politica; and C. A. Bayly and E. F. Biagini, *Giuseppe Mazzini and the Globalization of Democratic Nationalism, 1830–1920*.
4. Garibaldi collaborated with the English noblewoman Anna Winter and the physician Timoteo Riboldi in setting up the society.
5. Christopher Duggan locates the policy of Piedmontization within a largely "disingenuous" claim for the urgency of unification, writing that it was "indicative of a dangerous capacity on the part of Italy's rulers to divorce the claims of the nation, understood in an abstract, almost Platonic, sense, from those of the people that constituted it" (232).
6. Despite Wolfe's reservations about the theoretical bias underpinning the rights-based approach, it must be acknowledged that some important legal results have been achieved. In Italy, Paola Cavalieri is arguably the best-known representative of this stance. She collaborated with Peter Singer on *The Great Ape Project* and has also published *The Animal Question: Why Nonhuman Animals Deserve Human Rights*.
7. There is of course also room to nuance understandings of humanist goals, as evident in the 2008 volume of *Annali d'italianistica* featuring articles on "Humanisms, Posthumanisms, & Neohumanisms" and contemplating the "ethical question concerning the nature of humanism in its multifaceted expressions" (Lollini 22).
8. Derrida's text also takes issue with referring to animals with a singular term. This singular ignores that "heterogeneous multiplicity of the living" in order to "designate every living thing that is held not to be human" (31).
9. A number of special journal issues featuring Italian contributions to the conversation on biopower, humanism, and posthumanism offer evidence that an Italian tenor of thought crosses disciplinary boundaries and has been of particular interest to English-language audiences in recent years. For example, a special issue of *Angelaki: Journal of the Theoretical Humanities* on "Italian Thought Today: Bio-Economy, Human Nature, Christianity" includes meditations on life and biopolitics by thinkers including Roberto Esposito, Paolo Virno, and Giorgio Agamben. *Cosmos and History: The Journal of Natural and Social Philosophy* dedicated an issue to "The Italian Difference: Between Nihilism and Biopolitics," edited by Lorenza Chiesa and Alberto Toscano with essays by Antonio Negri, Gianni Vattimo, Esposito, Luisa Muraro, and Virno. This last was republished in volume form as *The Italian Difference: Between Nihilism and Biopolitics* (2009).
10. While Esposito acknowledges that Italian thought does, of course, address human language from a variety of angles, he claims that it is not limited to or by this question as, for example, analytic philosophy,

which "was created explicitly for the critical analysis of philosophical language" (5).
11. This creates what Timothy Campbell, in his introduction to the first of *Diacritics*'s two issues on Italian thought, describes as the "improper mix of concept and figure" that generates within Italian philosophy "movement and attraction" (4). Reluctant to impose a "forced unity" on Italian philosophy, Campbell proposes a consideration of the disciplinary "openness to the outside" of Italian philosophy (4).
12. Specifically, Esposito identifies three paradigms or axes within Italian thought as follows: (1) the "immanentization of antagonism," or the Italian refusal to negate the originary violence of order (24); (2) the "historicization of the nonhistorical," which, like Vico's "ricorso" or return, acknowledges the "unresolvable dialectic" between history's need to obscure the corporeal or living dimension of prehistory (26–27); and (3) the "mundanization of the subject," or the Italian tendency to resist the broader Western "construct that founds the unity of the subject on a separation between itself and its own biological substrate" (28–29).
13. Negri (somewhat theatrically) targets the "weak thought" made famous internationally by Gianni Vattimo, describing this "vile" thought as a plan "to repudiate the history of the insurgences and resistances that had accompanied the first construction from below of a public space in Italy" (14).
14. Gilles Deleuze echoes this association of the literary with animality: "Literature begins with a porcupine's death, according to Lawrence, or with the death of a mole, in Kafka. [...] As Moritz said, one writes for dying calves" (2).

Works Cited

Agamben, Giorgio. *Homo Sacer: Sovereign Power and Bare Life*. Trans. Daniel Heller-Roazen. Stanford: Stanford UP, 1998.

———. *Means without End: Notes on Politics*. Trans. Vincenzo Binetti and Cesare Casarino. Minneapolis: U of Minnesota P, 2000.

———. "No to Biopolitical Tattooing." Trans. Stuart J. Murray. *Communication and Critical/Cultural Studies* 5.2 (2008): 201–2.

———. *The Open: Man and Animal*. Trans. Kevin Attell. Stanford: Stanford UP, 2004.

Bataille, Georges. *Theory of Religion*. Trans. Robert Hurley. New York: Zone, 1992.

Bayly, C. A., and E. F. Biagini. *Giuseppe Mazzini and the Globalization of Democratic Nationalism, 1830–1920*. Oxford: Oxford UP, 2008.

Braidotti, Rosi. "Animals, Anomalies, and Inorganic Others." *PMLA* 124.2 (2009): 526–32.
Bussolini, Jeffrey. "Recent French, Belgian and Italian Work in the Cognitive Science of Animals: Dominique Lestel, Vinciane Despret, Roberto Marchesini and Giorgio Celli." *Social Science Information* 52.2 (2013): 187–209.
Campbell, Timothy. "Introduction." *Diacritics* 39.3 (2009): 3–5.
Cassano, Franco. *Southern Thought and Other Essays on the Mediterranean*. Trans. and ed. Norma Bouchard and Valerio Ferme. New York: Fordham UP, 2012.
Cavalieri, Paola. *The Animal Question: Why Nonhuman Animals Deserve Human Rights*. Trans. Catherine Woollard. Oxford: Oxford UP, 2004.
Cavalieri, Paola, and Peter Singer, eds. *The Great Ape Project: Equality beyond Humanity*. New York: St. Martin's, 1993.
Chiesa, Lorenzo. "Biopolitics in Early Twenty-First-Century Italian Philosophy." *Angelaki: Journal of the Theoretical Humanities* 16.3 (2011): 1–5.
Chiesa, Lorenzo, and Alberto Toscano, "Introduction." In *The Italian Difference: Between Nihilism and Biopolitics*, ed. Lorenzo Chiesa and Alberto Toscano, 1–10. Melbourne: re.press, 2009.
Costlow, Jane, and Amy Nelson, eds. *Other Animals: Beyond the Human in Russian Culture and History*. Pittsburgh: U of Pittsburgh P, 2010.
Deleuze, Gilles. *Essays Critical and Clinical*. Trans. Michael A. Greco and Daniel W. Smith. Minneapolis: U of Minnesota P, 1997.
Della Seta, Roberto. *La difesa dell'ambiente in Italia: Storia e cultura del movimento ecologista*. Milan: FrancoAngeli, 2000.
Derrida, Jacques. *The Animal That Therefore I Am*. Ed. Marie-Louise Mallet. Trans. David Wills. New York: Fordham UP, 2008.
Duggan, Christopher. *The Force of Destiny: A History of Italy since 1796*. Boston: Houghton Mifflin, 2008.
Esposito, Roberto. *Living Thought: The Origins and Actuality of Italian Philosophy*. Trans. Zakiya Hanafi. Stanford: Stanford UP, 2012.
Fiamengo, Janice, ed. *Other Selves: Animals in the Canadian Literary Imagination*. Ottawa: U of Ottawa P, 2007.
Gramsci, Antonio. *Il Risorgimento*. Rome: Riuniti, 1996.
Iovino, Serenella. "Ecocriticism and a Non-Anthropocentric Humanism." In *Local Natures, Global Responsibilities: Ecocritical Perspectives on the New English Literatures*, 29–53. Amsterdam: Rodopi, 2010.
Lollini, Massimo. "Humanisms, Posthumanisms, and Neohumanisms: Introductory Essay." *Annali d'italianistica* 26 (2008): 13–23.
Lundblad, Michael. "From Animal to Animality Studies." *PMLA* 124.2 (2009): 496–502.
Marchesini, Roberto. *Il tramonto dell'uomo: La prospettiva post-umanista*. Bari: Dedalo, 2009.

Mazzini, Giuseppe. *A Cosmopolitanism of Nations: Giuseppe Mazzini's Writings on Democracy, Nation Building, and International Relations.* Ed. Stefano Recchia and Nadia Urbinati. Princeton: Princeton UP, 2009.
Negri, Antonio. "The Italian Difference." Trans. Lorenzo Chiesa. In *The Italian Difference: Between Nihilism and Biopolitics*, ed. Lorenzo Chiesa and Alberto Toscano, 13–23. Melbourne: re.press, 2009.
Ortese, Anna Maria. *The Iguana.* Trans. Henry Martin. Kingston, NY: McPherson, 1987.
Scioscioli, Massimo. *Giuseppe Mazzini: I princìpi e la politica.* Naples: Guida, 1995.
Toscano, Alberto. "Chronicles of Insurrection: Tronti, Negri and the Subject of Antagonism." In *The Italian Difference: Between Nihilism and Biopolitics*, ed. Lorenzo Chiesa and Alberto Toscano, 109–28. Melbourne: re.press, 2009.
Wolfe, Cary. "Human, All Too Human: 'Animal Studies' and the Humanities." *PMLA* 124.2 (2009): 564–75.
———. *What Is Posthumanism?* Minneapolis: U of Minnesota P, 2010.
Woodward, Wendy. *The Animal Gaze: Animal Subjectivities in Southern African Narratives.* Johannesburg: Witwatersrand UP, 2008.

Part I

Ontologies and Thresholds

I

Confronting the Specter of Animality

Tozzi and the Uncanny Animal of Modernism

Deborah Amberson

Federigo Tozzi's novel *Adele* contains an affecting description of the brutal death of a dog, killed by agricultural workers in order to protect the grape harvest from this canine scavenger.[1] Tozzi describes the dog's mounting unease as he is secured with a rope and led away by the head worker and his son. While walking to his death, the dog recalls a bitch he had met that morning and pauses in order to find her scent again. Jerked forward by the peasants, he becomes sad because he does not understand what is happening. On arriving at a fig tree, the peasants tie the dog, who, apparently overcome by emotion, performs gestures of submission. At this point, the son takes his rifle and shoots the dog in the muzzle. The dog falls backward and, wheezing rapidly, spills blood from his mouth down his chest. When he stands again with a gentle expression in his eyes, the son shoots him in the head. As he tries once again to stand up, staring all the while at his killer, the father finishes him off by striking him four times on the head with a shovel (Tozzi 555–57).

The numerous nonhuman animals that inhabit Tozzi's literary world are, more often than not, subjected to a cruel fate not unlike that of the dog. These beasts, for the most part typical inhabitants of the Tuscan landscape, occupy a realm defined by a violence done unto them by the human. The bulk of this violence takes place in an agricultural domain constructed on a rational program of animal subjection and exploitation implemented in order to guarantee foodstuffs for humanity. Yet despite an apparent authorial denunciation of the instrumentalization and victimization of the nonhuman animal, Tozzi's animals are not merely pathetic entities who elicit compassion. Instead, their inscrutable gaze, their predatory violence, and their capacity for suffering come to constitute an unfathomable menace for Tozzi's young human protagonists struggling to negotiate the threshold of adulthood. In this unease before the animal, we might discern a quintessentially modernist or, more specifically, post-Darwinian anxiety before a purported biological kinship between human and nonhuman animality. Accordingly, the animal comes to constitute an uncanny presence, simultaneously familiar and alien, which provokes a series of often unpredictable human responses, including compassion, shame, repulsion, anguish, and violence. This essay charts Tozzi's bleak portrait of human–animal relations as they evolve in Siena and its environs during the first two decades of the twentieth century.

Exploiting the Beast

Turning initially to the domesticated animals of human agriculture, we discover a series of animal beings whom we might consider in the light of Jean-François Lyotard's claim that "the animal is the paradigm of the victim" (28). Situated within a discussion of the differend, defined by Lyotard as "a case of conflict, between (at least) two parties, that cannot be equitably resolved for lack of a rule of judgment applicable to both arguments" (xi), the animal is identified as a being "deprived of the possibility of bearing witness according to the human rules for establishing damages" (28). In the case of the aforementioned dog killed to protect the grapes, we note Tozzi's focus on the dog's inadequate attempts to communicate through whimpers (556) and "acts of submission," and his efforts to elicit compassion from his killers by holding their gaze even up to his death (557). This description, arguably the most pathos laden of all Tozzi's animal portraits, draws us into the mental interiority of the dog as he experiences a sense of disquiet on being bound and led away and a mounting sadness in the face of his failure both to understand his plight and to communicate his state of mind (556). What Tozzi seems intent on underscoring here is, very simply, the dog's suffering. In so doing, he seems to echo, at least to some extent, Jeremy Bentham, who famously repositioned philosophies of animality by considering not the nonhuman animal's lack of rationality or speech but rather his or her capacity for suffering: "[T]he question is not, Can they *reason*? nor, Can they *talk*? but, can they *suffer*?" (311). Tozzi suggests an ethical equivalence between the human and nonhuman animal, an equivalence noted by Franco Petroni, who writes that the nonhuman characters are almost always represented in the same manner as the humans, "almost as though their capacity for suffering was sufficient for them to be recognized by the narrative as our equals, endowed, like us, with a 'soul'" (42).[2]

This animal capacity for suffering prompts Tozzi's apparent denunciation of the agricultural exploitation of the nonhuman animal. Most pertinent here are the novels set in the world of farming—namely, the aforementioned *Adele*, *With Eyes Closed* (*Con gli occhi chiusi*), and *The Farm* (*Il podere*).[3] The well-known scene of the castration of the farm animals in *With Eyes Closed* constitutes perhaps the most graphic indictment of agricultural violence.[4] The young protagonist's father Domenico habitually orchestrates a sweeping castration of his "beasts," which shows little apparent discrimination, targeting cockerels, calves, dogs, and cats (72).[5] The event is a spectacle drawing the amused workers to see the "dejected" cockerels "with bloodied feathers" and the calves "stunned by the castration, distressed, their eyes darker and more sullen" (72). Toppa, the dog, is also targeted and stands afterward with his tail tucked between his legs growling at those other dogs who draw near to him (73). The workers approve of this bloody event, remarking that, as a result of the castration, the animals "will get even fatter" (72).

This premeditated fattening of the farm animals draws us toward the question of the slaughterhouse and the human consumption of animal flesh, an issue about which much has been said in the field of animal philosophy. In "'Eating Well' or the Calculation of the Subject," Jacques Derrida identifies the "*sacrificial* structure" of discourses that separate the "animal" from the "human" and, in so doing, open a place for "a noncriminal putting to death" of that "animal" (*Points* 278). Moreover, this is a gendered discourse that privileges the human male. In fact, Derrida identifies a "carnivorous virility" that underpins Western subjectivity, and accordingly, his "phallogocentrism" is reconfigured as "*carno-phallogocentrism*" (*Points* 280, italics in original). As such, the male subject "does not just want to master and possess nature actively" but also becomes the one who "accepts sacrifice and eats flesh" (*Points* 281).[6] *Adele* offers a scene in which a family of agricultural laborers slaughters a pig. Faced with the "cut up and bloody" pig's flesh, "their instincts become manifest" (550). Yet this particular reference to instincts does not reflect the commonplace and pejorative association of human physical appetites with "animal" behavior. Instead, it seems connected with a human instinct to dominate the animal world and, more specifically, the male acceptance of the animal sacrifice. This becomes clear when the father of the family threatens the dog when he sniffs around the meat. Apparently reinforcing a species hierarchy that places humanity at the top of the food chain, the father kicks the dog violently and drives him off with death threats: "If you touch this, I will shoot you" (551).

Violence, however, is not exclusive to humanity. Indeed, while Tozzi certainly underscores the suffering of agricultural animals at the hands of humanity, he also describes a nonhuman animal world defined by an internal brutality. Turning once again to *Adele*, we find a reference to a hen who unwisely entered a pig's trough only to be snatched up in the mouth of the pig who would have killed her had a human not beaten him in turn with a stick (536). In the same pages we read of two hens placed in a henhouse where they are tortured and almost killed by the other hens: "[T]hey tormented them all day long, forcing them to run along the fence of the enclosure, under a hail of pecks. The following morning they were found still alive but with their heads entirely skinned. Blood still dripped over their yellow eyes" (537). *With Eyes Closed* offers the example of the aforementioned dog Toppa, who killed more than one dog "by biting them savagely on the backbone" and tore to pieces two other dogs who had dared to eat his food (100). Thus Tozzi's animals, human and nonhuman alike, seem defined by a shared relation to violence. Accordingly, the world of living beings is not so much divided into humanity on the one side and animality on the other. It is, rather, divided across the various species barriers into predator (almost always male) on the one side and victim on the other, with each individual falling into the former category or the latter according to his or her position on a hierarchical chain of violent domination. The agricultural exploitation of the nonhuman animal, then, constitutes just one form, albeit probably the most systematized, of the violence and suffering that defines embodied being.

Tozzi's young human protagonists are closer in kind and in status to the oppressed animal than to the persecutor, repeatedly falling foul of a social and economic order constructed on a calculating violence—a violence, it bears repeating, that is almost always gendered as male. While this despairing identification with the animal victim certainly relates to the critically well-trodden question of the protagonists' failure (or refusal) to enter an adulthood personified in the figure of the hypersexualized and brutally tyrannical father,[7] it is also central to Tozzi's treatment of animality. Indeed, the sexualized brutality of human adulthood is frequently displayed by dominating a nonhuman animal, as is amply demonstrated in a single example from *With Eyes Closed*. Domenico inflicts what Luperini terms a "test of strength and virility" (7) on the young protagonist Pietro when he insists that the boy master an unruly horse. The father's whip, identified by Luperini as a sadistic-phallic emblem of the authority of the "father-master" (8), is raised to Pietro's nose as he is threatened by his father for ultimately failing to dominate the horse (Tozzi 34).

Pietro's failure or refusal to master this animal body constitutes, I would suggest, a broader rejection of a particular social (and agricultural) configuration personified by the brutal and sexualized father figure, whose duty, as Sandro Maxia underlines, is that of affirming, imposing, and guarding order and continuity (59). This rejection, moreover, is not limited to *With Eyes Closed* but is also apparent in the novels of inheritance—namely, *The Farm* and *Three Crosses* (*Tre croci*).[8] Indeed, Debenedetti extends his Oedipal reading with the claim that the "property" inherited by Remigio Selmi, protagonist of *The Farm*, and by the Gambi brothers in *Three Crosses* symbolizes paternal authority (98). More important, the heirs' failure or refusal to make an economic success of their inheritance suggests the negation of the capitalistic fetishization of property (86). Here, Debenedetti intuits what, I would argue, is a programmatic albeit subtle denunciation of a specifically capitalist rationalization of objects and beings as abstract resources. It is this principle of exploitative instrumentalization that Remigio attacks as he negates the economic properties of the farm.[9] Remigio's rebellion against the paternal model of exploitation of bodies becomes even more radical when he himself accepts the status of the sacrifice, a status more conventionally attributed to the nonhuman animal of agriculture. Walking in front of Berto, a farm worker who not only is armed with a hatchet but has made clear his hatred for the young farm owner, Remigio feels increasing fear at the proximity of his employee (399). He wants to turn around to smile at Berto, but he finds himself unable to do so. In fact, Remigio evidently senses danger, but he repeatedly does nothing to protect himself, as though he is already resigned to his fate as sacrificial victim. He continues to walk forward, and finally Berto, "enraged [. . .] struck him with the hatchet on the back of the neck" (399). In dying, Remigio appears to refuse the status of male subject who accepts and eats the animal sacrifice. Instead, he offers himself as animalized "thing" to Berto's hatchet and becomes a scapegoat for the violent exploitation of animal bodies needed to guarantee economic success in the domain of agriculture and, more generally, human supremacy in the world.[10]

The Unfathomable Animal

To characterize Tozzi's young protagonists as steadfast defenders of the animal victims of agriculture would, of course, be erroneous. Such a view does not begin to account for the anxiety and disgust frequently felt by the protagonists before the world of animality and, specifically, before the gaze of the animal. In Tozzi's literary universe, the animal gaze is disconcerting, encompassing that same enigmatic variety acknowledged by Derrida, who imagines himself observed naked by an animal gaze "behind which there remains a bottomlessness, at the same time innocent and cruel perhaps, perhaps sensitive and impassive, good and bad, uninterpretable, unreadable, undecidable, abyssal and secret" (*Animal* 12). Wherein lies this unsettling force of the animal gaze? For Derrida, when this "wholly other" animal being who dwells in "intolerable proximity" returns our gaze, it challenges human efforts at self-delineation from the throng of living beings. In short, the animal gaze discloses the precipitous and even preposterous edges of the category of the human: "[T]he gaze called 'animal' offers to my sight the abyssal limit of the human [. . .] the bordercrossing from which vantage man dares to announce himself to himself" (*Animal* 12). For Georges Bataille, the animal gaze carries a similar force, introducing a sameness that remains utterly unfathomable and opening before the human "a depth that attracts me and is familiar to me. In a sense, I know this depth: it is my own. It is also that which is farthest removed from me, that which deserves the name depth, which means precisely *that which is unfathomable to me*" (2, italics in original).

This presence of a familiar and simultaneously unknowable animality becomes even more disconcerting in light of Charles Darwin's publication of his theories on evolution, a scientific mechanism that, to state the obvious, insists on a biological continuity between human and animal species.[11] Carrie Rohman stresses the increased centrality of animality to a post-Darwinian world still reeling from the "catastrophic blow to human privilege vis-à-vis the species question" (1) and the related challenge to the "traditional humanist abjection of animality" (22). Identifying a multipronged attempt to shore up anthropocentrism, Rohman discerns a "residual humanism" in the Victorian "over-investment in the notion of progress" (3) and contextualizes discourses of race and gender within an imperialism that "animalizes the colonized other in an attempt to purify the European subject of its Darwinian heritage" (22). Yet despite these efforts to exorcize the specter of animality, a "lurking anxiety" remains concerning the possibility of "human privilege" (5). Literary modernism belongs squarely in the space of this anxiety, though its response can certainly not be reduced to a uniform attempt to purge animality. Indeed, Rohman describes ambivalent modernist operations of "displacement of," "confrontation with," and "recuperation of" the animal as these texts "variously reentrench, unsettle, and even invert a humanist relation to this nonhuman other" (12).

This ambivalent variety certainly defines Tozzi's literary portrait of the nonhuman animal. While his denunciation of the abjection of agricultural animals might be said to engage in a type of ethical "recuperation" of animality, the disquiet his protagonists feel before the nonhuman animal prompts a disgust that demands strategies analogous to modernism's attempts to "reentrench" the humanist relation to an inferior animal other (Rohman 12). Indeed, having paralleled the animals' agricultural exploitation with a subjugation to a tyrannical paternal model, Tozzi's young protagonists are obliged to consider the nonhuman animal as their equal. This becomes an equivalence that generates extreme discomfort. Now the ethical consideration of a shared capacity for suffering opens onto a broader state of incapacity—an incapacity that becomes more unsettling as it extends beyond the socioeconomic to encompass the ontological and the epistemological in a Tozzian universe characterized by a phobic repulsion before the needs of the flesh and a desolation before the limits of the intellect.

Derrida approaches Bentham's consideration of animal suffering and describes the question as one that is "disturbed by a certain *passivity*" (*Animal* 27, italics in original). Bypassing the customary philosophical considerations of the nonhuman animal as an entity deprived of those capacities deemed proper to man (reason, speech, etc.), Bentham's question regarding animal suffering "amounts to asking 'Can they *not be able*?'" and the ability to suffer becomes, then, a "possibility without power, a possibility of the impossible," a "nonpower" (Derrida, *Animal* 28, italics in original).

The "nonpower" that Tozzi's young protagonists share with the nonhuman animal reflects a particular mode of being in the world: a dark and desolate form of Heideggerian "thrownness." Tozzi's vision of being offers little or no prospect of assuming those responsibilities, making those choices, or ultimately finding that freedom that Heidegger deems proper to man. Instead, in refusing adult subjectivity and all the brutal mastery that that particular mode of being entails in Tozzi's universe, the protagonists remain subject to a reality that they cannot (or will not) transcend and shape to their will. Importantly, this reality is not simply the external world of objects and other bodies but also becomes the physical realm of the protagonists' own embodiment. Indeed, in failing to transcend or master reality, they appear condemned to an existence of *zoē*, a term Agamben defines as "the simple fact of living common to all living beings" (1).[12] More specifically, they appear ensnared at the level of their own incarnation, a bodily incarnation they share with the animal world. Here the post-Darwinian menace of animality triggers disgust before biological needs and realities such as nourishment and sensory experience—needs and experiences, it bears repetition, that are shared with the nonhuman animal. The gaze of the animal, then, becomes a constant reminder of what Heidegger describes in his "Letter on Humanism" as our "scarcely conceivable, abysmal *bodily* kinship with the beast" (*Basic* 230, emphasis added).

Derrida opens *The Animal That Therefore I Am* with a consideration of the "reflex of shame" he feels when being observed naked by a cat "that looks at you without moving, just to see" (4). This, however, is a doubled shame or rather a being "ashamed for being ashamed" that relates to the possibility of human nudity as against the impossibility of nudity for the animal, who "is not naked because it is naked" (4–5). The protagonist of Tozzi's *Beasts* finds himself succumbing to shame before the gaze of a lizard: "Odors of juniper, of hawthorn, of crab-grass, of horehound! On a low wall, I saw a green lizard. I stopped, so that he wouldn't flee. Then, looking at his frightened and intelligent eyes, I felt a painful disappointment. And my face turned red with shame" (602). While the fear in the lizard's eyes might suggest an ethically oriented shame that reflects the threat posed by humanity to the nonhuman animal, the character of the sensory pleasure taken by the narrator draws the discourse toward the question of carnality. Indeed, prior to seeing the lizard, the narrator related happily to a dematerialized natural dimension described as an "immense dream of my soul," and it is the gaze of the embodied animal that shatters this disembodied experience and draws the narrator back to his own material carnality (601). While the nudity and the specular shame of Derrida's staring cat do not feature in this example from *Beasts*, what does is a materiality common to human and nonhuman animals that in and of itself prompts shame.

Emmanuel Levinas describes the human experience of shame as reflecting the desire to hide something not from others but from ourselves, because shame is "primarily connected to our body" (64). Indeed, what defines shame is "the radical impossibility of fleeing oneself to hide from oneself, the unalterably binding presence of the I to itself" (64). Moreover, though Levinas does acknowledge a social component to shame, he focuses on the experience within the ambit of the self and, turning to nausea, writes that shame is prompted by the "very fact of having a body" and that, even in solitude, the subject is "still 'scandalized' by himself" (67). Human shame, then, is triggered by embodiment, a material condition highlighted by Tozzi at every turn. Indeed, Tozzi's bodies and in particular the bodies of his young protagonists underscore an insistent materiality in that they are consistently overwhelmed by involuntary actions and reactions such as stuttering, trembling, spluttering, twitching, and blushing.[13] Most pertinent here among these convulsive bodily behaviors is, not surprisingly, the blushing—a physical response that usually accompanies shame. However, it is crucial to bear in mind the full array of bodily convulsions precisely because it seems that Tozzi suggests that this wayward materiality is the problem, and not specific triggers in the external world. This point emerges in *Memories of an Employee* (*Ricordi di un impiegato*).[14] On seeing the young Leopoldo blush when she threatens to tell his father about his romantic relationship with Attilia, Leopoldo's mother tells her son: "You are ashamed even of yourself!" (405). In effect, she appears to be entirely correct, as the shame felt by the protagonist stems not from external circumstance but from the very fact of having an inescapable body with determined needs and desires.

The related fact of disgust functions in a similarly all-pervading manner. On the one hand, it is projected outward by Tozzi's protagonists, transforming the external world of bodies, human and nonhuman, into sources of nauseating repulsion.[15] On the other, however, disgust revolves consistently around the consumption of food, as suggested by a further example from *Memories of an Employee*.[16] Upon hearing a colleague's insistence that "here we are all equal," Leopoldo becomes disgusted by the food he is eating: "I feel disgusted [. . .] I can hardly chew the last mouthfuls" (414).[17] Describing the mouth as a "specially charged border of the body," Martha Nussbaum writes that disgust reflects our "interest in policing the boundary between ourselves and nonhuman animals, or our own animality" (202). Leopoldo's disgust certainly manifests an interest in "policing" the borders of his body, as he rejects his own materiality, the embodiment he shares with human and nonhuman animals alike, now mirrored in that of his colleague who insisted on their sameness. However, his discomfort in the flesh reaches phobic proportions, as evidenced by his refusal to eat ("I am hungry and I do not eat" [428]), a behavior that immediately follows his observation of the gradual putrefaction of a cat lying dead on the roof outside his window (427). His phobic horror is also triggered on seeing the drops of blood left by a dentist who performs tooth extractions in the bedroom he rents (415).

This reference to the potent effect of blood resonates with Freud's theory of a human "organic repression" that serves as a "defence against a phase of development that has been surmounted" (*Civilization* 46). As man assumes an "upright gait," the role played by the "olfactory stimuli" is assumed by "visual excitations," and a resulting "incitement to cleanliness" prompts the rejection of blood, specifically menstrual blood, and excrement (46–47). Thus as man develops beyond the animal phase of existence, represented here by the dog, whose "dominant sense" remains that of the olfactory and who shows "no horror of excrement," man must constantly guard against the threat of animality (47). This threat, moreover, becomes especially pertinent if, to return to the point made in the first part of this essay, a human adulthood constructed on top of the domination of animal bodies has been rejected by the protagonist. In effect, having rejected the only available model for human behavior, the young protagonists have painted themselves into a corner in which their only company is that of the nonhuman animal. Given this predicament, the phobic attitude before food, blood, and bodies seems to reflect a fear on the part of the human protagonists of an atavistic regression to bestiality.

Three Crosses becomes the most pertinent text here, as the animalistic consumption of food rejected by the phobic Leopoldo becomes the raison d'être of the Gambi brothers. References to the desire for food are constant. Niccolò lusts after fruit he sees, and its smell "made him loosen and tighten his nostrils, and his knees gave way beneath him" (166). He wakes only to eat (161) and would like to have two stomachs, as one is not sufficient for the quantities of food he desires (165). Enrico claims that the worst thing about their imminent ruin is the impact it will have on their prospects for eating; nothing else matters, he says (235). Giulio also has a weakness for a "well set table" and rushes home from work to ensure that he not miss out on the "tastiest morsels" (171). This sustained focus on food is accompanied by a noteworthy number of animal parallels. Enrico laughs like a mouse (205), he is described as a boar (216), and his teeth are compared with those of a wolf (249). Niccolò's yawn ends in a braying sound (201), and he snarls (225). He also suffers from uncontrollable rages, which he describes, rather significantly, with the Italian phrase "*vado in bestia,*" or "I become a beast" (173). Moreover, *Three Crosses* is a text that, unlike the other novels, revolves principally around dialogue—a dialogue that is animalistic in that its convulsive and raucous excess skirts the borders of nonsignification.[18]

Tozzi's juxtaposition of the consumption of food and the threat of animality in *Three Crosses* requires, however, further qualification. Although the Gambi brothers spend inordinate amounts of time obsessing about food, they never appear to take pleasure in eating and are generally represented either before or after their meals.[19] This insistent denial of gustatory satisfaction appears as a programmatic negation of the faculty of taste.[20] If the act of eating underscores the threat of the materiality shared with the animal world, as in the aforementioned examples of the refusal to consume, the sense of taste might be considered in terms of a particularly human possibility of discernment. In short, it reflects the commonplace that the animal will eat anything, including excrement, while the human rejects that which is unpleasant. As such, the absence of taste here seems to advance the animalization of the brothers to the level of epistemology. If they cannot appreciate or even discern flavor when food is their primary mode of interaction with the world, how can this reality encountered first through the sensory ever be expected to make sense? Moreover, what now differentiates them on the epistemological level from the very animality that threatens to overwhelm them?

Much has been said in the field of philosophy about the cognitive distance between man and animal. Indeed, as indicated before when addressing the importance of Bentham's question about animal suffering, animals have long been defined in terms of what they lacked with respect to humanity rather than in terms of what they possessed in and of themselves. Heidegger's characterization of the animal as being "poor in world" is arguably one of the most well-known philosophical considerations of animal being (*Fundamental* 176–77). Indeed, working frantically to elevate humanity above the animal, Heidegger describes man as "not merely a part of the world" but also "master and servant of the world in the sense of *'having'* world. Man has world" (177, italics in original). While this description of world mastery certainly resonates with the brutal adulthood rejected by Tozzi's young protagonists, we note that, for Heidegger, the distinction is principally cognitive. In short, the distinction between man and animal lies, first and foremost, in the possibility of *"apprehending something as something"* (306, italics in original). He famously describes the gnoseological limits of a lizard lying in the sun: "[I]t is doubtful whether it really comports itself in the same way as we do when we lie out in the sun, i.e., whether the sun is accessible to it *as* sun, whether the lizard is capable of experiencing the rock *as* rock" (197, italics in original). William James, a philosopher dear to Tozzi, argues for the same cognitive limitation to animality. In *Some Problems in Philosophy*, he writes that, without the distinctively human substitution of concepts for perceptual impressions, we would exist as the animal does, "simply 'getting' each successive moment of experience, as the sessile sea-anemone on its rock receives whatever nourishment that wash of the waves may bring" (*Writings* 1015).

In programmatically negating the efficacy of sensory perception, whether that sense be taste, sight, hearing, or touch, Tozzi abandons his human protagonists in an epistemological dimension comparable with the experience of Heidegger's lizard or James's sea anemone. In short, like the anemone, they can only "get" wave after wave of disjointed sensory input. Moreover, for the young protagonists ill at ease in their own flesh, this sensory experience acquires an intensity that very frequently skirts the borders of the violent. Maxia, in fact, describes the sensory relationship with the world in terms of an assault, writing that the protagonists do not hear a sound but are instead deafened by it, and that color is a blinding experience (68–69). One example will suffice here. The narrator of *Beasts* describes the violence of a sun that "cuts the eyes with its pieces of glass" (612). This sensory assault closely resembles James's well-known description of the human baby, who lives "assailed by eyes, ears, nose, skin, and entrails at once" and experiences the entire world as "one great blooming, buzzing confusion" (*Principles* 462). At issue here is the absence of an organizing framework of conceptual categories and causalities: a level of self-transcendence at which the "whole system of relations, spatial, temporal, and logical [...] gets plotted out" (James, *Writings* 1016). It is precisely this conceptual organization of reality that affords us not only the possibility of interpreting the world but also the agency to shape it or, to say it with James, to "actively turn this way or that, bend our experience, and make it tell us whither it is bound" (*Writings* 1015). In effect, it elevates us to the mastery that defines the humanity that, for Heidegger, "has" world.

For Tozzi's protagonists, the animal gaze is, then, that of a terrifying counterpart, first equal in suffering and now identical in terms of its ontological and epistemological needs and limitations. As such, the animal acquires the unsettling force of the uncanny—a status, it should be underlined, that prompts acts of gratuitous violence on the part of the protagonists.[21] In light of Debenedetti's argument for the centrality of blindness to Tozzi's writing (95), it is more than mere coincidence that, in analyzing Hoffmann's "The Sandman," Freud had refuted Ernst Jentsch's association of intellectual uncertainty with the uncanny and had bound the uncanny to the "fear of being robbed of one's eyes" (*Standard* 230). In the context of *With Eyes Closed* and in the broader context of the Oedipal narrative of castration, blindness suggests a destabilization of human subjectivity. Indeed, what we see at the heart of the uncanny is precisely the blurring of traditional and carefully guarded conceptual oppositions such as subject–object, mind–body, and essence–appearance, all being, as Mladen Dolar states, "so many transcriptions of the division between interiority and exteriority" (6). The uncanny, then, becomes "something that shatters" these divisions and "cannot be situated within them" (6). In Tozzi's portrait of animality, the animal uncanny emerges on the heels of the final erasure of any demarcation between human subject and animal object. That human subjectivity so carefully constructed on the abjection and consumption of the animal object or thing disintegrates as the young protagonists prove unable to police the borders of their being and separate their interiority from the external world. Indeed, it is this interpenetration of their bodies and the world that renders their sensory perception so blindingly intense and, moreover, underpins their horrifying identification with the uncanny animal. Now unable to transcend their embodied selves, they inhabit a dimension that, for Bataille, is one of "immanence and immediacy," where, without demarcation between subject and object, they exist like the animal, who is "in the world like water in water" (23).

Writing Animal Being

In order to approach the enigma of animal immanence, their being "like water in water," Bataille suggests that the correct route is that of poetry (21). Akira Lippit coins the term "animetaphor" to account for the particular "vitality" that animal metaphors introduce into language: "[O]ne finds a fantastic transversality at work between the animal and the metaphor [...] Together they transport to language, breathe into language, the vitality of another life, another expression" (165). Coming from outside of language, the animal remains within it as a "foreign presence," and the "magnetic property of the animetaphor does not simply sway language but actively transforms it, assailing *logos* with the catachrestic force of affect" (Lippit 165–66). Derrida coins the term "animot" not only to contest that reductive tendency to speak of nonhuman animals in the singular as against a monolithic humanity but also to introduce into language a grammatically singular term that renders this "irreducible living multiplicity of mortals" and becomes "a sort of monstrous hybrid, a chimera waiting to be put to death by its Bellerophon" (*Animal* 41). The animal, traditionally excluded from reason and speech, has found a route into our human language and from within challenges language's organization, its constancy, and its categories. Similarly, Tozzi's writing, characterized by an expressionism focused on the sensory immediacy of the body, carries at its moments of greatest intensity the trace of this uncanny animal.

Tozzi's production is often divided into two six-year phases, or "*sessenni*," with critics largely favoring the first phase.[22] Central to this critical preference is the claim that the earlier period better illustrates Tozzi's expressionistic and antihierarchical parataxis of noncausality.[23] This nonhierarchical parataxis, I would suggest, should be considered in terms of a rendering of the sensory intensity that arguably characterizes animal being. Tozzi's parataxis, then, is the style of a body that perceives but does not access the conceptual transcendence and agency described by James. Robert De Lucca describes a Tozzian stylistics that becomes a gathering of "sounds, sights and smells," where the purely tangible becomes "words without the mediation of the intellect" (247–48). Unmediated sensory gathering lies at the heart of what Tozzi himself described as a rejection of conventional plot structures in favor of a "lyrical force," or "*forza lirica*" (1325). The following example from *With Eyes Closed* will serve as illustration:

A humid strip of sepia colored clouds separated the dark blue sky from a horizon that shone with evening rays. The foliage of the olive trees seemed a single veil held and enveloped in the open branches of each tree.
The cypress trees of the farmyard were black.
The flies and white butterflies brushed against the young girl's forehead and an unknown fragrance alternated with the hot stench emanating from the stables below.
From a peach tree whose flowers were damp and resinous, a cicada let out a shriek, as though it had been dreaming. (17)

In this assemblage of raw sensation, what emerges is an unmediated registering of the sights, sounds, smells, and tactile sensory experience of Ghisola. It is the domain in which, as Baldacci notes, verbs such as *appear, feel, seem,* and *believe* (*parere, sentire, sembrare,* and *credere*) prevail (*Tozzi moderno* 13). The narrator fades from view, and immediate sensuousness guides the movement from one sentence or clause to the next. Ghisola observes the clouds and then sees that the tops of the olive trees appear as a single veil over the branches. She then notes the blackness of the cypresses, an observation interrupted by the creatures that brush against her and the stench coming from below. She appears to locate the source of a cicada's cry, and then the narrator returns to reference a dreamlike state. Beyond the elementary classification of color, this passage could perhaps render the sensory experience of Heidegger's lizard. The temporal dimension also resonates with what we think we know of animal being. Put simply, the absence of causality means that temporality carries with it no inherent sense of narrative development or progress.[24] Indeed, in this passage, Ghisola's impressions could very easily be reversed, beginning with the screech of the cicada and ending with the clouds. As such, Ghisola seems here to resemble James's sea anemone, as she simply "gets" wave after wave of sensory input—input that is not organized into a hierarchical or causal conceptual temporality.

Given the variety within Tozzi's literary encounter with animality, it becomes impossible to classify his portrait of animal being under any single concept or tendency. His writing seems ethically oriented in its portrait of animal suffering and its condemnation of modernity's increasingly efficient abjection of animality; his expressionistic lyricism suggests the ontological and epistemological experience of animal being. Yet the body and the animal body in particular trigger such phobic disgust that the protagonists are driven to commit extreme violence to the animals. In effect, what we can identify in Tozzi's work is a painful anxiety before animality, an anxiety that verges on paralyzing anguish in the face of what we as humans share with the numerous animal species. By situating his work within a modernism fretfully negotiating after Darwin the threshold of humanity, we might account for the contradictory force of his consideration of animality. But his work seems to approach broader and less historically delimited questions. His unease before the animal bears comparison with Cora Diamond's discussion of the "difficulty of reality," a phrase she employs to render those "experiences in which we take something in reality to be resistant to our thinking it, or possibly to be painful in its inexplicability" (45–46). Returning to Derrida's consideration of the "nonpower" that humanity shares with animals, we find that this space also encompasses mortality, "the most radical means of thinking the finitude that we share with animals" (*Animal* 28). Thus in the eyes of animals large and small and despite all that separates us from them, we read our mortality, and their gaze triggers the "anguish of this vulnerability, and the vulnerability of this anguish" (*Animal* 28) before the moral obscenity of a life that ends inconceivably in death.

Notes

1. Written between 1909 and 1911, *Adele* was published in 1979 by Vallecchi.
2. Unless otherwise indicated, all translations in this essay are mine.
3. Written around 1913, *With Eyes Closed* was published in 1919 by Treves. *The Farm* was written in 1918 and published in volume form in 1921 by Treves.
4. An equally graphic example of cruelty toward nonagricultural animals can be found in *Beasts* (*Bestie*), where Migliorini, an agricultural worker, takes pleasure in torturing toads in a variety of ways, including impalement, evisceration, and burning (Tozzi 583). *Beasts* was composed in 1914 and 1915 and published in 1917 by Treves.
5. Giacomo Debenedetti offers a highly influential Oedipal reading of this particular scene, describing it as a condensation of the trauma of paternal mutilation (96).
6. In *Meat*, Nick Fiddes writes that "the most important feature of meat [...] is that it tangibly represents human control of the natural world. Consuming the muscle flesh of other highly evolved animals is a potent statement of our supreme power" (2). In the 2009 *PMLA* issue dedicated to animal studies, Marianne Dekoven addresses the gendered dimension of meat. She references two key texts—Carol J. Adams, *The Sexual Politics of Meat: A Feminist-Vegetarian Critical Theory* (1990), and Brian Luke, *Brutal: Manhood and the Exploitation of Animals* (2007)—that, she argues, "make the case that the objectification of and violence against animals parallel and undergird the objectification of and violence against women" (363).
7. Romano Luperini describes the Tozzian protagonist's rejection of an "adult genitality" that offers power and sexual gratification but also demands a posture of brutality toward others (13).
8. *Three Crosses* was written in 1918 and published by Treves in 1920.

9. Petroni sees Remigio's relationship with his farm as one that highlights use value rather than exchange value (83). Eduardo Saccone considers Remigio's interaction with the farm in terms of eroticism (77).
10. Petroni describes an ideology of sacrifice that dominates Tozzi's mature novels and writes that sacrifice becomes the only way to avoid engaging in violence (75).
11. *On the Origin of Species* was published in 1859. Though Darwin does not here explicitly address the evolutionary mechanism in the human species, the implied relevance to human action is obvious in the closing pages: "Light will be thrown on the origin of man and his history." Darwin, *On the Origin of Species* (Ontario: Broadview, 2003), 397. Darwin turns to evolution in the human species in his subsequent text, *The Descent of Man* (1871).
12. Borrowing the distinction from the ancient Greek philosophers, Agamben contrasts *zoē* with *bíos*, which he defines as "the form or way of living proper to an individual or group" (1).
13. I have discussed this issue elsewhere, providing details of the copious examples of these involuntary bodily behaviors. See Amberson 76–116.
14. Composed in 1910, *Ricordi di un impiegato* underwent revision in 1919. Giuseppe Antonio Borgese edited the first published version, which appeared in volume form in 1927 with Mondadori. Glauco Tozzi returned to the original manuscript, publishing the first integral edition in 1960.
15. While Tozzi's entire universe is populated by repulsive and frequently deformed bodies, one example will suffice here. *With Eyes Closed* offers a description of a company of beggars that includes a woman with a face like a mask of red skin and a woman with a case of eczema so extreme that only her enflamed eyes are visible and they look like wounds (Tozzi 89–91). For a more detailed consideration of examples of deformity, see Amberson 84–87.
16. Sexuality, whether in the form of their own desire or the behavior of others, also prompts embarrassment in the young protagonists. However, the question of sexuality is complicated by the association with the brutality of the tyrannical father. As such, it carries a significance that touches the social as well as the biological.
17. *Three Crosses* offers many cases in which food prompts a discomfort that approaches disgust. I would mention Giulio's embarrassment when Enrico arrives with his arms filled with fruit (171). *Adele* offers the example of the protagonist's encounter with a cherry tree; as she leaps up to grab the cherries, she crushes under foot a rose bush, and on seeing her own footprint on the bush, she is overwhelmed with a "disgust at the whole plant" (528).

18. Maxia describes this dialogue as consisting of "shouting, noise, venting of nervous infirmity, thunderous accompaniment to a gesticulation that is exaggerated and convulsive" (137).
19. The explicit act of eating or drinking features only three times in the text and in each case does not bring pleasure. On only one occasion are the brothers depicted at the table, and here no one actually eats. Instead, the brothers indulge in an excessive laughter that causes items to exit the mouth rather than enter it (190–91).
20. I have suggested elsewhere that each novel revolves around and negates the epistemological possibilities of a particular human sense. *With Eyes Closed* famously underscores blindness, *The Farm* suggests a faulty sense of smell, and *Memories of an Employee* and *Adele* show the limits of touch. For a fuller development of this argument, see Amberson 90–95.
21. This gratuitous violence differs from that of the agricultural machine. Two examples will clarify this distinction. In *With Eyes Closed* Pietro dismembers crickets (12) and Ghisola inexplicably crushes the heads of the birds she had earlier decided to protect (16).
22. The first phase stretches from 1908 to 1914, while the second "*sessennio*" begins in 1914 and ends with Tozzi's death in 1920.
23. Insistent that Tozzi is not a naturalist, Debenedetti describes a narrative economy that, rejecting principles of causality, records rather than explicates (92). Baldacci describes an antihierarchical organization in which no moment is privileged (*Tozzi moderno* 9). Maxia describes *With Eyes Closed* as a text whose structure is one of a paratactical and centrifugal episodicity (11). Cataloguing a series of characteristics including parataxis and a levelling of syntactical hierarchies, Luperini also identifies a centrifugal narrative organization (41–42).
24. Critics largely agree that Tozzi's lyricism fractures narrative temporality in order to posit a noncausal sequence of moments. Baldacci writes of the "sudden illuminations" that break narrative temporality ("Introduction" xxii). Petroni identifies a "symmetrical logic" that occasions the temporal reversibility characteristic of the working of the unconscious (147–48). He also describes a subject who lives not in an objective temporality but, rather, in a series of "temporal atoms each of which absorbs him, forcing him into a present that is devoid of developments" (40–41).

Works Cited

Agamben, Giorgio. *Homo Sacer: Sovereign Power and Bare Life*. Trans. Daniel Heller-Roazen. Stanford: Stanford UP, 1998.

Amberson, Deborah. *Giraffes in the Garden of Italian Literature: Modernist Embodiment in Italo Svevo, Federigo Tozzi, and Carlo Emilio Gadda.* London: Legenda, 2012.
Baldacci, Luigi. "Introduction." In *Il podere*, vii–xlvii. Milan: Garzanti, 2002.
———. *Tozzi moderno.* Turin: Einaudi, 1993.
Bataille, Georges. *Theory of Religion.* Trans. Robert Hurley. New York: Zone, 1992.
Bentham, Jeremy. *An Introduction to the Principles of Morals and Legislation.* Oxford: Clarendon, 1907.
Darwin, Charles. *On the Origin of Species.* Ontario: Broadview, 2003.
Debenedetti, Giacomo. *Il personaggio uomo.* Milan: Garzanti, 1988.
Dekoven, Marianne. "Why Animals Now?" *PMLA* 124.2 (2009): 361–69.
De Lucca, Robert. "Tozzi, Automatism, and Epistemology." *Quaderni d'italianistica* 16.2 (1995): 245–59.
Derrida, Jacques. *The Animal That Therefore I Am.* Ed. Marie-Louise Mallet. Trans. David Wills. New York: Fordham UP, 2008.
———. *Points . . . Interviews 1974–1994.* Trans. Peggy Kamuf and others. Stanford: Stanford UP, 1995.
Diamond, Cora. "The Difficulty of Reality and the Difficulty of Philosophy." In *Philosophy and Animal Life*, 43–89. New York: Columbia UP, 2008.
Dolar, Mladen. "'I Shall Be with You on Your Wedding Night': Lacan and the Uncanny." *October* 58 (1991): 5–23.
Fiddes, Nick. *Meat: A Natural Symbol.* London: Routledge, 1991.
Freud, Sigmund. *Civilization and Its Discontents.* New York: Norton, 1961.
———. *Standard Edition of the Complete Psychological Works of Sigmund Freud, Volume 17.* London: Hogarth, 1955.
Heidegger, Martin. *Basic Writings.* Revised and Expanded Edition. New York: HarperCollins, 1993.
———. *The Fundamental Concepts of Metaphysics: World, Finitude, Solitude.* Bloomington: Indiana UP, 1995.
James, William. *The Principles of Psychology.* Cambridge: Harvard UP, 1983.
———. *Writings 1902–1910.* New York: Library of America, 1987.
Levinas, Emmanuel. *On Escape.* Trans. Bettina Bergo. Stanford: Stanford UP, 2003.
Lippit, Akira Mizuta. *Electric Animal: Toward a Rhetoric of Wildlife.* Minneapolis: U of Minnesota P, 2000.
Luperini, Romano. *Federigo Tozzi. Le immagini, le idee, le opere.* Rome: Laterza, 1995.
Lyotard, Jean-François. *The Differend: Phrases in Dispute.* Minneapolis: U of Minnesota P, 1988.
Maxia, Sandro. *Uomini e bestie nella narrativa di Federigo Tozzi.* Padua: Liviana, 1971.
Nussbaum, Martha. *Upheavals of Thought: The Intelligence of Emotions.* Cambridge: Cambridge UP, 2001.

Petroni, Franco. *Ideologia e scrittura: Saggi su Federigo Tozzi*. Lecce: Manni, 2006.
Rohman, Carrie. *Stalking the Subject: Modernism and the Animal*. New York: Columbia UP, 2009.
Saccone, Eduardo. *Allegoria e sospetto: Come leggere Tozzi*. Naples: Liguori, 2000.
Tozzi, Federigo. *Opere*. Ed. Marco Marchi. Milan: Mondadori, 1987.

2

Cesare Pavese, Posthumanism, and the Maternal Symbolic

Elizabeth Leake

The oeuvre of Cesare Pavese (1908–50) is deeply concerned with questions of origins, human and otherwise. At the heart of this concern is an enduring anxiety about the female body—an anxiety that results, more frequently than not, in its violation, mutilation, and destruction. What is more, the female body is oftentimes more than merely a body for Pavese; it is a stand-in for the natural world—zoological, botanical, and geological— whose instincts, ripening, heat, and colors are available for manipulation and exploitation by men, except in those instances when its propitiation has been insufficiently or improperly enacted.[1] Beyond what we might thus call an anatomical anxiety about women is a functional one—that is, an anxiety that extends from female bodies proper to the generative function of the natural world writ large. Not surprisingly, this finds its most powerful expression in Pavese's continued preoccupation with female sexuality, and particularly maternity, made emergent and operative in the equation between women and animals in several of his novels as well as throughout his poetic oeuvre.[2] More unexpected, perhaps, is the idea that alongside female generative power is also depicted a male maternal function. This essay will examine the stakes of these concerns as they intersect the theoretical realms of posthistory, posthumanism, and feminist theory.

The premise of my argument is that in *The Harvesters* (*Paesi tuoi*, 1941), *The House on the Hill* (*La casa in collina*, 1949), and *The Moon and the Bonfires* (*La luna e i falò*, 1950), Pavese stages the symbolic matricide that feminist thinkers have identified as the suppression necessary for history and for phallogocentric humanism to prevail over the natural, the animal, and the maternal symbolic. Specifically, Pavese accomplishes this in two steps. First, his texts relegate the fecund female body to the irredeemable animal/

natural world, both by way of repeated recourse to their equivalence ("You, too, are hill / and path of stones" begins one of his poems)[3] and through the repeated destruction of the female body in various propitiatory rites (sacrificial bloodletting and the bonfire chief among them). Second, where the prehistorical was inhabited of necessity by subjects of woman born, the historical occludes the origin of that birth; this occurs by way of the reinscription of a generative, almost maternal (in that the birthing body is male) function onto some of Pavese's male characters. This double move—erasure of female maternity and its reinscription as the province of men—means, effectively, that the novels forestall the demise of history by maintaining the fantasy of male self-generation necessary for phallogocentric humanism to continue. When the two gestures are considered together, the texts appear to militate for the postponement of the end of humanism and the historical and, consequently, for the postponement of the advent of posthumanism and the posthistorical (to the limited extent that these can be considered sequential). To construct this argument, I build on a well-established foundation—namely, the oft-made observation that Pavese's novels sustain the alterity of women and nature with respect to men, an alterity on which the (male) subject of modernity is founded.[4] Put differently, Pavese's characters can be said to exhibit speciesist attitudes, where, as Rosi Braidotti argues, speciesism is akin to "sexism or racism in privileging humans, males, and whites over all others" (*Nomadic* 90).[5]

It is something of a critical commonplace to remark that by insisting on the alterity of women and nature, Pavese's opus articulates a crisis of the phallogocentric subject, even when he appears to militate on its behalf. According to this thinking, Pavese's longstanding interest in ethnography and anthropology, his reading of scholars such as Kerényi and Lévy-Bruhl, the engagement of critics like Furio Jesi, and not least, Pavese's own *Dialogues with Leucò* (*Dialoghi con Leucò*, 1947) emerge as evidence that the relations between myth and history—that is, between man and the mystical, the magical, and ritual—undergird his fiction. I take as my point of departure the observation that engagement with the relations between myth and history (conceptualized also as the cyclical time of nature and the linear time of history) is fundamentally a concern with origins. My claim is not so much that these concerns are heavily inflected with questions of gender (this, too, is well documented in the critical scholarship) but rather that the question of origins, doubly bound in biological questions and in temporal ones, is parsed as the possibility of parthenogenesis: of giving birth to oneself without need for the participation of an other.[6]

But Pavese and his works are not my sole objects of interest. Instead, I make these claims in order to make a larger, more theoretical point about feminism and posthumanism. For there are theoretical stakes to this move; it brings into high relief (and not for the first time) both modernity's founding epistemological gesture of erasure of the biological and modernity's constitutive instability: what Braidotti calls the "interconnected facets of structural otherness or difference as pejoration, which simultaneously construct and are excluded in modernity" (*Nomadic* 28). This chapter will argue that Pavese's resistance to posthistory via the fantasies of parthenogenesis and male maternity exposes the doubly illusory emergence and operation of phallogocentric humanism and illuminates the broader potential of a posthumanism in the joint service of feminism and nonhuman animals.

Prehistory

Feminist scholars (Cavarero, Braidotti, Lloyd, and others) assert that the emergence and operation of history and humanism is a function of form, or rather of relations of norm and nonconformity. As Braidotti asserts, "The dominant power structures in our system work by organizing differences according to a hierarchical scale that is governed by the standardized mainstream subject. Deleuze calls it 'The Majority subject' or the Molar Center of Being; Derrida calls it 'phallologocentrism'; Irigaray opts for 'the hyperinflated, falsely universal logic of the Same.' In such a scheme normality, as Canguilhem presciently put it, equals the zero degree of deviancy or monstrosity" (*Nomadic* 28). Another way to think about this is to say that the subject of modernity is organized around a series of exclusions: man is not woman, and man is not animal, for example. There follows an attendant corollary: woman is animal (also parsed as nature).

This last identification obfuscates the precedence of the biological before the symbolic: "Prior to thought and thinking, there is life and there is the living being. This living entity becomes a subject by entry into the symbolic system, which entails the inscription into the symbolic and thus is prior to its specific order" (Braidotti, "Foreword" xvii). This is, of course, the theoretical articulation of the foundational premises of Adrienne Rich (*Of Woman Born: Motherhood as Experience and Institution*, 1977) and Luisa Muraro (*The Symbolic Order of the Mother*, 1991): both birth and language originate with the mother. The humanist subject is unthinkable outside of the constitutive disavowal that distinguishes him, effectively, from himself (i.e., his humanity from his animality) in that "in so far as Man, the male, is the main referent for thinking subjectivity, the standard-bearer of the Norm, the Law, the Logos, Woman is dualistically, i.e., oppositionally positioned as his 'other'" (Braidotti, *Nomadic* 36). He is therefore doubly unstable, because the suppression of animality and his ineluctably biological origin requires an analogous discursive disavowal—the disavowal, in Braidotti's terms, of "the embodied, sexed, and corporeal nature of the living beings" ("Foreword" xvii). The moment the humanist term *man* is meant to include both men and women, it can in actuality mean neither. Thus here, too, the definition of *man* calls into question the very possibility of man ("the central program of phallogocentrism: the masculinization of the site of origin of the subject and the reduction of masculinity to an abstraction" [Braidotti, "Foreword" xviii]).

A (modernist) vision of woman as natural or animal, of woman as body, consequently has as its corollary one of man as thought.[7] Pavese's novel *The Harvesters*, composed between June and August 1939 and published in 1941—a novel about the incestuous rape and eventual murder of the victim Gisella by her brother Talino—stages the diminishment of female characters to their physical materiality through its insistence on the visual element of spilled blood, specifically of the earth red with Gisella's blood. In the first of the passages that follow, Berto recounts hearing about Talino's first assault on Gisella. In the second and third passages, the invocation of blood in the countryside, and in connection with dust and hay, prepare us for the scene that follows soon after (the last three quotes) in which Talino plunges a pitchfork into his sister's throat:

> Miliota herself [. . .] was telling us that her sister bled for a whole week. (*Harvesters* 119)

> As I watched him coming towards me in the bright sunshine, the thought struck me that the shedding of blood seemed less shocking in the country than in the shadow of a house in Turin. Once I had seen blood on the wheels of a tram after an accident, and it was terrifying. But here, the idea of someone sinking down and pouring out his life-blood on the stubble seemed more natural, as in a slaughter-house. (122)

> [A]fter five or six trips through the doorway there was a red haze before my eyes. In my mouth was the taste of grain, dust, and blood. (135)

> A sudden ferocious glare blazed up in Talino's eyes, he jumped back to give himself room, and [. . .] he had driven the pitchfork into her throat. [. . .] Gisella let the bucket fall and the water swilled over my shoes. I thought it was blood, and leapt aside. Talino sprang away, too, and we heard Gisella's voice come bubbling up in her throat. "Holy Mother!" she gurgled, then coughed until the pitchfork dropped away from her neck. [. . .] Gisella was coughing and bringing up blood, and the prongs were dark with it. (136–37)

> Where she had fallen with her bucket, the earth was so dark with blood that the very sight of it sickened me, and the trail to the corn-stack was still more red, more vivid. (139)

> The bloodstains could still be seen in the doorway of the shed. "It's a strange thing," I reflected, "that every day blood is spilt on the roads. The ground soaks it up, and we think no more about it. But to look at it now, and realise

that this mud-patch is where Gisella's warm life-blood ebbed away, turns me cold with horror." (148)

Gisella's death at the hands of her pitchfork-wielding brother is witnessed by Berto and members of her family. But before her death, we learn, she had already once submitted to a similar, violent assault by her brother and lost a significant quantity of blood ("her sister bled for a whole week"), a repetition that is evoked in the double recontextualization of blood in the second quotation: from countryside to city ("the shedding of blood seemed less shocking in the country than [. . .] in Turin") and back again ("on the wheels of a tram after an accident [. . .] on the stubble"). This repeated comparison serves to underscore the idea that the normal, or rather, the unremarkable context for bleeding is a rural one—an observation made more complex when considered in the context of the overarching preoccupation, across Pavese's oeuvre, with rural violence.[8] In other words, that Gisella's blood is repeatedly spilled in the countryside is not the point so much as the idea that the countryside is the habitual site of violence, a violence intensified both by the fact that she survives the first time but not the second and by the comparison with the slaughter of a pig: "'A pity,' the doctor went on. 'Physically, she was in excellent health. [. . .] Even pigs cannot endure so much'" (*Harvesters* 148–49). The spilling of blood on the earth, too, implies the realms of sacrifice (we will see this later with Gisella's juxtaposition with a goat) and propitiation, measures meant perhaps to counter the acts of incest and their attendant violence to the social order.[9]

These images, by virtue of their quantity and concentration, serve to establish Gisella's gendered, bleeding body as a kind of shorthand for the conflation of nature (both nature in contrast to the culture of the city and nature as animal), sex, and violence. As such, she must be repressed—here, tellingly, through an act of violent bodily penetration of her throat, and thus at the site of the acoustic production of language/speech. What's more, that repression is within Talino's rights, insofar as, for the speciesist subject, "it is not up to the rationality of the law and the universalism of moral values to structure the exercise of power, but rather the unleashing of the unrestricted sovereign right to kill, maim, rape, and destroy the life of others" (Braidotti, *Nomadic* 336). Indeed, Talino's incestuous rape of Gisella is configured almost as the exercise of his droit du seigneur, when Berto remarks to himself about their tryst, "Never mind. If it hadn't been for him, perhaps Gisella wouldn't have come with you" (*Harvesters* 125–26). Here we could make observations about the mythification of the countryside so prevalent in Pavese's novels or the conflict he articulates in his narrator between the desire to act (to protect Gisella, for example) and its impossibility (a function of the inexorable existential solitude that characterizes his heroes). I prefer, rather, that we note the resemblance, mutatis mutandis, of Gisella's position to that of the "ungrievable" lives described by Judith Butler in *Frames of War*—that is, "those that cannot be lost and cannot be destroyed, because they already inhabit a lost and destroyed zone; they are, ontologically, and from the start, already lost and destroyed, which means that when they are destroyed in war, nothing is destroyed" (xix). Though the circumstances are quite different (Pavese's family drama versus Butler's tabulation of war dead), the implications for Gisella as animal and for Butler's ungrievable lives (women and children chief among them) are the same. What is more, the logic of "disavowal and rationalization" (Butler, *Frames* xxi), necessary for the notion of lives that do not count as such to adhere, underscores that before the text even poses the question of humanity, it must first make operative a (rationalized and disavowed) definition of *life*.

In both cases, such a definition is species-specific, predicated on power relations among humans for Butler and in the speciesism Pavese's texts evince. Throughout his opus, Pavese demonstrates a near obsessive identification of one particular feature of the natural landscape—the hills, in which the majority of *The Harvesters* (but *The House on the Hill* and *The Moon and the Bonfires* equally) takes place—with female breasts. Their appearance, whether human or telluric, is at once eroticized (as is the case with Gisella and the equation hill-breast) and maternal (as is the case with Adele, who nurses her infant constantly throughout the novel; the indirect comparisons of Gisella to a cow or a goat; and the equivalence earth-mother), suggesting both the return to the mother (earth) of sexuality and of death:[10]

> There was a big hill shaped like a woman's breast. (*Harvesters* 30)

> "Where's the hill that looked like a breast?" "This is it," said Talino. [. . .] I turned and looked back at the hill where we had left the train. Now it looked bigger and exactly like a breast, all smoothly rounded on each side and with a clump of trees making a dark ring at the peak. And Talino laughed in his beard like an oaf, as if he really were facing a woman with her breast bare. (31–32)

> I looked up at the bats flying round, and there, before my eyes, was the hill I had seen from the train, with its peak like a nipple and lights gleaming from its side. I turned round, but the house hid the other hill that could be seen from the threshing floor. "We're between two breasts," I said to myself. "Nobody here thinks so, but we're between two breasts." (44)

> From where I lay I could see the first hill, all scorched and bare—that's where all the vineyards were—and at the top of it the nipple that was so pretty to look at. (57)

> Gisella placed the pail underneath a cow and began milking her, handling the teat as if it were her own. It made my mouth water to see her leaning forward like that. (79)

> Gisella [...] had a way of responding with such flashing eyes that she could have set fire to the Grangia, like Talino. I haven't said this before, but when I was watching her milking in the cow-shed, I cupped my hand round the teat and her fingers as well, pulling with her until the milk came. (84–85)

In these passages we perceive a further gloss on the nodal point composed by nature, sex, and violence. Milk supplants blood (we cannot help thinking of the Kristevan abject), though not in order to reclaim symbolic maternal precedence so much as to eroticize, and thereby devalue, debase, and displace maternity as the inaugural event of patriarchal history. Though it is tempting to read the figure of the nursing mother as the sign of female resistance against the erasure of maternity from the foundations of order, Cavarero claims the opposite when she reads nursing as its validation: "[T]he maternal power to generate life was transformed into a transitional site on the way to a life generated by fathers, into a nurturing cell. Breastfeeding is a continuation and a confirmation of this power" (72). The telluric and the anatomical elide into a single, undifferentiated category (the embodied) as over and against the conceptual, the spiritual (the philosophical, Cavarero would say), the universalizing of culture, of history. Whatever its form, embodiment is irredeemably dissociated from the patriarchal subject.[11]

Here, too, we might locate the recurrence of violence and in particular the recurrent discourse of violent consumption, whether explicit or implied, in the relations to Gisella (breast, blood, milk, goat) exhibited by the narrator and by Talino. For Braidotti, the threat and promise of violent consumption are not symptoms of the patriarchy so much as they are structural components of it. Between the patriarchal subject and the animal (i.e., natural, material, embodied) there exists

> an intimate relationship, framed nonetheless by the dominant human and structurally masculine habit of taking for granted free access to and consumption of the bodies of others, animals included. As a mode of relation, it is structurally violent and saturated accordingly with projections, identifications, and fantasies. These are centered on the dyad fear and desire, which is the trademark of the Western subject's relationship to the phallic law, the lack and the power of the master signifier, as Lacan astutely noted. It is also a token of this same subject's sense of supreme ontological entitlement. Derrida also referred to this human power over animals in terms of: "carnophallogocentrism." (*Nomadic* 81)

No wonder, then, that Gisella is also depicted both as fruit and as bearer of fruit, and as (bearer of) water, consumables whose symbolic valences are readily apparent:

> Gisella, who now smiled at me, seemed to live on fruit instead. When I had finished I asked Talino if he hadn't any apples and he took me into a loft where the whole floor was covered with them like a mosaic, all red or turning brown. I picked out a good one and bit into it. It tasted sharp, as I like apples to be.
> "They're Gisella's apples," Talino remarked as we went back to the table.
> "Why? Do you cultivate apples?" I asked Gisella.
> They hardly understood what I meant. Instead, the old man explained to me that when a girl is born a tree is planted, so that it grows as she does. (*Harvesters* 56)

> I went off by myself into Gisella's apple loft, picked out the best fruit I could see and bit into it frantically. "Tonight," I was thinking, "I'll fill my pockets with them." (162)

Here again we see the same, bidirectional identification of the female body with the animal—with the natural as portable ("I'll fill my pockets with them"), consumable good. Gisella looks like fruit, the apples (with their Edenic overtones) taste like her, and, more to the point, it is implied that she herself gives birth to them, whether by hatching them like a chicken ("Do you cultivate [*covate*] apples?") or in the act of her own birth, on which occasion the fruit-bearing tree was planted.[12] Water functions similarly, as on multiple occasions Gisella is depicted as both the provider of water and its very substance, as is evident in the first example following. Further, the same conflation between the animal, the natural, the erotic, and the violent that was at play in the images of the apples and of female breasts (note the recurrence of the hill-breast equation as well as of the goat that appears soon after the conclusion of the second passage) is mobilized in the suggestion of blood implicit in the water that is as sweet as cherries; indeed, Gisella is in the act of passing a drink of water to Talino when she is killed:

> [S]he leaned over to lift it and I could see her bare legs. I stood close against her to help her lift it over the rim. The water mirrored our faces, and when we drank it was sweeter than cherries. If all those children hadn't been there (not to mention Talino), I would have made the most of it. (*Harvesters* 57–58)

"But here, in the moonlight, she won't be willing [...] Suppose she only wants to talk?" But I laughed, for if I told her about the hill shaped like a breast, I should be able to steer the conversation along the right lines. (74)

In the second citation, Berto awaits Gisella at their first assignation, but he waits in vain; instead of Gisella, a goat arrives. The close association of Gisella with the animal/natural world is typical of the humanist/phallogocentric conception of the body, as Elizabeth Grosz puts it, as bodies cannot be adequately understood as "ahistorical, precultural, or natural objects in any simple way; they are not only inscribed, marked, engraved, by social pressures external to them but are the products, the direct effects, of the very social constitution of nature itself" (x). Taken together, these Pavese passages disclose the novel's concern with the occlusion of the feminine, an occlusion not exclusive to *The Harvesters* (Cate of *The House on the Hill* is deported and presumably dies in a prison camp; Santina of *The Moon and the Bonfires* is shot and her body burned; in the same novel, her sister Silvia dies after a botched abortion, Mentina dies in childbirth, and Rosina is kicked to a bloody death: "she was dead and blood came out of her mouth" [169]). The novels evince concern about a crisis of masculinity through the repeated staging of a symbolic matricide. Pavese stages relations between men and women as a conflict on the verge of eruption: always uneasy, marked by violent skirmishes, and more than occasionally lethal. Though they do so at great personal cost (no Pavese character is ever happy), Pavese's men survive the threat to their sovereignty posed by gendered origins. In contrast, his women, almost inevitably, must die or at least disappear. The apotheosis of the masculine as neutral and universal serves to conceal sexual difference and, more important for our purposes, to conceal the maternal function at the root of all existence. Moreover, Pavese's characters' male maternities (announced several years earlier in his poetry)[13] rehearse the symbolic matricide of which Cavarero, Irigaray, Muraro, and others speak, the more fully to resist a retroactive imputation of matrilineality and thus to remain firmly entrenched in a modern sensibility.[14] Braidotti assesses it as follows: "Cavarero joins forces with Irigaray here, in the pursuit of a female-sexed materialism which functions as the substratum of and is prior to the phallogocentric order. [...] Instead of recognizing the embodied, sexed, and corporeal nature of the living beings, phallocratic thinking replaces the maternal origin with the highly abstract notion of man being at the origin of himself" ("Foreword" xvii). Contrast these positions, in which symbolization and embodiment vie for *sequential* primacy, with one such as Butler's (in *Bodies that Matter*) in which symbolization, rather, *constitutes* living being. The distinction is important insofar as the ontological argument anticipates the possibility of male maternity (to which we will return presently) by positing a generative practice not based in sequentiality/temporality but rather simultaneity.

We might alternatively articulate the constitutive disavowal endemic to the masculinization of the site of origin, following François Jacob: "[A]long with sexual reproduction death would provide the necessary condition for life, most notably in the perspective of evolution: 'Not death coming from the outside as the consequence of some accident,' he elucidates, 'but rather death coming from within as a necessity prescribed, already in the egg, by the genetic program'" (qtd. in Baracchi 320). Jacob's introduction of death into birth is crucial here, in its articulation of the suppression or destruction of the maternal symbolic (death to birth-giving—birth no more, Cavarero would say). The identification of the masculine with the human both obscures the initial symbolic matricide and serves to endorse a kind of symbolic parthenogenesis (Braidotti's "man being at the origin of himself"). From matricide, then, we move to male maternity. Pavese stages in *The Harvesters*, *The House on the Hill*, and *The Moon and the Bonfires* the matricide necessary for history and for phallogocentric humanism to prevail over the natural, the animal, the maternal symbolic.[15] He attributes a maternal function to some of his male characters and relegates the female body to the irredeemable animal/natural world by destroying it in propitiatory rites. Like the dual nature of sacrificial bloodletting in *The Harvesters*, *The Moon and the Bonfires* renders bonfires whose goals conflate the realms of the telluric and the human: those bonfires regularly lit to render more fertile the earth and the single, unrepeatable bonfire in which Santina's body is destroyed to prevent posthumous desecration in the form of necrophilia, itself an example of humanist category confusion, in that if the body is pure (feminized) materiality, then its sentience is irrelevant to the question of desecration. The point, I repeat, has to do with these symbolic matricides and, as we will see, the temporal characteristics of the move to postpone posthistory and maintain a fantasy of male self-generation.

In these novels, male protagonists evince increasingly (male) maternal functions, by which I mean the ability to spawn, as it were, both themselves and their younger doubles, without however undergoing feminization. In a move reminiscent of a gender-inverted *affidamento* or entrustment à la Muraro,[16] boy children are produced—whether literally sired, metaphorically entrusted, or both—by men, in environments where mothers, if indeed they exist, are radically redimensioned as secondary presences. *The House on the Hill*, for example, starts with a protagonist who is psychologically split, fully identified with his adult self as well as with his child self (not to mention the author's doubling in the dog Belbo, which is also the name of Pavese's natal village—Santo Stefano Belbo): "I was finding my boyhood just to have a companion, a colleague, a son. I saw this country where I grew up with new eyes. We were alone together, the boy and myself" (66). Soon thereafter, however, the identification loosens and the narrator marks his distance from that youth: "[T]he rash young man who ran away from things thinking they might still happen anyway, who thought of himself as a grown man and was always waiting for his life to begin in earnest; this person amazed me. What did the two of us have in common? What had I done for him? [...] Well, I thought as soon as I was alone, you are not that boy any longer, you aren't taking the old chances" (69–70).

Eventually, that doubling of adult self and child self is expanded to encompass two characters, Corrado and his putative son, Dino, at the price of mother Cate's erasure:[17] "'His name is Corrado,' I said. [. . .] 'It's my name,' I said" (*House* 88); "It had taken me a month to discover that Dino was short for Corrado" (89); "I took him by the head to hold him upright. I seemed to be holding myself as a boy: the same short hair and long shoulders" (104); "If nowadays Dino accepted me without much enthusiasm it was because I was too close to him, making myself act the father" (107); "And now Dino had no one except me" (151). The move, in other words, is from the simultaneous presence of two generations of one man *in* one man to the simultaneous presence of the two generations possible only in a sequential relationship (first Corrado, then Dino).

This temporal shift, again dependent on the occlusion of the mother, is spelled out more clearly in *The Moon and the Bonfires*. Cinto loses his mother in childbirth and is terrorized by his father. In place of these absent and unparentlike parents, Cinto is instead immediately and repeatedly identified with Anguilla. He grows up in the house in which Anguilla was raised, in similarly breathtaking poverty; upon first meeting, Anguilla declares "I was a boy like you" (37); "I began to laugh and told him I'd done the same trick when I was a boy" (39); "It was just as if I knew the dreams he had at night and the things that crossed his mind while he limped across the square" (118). Later, Anguilla and Nuto undertake responsibility for Cinto's education and well-being: "I told him right away that it was up to us to take care of Cinto, that we should have been doing it anyway" (171). Indeed, Cinto's horizontal affiliation/identification with Anguilla extends now to Nuto as well, after whom he will model himself: "Nuto took Cinto into his house to show him carpentry and to teach him to become a musician" (194). In this novel, we observe a more exasperated version of the tension between sequentiality (Cinto being "fathered" by Nuto and Anguilla) and simultaneity (Cinto *as* Nuto and Anguilla). The most egregious example of the latter (echoing the permutations in the Corrado-Dino dyad) is when Nuto says to Anguilla, "Your father—that's you" (11).

Posthistory

What are the relations between these issues of temporality and the animalization of woman, the womanization of the telluric, symbolic matricide, and paternity, and what purposes do they serve in Pavese's fiction? What threat does these novels' commitment to the modern subject attempt to forestall? In my reading, Pavese anticipates the notion, here articulated by Braidotti, that "[m]an as the privileged referent of subjectivity, the standard-bearer of the norm/law/logos, represents the majority, i.e., the dead heart of the system. The consequences are [. . .] that masculinity [. . .] can only be the site of deconstruction or critique" (*Nomadic* 36). We have seen how Pavese depicts the crises of masculinity, on the one hand, around questions of origins, identity, and genealogy and, on the other, around the construction of a speciesist framework dependent on the repression of female subjectivity. What remains to be seen is how these converge with discourses about posthistory currently in circulation, and more specifically, how these convergences can be read to militate in a feminist key.

Giorgio Agamben articulates the notion of the constitutive instability of history and thus of humanism by way of Kojève's engagement with Hegel:

> [I]n Kojève's reading of Hegel, man is not a biologically defined species, nor is he a substance given once and for all; he is, rather, a field of dialectical tensions always already cut by internal caesurae that every time separate—at least virtually—"anthropophorous" animality and the humanity which takes bodily form in it. Man exists historically only in this tension; he can be human only to the degree that he transcends and transforms the anthropophorous animal which supports him, and only because, through the action or negation, he is capable of mastering and, eventually, destroying his own animality (it is in this sense that Kojève can write that "man is a fatal disease of the animal"). (12)

There are two elements of interest here: the idea that the existence of man entails by necessity an act of partial self-destruction or disavowal, and further, the notion, to which we alluded before, of the human as that which is instantiated only within that disavowal. The conceptualization of the human as distinct from the animal requires the existence of the animal insofar as the distinction defines the terms, and yet no distinction is possible. The human exists, if you like, in an aporia analogous to the simultaneous presence of wood and ashes[18]—a state of affairs possible only in an epistemological temporality that permits conditions to be both simultaneous and sequential. History, in other words, presents the logic of both *and* and *or* at the same time. Another way to understand this aporia that is history is from the perspective of posthistory; Kojève provides a clarifying contrast when his interest in the end of human history leads him to meditate on, in Agamben's words, the "figure that man and nature would assume in the posthistorical world" (6). Kojève opines, "Man remains alive as animal in harmony with Nature or given Being" (qtd. in Agamben 6)—with an emphasis on simultaneity.

Posthistory, then, implies both a different temporality than that of history as well as the correction of a kind of category error by way of a return to the identification of man and animal. If man "has become animal again at the end of history" (Agamben 6), it must be because, following Hegel, "the completion of history necessarily entails the end of man" (Agamben 7): an ending, in other words, and a return to a previous state. In contrast, Agamben formulates the end as a series of conceptual uncouplings:

> In our culture, man has always been thought of as the articulation and conjunction of a body and a soul, of a living thing and a *logos*, of a natural (or animal) element and a supernatural or social or divine element. We must learn instead to think of man as what results from the incongruity of these two elements, and investigate not the metaphysical mystery of conjunction, but rather the practical and political mystery of separation. What is man, if he is always the place—and, at the same time, the result—of ceaseless divisions and caesurae? (16)

Of interest to us here are the question of political ramifications (and we question, in passing, the implication of transcendence in the term *mystery*) and the idea introduced here of man conceived as instrumentality. What is important about the move from history to posthistory, Agamben avers, is that we must learn to rethink man, and not that man has changed in some fundamental way.

This rethinking has far-reaching repercussions. Beyond the definition of man, it calls into question the very *possibility* of man: "The messianic end of history or the completion of the divine *oikonomia* of salvation defines a critical threshold, at which the difference between animal and human, which is so decisive for our culture, threatens to vanish. [. . .] If animal life and human life could be superimposed perfectly, then neither man nor animal—and, perhaps, not even the divine—would any longer be thinkable. For this reason, the arrival at posthistory necessarily entails the re-actualization of the prehistoric threshold at which that border had been defined" (Agamben 21). Moreover, it reintroduces the temporal logic of return in its suggestion of a "re-actualization of the prehistoric threshold": posthumanism must countenance prehistory as well as posthistory. The end of history moves us into an economy of time at once transcendent and immanent, and here we might recall the title of Pavese's last novel, *The Moon and the Bonfires*, whose two terms resonate with the same antinomic logic (the cyclical or immanent moon coexists with the linear or transcendent bonfire)—reason and season, as Gian Paolo Biasin would say (220–21). As for the "practical and political mystery of separation" (Agamben 16), Cavarero counters the death focus of history with a prehistory that reinstates, and repoliticizes, birth from the mother: "As a recuperation of the sense of human engendering from the mother, a philosophy of birth has thus the main purpose of disinvesting the concrete individuality of each human from societal totalization. Birth, love, and death belong irreducibly to humans, despite state claims that they are legal matters subject to regulation. [. . .] But turning the gaze toward the mother, one can acknowledge that these are separate from the site of negotiable common living, and not subject to societal regulation. They are *physis* rather than *polis*" (82). Thus this recuperation of birth from the mother represents a crucial synthesis of the temporal aporias discussed before. Reviving the possibility of coexistence of both the vertical and the horizontal axes are, in effect, profound political gestures.[19]

Posthumanist vision enables recognition of the animal, of the other, and of the relations of disclosure and openness.[20] Though these are not her terms, I would argue that the recuperation of the maternal symbolic theorized by Cavarero serves the objectives of posthumanism, when the latter is conceived as a (Kojève/Agamben-inflected) absorption/acknowledgement of the proximity and mutually informative affirmation of the human and the animal (or the natural), over and against the historical position by which the human supersedes the biological, or (in different terms) by which *logos* supplants *physis*. Similarly, posthumanism supports the feminist cause, in that the former militates for a recuperation of the "embodied, sexed, and corporeal nature of living beings" (Braidotti, "Foreword" xvii). "[H]uman being is first of all embodied being," declares Katherine Hayles (283). Cavarero's attempt to restore the maternal function to a foundational position—"Prior to thought and to thinking, there is life and there is the living being" (Braidotti, "Foreword" xvii)—moreover, summons the capacity of posthumanism to resist the "death-based" worldview of phallogocentrism (Braidotti, "Foreword" xviii). Pavese's insistence on the primacy of standardized universalist subjects displays an enduring interest in the forestalling of the end of history and thus of that reciprocal confirmation between posthistorical and feminist concerns.

Notes

1. Consider Baracchi's observation regarding the artistic convention by which the body of the Greek deity Artemis is represented as being covered by folds of fabric ("veiled" is Baracchi's term): "[T]his imaginal configuration announces that nature may become matter, body, indeed, a woman's body—the object of scientific examination, undressed, inspected with increasingly sophisticated instruments in all her folds and receptacles" (323).
2. Examples of the equivalence between women and animals abound in his poetry; consider "The Billy Goat-God" ("*Il dio-caprone*," 1933), in which women figure as goats, or "Instinct" ("*L'istinto*," 1936), in which they are likened to dogs. Pavese's attribution of animal traits to humans is not unique to women. In *The Harvesters*, for example, Talino is compared to a barn animal (8), a calf (15), a dog (36 and 80), a goat (46), and a beast (78). Page numbers here refer to *Paesi tuoi* (2001).

3. This is the first line of a 1945 poem in *Earth and Death* (*La terra e la morte*), republished in *Tutte le poesie* (1998), 123. My translation.
4. In Rosi Braidotti's words, "The emancipatory project of modernity entails a view of 'the knowing subject' [. . .], which excludes several 'boundary markers' also known as 'constitutive others.' These are sexualized others, also known as women, ethnic and racialized others, and the natural environment" (*Nomadic* 28).
5. With regard to the term *speciesism*, Braidotti remarks, in a discussion of the work of Mary Midgely, that the latter "does not like the term *anthropocentrism* and prefers to it 'human chauvinism; narrowness of sympathy, comparable to national, or race or gender—chauvinism'" (*Nomadic* 88).
6. Thus I do not use the term as, say, a Marinetti might; the distinctions between Pavese's and Marinetti's parthenogenetic visions are at once aesthetic and political.
7. Elizabeth Grosz clarifies this point:

   The male/female opposition has been closely allied with the mind/body opposition. Typically, femininity is represented (either explicitly or implicitly) in one of two ways in this crosspairing of oppositions: either mind is rendered equivalent to the masculine and the body equivalent to the feminine (thus ruling out woman a priori as possible subjects of knowledge, or philosophers) or each sex is attributed its own form of corporeality. [. . .] Patriarchal oppression [. . .] justifies itself, at least in part, by connecting women much more closely than men to the body and, through this identification, restricting women's social and economic roles to (pseudo) biological terms. Relying on essentialism, naturalism and biologism, misogynist thought confines women to the biological requirements of reproduction on the assumption that because of particular biological, physiological, and endocrinological transformations, women are somehow *more* biological, *more* corporeal, and *more* natural than men. The coding of femininity with corporeality in effect leaves men free to inhabit what they (falsely) believe is a purely conceptual order while at the same time enabling them to satisfy their (sometimes disavowed) need for corporeal contact through their access to women's bodies and services. (14)

8. The most spectacular example of rural violence is probably Valino's murderous rampage, arson, and suicide in *The Moon and the Bonfires*; the convergence of sex and violence can be observed in the massive blood loss that causes Silvia's death in the same novel.
9. *The Moon and the Bonfires*, too, culminates in the consumption by fire of Santina's body as a gesture of appeasement toward the earth.

10. Carlo De Matteis emphasizes the connection of the maternal not with violence per se but with its extreme outcome, death, when he argues that Gisella "is lover, but is configured as a mother at the same time [...] with respect to Berto; she is likewise sister lover for Talino, with a naturalness that is accepted without taboo by the community in which she lives; finally, her figure bears profound meaning to the extent that she embodies the values of fertility and life, on the one hand, and blood and death, on the other. This multiple yet implicit interweaving of motifs renders some of her features similar to those of the Greek mythological figure of Kore [...]. The maiden mother as life, the maiden man as death, death as a celebration of the alternation of the earthly seasons, the relationship to the sun (in whose presence the killing takes place in the novel) and to the moon (which is hidden in the myth and in the novel appears frequently in connection to the maiden), the link to grain perceived as fertility, the equivalent of nuptials and murder" (qtd. in Pavese, *Paesi tuoi*, 128).
11. As noted before, it is not my contention that Pavese does not attribute animal-like qualities to his male characters. Talino's animality (addressed in note 2) is closely connected to the theme of the contrast between city and country at the heart of the novel. Note, too, that in *The Moon and the Bonfires*, Nuto's observation removes the question of gender from that of animality: "blood is red everywhere" (116).
12. The Italian *covare* means to sit on eggs. See also Pavese's poem, "Grappa in September" ("*Grappa a settembre*"), in *Hard Labor* (*Lavorare stanca*), in which women are compared to fruit ripening in the sun (*Tutte le poesie* 29).
13. See "Maternity" ("*Maternità*," 1934) and "Paternity" ("*Paternità*," 1935), both from *Lavorare stanca*, republished in *Tutte le poesie*, 54 and 103, respectively.
14. Pavese himself engages with the relations between animals, humans, and prehistory invoked here when he says, in his diary (addressing "The Billy Goat-God" cited in note 2), "Reading Landolfi makes it clear that your motif of the goat was the motif of the *bond between man and the animal kingdom*. Hence your taste for prehistory, the period that gives a glimpse of a community of interests between man and wild beasts" (qtd. in Biasin 267).
15. Regarding *The Moon and the Bonfires*, we might mention analogous instances of the collapse of natural/animal/female, such as when Nora's voice is likened to the chirping of crickets or when the moon is compared to a knife wound that fills the plain with blood and when the moon is connected with the bonfire. These images serve as a parsing, a promotion of the deep interconnection between the feminized and the natural life. Another way to consider this dyad

is as it aligns gender and embodiment along the axes of myth and history.
16. Muraro defines *affidamento* as a relationship that "occurs when you tie yourself to a person who can help you achieve something which you think you are capable of but which you have not yet achieved" in her 1985 "Bonding and Freedom" (qtd. in Bono and Kemp 123). Important for our purposes is the hierarchical nature of the relationship between helper and person being helped.
17. Although Cate never confirms Corrado's suspicion that he is Dino's father, it is likely.
18. This is Emanuele Severino's image in *Tautótēs* (1995).
19. "By showing that what are erased in the process of erection of the transcendental subject are the maternal grounds of origin, Irigaray simultaneously demystifies the vertical transcendence of the subject and calls for an alternative metaphysics. Irigaray's transcendental is sensible and grounded in the very particular fact that all human life is, for the time being, still 'of woman born'" (Braidotti, *Nomadic* 146).
20. On the question of disclosure, "Nature [...] gives life *and* withdraws into death. In this dynamic contrast we glimpse at nature as the mystery of *metamorphosis*—the mystery, literally, of becoming as relentless becoming-other" (Baracchi 320).

Works Cited

Agamben, Giorgio. *The Open: Man and Animal*. Trans. Kevin Attell. Stanford: Stanford UP, 2004.
Baracchi, Claudia. "Looking at the Sky: On Nature and Composition." *Annali d'Italianistica* 26 (2008): 319–32.
Biasin, Gian Paolo. *The Smile of the Gods: A Thematic Study of Cesare Pavese's Works*. Trans. Yvonne Freccero. Ithaca: Cornell UP, 1968.
Bono, Paola, and Sandra Kemp. *Italian Feminist Thought: A Reader*. Oxford: Basil Blackwell, 1991.
Braidotti, Rosi. "Foreword." In *In Spite of Plato: A Feminist Rewriting of Ancient Philosophy*, by Adriana Cavarero, trans. Aine O'Healy and Serena Anderlini-D'Onofrio, vii–xix. Cambridge: Polity, 1995.
———. *Nomadic Theory: The Portable Rosi Braidotti*. New York: Columbia UP, 2011.
Butler, Judith. *Bodies That Matter: On the Discursive Limits of "Sex."* London: Routledge, 1993.
———. *Frames of War: When Is Life Grievable?* London: Verso, 2010.
Cavarero, Adriana. *In Spite of Plato: A Feminist Rewriting of Ancient Philosophy*. Trans. Aine O'Healy and Serena Anderlini-D'Onofrio. Cambridge: Polity, 1995.

De Matteis, Carlo. "Simboli e strutture inconsce in *Paesi tuoi*." *Studi novecenteschi* 4.11 (1975): 185–205.
Grosz, Elizabeth. *Volatile Bodies: Toward a Corporeal Feminism*. Bloomington: Indiana UP, 1994.
Hayles, N. Katherine. *How We Became Posthuman: Virtual Bodies in Cybernetics, Literature, and Informatics*. Chicago: U of Chicago P, 1999.
Pavese, Cesare. *Hard Labor: Poems by Cesare Pavese*. Trans. William Arrowsmith. Baltimore: Johns Hopkins UP, 1979.
———. *The Harvesters* [*Paesi tuoi*]. Trans. A. E. Murch. London: Peter Owen, 1961.
———. *The House on the Hill* [*La casa in collina*]. Trans. R. W. Flint. New York: New York Review of Books, 1996.
———. *The Moon and the Bonfires* [*La luna e i falò*]. Trans. Marianne Ceconi. Westport, CT: Greenwood, 1975.
———. *Paesi tuoi*. Turin: Einaudi, 2001.
———. *Tutte le poesie*. Turin: Einaudi, 1998.
Severino, Emanuele. *Tautótēs*. Milan: Adelphi, 1995.

3

Montale's Animals

Rhetorical Props or Metaphysical Kin?

Gregory Pell

To Anthropomorphize or Not, That Is the Question

This essay seeks to reconcile an anachronism: a reading of the work of Eugenio Montale in the light of contemporary posthumanism. A series of crucial questions will be considered. Does Montale let animals just be themselves, employing their image with an indifference whereby they speak for and of themselves? Do Montale's animals become props for questions concerning humanity that Montale could not otherwise iterate? If or when Montale employs nonhuman animals as verbal conduits, does he perform them a disservice, or does he paradoxically show his dependence on them? This essay acknowledges that Montale is, at times, guilty of a poetic use of nonhuman animals that does not encompass their individuality or dignity. But more important, it argues that Montale consistently interrogates his own misuse of animals as species rather than as individuals and, in the process, develops a sensibility comparable with that of contemporary scholars of animality. It is this poetic interrogation that keeps Montale's oeuvre from falling into what John Simons terms "trivial anthropomorphism" (119) and allows the poet to move toward what Donna Haraway might call proper "engagement" with animality.

Paul Shepard suggests that anthropomorphism creates "the imaginary continuity between animals' lives and our own" and "binds our continuity with the rest of the natural world" (88). Shepard suggests that without the stimulus of the anthropomorphic imagination, humans would be alienated from the subjectivity of other animals and fail to develop empathy—fail, in other words, to become fully human. Roberto Marchesini and Sabrina Tonutti have a complementary position: "Anthropopoiesis becomes a process through which the human realizes itself in the very act of anthropodecentralization. In this way the nonhuman altern assumes an identity role in that it: a) is considered a dialogic entity, b) is recognized as a plural entity, c) is interpreted in its being carrier of other perspectives on the world" (150).[1] Montale's grappling with human identity seems equally bound up with the nonhuman animal who remains central to a decades-long poetic interrogation of humanity, animality, the metaphysical, and the divine.

Will the Real Animal Please Step Forward?

Montale's poem "Animals" ("*Gli animali*," published in *Notebook of Four Years* [*Quaderno di quattro anni*], 1977) highlights the poet's tendency to conflate and place in constant tension various interspecies attributes under the aegis of a deep-seated concern regarding the possibility of a God and a Christian salvation. The poem opens with a consideration of those rare animals under threat of extinction who "raise consternation / in whoever suspects that their Father might have broken their mold" (*Tutte* 600). The poet then writes that these threatened animals have not all been victims "of man and of climate, / or of some divine craftsman"; instead, their possible disappearance stems from the following: "Whoever created them believed them useless / to the most unhappy of his products: us" (*Tutte* 600). "Animals" alludes to the classic Montalian *male di vivere* (pain of living) in the most unhappy product of the creator, whereby the final "us" clearly means "we humans." The work sarcastically underscores an anthropomorphic bias through the endangered animals deemed useless for *us*, as if they were created solely to serve humans. Here, the poet parodies the tradition of speciesism, in this case founded on a Judeo-Christian world of creation with a Godhead. Yet by employing the third-person plural possessive, he places distance between "their" god, "their Father," and "his." Why not "*il Padre*" ("the Father" or implied "our Father") instead? Given the "us" at the end, why not use "*nostro* [our] *Padre?*" Montale's capital *P* evokes reverence for that divine "Father"; additionally, the poetic voice imagines the divine, anthropomorphized Father as a god of animals, not his god. Quite rhetorically, Montale positions his reader to take for granted that the humans are not themselves "animals," and further, that they are crass and unsympathetic, thinking only of utility in their social, political, and economic interactions with others. A creator ("Whoever created them") deemed "animals" no longer valuable in a market of putatively rational pragmatism populated by human animals—the "unhappiest of his products." Thus Montale denounces the industrial anthropocentric world, wherein, as the faux apologia insinuates, animals risk uselessness.

Further complicating his view on the nonhuman animal, Montale here endorses a nonteleological, Darwinian world of evolution by breaking "the mold" of creation, as if there were a fluid dynamics as opposed to a strict entelechy. Ironically, however, from the beginning of his career, Montale's poetic world almost completely removes the human predicate from the picture, relating to other humans through allegorical creatures and situations in which humans are poetic props rather than concrete individuals— just as nonhuman animals are props or analogues. In that respect, we might see Montale as an equal opportunity discriminator, using both *humans* and *animals* as means to his poetic ends. Here we might turn to the thought of Les Murray, who in a poem titled "Existential Beasts" permits us to understand how unusual it is to just let "animals" be animals: to not anthropomorphize them; to not theriomorphize us; to not raise (or lower) them to a level inconsistent with their own *just being*. Murray writes, "Metaphysical creatures with their habit / Of Being Themselves in lofty, solemn ways / Amuse me a bit, though the vogue for them is strong / Being oneself is intricate, God knows, / But—praise a beast for being wholly Rabbit?" (28). In a formulation that echoes Murray, Antonio Faeti, in the preface to Moravia's *Histories of Prehistory (Storie della preistoria*, 1982), advocates a righteous indifference toward nonhuman animals, conferring on them a status neither romanticized nor inferior: "Whoever even thinks about rats [note that Italians often refer to mice and rats indiscriminately], about those big sewer rats with fierce snouts [. . .] while reading the adventures of Mickey Mouse? And, yet, Mickey Mouse is but a rat [. . .]. Real animals have little in common with those that are described, filmed, drawn. A good rapport with animals is achieved when one learns to appreciate their diversity, when we feel them quite distant from ourselves, when we do not feel the need to humanize them at all costs" (Faeti 5–6). Montale's world is theriomorphic rather than anthropomorphic, but his is not a romanticized use of animals. Instead animals are a sort of catachrestic default, supplying the only possible descriptive corollaries to his human protagonists. Yet Montale seldom uses similes with animals; no one is "like" this or that animal. Animals appear as themselves or as vehicles for some theriomorphic pseudogoddess. So even when he appears to revere animals, or when that reverence is corroborated by his usage of them as *senhals* for his various poetic women (Clizia, Volpe, etc.), his allusions and metaphors are not part of a unified ideology for or against an anthropomorphic paradigm. So, we might ask, are other-than-humans only useful in terms of better defining humans? If so, do they signal a lack in the human?

In *The Animal Part* (2010), Mark Payne alludes to the ease with which "being or becoming something other than a human being is possible," for the "human body is imagined either already to contain the nonhuman or to be capable of transformation into it" (23). We tend to accept a disparaging theriomorphosis, whereby a "bestial" characteristic is noted in a human, as when a voracious human glutton eats "like a pig." However, pigs do not eat when not hungry, and humans do not eat only to satisfy a biological need. Marchesini writes, "Animality becomes rather a great container to apply to art for the purpose of discriminating, subjecting, killing and branding with infamy: it is still quite common to use the term 'bestial' when referring to reprehensible behaviors, even when those behaviors have no counterparts but in mankind" (*Tramonto* 43). So if a nonhuman animal acts according to its nature, it is a "beast"; if a human acts negatively according to its nature, it too is a "beast"? Is there no word to refer to deplorable human behaviors without paradoxically resorting to nonhuman species that do not exhibit them?

The complexity of this allusive/symbolic relationship features in Montale's work. Though nonhuman animals are frequently thought of as "lower" beings, the culmination of loyalty is found in the analogy of a specific nonhuman animal—the dog, characterized as "baying loyalty" in "The Ark" ("*L'arca*"; *Collected Poems* 291). Here Montale evokes canine fidelity to express his commitment to Clizia, his beloved. But years later, in "I Have Never Understood Whether I Was" ("*Non ho mai capito se io fossi*"), we face a more problematic usage of the dog: "I have never understood whether I was your faithful and mangy dog or if you were it for me" (*Tutte* 293). Is the human the animal or the animal the human? Andrea Giardina appreciates this indeterminacy: "If a dog is not human, then neither is it animal" (148). Yet the real issue seems to be a cavalier use of the dog whereby the poet, oblivious to any "real" dog, wrestles with the notion of who was, ironically, the "better" (or "worse") human by being the dog. Strangely, it is Montale's companion and eventual wife, Drusilla Tanzi (a.k.a. "Mosca"),[2] to whom he dedicates the poem, and not Clizia / Irma Brandeis. Montale was unfaithful to Mosca in poetry and in life, as he attempted to cultivate a real-life relationship with his rhetorical *senhal*, Irma Brandeis. Hence the poem can be read in a few different ways: (1) Mosca was loyal, like a dog, and consequently treated "like a dog," or taken for granted; (2) Montale behaved badly (like a dog, but in its negative connotation), yet somehow Mosca stayed faithful to him (more like the figurative, Platonic dog) through the years, thus showing her unconditional loyalty to a master who is more a beast than she; and (3) Montale has, like a dog, acted "bestially," yet the so-called beast of comparison may actually demonstrate loyalty better than the human.

Montale's exploitation of the dog image is therefore ambiguously either laudatory or vilifying, depending on the referent. We have moved beyond the Platonic, universally representative dog that speaks for all dogs and arrived at a complex variety of abstract dog behaviors that are (mis)applied to humans, or vice versa. Giorgio Manganelli explains a tendency of which Montale's poem is an exemplar: "For centuries now dogs have ceased being animals, at least in the way that one calls tigers and giraffes animals. The dog [. . .] has become a symptom [. . .]. Precisely: there were millennia in which the dog was 'natural,' like water and a flower; but today it is not natural, it is like us; an artificial finding or invention. Perhaps in this world, man and dog are the only beings who have attained a total, irreparable unnaturalness" (206–7). However idiosyncratic or specific the dog becomes in this poem, it is no better than Montale's other props/animals, for Montale depends on the rhetorical dog that exists in language as a commonplace. After all, Montale quickly shifts from the dog imagery to Mosca's being likened to a blind bat. However enviable the bat's radar senses, the bat, objectified for poetic ends, is more valuable as a species than as an individual. Thus one needs to examine whether Montale does a disservice to animals by only employing them as a means to his poetic ends.

Trivial Anthropomorphism or Righteous Indifference?

John Simons examines how people often presume texts that include non-human animals to be ipso facto advocates of them, when in reality authors merely—and contradictorily—use animals as "props" to illustrate a human trait for which humanity lacks an appropriate metaphor: "Every time we represent an animal we are [. . .] engaging in an act which, to a greater or lesser degree, appropriates the non-human experience as an index of humanness [...] Obviously to write about a fox is a very different act from hunting one to death with hounds, but it is, none the less, a use of the animal for a means designed to further the aims of the human even where the intention is to alleviate the suffering of foxes" (87). To describe this attitude, Simons coins the aforementioned term "trivial anthropomorphism" (119); although texts that employ animal figures—many of which are children's literature—frequently seem to blur the boundaries of humans and nonhuman animals, they do not "press against and force us to question the reality of [this] boundary" (119).

Because Montale's opus tends to resist critical and ideological approaches at every turn, it is difficult to ascertain precisely which theoretical aspects of the animal–human boundaries he presses the reader to question. As for example with his "hedgehogs" who "quench their thirst on a trickle of piety" (*Tutte* 192), there is a conflation that oddly sets up and then pulls down the anthropomorphic God of tradition. As Stelvio Di Spigno observes, the anthropomorphic religious tradition does not serve as his only paradigm, especially in the poet's later work where, rather than "*il Dio*" ("the God"), one could speak more readily of "*gli Dei*" and "*Iddii*" (both versions of "gods"): "More than a Christian paradise there is the idea of a repetitive human existence that terrorizes the poet [. . .]. That which remains to do is to conceive of, in a new way, that which regards the condition of mankind on Earth and even outside of this Earth: to strip thinking itself of its anthropomorphic characteristics, to accept Nothing as other animals do, to oppose it with a rock-solid faith in things terrestrial" (171–72). Even when Montale sees God as having that superaltern position, as a "Fisherman" ("Kingfisher,"[3] *Tutte* 487) his agenda is not one easily associated with the

New Testament. Instead, a great irony is played out: whereas Montale had little luck hooking real fish, now the fisher of souls vacillates before hooking them. The poet expresses autoironic playfulness, seeing himself as a dish "in foil" or "marinated," but "the Fisherman hesitates because our pulp / whether in foil or marinated is no longer in demand." No longer is the problem "that of preferring / but rather of being preferred" ("One Must Prefer" ["*Si deve preferire*"], *Tutte* 512).

This leads to other reversals whereby the poet becomes prey/dinner or poems in which he rethinks his youthful cavalier attitude toward hunting animals. We take as example the badger of "*Schiappino*":[4] "In the dead of night the badger tried to get out / and Schiappino shot but the badger / balled up and disappeared rolling / onto the nearby shore" (*Tutte* 699). The badger returns in "*La belle dame sans merci II*": "I searched in vain for / an archetype, whatever it might be, living or extinct, of you, of your secret. / Among all the animals perhaps the unicorn that lives in heraldic insignias but not beyond them. / I no longer had any doubt: I was the badger / that balls up and falls from the crest / to the shore trying to flee" (*Tutte* 834). Yet even in a moment of potential pathos, Montale fails to complete his gesture of empathy, as this was but another rhetorical game: the archetype of the poetic "*tu*" was "the unicorn"—mythological and as such unobtainable— and the poet's archetype was this "badger," in the latter of the two poems rendered more clumsy not in an attempt to portray the panic and difficult terrain of the badger's escape but to highlight, with typical self-effacement, the poet's own awkwardness.

However, this change of mind-set owes not to any inherent value in the animal but to the potential harm that could be done to a human woman while visiting the poet in her animal incarnation, as we will witness in "The Bat" ("*Il pipistrello*") and "Clizia in Foggia" ("*Clizia a Foggia*"). The possibility of metempsychosis forces Montale to see how quickly humanity can turn catachrestically "bestial"—how quickly a human can go from "stuffer" to "stuffing" (*Tutte* 276), as he writes in "The Prisoner's Dream" ("*Il sogno del prigioniero*"). In this poem, the truly "deplorable nonhuman" is found precisely, even exclusively, in humanity—retrospectively in the concentration camps of the Second World War and the Gulags of the Cold War Soviet Empire. Agamben's work is pivotally important here, with regard to this Heideggerian "conflict [...] between the *animalitas* and the *humanitas* of man" (75), which evokes the tension in Montale's stuffer/stuffing duality. Agamben contends that Heidegger was the last to believe that "the anthropological machine, which each time decides upon and recomposes the conflict between man and animal, between the open and the not-open, could still produce history and destiny for people" (75). Man's presumption to a "total management" (Agamben 77) of animal and human systems can lead to humanizing the "animality" of humankind to the point where aberrant behaviors can be justified (77). When, in the name of the so-called good, humans render palatable that which they would normally associate with "lower" classes of animals, we can say that these humans have "animalized" themselves, for they have become the "signified" of "animal," even if the "signifier" (*human*) absolves them of any culpability.

In "The Prisoner's Dream," humans become equivalents of geese, the meal of cannibalizing humans, slaughtered to become "pâté destined for the pestilential Gods" (*Complete Poems* 409). The culinary metaphor of pâté in the context of torture and slaughter of fellow humans adds grotesque humor to an otherwise grim poem: humans are not ready to deal with cruelty to *nonhuman* animals, for they have yet to remedy their cruelty to *human* animals. When human language cannot do justice to torturous captivity and/or death, the poet makes recourse to animal imagery, imagining himself, in "The Prisoner's Dream," fused with the flight of a moth ("I've become the flight of the moth"; *Collected Poems* 409). The poet feels a sense of guilt or complicity—as a member of the same "species" of contemptible humans—so that the moth to whom he is fused is the same one the poet has crushed under his shoe: "[M]y sole is turning into powder on the floor" ("The Prisoner's Dream," *Collected Poems* 409). As the crushed kin of the moth, Montale shifts from merely seeing animals as poetic *senhals* to considering them actual incarnations of absent or deceased humans in the form of visiting angels. Yet Montale's angels preserve an iconic image of the winged human form. Without realizing it, in fact, perhaps all along our so-called anthropomorphic religious culture has celebrated the hybridization and contamination of nonhuman animal forms.

Angels and Curious Creatures

From as early as *The Occasions* (*Le occasioni*, 1939), Montale's use of animals developed from one of "bestial" objective correlatives—found in *Cuttlefish Bones* (*Ossi di seppia*, 1925)—to the representatives of female presences as *senhals*. Where Esterina of *Cuttlefish Bones* was an earthly creature, wholly real, the poetic persona in *The Occasions*, as Paolo Sica observes, "addresses the sublime Clizia to receive from her the signs that save him from his own destructive masculinity" (237). Furthermore, even as Clizia becomes an angelic absence-presence, the poet seeks signs of her in the objects, phenomena, and animals of his environment, especially in the *Motets* (*Mottetti*), among which the quintessential expression of Clizia's presence is the sixth *Motet*: "The hope of even seeing you again" ("*La speranza di pure rivederti*"). Here the hope of catching some revelatory sign from Clizia, "some flash *of yours*" (*Collected Poems* 197), is fulfilled by observing two jackals being walked on a leash in Modena. The odd appearance of these "beasts" truly occurred, according to Montale, but why would the poet equate their presence with a revelation of Clizia? In 1950, in the *Corriere della Sera*, Montale came clean: "Clizia loved quaint animals. [. . .]

And from that day hence he never read the name Modena without associating that city to the image of Clizia and of those two jackals. [. . .] Could those two little beasties have been sent by her, almost like an emanation? Could they have been an emblem, a hidden message, a *senhal* of her?" (*Sulla poesia* 85). Clizia appears ambiguously as bird or angel, a figure reprised in later works: in "The Bangs" ("*La frangia dei capelli*"), the "*frangia*" is synonymous with "the wing on which you fly" (*Complete Poems* 281); in "Your Flight" ("*Il tuo volo*"), the "*ciuffo*" (*Tutte* 210) could be read as "forelock of hair" or as "tuft of feathers"; and in "Dark Angel" ("*L'angelo nero*"), the poet conflates forehead and bird tuft in "the fringe of your feathers" (*Tutte* 378).[5] Last, in "The Fan" ("*Il ventaglio*"), the poet notices how "the feathers on your cheeks are whitening" (*Complete Poems* 287). For angels to have human form is one thing; for them to have birdlike wings may be taken as conventional wisdom by followers of anthropocentric religion. However, in this context, a sort of hybridization is implied, and it is unclear whether Clizia has been reincarnated as a bird or returned from the beyond as an angel. These hybridizations and encounters culminate in the poem "The Eel" ("*L'anguilla*"), where Clizia is the eel as much as the "sister" of the eel. But in order to further this discussion, it will be necessary to speak of the notion of language and how poetry functions.

Animals "in Language": Incarnations and Guilt

It would be incorrect to assert that humankind uses language whereas nonhuman animals do not. However, what appears to separate humans from nonhuman animals is the transcendent usage of rationalizing rhetoric.[6] In *Language as Symbolic Action* (1966), Kenneth Burke made two relevant points in this regard: first, that there "are no negatives in nature, and that this ingenious addition to the universe is solely a product of human symbol systems" (9); second, "animals can communicate and use tools (apes, e.g.), but they do not use words about words" (14). That is, human language has morphosyntactic features that animal language arguably lacks. Thus the most meaningful hybridizations of the human-versus-animal world happen paradoxically in the anthropomorphic world of humans. Ironically, only in language that "talks about" language can we truly get beyond the animal divide to an ahumanity, or to a posthumanity.

Let us consider two examples, the first of which is taken from "The Eel." Here, we see the "eel" as a "spark/*scintilla*" that is the "twin/*gemella*" to Clizia's "*iride*" ("rainbow, iris");[7] then the "twin" becomes the "sister/*sorella*," a reprise of the earlier "siren/*sirena*" (*Collected Poems* 206). All this occurs courtesy of a smooth flow of consonance of "-illa/-ella," "sor-/sir-," and /i/ and /e/ assonances. Through poetic metamorphosis, each eel-become-human is theriomorphized. The second instance is from "If They've Compared You" ("*Se ti hanno assomigliato*"), where the poet employs what, at first, seems like a rather superficial pun (*"donnola"* [weasel]: *"donna"* [woman]; *Tutte* 267), which "is drawn from the audible rather than the visual qualities of the image" (Almansi and Merry 115). The brevity of the pun opens a vast discourse on human nature: "The point is," remarks Cambon, "that she is not *only* a woman or *only* a wild creature but something more, a being that encompasses the merely feral and the merely feminine in a kind of unorthodox transcendence" (174). Regarding transcendent beings among us, Montale opines, "The Greeks had resolved the problem in a different way: inventing the Gods, ad hoc deities made in their image. [This was] not different from a theory of Hölderlin who believed in the existence of terrestrial deities, living in cognito among us. But it is not easy to run into any; such a possibility is granted only to poets. And to this day that is still the way in which one might have a concrete experience with the divine" (*Auto da fé* 350). Perhaps, then, Montale's animals were always totemic emblems of the terrestrial divinities. Thus Montale's position evolves from an intuition to a rationalization and produces a posthuman vision of Clizia (not exclusively animal or human, and perhaps god[ess]-like) on a linguistic plane. Rather than a guardian angel, Clizia is more specifically a guardian animal—one that suffers vicariously for the poet as much as she represents a cryptic salvation.

In "The Capercaillie" (*"Il gallo cedrone," The Storm* [*La Bufera*], 1956),[8] the delicate nature of the relationship between poet and goddess is incarnated in the wood grouse: the poet realizes his culpability in the sacrifice that she makes for him. After she/it is shot by a human hunter—"Where you fall after the sharp shot"—the poet suddenly feels empathy: "I too lie low, burn in the ditch with you" (*Collected Poems* 383). The mood is dominated by an attempt at atonement, as the poet pledges avian solidarity in the midst of a hunt: "I feel your wound in my own breast, under / a clot of wing; I try to lumber / over a wall and all that lasts of us / are feathers on the frosted holly" (*Collected Poems* 383). Zambon appreciates Montale's enigmatic subtlety: "The sense of guilt for acts of cruelty committed in killing these little creatures, certainly also tied to relationships with his father and other people dear to him, comes with an awareness of his own affinities with the 'sacrificed' animals" (130).

No work of Montale's, however, captures the notions of incarnation/metempsychosis and expiation for sins against nonhuman animals better than his aforementioned prose work, "The Bat" (*Butterfly of Dinard* [*Farfalla di Dinard*], 1956).[9] In this tale, the protagonist finds himself in a hotel with his wife, cast as the hysterical agrizoophobe. When a bat somehow enters the hotel room, she screams: "'A bat! [. . .] Send that nasty beast away, send it away!' she yelled from under the sheets, for fear of being grazed by such a foul flight" (*Farfalla* 127). At one point, the woman asks, "Has the monster gone away?" (128); then, in referring to it as "that vampire" (128), she creates a double helix of anthro- and theriomorphism.[10] The man, in a clumsy attempt to send the beast out the window, lands a magazine blow in the vicinity of the bat, causing it to fall disoriented into a wastepaper basket. Yet the bat continues to flutter about, and with great pathos, the husband wonders whether his dead father might have returned to see him in bat form (130). This motif is repeated in a later poetic work, "*Annetta*," in which the more mature poet has solidified his empathy toward nonhuman animals—in this case, the rock thrush that he once heard singing and the rock thrush that he later killed: "the only crime / for which I cannot forgive myself. But I was crazy / and not about you, but from youth, / crazed by the most ridiculous season / of our lives" (*Tutte* 501–2).

In "The Condemned" ("*Il condannato*"), however, Montale approximates an animal's putative narrative, in this case a lobster, not as an analogue for the poet but as an animal *qua* animal, the lobster as itself—although the language used to report the different viewpoints is not the lobster's. The story is simple: a group of people observe a lobster in a tank with its pincers bound by string. As one or another person raises a finger to the tank, the lobster raises a claw but then lowers its "terribly sharp shear" back into the water, realizing that the string impedes its snapping action (*Farfalla* 208). "'In a half hour it will be in the pot,' said the man with glasses 'and meanwhile it still tries to inflict harm. You can tell that one can not negate the aggressive instinct of men and beasts'" (208). The discussion continues: "'I think he's playing like a cat,' said the second man. 'He doesn't want to hurt anyone. Even a cat can scratch you when it's playing. Perhaps the lobster doesn't even know it's been sentenced to death'" (208–9). During their discussion, a young child seems to confirm the hypothesis that the lobster was behaving like a cat, as if it were engaging in a sort of "reciprocal induction" (in Donna Haraway's terms [232]) in which the hominid fails to perceive the crustacean's overture. In a locus where discrete, morphosyntactic language has no currency, the adult humans presume the worst of the animal, when perhaps they should be more unprejudiced: "'Oh, what a pretty shrimp!' said a child. 'May I touch him, father?' And before his father said either yes or no, he was already immersing his finger in the tank, sticking it right into its claws from which the child had inadvertently untied the safety tethers in the process. The lobster squeezed its snipper, hesitating an instant on the child's finger, as if to caress it; then he let go of his prey. Everyone was screaming: 'Look out!' let it go,' but the finger bore not one single scratch" (*Farfalla* 209).

Continuing Haraway's line of argument, we may presume that this moment stands as a fantastical exemplar of animal–human "contact zones degenerat[ing] into impoverishing border wars" (232). The humans can only presume that the child had a narrow escape, thus confirming that the animal, only capable of inflicting pain on humans, has earned its rightful place on the dinner plate: something to eat with bread (*cum panis*) but not an entity with whom to break bread (*companio*).[11] In the meantime, the fishmonger wraps the lobster for a customer to take home. At this the young child asks, "They are cooking him? But why? With me he just wanted to play" (*Farfalla* 210). Haraway, in discussing human–animal play, refers to "metacommunication, communication about communication, the sine qua non of play. Language cannot engineer this delicate matter; rather, language relies on this other semiotic process, on this gestural, never literal, always implicit, corporeal invitation to risk copresence, to risk another level of communication" (239). The question is whether the lobster wanted to play as a lobster or as the incarnation of one of Montale's many shades, like the "floating shadow" (*Farfalla* 127) that may have been none other than the presence of his father in "The Bat." Why would the alter ego of the bat story have been anxious about killing the bat, believing it was an incarnation of his father, if he did not believe in metempsychosis? And what if we humans were the problem in failing to add metacommunicative subtext to our interaction with a crustacean or bat, or any other creature, for that matter?

Metempsychosis, Metacommunication, and Professorial Presumption

"Clizia in Foggia" addresses the issues of metacommunication, animal perspective (the default anthropocentric attempt to empathize with the animal or to see from its point of view), and metempsychosis. The story imagines Clizia in the city of Foggia awaiting a train connection. To avoid the oppressive heat, she "escapes" into the town hall, where two professors hold a lecture/debate on metempsychosis. During the event, Clizia either falls asleep and dreams or is put under hypnosis by the two doctors—the story does not clarify which. The story that ensues tells of her life as a spider, presumably an erstwhile stage of her soul's transmigration. Montale shifts the point of view to that of a spider, deconstructing one of the creatures that most commands fear in the mind of humans. While humans might see lobsters as threatening to humans (unidirectionally, despite the fact that in the history of culinary science no lobster has ever boiled a human in a pot) and incapable of play, the young lad in "The Condemned" helps rethink the directionality of communication with animals. Though the story is purely fiction, John Simons would probably agree that Montale has "pressed" humans to question the boundary of the human and the nonhuman. In "Clizia in Foggia," Montale does the same thing, albeit more explicitly shifting perspective from hominid to arachnid.

Incarnated in a spider, Clizia "saw the world according to a horizontal perspective, no longer vertical as she seemed to recall that of men planted atop two stilts and who proceed at right angles with the earth" (*Farfalla* 92). Then the spider-Clizia arrives in a courtyard with a fountain and vegetation where a young man admires the aesthetics of her web, a clearly anthropomorphized view that removes species function from issues of beauty. The spider, caught in a honey-like substance, tries to break free when a hand on Clizia's arm suddenly wakes her from her hypnosis-induced dream/trance.

At the professors' bidding, Clizia recounts her past life: "You see, I believe I dreamt of being a spider, yes, a spider in the courtyard of Pythagoras' house" (*Farfalla* 94). Yet the professors accuse her of poking fun at science and lying: "Do you realize the perfection that would be required to pass in one shot from the stage of a spider to that of a human being? Be serious, tell us then *who* you dreamt of being" (94), the presumption being that Clizia had to have been *someone* and not *something*—that is, a nonhuman animal. To the jeers of audience members, the professor accompanies Clizia out of the room. Though the scientist is dogmatically inflexible, his science proposes three not wholly coherent points with regard to the human–animal relationship: (1) evolution exists; (2) metempsychosis exists; and (3) there is, contrary to evolution, a teleologically driven perfection to which all this is directed. According to the professors' anthropocentric science, the evolutionary jump from "mere" spider to man offends the notion of man's (putative) perfection.

Between "The Condemned" and "Clizia in Foggia," we see the irony of communication in "mere" animals: in one gesture, a *lowly* lobster communicates with the young boy; yet, relying on complex morphosyntactical language, Clizia earns only derision from the professors and the audience. Proponents of human exceptionalism, the professors in reality fail to comprehend. Metempsychosis fits neatly into their anthropocentric, teleological world; yet they do not notice the metaphysical kin around them, nor do they deign to imagine the animal already in their human body.

Most striking about Clizia-as-spider is the way she would have presumably met her demise in the story, had she not been awoken: engaging in "human" behavior brought her into a fatal trap. The spider and the humans (potentially Pythagoras and his fellow students) seemed to coexist nicely in the courtyard: "While [Pythagoras] observed the spider's handiwork, his enormous youthful face never lost its absorbed and intense expression. It seemed as though the web were almost an extension of his thoughts, as if it wove itself right into the topics of the book that he was reading" (*Farfalla* 93). Yet one day the spider, who only eats living prey, noticed "a sweet, blond, resplendent pulp" (93) on a plate and lowered itself to eat this sort of manna: "She hung from her web and lowered herself, alas!, with such haste out of greediness, down the thread that kept extending downward [. . .]. By the time she realized what was happening, her destiny was sealed. The golden sticky nectar had already claimed her hairy back [. . .] [N]ext came a leg that sank into the viscous marsh [. . .] In a fit of supreme desperation, of an unthinkable revulsion, she found herself throwing her head backwards to hasten her death" (93–94). The spider almost meets its demise having tried to appropriate that which normally would not be part of its diet. Thus Montale's story provides clarifying resonance to Antonio Faeti's warning about the dangers of anthropomorphism: "A good rapport with animals can be obtained just when [. . .] we feel them quite distant from ourselves, when we do not feel the need to humanize them at all costs" (6). The putative Pythagoras of "Clizia in Foggia" is a "young man" who may or may not have left the fateful "human" food there for the spider, not properly perceiving the spider's predatory nature.

Montale Rereads Himself: Animals as Individuals or Collective Species

Montale's complex relationship to nonhuman animals culminates in "*La busacca*" (*Farfalla*). In this story, the eponymous bird is the only creature in Montale's oeuvre *not* based on a real animal or one acquired from a preexisting cultural mythology—this is the closest Montale gets to the fantastic of Landolfi's "*porrovio*" or "*labrena*," Cortázar's "Abdekunkus," or Borges's "hide-behind."[12] In this fairy-tale story, the bird is mysterious and elusive but ultimately the banal target of the oxymoronic, threatening innocence of a child: "children" are defined as "the most natural and decisive friendly enemies of beasts" (*Farfalla* 29). Montale's companion in the tale is Zebrino, who, "with some local birds—goatsuckers, the *busacca*—had become very friendly in his early years" (30). Despite the fact that Zebrino "pitied some of the dead birds and had no intention of going down the road of St. Hubert [the patron saint of hunters]," he attempts to shoot the elusive "*busacca*" (30). Why would Zebrino, "who found himself living in a land quite lacking in exotic zoological species" (29), not appreciate this avian rarity by studying it or protecting it? Why waste time hunting this "unbaggable demon" (30)? He seems to want to hunt and kill it out of a grotesque, innately human pride. The fact that Zebrino is a friend of the narrator but not synonymous with the narrator is important: the story presents a moment in which an adult Montale, distanced from his misguided youth, rethinks his relationship with nonhuman animals. Perhaps it was just as well that Zebrino's rifle malfunctioned, for this must have been more than just a bird but a strange deity, a sacred beast, a species unto itself—"singular by definition" (32). The "*busacca*" bird contrasts the whole basis of memorial fauna in Montale's prior work, where the abstract species counted more than the concrete individual: the poet mentioned prior to the publication of *Farfalla* how "[a] blackbird, and even a dog long dead, can return, because for us they count more as a species than as individuals" (*Sulla poesia* 80). But the "*busacca*," like a deity, is both species and individual in one, a sacred beast, either in its singularity or in its metaphysical link to a divine state that poses resistance to the poet's *male di vivere*.

This brings us to conclude with the badger from a lesser-known short story by Montale, "A Ligurian Beach" ("*Una spiaggia in Liguria*"),[13] in which a young "Montale," left ashore during a night-fishing expedition and armed with a shotgun, is forced to "hunt" for the first (and last) time. He hears a shot, after which the intended prey of a hunter, a badger, slips down a slope in an attempt to flee, revealing itself as a potentially easy target for the youth.[14] He raises his "double-barreled muzzle-loaded musket" but instead discovers something "with its hands (or its paws?) resting on a large slab, a being never before seen that observed me with human eyes" ("Spiaggia" 214). Thus Montale purposefully shoots high, sparing his target and incurring the exasperation of the hunter who had originally flushed out the badger. What the young Montale saw was "half-angel, half-beast" (214), but he does not exclude having seen it as somehow either inanimate or human: it was, after all, a "something," perhaps a "*someone*" (214, italics in original), "the being without a name" (215), to which/whom Montale spares suffering. Could the imminent animal suffering that drew Montale's pity have been a reiteration of the "hardened nameless sufferance" from the poem "I've Paused at Times in the Caves" ("*Ho sostato talvolta nelle grotte*," *Collected Poems* 71)? In the occult badger, young Montale found a sort of kin that mirrored him—something that, as Marchesini stated it, forces "the human system to not close itself narcissistically within the species, but to realize a cognitive state of non-equilibrium that renders man a participant in the universe" (*Post-Human* 63).

That which causes the Montalian alter ego to reconsider shooting the "beast" was the eye contact that each made, one with the other. In Haraway's words, "Derrida correctly criticized two kinds of representations, one set from those who observe real animals and write about them but never meet their gaze, and the other set from those who engage animals only as literary and mythological figures" (21). With his "badger," Montale demonstrates a sensitivity for nonhuman animals beyond their use as simple rhetorical props, instead raising consciousness of points of confluence and correspondence in the animal-human kingdom. Without a doubt, more attention should be paid to this relatively unknown prose work that predated many contemporary discussions on nonhuman animals. In this story, Montale met the gaze of the animal, but instead of engaging that nonhuman gaze, the animal engaged *Montale*.

Notes

1. Unless otherwise indicated, translations are my own.
2. The nickname *Mosca* ("Fly") was given to Drusilla by her friends because of her large eyeglasses that resembled the eyes of the common insect.
3. The original title takes the English word.
4. The nickname *Schiappino* is the diminutive of *Schiappa*, which translates as "fumbler" or "dimwit."
5. Since *frangia* can mean both "bangs" and "fringe" in Italian, the anthropotherio divide is much more ambiguous in the original.
6. For an exhaustive study on this subject, see Stephen R. Anderson, *Doctor Doolittle's Delusion* (2004). See also Hauser, Chomsky, and Fitch, who argue "that no species other than humans has a comparable

capacity to recombine meaningful units into an unlimited variety of larger structures, each differing systematically in meaning" (1576).
7. Here, Galassi has used both "rainbow" and the ocular "iris," for *iride* in Italian has both meanings, and clearly Montale meant both to be intimated.
8. A capercaillie is more commonly known as a European wood grouse.
9. For a useful comparison of the terms and stylemes common to Montale's poetry and prose, cf. Cesare Segre, "Invito alla *Farfalla di Dinard.*"
10. Though vampires are associated with the bat, legends of the former are much older, the latter having been added to the succubor myth in the 1600 or 1700s. So the vampire bat is by definition an anthropomorphized animal. But to see the bat and resort back to the predating legend is to theriomorphize. For further reading on the mythologies involving shapeshifting and vampires, see Judyth McLeod, *Vampires: A Bite-Sized History.*
11. Though Haraway does not use the word *companio*, I borrowed her insight on "*cum panis*" (16–17), which is the Latin etymology for *companion*. Her use of *cum panis* is part of a larger discussion on the category of "companion species" (16).
12. Landolfi's fantastical creatures are found in, respectively, the novels *Cancroregina* and *Le labrene*; Cortázar's "Abdekunkus" comes from the short story "Now Shut up, You Distasteful Abdekunkus"; and Borges's "hide-behind" is found in the short story "Fauna de los Estados Unidos" in *Manual de zoología fantástica* (1971).
13. This story appeared as "Memory of a Beach" ("*Ricordo di una spiaggia*") in *Il popolo di Roma* (August 27, 1943); it appeared as "Mesco Promontory" ("*Punta del Mesco*") in *La Patria* (May 19–20, 1945); and it again appeared as "*Una spiaggia di Liguria*" in *La lettura* (December 27, 1945). More recently it was included as "A Beach in Liguria" in Luperini, *Montale o l'identità negata* (1984).
14. This event is also included in the poem "*Schiappino*" (*Altri versi*, 1980).

Works Cited

Agamben, Giorgio. *The Open: Man and Animal.* Trans. Kevin Attell. Stanford: Stanford UP, 2003.

Almansi, Guido, and Bruce Merry. *Eugenio Montale: The Private Language of Poetry.* Edinburgh: Edinburgh UP, 1977.

Anderson, Stephen R. *Doctor Doolittle's Delusion: Animals and the Uniqueness of Human Language.* New Haven, CT: Yale UP, 2004.

Bonora, Ettore. *Lettura di Montale. 1. Ossi di seppia.* Turin: Tirrenia-Stampatori, 1980.

Burke, Kenneth. *Language as Symbolic Action*. Berkeley: U of California P, 1966.
Cambon, Glauco. *Eugenio Montale's Poetry: A Dream in Reason's Presence*. Princeton: Princeton UP, 1983.
Di Spigno, Stelvio. "L'inganno del Tempo nel secondo Montale." In *La poesia italiana del secondo Novecento: Atti del Convegno di Arcavacata di Rende (27–29 maggio 2004)*, ed. Nicola Merola, 167–74. Soveria Mannelli, Catanzaro: Rubbettino Editore, 2006.
Faeti, Antonio. "Una saggezza bestiale." In *Storia della preistoria*, by Alberto Moravia, 4–9. Milan: Bompiani, 2001.
Giardina, Andrea. "Il viaggio interrotto. Il tema del cane fedele nella letteratura italiana del Novecento." *Paragrafo. Rivista di letteratura & immaginari* 1.1 (2006): 145–65.
Haraway, Donna J. *When Species Meet*. Minneapolis: U of Minnesota P, 2008.
Hauser, Marc, Noam Chomsky, and W. Tecumseh Fitch. "The Faculty of Language: What Is It, Who Has It, and How Did It Evolve?" *Science* 298 (2002): 1569–79.
Manganelli, Giorgio. *Improvvisi per macchina da scrivere*. Milan: Adelphi, 2003.
Marchese, Angelo. *Visiting Angel: Interpretazione semiologica della poesia di Montale*. Turin: Società editrice internazionale, 1977.
Marchesini, Roberto. *Post-Human: Verso nuovi modelli di esistenza*. Milan: Bollati Boringhieri, 2002.
———. *Il tramonto dell'uomo: La prospettiva post-umanista*. Bari: Dedalo, 2009.
Marchesini, Roberto, and Sabrina Tonutti. *Manuale di zooantropologia*. Rome: Meltemi Editore, 2007.
Montale, Eugenio. *Auto da fé. Cronache in due tempi*. Milan: Casa Editrice il Saggiatore, 1966.
———. *Eugenio Montale: Collected Poems, 1920–1954*. Ed. and trans. Jonathan Galassi. New York: Farrar, Straus and Giroux, 1997.
———. *Farfalla di Dinard*. Milan: Leonardo Editore, 1994.
———. "Una spiaggia in Liguria." In *Montale o l'identità negata*, by Romano Luperini, 211–16. Naples: Liguori, 1984.
———. *Sulla poesia*. Ed. Giorgio Zampa. Milan: Mondadori, 1976.
———. *Tutte le poesie*. Ed. Giorgio Zampa. Milan: Mondadori, 1990.
Murray, Les. *The Weatherboard Cathedral*. Sydney: Angus and Robertson, 1969.
Payne, Mark. *The Animal Part*. Chicago: U of Chicago P, 2010.
Segre, Cesare. "Invito alla Farfalla di Dinard." In *I segni e la critica*, 135–51. Turin: Einaudi, 1969.
Shepard, Paul. *The Others: How Animals Made Us Human*. Washington, DC: Island, 1997.

Sica, Paola. "The Feminine in Eugenio Montale's Juvenile Work: 'Sensi e fantasmi di una adolescente.'" *Rivista di studi italiani* 2 (2000): 236–49.

Simons, John. *Animal Rights and the Politics of Literary Representation*. New York: Palgrave MacMillan, 2002.

Talbot, George, ed. *Eugenio Montale: Selected Poems*. Dublin: UCD Foundation for Italian Studies (Belfield Italian Library), 2000.

Tugnoli, Claudio. "Il postumanesimo di Roberto Marchesini." In *Zooantropologia: Storia, etica e pedagogia dell'interazione uomo/animale*, ed. Claudio Tugnoli, 64–72. Milan: FrancoAngeli, 2003.

Zambon, Franco. *L'iride nel fango: L'anguilla di Eugenio Montale*. Parma: Nuova Pratiche Editrice, 1994.

4

The Word Made Animal Flesh

Tommaso Landolfi's Bestiary

Simone Castaldi

Few twentieth-century bodies of work feature animal creatures as consistently and as extensively as that of Tommaso Landolfi. From the early stories of *Dialogue of the Greater Systems* (*Dialogo dei massimi sistemi*, 1937) to collections such as *The Geckos* (*Le labrene*, 1974), animals appear in Landolfi's fiction as a destabilizing presence: they signal a chance for change, as with the weregoat of *The Moon Stone* (*La pietra lunare*, 1939), or mark points of crisis, like the mysterious *porrovio* in *Cancerqueen* (*Cancroregina*, 1950). These narratives display a constant, albeit nonlinear, movement toward the other-than-human that invests not only man but also objects and eventually language itself. These metamorphoses are not Ovidian in nature; they are neither mythic nor anthropocentric but rather blur the boundaries of the human. In this displacement of what constitutes man, language is central and thus becomes a fulcrum of repositioning into the animal. This process of theriomorphosis of the verbal sphere suggests that when language becomes animal the human follows. And this is the alternatively threatening and liberating function of fantastic animals such as the untranslatable *vipistrelli*, the *canie*, or the *porrovio*—this latter, which, Landolfi informs us, "is not a beast; it is a word" (*Cancroregina* 77).[1] Thus the animal presence threatens the dissolution of the ties between signifiers and signified and points to the beginning of a reformulation of the boundaries of verbal expression, which is mapped by the development of Landolfi's literary work through the years.

Although Landolfi's bestiary comprises a limited variety of species, the author's fascination with the animal encompasses a wide range of literary references and influences. Among these are the anthropomorphic animals of fables, from Aesop to La Fontaine; the theriomorphic characters of Gogol and Kafka; those belonging to the legacy of surrealism and presurrealism, from the Comte de Lautréamont to Alberto Savinio; and the bestiaries of Giacomo Leopardi and Eugenio Montale. The key role played by intertextuality in Landolfi's work is an aspect that still needs to be analyzed in depth, but nowhere is it so evident as when animals enter the narratives. In this essay, I will concentrate on the central role played by animals in Landolfi's work and, more specifically, on the meaning and implications triggered by their presence. I will proceed by dividing the animal presence into three categories: (1) animals proper and fantastic animals; (2) anthropomorphic and theriomorphic creatures and objects; and (3) *animots*[2] and theriomorphic language. By necessity, these categories are only roughly fixed, and occasionally the designations overlap.

Animals Proper and Fantastic Animals

Among Landolfi's cast of domestic and farm animals, the dog is the most recurrent creature, while within the category of wild animals, insects, reptiles, and rodents constitute the majority.[3] Dogs often appear in connection with another of the author's recurring elements: the semiautobiographical country house where the protagonist retires, either to write or as the result of economic difficulties.[4] Almost infallibly, the villa becomes the "mental space" (Andreozzi 210) for the confrontation with the "animal other" and the corresponding gradual mental breakdown of the protagonist. At the scene of this unraveling, the dog is often a silent, passive witness, as exemplified in early stories such as "Maria Giuseppa" (1930; *Dialogo*)[5] and "Week of Sunshine" ("*Settimana di sole*," 1937; *Dialogo*).

A different typology of more active dog characters emerges with the dog-as-narrator of "Fable" ("*Favola*," 1938; *Mar*). Here the animal is given a voice by way of internal focalization so that canine thoughts are expressed in human language. One can certainly detect the influence of Kafka's "Investigations of a Dog" (1931), where the canine protagonist is also the first-person narrator. Despite their use of language, both Landolfi's and Kafka's dogs retain the complexity of their canine ethology and are hence more multilayered than the purely allegorical animals in Aesop's and La Fontaine's fables.[6] Châli, the dog in "The Storm" ("*La tempesta*," 1939; *Mar*), belongs instead to the category of animals interacting verbally with human characters.[7] Here the reader is presented with a dog that is (almost) able to articulate human language, and as such, the story represents an important nodal point to understand the gnoseological relevance of the animal in Landolfi's work. The tone of the narrative is light and farcical (albeit ripe with grotesque overtones), and the tale is presented in the guise of a vaudeville vignette. A man, accosted by an acquaintance who claims his dog can speak, reluctantly agrees to witness a demonstration. Terrified when the dog utters what sounds like mysterious scraps of human language, he interrupts the experiment. The employment of human verbal language by animals is unsettling because it represents both a breakdown of boundaries between the human and the "other" and stands as a sign of corruption of the referential powers of language.

In "New Insights into the Human Psyche: The Man from Manheim" ("*Nuove rivelazioni della psiche umana. L'uomo di Manheim*," 1942; *Spada*) the talking "dog" is actually a human. The setting is a scientific conference in which a researcher reports on his experiments with a talking animal. The twist is that both the scientist and his audience are dogs and the talking animal is actually a human in a dog-run society where men, having lost verbal language, live as pets. Though more lighthearted than "The Storm," this story still suggests not only that language is at the contentious heart of an opposition between what is human and what is not but that human verbal language itself represents a burden. The talking human of the story is a satisfied, placid being, reluctant to show off his linguistic ability, and in the end, he is killed by the very effort of producing language. On the opposite side, the dogs, who are now carriers of language and eager to defend their distance from the human "other," have acquired the characteristics of real-life humans. It is clear that there is no movement toward the animal if a highly referential, normative verbal language is present as an element of resistance. Being the closest to man, and consequently the most prone to domestication, dogs often fail to function as a pathway to the animal other. The assimilation works only one way: toward the human. In fact, dogs are often agents of man's hegemony over the animal; one is reminded of the protagonist's dog in "Maria Giuseppa" unleashed against the cats or the one in "Hands" ("*Mani*," 1937; *Dialogo*) who hunts down a mouse.

Rodents and insects belong to a wholly different order: at once menacing and enticing, they are the ones that Landolfi most often employs to stage critical moments of contact with or obliteration into the other. In the realm of wild animals, we can distinguish between passive animals, which suffer the violence of man, and active ones, slithering and crawling and threatening to infiltrate and dissolve the unity of human identity. But even the passive animals constitute a threat, as in "Hands" or "Fear" ("*La paura*," 1942; *Spada*). In the former, the semiautobiographical dweller of the "large abandoned house" (93) comes home and finds that a country mouse has entered the house. The man sets his old dog to hunt the intruder, and after a meticulously described chase, the mouse, leaving a trail of shiny entrails behind him, is killed by the dog. However, during the chase, the mouse acquires characteristics that draw him closer to the human. The narrator uses the word "hands" referring to his paws: "[H]e was shielding himself with his hands (mice have human-like and floppy hands)" (*Dialogo* 97). The transferal of this physiological trait from human to animal provides the starting point for the unraveling of species boundaries.

The animal further crosses the borders of the human when the narrator describes his final defeat by the dog: "[T]he mouse looked like a baby who's about to cry, yet with no sadness" (*Dialogo* 98). As the mouse approaches death, Landolfi's description takes the narrative into a space where the abject provides a chance to reconnect the human with the animal. In *Civilization and Its Discontents*, Sigmund Freud claims that man's break from animality happened thanks to a shift from the quadruped position to the current erect bipedal one. This separation from the ground also involved the rejection of the formerly stimulating smells of blood and feces, the lure of the organic that man had to repress in order to emancipate himself from the animal state (63–68). By witnessing and participating in the hunting and killing of the animal, and its wounding that revealed the animal's entrails, the human protagonist of "Hands" reclaims the experience of blood and feces and breaks away from the Freudian "organic repression": "There is nothing that gives one the perception of flesh and blood as entrails do, with their warm stench. Federico felt suffocated, throttled by mouse flesh; the taste and putrid smell of fat and tallowy flesh had become a condition of his being, and he savored it directly through his blood, irreparably" (*Dialogo* 100–101).

Tellingly, the animal presence that has now invaded the thoughts of the protagonist disrupts his ability to negotiate verbal language. At first the protagonist fails to sustain an imaginary conversation in French, a prandial habit developed over long months of solitude: "*Ah oui Monsieur, je vous l'assure, c'est un spectacle dont vous devriez vous régaler* . . . and he went on with his mouth full, staring across the table. But the sudden thought of the mouse flashed through his mind: more than a thought, an intimate and subterranean sensation, something that clanged unexpectedly inside him, gave signs of wanting to burrow deeper and rapidly disappeared" (*Dialogo* 99). Here thought itself behaves in animal fashion, like a rat "burrowing" and "rapidly disappearing." Now the presence of the mouse has found its way into the psyche and inhabits it in the same way it did the house. Next, the protagonist tries to read but finds that the enjoyment of Flaubert's *Sentimental Education* is also sabotaged by the memory of the contact with the animal "other." The coming closer to the animal corresponds again to a breakdown of human language. At the end of "Hands" we are given a glimpse of this language, one completely identified with the pack of mice with whom the protagonist is trying to communicate, a language soft and thunderous whose lexemes are the unpredictable trajectories of each individual mouse: "Sometimes, even after his hair had turned grey, he roamed at night through the inhabited rooms of his house [. . .], calling: 'Come to me, little mice! Oh come little mice, and rest in my arms!' The little mice, whenever he chanced to run into them, were amused and frightened, and gazing at him with their tiny round glistening eyes, trotted delicately ahead of him with a faint roll of thunder" (*Dialogo* 103).

"Hands" reveals the symbolist connection that ties Landolfi's work, through Mallarmé, to Hugo Von Hofmannsthal, the Viennese author whose works Landolfi translated later in his career. On the one hand Landolfi shares Mallarmé's fascination with the possibilities that the autonomy of language magically discloses, but on the other, as with Hofmannsthal, the coming apart of the referential ties of language unveils a vertiginous abyss. The word made animal flesh, like Landolfi's insects and rodents, is the object of both enthrallment and abjection. The model here is Hofmannsthal's *The Lord Chandos Letter* (1902), the short story that marked the writer's farewell to poetry and the short story medium in favor of drama. The semiautobiographical story, set as an early seventeenth-century epistolary exchange between the fictional Lord Chandos and Lord Francis Bacon, deals with the writer's progressive loss of the power of language as an epistemological tool. The pivotal point of the story is the description of the poisoned rats trying to escape the narrator's cellar: "Suddenly this cellar unrolled inside me, filled with the death throes of the pack of rats. It was all there. The cool and musty cellar air, full of the sharp, sweetish smell of the poison, and the shrilling of the death cries echoing against mildewed walls. Those convulsed clumps of powerlessness, those desperations colliding with one another in confusion. The frantic search for ways out. The cold glares of fury when two meet at a blocked crevice" (123). As Deleuze and Guattari maintain regarding this very passage in their chapter on becoming-animal in *A Thousand Plateaus*, "Hofmannsthal, or rather Lord Chandos, becomes fascinated with a 'people' of dying rats, and it is in him, through him, in the interstices of his disrupted self that the 'soul of the animal bares its teeth at monsterous [sic] fate': not pity but *unnatural participation*. Then a strange imperative wells up in him: either stop writing, or write like a rat ... if the writer is a sorcerer, it is because writing is a becoming, writing is traversed by strange becomings that are not becomings-writer, but becomings-rat, becomings-insect, becomings-wolf, etc." (240, italics in original). And in fact, the language which closes Landolfi's story, after the presence of the mouse becomes tied to the narrator's soul with "deep and indissoluble ties" (*Dialogo* 101), is the language of the pack of rats, that "light rolling of thunder" produced by a multitude, unpredictable, going in many directions at once.

Other animals playing the roles of "paradigmatic victims" (Lyotard 28)[8] are the dog in the autobiographical *The Fisherman's Beer / The Sinner's Coffin* (*La Biere du Pecheur*, 1953), a pet animal run over by a car and abandoned in the street by Landolfi, who is terrorized by the prospect of witnessing its blood and entrails (again!), and the toad of the grotesque story "Fear." In the latter tale, a group of friends, sitting late at night in a car, witnesses the puzzling scene of an old woman who, waiting up for her dissolute daughter to come home, is trying to kill a toad by covering it with burning coals. The reproachful spectators, however, cannot act, frozen by fear as the toad hops around and is time and again covered with coals. Here the terror is produced not only by the grotesque figure of the old woman and her obscure motives but by her efforts to erase the animal by literally covering it up. Even more fearful is the ability of the animal to resurface each time (the temptation of a Freudian reading is hard to resist) and its unpredictable jumping that takes it, at the end of the story, back to the feet of its persecutor.

The category of active animals features primarily insects and reptiles. Among the insects, the most menacing are the cockroaches of "The Cockroach Sea" ("*Il mar delle blatte*," 1930; *Mar*) and the spiders of "The Death of the King of France" ("*La morte del re di Francia*," 1935; *Dialogo*). Just as the animals-as-victims manage to penetrate the psyche and progressively dissolve the distinction between human and nonhuman, the active animals are qualified by their intrusiveness. Slithering and crawling, equipped with suction cups rather than claws, they attach themselves to the body or threaten to penetrate it. As in Lautréamont's presurrealist opus, *Maldoror*, the suction cup corresponds to the lure of blood and the claw to the lure of the flesh (Bachelard 33). But in Landolfi, the intrusion of the suction cup prevails over the laceration of the claw. In "The Cockroach Sea," the snakes sucking the milk oozing from Lucrezia's breasts do not bite with their teeth but rather adhere to the body feeding like leeches:

> From the basket rose two sleepy snakes, [. . .] they turned their heads to the left and then to the right, as if orienting themselves, then started surely toward the girl. Each took possession of a nipple and they stood there sucking the milk [. . .] "Throw away these animals!" ordered the Variago. The seaman with the pasta noodle grabbed a pair of tongs and stepped closer. The animals refused to let go. Finally, they were pulled away, bloated like leeches, monstrous. [. . .] However, around the tip of Lucrezia's breasts, on the delicate texture of the areolas, there lingered a small bright-red circle, like a halo. (*Mar* 21)

The imagery of the suction cup also dominates "The Death of the King of France," wherein the spiders that so terrorize the protagonist have bodies like grains of pepper and long skinny legs "evidently equipped with suction cups" (*Dialogo* 63). Beneath the terror of intrusion lurks the fear of losing one's bodily unity, of melting into the animal "other." Both "The Death of the King of France" and "The Cockroach Sea" are then parables of penetration. In the latter story, in addition to the snakes, we note the presence of the worm, which, as Lucrezia's lover, triumphs over the protagonist in the lovemaking competition because of its superior ability to penetrate the woman's body. Similarly the eponymous cockroaches are horrifying chiefly because they threaten to infiltrate the ship and the body: "The cockroaches were entering everywhere, climbing everywhere, filling every nook, they were hanging from the rigging and the tents, they were blackening the sails. Lucrezia, standing on the forecastle was shielding herself the best she could [...]. The cockroaches were now at her hips, they were climbing her chest, had settled in her hair, were crossing her forehead. She could feel them between her thighs, they were filling the hollow of her armpits, forcing her lips, soon they would be in her mouth" (*Mar* 46–47).

"The Death of the King of France" also displays a wide repertory of leeching, sucking, and invasive creatures, including both real and fantastic animals: the fleas that torment the protagonist, the suction-cup-footed spiders, the phallic beasts that populate the dreams of the heroine. The latter also penetrate, cling, and suck rather than lacerating: "So this is the beast that can penetrate anywhere, nestle under a sleeper's pillow, in the hollow of one's armpits, between one's . . . yes between one's warm thighs [. . .] the beast takes possession of Rosalba. It jumps up to bite her most tender bud [. . .]. But the beast hasn't torn off anything, it hasn't torn off her most tender bud, there, in the crevice of her thighs, to eat it. The beast wants to suck her everywhere" (*Dialogo* 52–54). At the end of the story, even the vegetation acquires an animal, arachnoid quality. The low branches of the trees and shrubbery in the woods where the protagonist meets his fate are "viscous and prehensile like tentacles" (*Dialogo* 67); they scratch and lash (they don't tear because they seek to adhere and penetrate)—obviously a projection of the spider legs. Again, the intrusion of the animal "other" denotes a loss of boundaries signaled by the return of the aforementioned "repressed organic." The spiders are horrifying not only for their capacity to crawl inside the body but also because they reveal their bowels, their blood. The spiders with their bodies turned inside-out trigger the abjection for the entrails already seen in "Hands" and *The Fisherman's Beer / The Sinner's Coffin*. The revealing of the spider flesh itself is sufficient to pose the threat of a process of osmosis with the human body: "[T]hose yellow spiders with legs too weak to support their bloated bodies; which are nothing but a small blister of purulent matter [. . .] [T]his is perhaps the essence of spiders. That blister is like the skin of a too-taut boil which absolutely must be pierced *to prevent the pus from spreading to the rest of the body*" (*Dialogo* 65, my italics). Inside the process of animalization that informs Landolfi's work there is also, notably, a process of arachnomorphosis. In "The Death of the King of France," not only does the protagonist dread osmosis with spider flesh, but both his son and the vegetation eventually acquire spider features. Similarly, the monstrous creature in "Kafka's Daddy" ("*Il babbo di Kafka*," 1942; *Spada*) has a human head mounted on a gigantic spider body, and the monkey in *The Two Spinsters* (*Le due zittelle*, 1946) is likened to a grotesquely oversized spider (44).

It would be tempting to locate the generating myth of Landolfi's spiders in the story of Arachne as told by Ovid. The fate of young Arachne, transformed by the goddess Pallas into a spider and sentenced to spin geometrically complex webs forever, might be read as a parable on the doom of the writer caught in his own web of language. But spider webs are centripetal, and the power of the spider image in Landolfi is instead based in its centrifugal quality. In fact, Landolfi's spiders never spin webs or bait traps; instead, they lurk and unpredictably attack. In their clinging, osmotic, leeching attributes, Landolfi's spiders are the direct descendants of the ones populating the cantos of *Maldoror*: "Each night [...] an ancient spider of large species slowly pokes its head out of a hole set in the ground at one of the corner intersections of the room. [...] I who make sleep and nightmare recoil, feel the whole of my body paralysed when it climbs up the ebony feet of my satin bed. It grips my throat with its legs and sucks my throat with its belly" (Lautréamont 180). In Lautréamont's bestiary, as in Landolfi's, the weapon of the predatorial spider is the suction cup, its action revealed by the swelling pouch of the spider's belly.

Anthropomorphic and Theriomorphic Creatures

In an opus preoccupied with the muddling of boundaries between the human and the animal, the cases of shifts from animal to human are remarkably few, although the few there are occupy a position of relevance. Among the talking dogs examined in the first section, for example, both the one in "The Storm" and the one in "New Insights into the Human Psyche" tend toward the human by virtue of their use of language. But the dog in "Fable," like the talking animals of "The Torn Butterfly" and "The Tale of the Crab," falls outside this category because it gravitates toward the metaphoric employment of the animal typical of the Aesop and La Fontaine tales wherein, according to Trama, "the talking animal is a pretext, the hypothesis of a behavior that is ultimately human" (29).

The most significant example of anthropomorphism in Landolfi's bestiary is represented by Tombo, the monkey protagonist of *The Two Spinsters*. As with many of Landolfi's animal narratives, this one, too, reveals a pronounced intertextual component. Not only can one detect a nod to Aldo Palazzeschi's 1934 *The Materassi Sisters* (*Le sorelle Materassi*) in the triangulation between the two spinsters and Tombo, but structurally the two parts into which the novella is organized visibly draw on, and subvert, Edgar Allan Poe's "The Murders in the Rue Morgue" (1841) and (again) Hofmannsthal's *The Lord Chandos Letter* (1902), respectively. Although, on the surface, the plot of *Spinsters* can be read as a parodic inversion of Poe's story—the orangutan, slayer of the two women, becomes the monkey victim of Landolfi's spinsters—in both narratives, the same two central motifs are at work: the imitative behavior of the animal, which suggests a transgression of the boundaries between human and other, and the question of language as a *discrimen* between species. Poe's escaped animal seeks to imitate the ritual of the shave, and its possession of the razor leads to the slaying. In Landolfi it is the fascination with the rite of the mass that leads the monkey to its multiple escapes and the sacrilegious act: the symbolical theriomorphization of the rite itself, the performance of which will later seal its fate.

The question of language stands as a fundamental element in both narratives. Both Poe and Landolfi are aware that it is ultimately the control over verbal language that attributes citizenship to the human or animal realm. In "The Murders in the Rue Morgue," the witnesses claim to have heard two distinct voices at the murder site. The first one, speaking in French, is later identified as the voice of the orangutan's owner. The other is reported by witnesses of different nationalities as expressing itself in a foreign language: the Italian claims the language was Russian; the Spanish claims it was the voice of an Englishman, although he "does not understand English, but judges by intonation" (Poe 202); for the Englishman the voice is that of a German and "might have been a woman's voice" (201). Dupin quickly realizes that all emphasize the *foreign* quality of the language heard. And in fact, this language without referents, this *parole* without *langue*, is so foreign that it must belong to the *really foreign to man*, "the wholly other" (Derrida 11): it consists of the shrieks of the orangutan trying to cover up his crime. It is the erroneous individuation of language that makes it possible to mistake an animal for a man and makes the solution of the puzzle impossible—at least until Dupin's deductive powers are set in motion.

The first part of *The Two Spinsters* is a tale of cross-metamorphosis, configuring both becomings-animal and becomings-human. The mother of the two eponymous spinsters is the powerful matriarch of the house, who gradually takes animal shape. The completion of this metamorphosis is marked by her loss of language. Additionally, as she ages, the matriarch loses the ability to move her limbs with the exception of her forearms, which she bangs on her chest to signify yes or no. The transformation of the woman from human to animal is gradual but eventually complete. When still able to talk, she "squawks": "[A]s soon as Luilla would start getting ready to sneak out briefly she would start to screech" (23). Later, the sound of her beating her chest in the fashion of a gorilla resembles the jungle sounds of "an African drum" (23); the narrator informs us that her sensitivity "was more than animalesque" (22): and finally, when she dies, her head is reduced to a furry skull "bearded beyond all imagination" (26). When the monkey lowers his head close to that of the dying matriarch, he receives the scepter of power, thus beginning his process of anthropomorphization. But Tombo is also a textual figure and therefore, as with many animal presences in Landolfi, the displacement of human characteristics he embodies carries with it a verbal displacement, a linguistic glitch whose reflections muddle the surface of the text. Tombo is, in fact, referred to as a "*scimia*" as opposed to "*scimmia*," the standard Italian for monkey. The loss of the double *m*, as Trama notes, belongs to a series of concrete and symbolic emasculations to which the animal is subjected, such as castration per se, the filing of teeth, and confinement in a cage (145). This orthographical infraction also points to the potential subverting force that the animal brings, a force that is exerted both on the diegetic and on the structural level of the text.

As a replacement for both the overall authority figure of the family (the dead matriarch) and for the male authority figure (the prematurely deceased brother), Tombo is propelled toward a process of anthropomorphization and consequently endeavors to learn a language. Physiologically incapable of speech, the language he finds the most available is the one of the rite of the mass, a code he strives to master in every detail. Ultimately, it is this attempt to use a human semiotic code, therefore blurring the border between beast and man, which will lead to his demise. The second act of the novella coincides with a sharp shift in the narrative, as it is almost entirely occupied by a theological disquisition between an old representative of Christian orthodoxy and a young priest, Father Alessio. The nonanthropocentric argument of Father Alessio, who is trying to defend the monkey from the charge of blasphemy, soon turns into a wider exposition of the priest's pantheism. Clearly, the model is again *The Lord Chandos Letter*, and as in Hofmannsthal's story, the epiphanic point of departure is offered by the capability of the animal to offer a perspective other than that of the subjectivity of the self. In Hofmannsthal's story it is the aforementioned passage about the rat pack that affords Lord Chandos a glimpse at a nonidentitarian, polymorphous point of view—a *pack epistemology*. Lord Chandos's animism derives from a fracturing of the experience of the sensuous world: "A dog, a rat, a beetle, a stunted apple tree, a cart path winding over the hill, a moss-covered stone mean more to me than the most beautiful, most abandoned lover ever did [...]. These mute and sometimes inanimate beings rise up before me with such a plenitude, such a presence of love that my joyful eye finds nothing dead anywhere. Everything seems to mean something, everything that exists" (125). Father Alessio's apology for the monkey echoes Lord Chandos's claims:

> How many times have I found myself kneeling before a cat washing its face, before a squirrel [...]. Or before any other thing, before a blade of grass as well as a house of a man, before a starry sky as well as the refuse from a living body. There, I say to myself, this cat is like this and it cannot be any other way, and it is perfect: another thing or another shape would never make a cat more perfect or more beautiful than this, it would only be something different, it wouldn't be a cat. But this other thing would be equally perfect in itself... I have no hope of making myself understood. (*Zittelle* 82)

However, Landolfi translates the tragic dimension of Lord Chandos into the grotesque stage presence of Father Alessio, whose argument ultimately becomes the blathering of a madman, thus sealing the fate of the monkey he had set out to save. Hence the quintessentially modernist Hofmannsthal is reread by an already postmodern Landolfi, a writer who pays homage and at the same time turns his models to parody.[9] One thinks not only of the treatment of Hofmannnsthal and Poe in *The Two Spinsters* but also of that of Gogol in "Gogol's Wife" ("*La moglie di Gogol*," 1954; *Ombre*) or Kafka in "Kafka's Daddy."

The exemplary Landolfian borderline creature is the "weregoat" of *The Moon Stone*. Landolfi's first great symbolist novel is traversed by infractions of human–animal boundaries. Gurù, the girl belonging to the "*veranie*," a species of weregoat, is human only in the upper part of her body; from the hips down, she has the body and the coarse fur of a goat. Yet unlike the awkward human spider of "Kafka's Daddy," Gurù is wholly harmonious, so much so that the protagonist is disconcerted to discover that the naked body of his lover appears so natural. Borderline creatures abound throughout the narrative: beyond the "*veranie*," there are frightening, diaphanous creatures with human bodies and heads and limbs of wolves, birds, cows, and snakes that appear in the lair of the bandits, who themselves wear goatskin leggings that make them resemble fauns. This proliferation of theriomorphic beings is related to surrealist iconographies, especially the figures populating Max Ernst's *A Week of Kindness* (1934), a work that appeared three years before the composition of *The Moon Stone* and one that Landolfi probably knew thanks to his frequenting of the Florentine artists associated with Giubbe Rosse. Equally relevant are Alberto Savinio's figures with animal heads. Savinio inaugurated this series of paintings at the beginning of the thirties, and again the influence of the painter is confirmed by the proximity of the two artists to the Giubbe Rosse environment.

Gurù, as the love interest of *The Moon Stone*, embodies both the attraction/dread of sexual initiation and Landolfi's overarching fascination and repulsion with respect to menstruation, which also permeates "The Death of the King of France." Again, a Freudian reading is courted by the text's symbolism. The virginal Gurù, turning into a sexually predatorial weregoat during the nights of the full moon, represents a movement against Freudian "organic repression" and its taboo of menstruation, suggesting a return to the dominance of the olfactory and to the periodicity of the sexual process that was proper to men in their pre-erect-posture state (Freud 66). Moreover, Gurù belongs to that group of creatures that corresponds to a project of production, *ex-novo*, of one's own totemic animals—an effort that yields its most relevant fruits in the category of word-animals discussed in the next section. Joining Gurù in this class of enigmatic, appealing, but disturbing characters are the mysterious armadillo women of "The Cockroach Sea." While in this story the main complex articulated through the animal presence is that of penetration, these creatures, able to enclose a man entirely within their bodies, correspond to the diametrically opposite obsession: that of being completely enveloped.

In addition to the more obvious theriomorphic creatures such as these, Landolfi's narratives display a pervasive tendency to attribute animal qualities to their human characters. This metamorphic drive is essential, for example, in "Maria Giuseppa," wherein the title character participates successfully in that process of animalization that is experienced only partially by the protagonist. Maria Giuseppa is often "*immusonita,*" "*a grugno duro,*"[10] and she obeys "like a dog when threatened with a stick" (*Dialogo* 16). The story can be read as an encounter (or a failed encounter) between two humans on the animal plane.

Not even objects are immune to this drive toward the animal. As discussed, one of the most pervasive presences in Landolfi's animal pantheon is that of the spider, so much so that a great number of his fictional beings fall under the influence of this animal. In addition to the bushes with spider legs in "The Death of the King of France," in "The Tale of the Werewolf" ("*Il racconto del lupo mannaro,*" 1939; *Mar*) the moon itself, once caught by one of the werewolves, comes to resemble the belly of a spider, "a big round object resembling a pulsating boil of lard" (*Mar* 98). In "The Wax Tooth" ("*Il dente di cera,*" 1939; *Mar*), a prosthetic tooth becomes a lurking, crawling presence—a creature that needs to be caught before it contaminates its surroundings: "[W]ill it forever remain in my room, this tooth?" (*Mar* 116). Finally, exempt from the complex of the spider image but still significantly caught in a process of animalization is the eponymous starship of *Cancerqueen*. Even though it eventually acquires the use of language, Cancerqueen is essentially an inanimate being turned animal. From its first appearance it is described as a "machine with bizarre moods" (32), and preparing for its first flight it displays an almost catlike behavior— "grumbled a bit, sneezed, yawned lazily, as if she did not fancy flying about just to be exhibited" (34)—and the sound of its engine is one of "fierce and menacing growls, wheezings, howlings" (51).

Animots

Nowhere is the process of becoming-animal as clearly registered as a destabilizing practice as with the appearance of what we can call (bending to our purposes the term coined by Derrida) *animots*—animal words. Here, the anxiety at the loss of the referential power of language is accompanied by a progressive animalization of language itself.[11] A word that refuses to conform to its assigned referent is an animal word, impish and unpredictable, endowed with the same magnetic drive of the animal, yet dangerous because, like a cancerous cell, it threatens to contaminate the whole structure of language.

This last category occupies such a central role in Landolfi's opus that it encompasses many of the instances discussed before. The majority of Landolfi's animal presences are in fact motivated by linguistic concerns, and they inhabit the space of the narration as textual occurrences spawned by linguistic infractions. The prosthetic tooth of "The Wax Tooth," for example, becomes an *animot* because it is made of "*cera giassa*," a wax qualified by the mysterious term "*giassa*";[12] hence the narrator's determination to find the *animot* before it contaminates his house and the exchange between language and reality. Tombo of *The Two Spinsters* is referred to with the aforementioned orthographically incorrect "*scimia*." It is this morphological infraction, reverberating on both the diegetic and structural levels of the text, that qualifies Tombo as a metalinguistic creature. As an *animot*, Tombo becomes a polymorphous animal creature: all animals and no animal in particular, he becomes the wholly other. He is therefore a spider, a "*buprestidae*" and a "*cerambycidae*" (here Landolfi exploits the estranging effect of the zoological names of two species of common insects) at first, and then after he attempts to break the boundaries of the human–animal divide, he becomes in turn a hen (56), a rabbit, a cow, a pigeon, and a rat (91). In the end, Tombo is punished specifically because of his polymorphous function: on a metanarrative level, because of his refusal to signify always and exactly *monkey* and always and exactly *animal*. Since the *animots* represent a loss of control over the normative function of language, they infallibly materialize as obsessive presences. In addition to the fantastic *silenziotti* in "Week of Sunshine" and the *canie*, the phallic potato-dog creatures in "The Death of the King of France," the most emblematic *animot* in Landolfi's work is probably the *porrovio*, a fantastic animal composed of pieces of other creatures but ultimately brought to life by the impossible adhesion to any referents engendered by its signifier:

> The porrovio! What kind of beast is the porrovium? I am sorry to admit that I myself do not know [...] He appears when the night scurries like a hare in the sun, with its ears transfused by the light [...] crouching like a cat, or better, like a cowpat, with yellow eyes. For a long time my life has been obsessed by the search or ordering of words. The porrovio prowls, grey, in the darkness, the porrovio comes, goes, the porrovio is a mass that I cannot swallow. The porrovio is not a beast, it is a word. (*Cancroregina* 77)

As a powerful totemic animal, the *porrovio* embodies the coming apart of the referential binds of language. As such, it marks a shift in Landolfi's literary output from the fictional to the autobiographical. Yet the *porrovio* returns years later in the autobiographical *Rien Va*, indicating both a continuity of poetics and the persistence of a feeling of inescapable vertigo at the outer reaches of language:

> Last night I met the lightning beast.
> Once I called it Porrovio and claimed it was a word.
> I was lying. It's my beast ... LIGHTNING BEAST ...
> Where do these strange words that I cannot control come from, words appearing instantly and totally alien to me? Where but from the depths of my madness? ... Lightning Beast: although meaningless, this expression seems fairly definitive, able to last for as long as one gives credit to it. But first of all, it does not have any logical ground, nor is it premeditated in any way. (307–8)

Two important Landolfian parables are expressly centered on the becoming-animal of language—namely, "Agitated Words" ("*Parole in agitazione*," 1968; *Più belle*) and "The Stroll" ("*La passeggiata*," 1965; *Più belle*). "Agitated Words" features an animalization *en abîme*, as *animots* literally come out of the protagonist's mouth, writhing and running around like "rabbits in a cage or young otters in the rapids" (*Più belle* 397). With a body of their own and the ability to speak, the fugitive words introduce themselves as signifiers revolting against their own signified. To avoid confusion, the narrator decides to force them to accept new aleatory meanings. However, the tale ends when the narrator realizes he has forgotten which signified went with which signifier. These *animots* end up as a lurking, menacing presence, eventually bent on returning to their point of origin to subvert the order of language: "[T]hey know what they mean, but I don't. It's terrible. Besides, I am a bit worried. I told you that [...] they fled who knows where, but they must still be in the house, and one day, you'll see, they'll ambush me" (*Più belle* 398).

The second parable of theriomorphic language does not feature animals per se but displays in full a verbal becoming-animal. In "The Stroll," Landolfi composes a story by way of what appear to be obscure neologisms. Seemingly composed of pure signifiers, the language employed functions by way of free associations and aural suggestions. The reader is hence allowed to witness what would happen if the "Agitated Words" were to take over. This walk through a phonosymbolic landscape takes the reader down many different paths at once. Words now merely suggest rather than strictly denote, as in the following passage provided in both Italian and English:

> Procedetti e principiarono i camepizi, le bugole, gli ilatri, i matalli, gli zizzifi anche, benchè, a vero dire, guasti alquanto dall'exoasco o dall'oidio; e zighene e arginnidi (pafie o latonie) e le piccole depressarie passavano di luogo in luogo e, accanto e sopra me, trochili e peppole, parizzole e castorchie, e l'aria era tutta uno zezzio, uno zinzilulio. (*Più belle* 381)

> I kept walking on and soon I could see tall weeds, the blue flowers of the bugles, the short *matallo* trees and the jujube trees, the latter though, infested with fungi and parasites; and butterflies were flying from place to place, and around and above me were hummingbirds and finches, chickadees and

shrikes, and the air resonated with the whistling of the breeze and the song of the swallows.

Here, Landolfi exploits the estranging effect that the readers experience in the presence of a language that is both familiar and mysterious. The phonolinguistic effects are obtained by way of alliterations (*campezi, zizzifi, zighene, parizzole, zezzio, zinzilulio*), assonances, and a stylistic register that runs from the colloquial to a turn-of-the-century high-literary one. Landolfi, however, wary of completely loosening the reins of language, anchors his theriomorphic language to a normative docking, and in fact, all the terms used in "The Stroll" are authentic Italian words, albeit of extremely low-frequency use.[13] The idea of a purely phonetic language made of signs with multiple or interchangeable referents runs as a leitmotif throughout Landolfi's opus. If this language is attainable, he suggests, then it will be as far from the human as possible: an animal language with an animal shape. This option of utilizing a nonanthropocentric language as a heuristic tool appears right from the beginning of Landolfi's career. The opening section of "Night Must Fall" (1937; *Dialogo*) is occupied by a musing on the song of the owl. For the narrator, the monotone song of the bird corresponds to a single-word language, whose meanings remain fresh although the single word is repeated over and over, unchanged.[14] Just like the language of the dog Châli, or the nonreferential inventions of the narrators of "Maria Giuseppa" and "Week of Sunshine," the pure animal language of the owl escapes the entropic exhaustion of human language by renewing its meaning with each utterance.

Toward the end of his career, in the volume of poetry *Violet Tone of Death* (*Viola di morte*, 1972), Landolfi referred to language as "mere verb, heavy with fixed meanings, forbidden to roam, bound in hell" (35). The animal presence then—and hence the becoming-animal of language—represents the other side of the coin of literary expression as both prison and impregnable fortress. As with Landolfi's ancestral home, the house of literature is traversed by the subverting presence of the animal as an intruder. Tombo, Gurù, the *porrovio*, the mouse of "Hands," the spiders of "The Death of the King of France," the arachnoid creature of "Kafka's Daddy," and the owl and its monoverbal song all ultimately mark not the failure of language but the chance for a reformulation of its limits. These presences, not wholly contained by the language that conjures them, work as a bridge connecting with a reality other than the one to which words confine us—for Landolfi, the final goal of any literary endeavor. As such, Landolfi's animals are indispensable disruptive elements: presences that upset the game of solitaire that the author cannot help but play with literature.

Notes

1. Unless otherwise specified, translations are my own.
2. I am here borrowing Derrida's neologism introduced in *The Animal That Therefore I Am*.
3. The ornithological presence, although far less present, is also relevant.
4. The isolated country villa is the counterpart of Landolfi's real-life house in Pico, where the writer often retired to work and where he spent the last years of his life.
5. At first reference, short stories will be identified by year of first publication and by the abbreviated title of the volume subsequently collecting them.
6. Animal narrators are not uncommon in Landolfi's fiction; other noteworthy examples include the cockroach in "*Il racconto della piattola*" ("The Tale of the Crab," 1942; *Spada*) and the butterfly of "*La farfalla strappata*" ("The Torn Butterfly," 1939; *Mar*).
7. The dog Châli (in real-life the name of Landolfi's own hunting dog) is named after a character in the eponymous Guy de Maupassant short story. On the subject, see also Idolina Landolfi, 77–90.
8. Lyotard argues that animals are paradigmatic victims because, unable to speak for themselves, they cannot denounce the injuries suffered.
9. On this issue Andreozzi identifies "a sort of ambiguous literary alienation separating Landolfi irreparably from his masters" (212).
10. Both expressions translate roughly as "with a brooding expression on her face"; however, Landolfi employs two terms, "*grugno*" and "*muso*," which in Italian refer to animal faces.
11. This "anxiety of nonreferentiality" is a pervasive concern in Landolfi's work, and nowhere is it as clearly spelled out as in the autobiographical story "*La penna*" ("The Pen"): "Black, dark words. In vain [...] I try to penetrate them and to establish a correspondence with some kind of reality, they only correspond to nothing [...] Sometimes, in certain harvest years, the nuts harvested from the hills are all empty because of a hidden parasite: greedy boy that I was, I was left with handfuls of empty shells, nothing but shells" (*Più belle* 403).
12. The word *giasso/a* is a Landolfian neologism. However, the term *giasso* in Ligurian dialect means "ice." One could, then, postulate a reference to Punta del Giasso, a rocky promontory close to Portofino traditionally held to be in the shape of a tooth.
13. A few years after the publication of the story, Landolfi revealed the trick in the essay/story "*Conferenza personalfilologicodrammatica con implicazioni*" ("Personalphilologicaldramatic Lecture with Implications"), now included in *Le labrene* (1974).
14. It is probable that Landolfi is paying homage to the most illustrious monoverbal literary animal: Poe's raven.

Works Cited

Andreozzi, Giorgio. "Il ragno, l'animale-totem." In *La liquida vertigine*, ed. Idolina Landolfi, 209–16. Florence: Olschki, 2002.
Bachelard, Gaston. *Lautréamont*. Salerno: Edizioni 10/17, 1989.
Deleuze, Gilles, and Félix Guattari. *A Thousand Plateaus: Capitalism and Schizophrenia*. Minneapolis: U of Minnesota P, 2009.
Derrida, Jacques. *The Animal That Therefore I Am*. Ed. Marie-Louise Mallet. Trans. David Wills. New York: Fordham UP, 2008.
Freud, Sigmund. *Civilization and Its Discontents*. Mansfield: Martino, 2010.
Landolfi, Idolina. "Tommaso Landolfi e il mondo francese." In *Gli altrove di Tommaso Landolfi*, ed. Idolina Landolfi and Ernestina Pellegrini, 77–90. Rome: Bulzoni, 2004.
Landolfi, Tommaso. *La Biere du Pecheur*. Milan: Rizzoli, 1989.
———. *Cancroregina*. Milan: Guanda, 1982.
———. *Dialogo dei massimi sistemi*. Milan: Adelphi, 1996.
———. *Le due zittelle*. Milan: Adelphi, 1992.
———. *Il mar delle blatte*. Milan: Adelphi, 1997.
———. *Ombre*. Milan: Adelphi, 1994.
———. *La pietra lunare*. Milan: Adelphi, 1995.
———. *Le più belle pagine di Tommaso Landolfi*. Milan: Rizzoli, 1982.
———. *Rien va*. Milan: Adelphi, 1998.
———. *La spada*. Milan: Adelphi, 2001.
———. *Viola di morte*. Florence: Vallecchi, 1972.
Lautréamont, Comte de. *Maldoror*. Cambridge: Exact Change, 1994.
Lyotard, Jean-François. *The Differend: Phrases in Dispute*. Minneapolis: U of Minnesota P, 1988.
Poe, Edgar Allan. *The Fall of the House of Usher and Other Writings*. London: Penguin, 1986.
Von Hofmannsthal, Hugo. *The Lord Chandos Letter*. New York: New York Review, 2005.
Trama, Paolo. *Animali e fantasmi della scrittura. Saggi sulla zoopoetica di Tommaso Landolfi*. Rome: Salerno Editrice, 2006.

5

Animal Metaphors, Biopolitics, and the Animal Question

Mario Luzi, Giorgio Agamben, and the Human–Animal Divide

Matteo Gilebbi

The "animal question" is a broad philosophical debate that erodes the purportedly tidy, sharp division between the human and the nonhuman, calling into question a widely accepted anthropocentrism and mankind's supposed ontological privilege. This approach to human–animal interaction is taken, therefore, to sabotage speciesism, the prejudice that animals are inferior to humans, which justifies the discrimination practiced by man against other species. Also, by making the borderland between humans and animals mobile—and, to a certain degree, unsafe—the animal question problematizes human identity and subjectivity. For this reason, one of the main goals of the animal question is to radically challenge the discontinuity between animals and human beings. This criticism should then lead to a displacement of the human realm and open a debate on repositioning anthropocentrism or even making it obsolete. Among the many voices that have raised animal questions in Italian culture, two make themselves particularly significant due to the clarity of their arguments and the consistency of their positions. Poet Mario Luzi and philosopher Giorgio Agamben pose the question of interspecies relations in terms that are not only radical but also complementary, giving us a transdisciplinary understanding of the human–animal divide.

From Animal Metaphor to Ecumenical Biocentrism

The presence of animal figures in poetry and other literary genres does not always serve to raise the animal question in an ontological sense; in literature, animals have been used primarily as symbols, metaphors, and allegorical figures that help define human qualities, feelings, or behaviors. To reference a canonical example, the three beasts encountered by Dante in the first canto of the *Inferno* are allegories of his sins. Similarly, Charles Baudelaire's albatross is a metaphor for the tragic implications of being an artist. In some cases, however, an animal image exceeds a rhetorical function and therefore stimulates an analysis of human–animal interaction, making the reader consider aspects of the animal's status, call into question human identity, or expose speciesism. In sum, the use of animal images can potentially raise animal questions.

On this matter, Jacques Derrida and Akira Lippit have argued that animal metaphors are a special kind of metaphor. According to Derrida, an animal image inside a metaphor carries an alien element, an element that does not belong to the human linguistic system. The animal we embed in our language is an *animot*: a homonym of *animaux* ("animals" in French) that marks the invasion of animality within the word (*mot*; Derrida 41–51). Entering human language, the animal "animates" it, shows its potentials and limits in describing and interpreting reality, and marks the otherness that the animal represents from a human standpoint. Synthesizing Derrida's thoughts, Akira Lippit points out that, when an animal metaphor stimulates this kind of animal question, it also challenges the function of human linguistic strategies and abilities. In these cases, the animal metaphor is an antimetaphor, a new and hybrid linguistic element that Lippit defines as "animetaphor" (169). In sum, an animetaphor involves the use of animal images to question human use of language and tropes as well as the anthropological status of language and how it influences the human–animal divide.

This active role of animal images is carried further by Roberto Marchesini and his zooanthropological theories. According to Marchesini, partnership with animals has been crucial in the human evolutionary process. Moving from recent developments in ethology and cognitive science, Marchesini argues that human and nonhuman animals share a partnership that intrinsically defines our ontological status. This means that "anthropopoiesis"—that is, the process of "becoming human"—was a historical event made possible by interactions with other species and by the subsequent acquisition of knowledge by humans. According to Marchesini, the development of human culture depends on the innate ability of our species to learn from interaction with others. This acquisition of knowledge is defined as "zoomimesis," since it is essentially a mimetic process. Marchesini explains that being human is the result of the observation, imitation, and hybridization of the behavior of other species. By observing, imitating, and developing a solid partnership with other animals, man not only learned to hunt, build, farm, and survive but also developed social interactions within the species. The organization of human society itself is the result of our imitation of other animals' social structures. Human culture and identity are built in partnership with other animals and could not exist without them. In conclusion, the role of the animal is what Marchesini defines as an "epistemological operator": a means that has offered humans the key to access knowledge and to develop a specific cultural background (105–40).

This interaction and partnership with animals also takes place in the animal images in language. Often, animal metaphors are indeed the result of human observation and imitation of animals. Animal images are used to store, communicate, and expand the knowledge acquired through zoomimesis. This is why animal metaphors, like the animals they represent, can become epistemological operators as well. When this happens, as Marchesini points out, these images assume the function of "theriomorphisms," which means that they not only help define human qualities but also reveal the process of knowledge acquisition and cast new light on the human–animal relationship:

> Where does human imagination originate, and how is it fed? Usually we think that ideas come from nowhere, or that they are contained in a parallel universe, or even that they take shape as an emanation of the anthroposphere. And yet the excess of theriomorphisms in human culture, in symbology as well as technology, in science as well as in art, should raise some suspicion. It is in the very moment that we face the unknown or represent that the animal comes to our aid, offering an opportunity to imagine alien forms, build taxonomies, give shape to new projects, and formulate thoughts that go beyond our intuitive limits. (Marchesini 105)[1]

Therefore animal metaphors can be tropes used to simply define a human trait, but they can also be used to raise an animal question. Following Derrida, then, I define *animetaphor* as an animal metaphor that raises questions about the bond between the human–animal divide and language. Inspired by Marchesini, I define *theriomorphism* as an animal metaphor that puts into question anthropocentrism and reconsiders the human–animal partnership.

Mario Luzi's poetry represents one of the most compelling examples of a gradual transformation of simple animal metaphors into animetaphors and theriomorphisms, from rhetorical elements to animal questions. Essentially, Luzi's entire poetic production appears as a long journey toward the discovery of human nature, considered by the poet as an enigma. The poem "Man—or Shadow" can help us broach this crucial aspect of Luzi's poetry: "Man or shadow, shadow / or man cannot distinguish outside / or inside himself, he gets lost / in the enigma of his species. / But / a subtle flame unites them, / a single light eliminates them" (lines 18–25, *Earthly* 39). The anthropological dimension manifests itself as indistinguishable from its "shadow," in symbiosis with its obscure component and lost in its own enigma. This enigma is what generates Luzi's poetry. In addition, as is clear from these lines, light and fire—symbols of faith—have the capacity to merge the positive and negative sides of humanity and also to extinguish them. By uniting and destroying the two elements, faith would become the most important tool in trying to solve the human enigma.[2] In the light of faith, "man" and "shadow," purity and sin, reason and instinct, and humanity and animality inside man are transformed from oppositional to symbiotic elements. Of all God's creatures, man is the one that has constructed a false dichotomy between human and animal nature, both "outside / or inside himself." Luzi's faith tells him that God has created humans as single entities, not divided between culture and nature. By interpreting these two elements as indistinct, they disappear ("a single light eliminates them"). However, in Luzi's poetry, the human figure emerging from the disappearance of the opposition between humanity and animality cannot be easily defined; it remains hidden behind this mystery and can be approached only by displacing man from his ontological centrality (anthropocentrism) and engaging in a process of investigation that continues to question human nature from a religious perspective. As Gloria Manghetti points out, Luzi's faith and his religious investigation do not bring a simple, serene, and harmonic solution to the human enigma; instead, this faith fosters uncertainty, anxiety, and unanswered questions (18). Light and fire can unite but also destroy. Since faith cannot completely unravel the mysterious nature of being human, poetry becomes involved in the search for clarity. For this reason, poetry becomes, for Luzi, the instrument through which the investigation of human nature can be refined and improved in order to arrive at answers that are less uncertain: less lost in the enigma.

Animal metaphors used in poetry become part and parcel of this process of investigation that defines Luzi's poetry. In his first book, *The Boat* (*La barca*, 1935), animal images are rare and rarefied, and generally used to explore female characters. This metaphorical relationship between women and nature emerges exemplarily in the opening lines of the poem "Fragility" ("*Fragilità*"). The poet offers a description of nature where "[c]reatures dip into the fields / inebriated by the strength that makes them bloom / between soft burdens that swing / when hit by the spring" (lines 1–4, *Tutte* 27).[3] This is immediately followed by the appearance of the female element: "Young girls with pensive faces / sew between hedgerows where gleams / in open garlands / the billow that ravishes beauty" (lines 4–8, *Tutte* 27). The enigma that this female image bears emerges from an interpretation of nature linked to symbolic strategies. Luzi's "young girls" and the landscape surrounding them belong to an arcadia: a place that is at the same time magical, inviolate, and unreachable. Humans, animals, and natural environments are used to convey sublime or tenuous feelings.

For example, in the poem "Serenade in D'Azeglio Square" ("*Serenata in Piazza d'Azeglio*"), Luzi appeals to the image of a "fresh, slippery turtle dove" (*Tutte* 15–16) in order to summon the portrait of a long-lost love. In another poem of the same book, "Terrace" ("*Terrazza*"), the image of a "large dove" (*Tutte* 41) unable to take flight is used as a metaphor for a depressing day during which the poet becomes aware of his loneliness.

Luzi also keeps animal images encaged inside a strict rhetorical function in his second book, *Nightly Advent* (*Avvento notturno*, 1940). The only difference is that here animal images acquire the capacity to summon an intimate iconography and a fantastic and surreal inner world, slightly changing their previous symbolic function of merely expressing the poet's human feelings. This world is described as an alternative reality and is used by the poet to replace the real world that was falling into imminent worldwide conflict. In this context, imaginary animals appear for the first time in Luzi's poetry, such as "dragons rebelling from the innermost / of my binary and painless life!" ("*Miraglio*," *Tutte* 74).[4] The poet taps into an imaginary bestiary to populate a visionary reality where his uneasiness and fears can find expression and consequently be vented.

This expanded metaphorical and symbolic use of animal figures is also maintained in his two short books published in the fifties: *Desert's Early Fruits* (*Primizie del deserto*, 1952) and *Proper Perspectives* (*Onore del vero*, 1957). However, at this point, a new element begins to emerge. As noted by Lisa Rizzoli and Giorgio Morelli, Luzi begins to move away from a symbolic imagination toward a more "natural reality" (71). Animals are for the first time described in their biological existence, and the human being is defined by the perception of an innate but new feeling: "the dark animal eternity / which moans inside us" ("And the Wolf" ["*E il lupo*"], *Tutte* 249). Here, Luzi's poetry begins to investigate the human enigma from the perspective of a biological interaction with animals and nature. However, the poet underlines how complex this interaction is in "Invocation" ("*Invocazione*"): "This is the right time, if you come, / stomp on the sad mildew, on the dry shrubs, / smash their nobs, tear the twines, / but hurt yourself, bleed you too, / cry with us, go dark in the depths" (lines 46–50, *Tutte* 180). In order to achieve a closer relationship with nature, man has to understand the deepest and most obscure aspects of biological reality. This stanza carries both a literal meaning, as the reader sees a desperate man ("cry with us") running away like a scared animal into the depths of the woods, and a symbolic meaning, as the reader understands that finding his inner "animal eternity" means examining what has always been considered the obscure side of human nature. In this stanza, Luzi indicates how man can move toward his inner animality and rediscover it, embracing this "darkness" through the act of sharing a common sufferance with animals and men ("bleed you too, / cry with us"). This can happen only because Luzi becomes aware that man and animal are elements of the same environment, so much so that they can share the same biological rhythm and become two very similar creatures ("In One Point" [*"In un punto"*], *Tutte* 225), sometimes even indistinguishable from each other ("Fog" [*"Nebbia"*], *Tutte* 196). These ideas, present in many poems of these two books, prove that the human–animal divide emerges here, slowly becoming one of the focal points of Luzi's poetry.

The poet accomplishes the final passage from animal metaphors to animetaphors and theriomorphisms in his following book, *In the Magma* (*Nel Magma*, 1963). Here, Luzi describes *anthropos* as the result of the connection and partnership between humans and animals. Being human means being one of many species inhabiting the biosphere, with no particular privilege, prestige, or superiority, so that speciesism can be considered specious, presumptuous, and illogical. Man is just an animal "born human" ("Terrace," *Tutte* 345), and his life is defined as the "long coming and going / between home and outside, between burrow and field" ("Between Night and Day" [*"Tra notte e giorno"*], *Tutte* 328). Through these images, Luzi defines man as a human animal: a creature biologically and ontologically tied to all creatures, whose home is no different from an animal den. The enigma that surrounded man becomes less substantial, and the shadows covering it partially dissipate. This happens because, by considering man as a human animal, Luzi simplifies the anthropological dimension by narrowing it to its biological status.

In addition, ideological and metaphysical superstructures lose a great part of their relevance, since the human being is now stripped down to his mere natural reality. The only nonbiological aspects that survive this process are faith and religious sensibility. They not only survive, but their role is even greater since, according to Luzi, the spiritual sphere is intrinsically intertwined with the biological one. The first and most powerful manifesto of this relationship between faith and nature is Luzi's poem "Me Abjure? Who Can Say" (*"Abiura Io? Chi può dirlo"*), from *For the Baptism of Our Fragments* (*Per il battesimo dei nostri frammenti*, 1985). The poem opens with an interrogation of faith, its nature, and its pitfalls: "Me abjure? Who can say / what is the right observance / of a faith—and then what kind of faith was it / it was only my cheerful / falling in love daily—which / then the legitimate seal: / to lose it, I maintain, deny oneself the privilege / of having it, maybe not it, / its sufficiency, its theological super-pride" (*Baptism* 21). This poem then turns explicitly to the world of animality, human and nonhuman, as Luzi challenges the assumed privilege of human faith: "And / then how can one accept, / how can one even think / that I have what the breakstones do not have / or the fireflies or the carps, / or even the poor human animal / dispirited and drained / on a bed in a convalescent hospital, / nor the rest which matures with us / through matter's single common process" (*Baptism* 21). This challenge develops into a portrait of the apparent authenticity of a more inclusive being: "[H]e glows with an almost / ribald love, / wilderness burning / even more celestial in his eyes— / poet, my only humble master, or more" (*Baptism* 21).

In this poem, Luzi questions the validity of a religious feeling that considers man the privileged subject of godly love. The faith built on this assumption is defined as a personal "falling in love daily," a superficial enjoyment that results in a "theological super-pride." The poet suggests that man must abandon this supposed privilege in order to have access to a renewed and more genuine faith—to experience that "celestial" love emerging from human "wilderness" ("*quid silvestro*" in the Italian original). Luzi reconciles the human–nature divide by repositioning humans at the same level as all the other beings, as all together becoming equal parts of a universe defined as "matter's single common process." Faith must recognize this common, ecumenical structure of the world by ending its validation of that shallow anthropocentrism that justifies the destruction of nature and our "*quid silvestro*." In fact, by validating this anthropocentrism, faith also authorizes speciesism and actually makes man more distant from the divine sphere. This happens because, according to Luzi's poetry, a separation between the biological and the theological spheres cannot exist in reality. The human animal, following a superficial belief that prejudicially gives him an ontological privilege, wrongly separates the natural sphere from the spiritual one. Luzi's philosophical position states that this discontinuity is faulty and that any theological perspective must be considered *sub specie naturalis*.

This is the most important aspect of Luzi's animal question that deeply informs all his late works, especially the section "Animalia" of the book *Under Human Species* (*Sotto specie umana*, 1999) and the two books *Doctrine of the Extreme Beginner* (*Dottrina dell'estremo principiante*, 2004) and *Leave Me, Do Not Hold Me Back* (*Lasciami, non trattenermi*, 2009). Through the constant use of animal images as theriomorphisms, Luzi gradually expands the animal question until it becomes a *weltanschauung*: he delineates an all-embracing biological vitality that includes the divine. In this interpretation of the world, humans and animals are not juxtaposed; they become equal subjects of an ecumenical and biocentric cosmos that they share with spiritual entities. A few lines from the poem "Where Are You? I Can't Find You" ("*Dove sei? Non ti trovo*") illustrate this point: "I feel / the elements, sun, air, winds / the many protagonists / of being, animal, / men, plants and angels / murmuring / sometimes restless" (lines 9–15, *Dottrina* 129). Luzi projects everything inside the contingency of a biological life that embraces the human, the animal, and the divine. Through this peculiar biocentrism, reality is interpreted as a harmonic unity where the separations introduced by the human animal are deceitful. Of those separations, anthropocentrism and speciesism are the most absurd, because they are against the normative order of things. In order to reach this conclusion, to rethink the position of man and his relationship with animals and the entire cosmos, Luzi had to reconfigure the use and function of animal images in his poetry. He was able to move from simple metaphors that described human qualities to epistemological operators that conveyed the complex animal question on biocentrism.

Biopolitics and Posthuman Idleness

This passage from the symbolic and metaphorical use of animals to their function as epistemological operators has important repercussions for ideological and political mechanisms. As evidenced in Luzi's poetry, when animals are not constrained inside the cage of metaphor, their presence as bare creatures can problematize human status, identity, and privilege. Therefore, as epistemological operators, animals help raise animal questions that, in addressing the anthropological condition, expose the biopolitical implications in human society and human–animal interaction. The term *biopolitics*, developed by Foucault and elaborated in *The Birth of Biopolitics: Lectures at the Collège de France, 1978–1979*, refers to the broad investigation of the impact of power apparatuses on the biological dimension of human and nonhuman animals. Simply put, these biopolitical implications are the effects of political and ideological power on the lives of both man and animal.

Close attention to biopolitics characterizes the bulk of Giorgio Agamben's philosophical enquiry. In the introduction to *Homo Sacer: Sovereign Power and Bare Life* (1995)—his first study completely dedicated to biopolitics—Agamben appropriates a useful definition of life from ancient Greek philosophy. The term *zoē* indicated biological life in its simple form—that is, the mere state of being alive. The term *bíos* was used, instead, to define everything beyond this mere state that is typical of each individual or of a group of people. *Zoē*, then, referred to bare life, while *bíos* referred to social and political life (*Homo Sacer* 1). Human life is therefore the combination of *zoē* and *bíos*. This is a crucial distinction, because it allows Agamben to pinpoint the exact aspects of human life targeted by political power. In fact, taking inspiration from Foucault's *The History of Sexuality I: The Will to Knowledge* (1976), Agamben notices how, in the modern era, politics began wielding its authority and taking control not only of *bíos* but also of *zoē* (3–4). Politics became biopolitics, and citizens became bodies. The most tragic results of biopolitical legislation are Nazism's scientific racism, eugenics, and extermination camps. As Agamben points out, the extermination of the Jews was not undertaken for religious or ideological reasons; it was the result of a biopolitical strategy of power and control: "The truth—which is difficult for the victims to face, but which we must have the courage not to cover with sacrificial veils—is that the Jews were exterminated not in a mad and giant holocaust but exactly as Hitler had announced, 'as lice,' which is to say, as bare life. The dimension in which the extermination took place is neither religion nor law, but biopolitics" (*Homo Sacer* 114).

As the equivalence of Jew to louse exemplifies, biopolitics can exercise its power on men when it transforms their *bíos* into *zoē*. A citizen can be more easily controlled by reducing him or her to the condition of an animal. Agamben defines this biopolitical mechanism as the "anthropological machine," a symbolic and material mechanism at work in scientific and philosophical discourse that determines the human–animal distinction (*Open* 33–37). Agamben distinguishes between a premodern and a modern anthropological machine. The former, running from Aristotle to Darwin, humanizes animal life. What we now consider human beings were seen as animals with human characteristics: slaves and barbarians are two clear examples of this distinction.[5] The modern anthropological machine is instead post-Darwinian, and it works in a similar but inverted form. It implies an animalization of some modes of human life and attempts to point at the animal aspects present within human beings themselves. The modern anthropological machine produced the *Pithecanthropus alalus*— that is, the missing link in the human evolutionary process—and the most violent animalization of the last century: the persecuted Jew. Agamben concludes this definition by observing that "it is not so much a matter of asking which of the two machines (or of the two variants of the same machine) is better or more effective—or, rather, less lethal and bloody—as it is of understanding how they work so that we might, eventually, be able to stop them" (*Open* 38). Having identified the target (*zoē*) and the logic (animalization of men / humanization of animals) of the anthropological machine, Agamben considers it important to explain how the mechanism is put into practice—that is, how the anthropological machine becomes biopolitical. The way the modern anthropological machine works can be understood by considering Agamben's *State of Exception* (2003). Inspired by Carl Schmitt's considerations, Agamben defines "state of exception" as "a suspension of the juridical order" (*State* 4). The state of exception is not a special law but rather a temporary or definitive abeyance of legality. It creates a space without law, generally justified by political power as a means to build defense or restore order in situations of emergency. Agamben had already mentioned examples of the state of exception in *Homo Sacer*: Hitler's suspensions—not abrogation—of the Weimar Constitution, as well as the immigration detention centers in Bari, Italy, where football stadiums were used to imprison asylum seekers. By suspending the juridical order in these spaces of exception, it became easy to blur the distinction between *bíos* and *zoē* and to negate human rights, reducing men to animals. The anthropological machine can operate more easily in states of exception.

It is clear that, from Agamben's perspective, man's social life—his *bíos*—is intrinsically connected to the political understanding of the human–animal divide and to the control politics wields on any *zoē*. If, following the assumptions of speciesism, the animal is considered an inferior being, humans can also be considered inferior when identified as animal. The modern human animal described by Agamben is not a creature enriched by close contact with the biological sphere but a harassed citizen who, under the sovereignty of a biopower, can be fairly easily placed in a state of exception and stripped of his rights.

In order to better understand the ramifications of this relationship between politics and the human–animal divide, as well as the biopolitical effects of the anthropological machine, it is necessary to analyze Agamben's considerations of animal status and how it relates to the anthropological dimension. In *Profanations* (2005), Agamben elaborates on the political implications of the term *species*, beginning with its etymology. He refers to the Latin *species* that originally meant "kind" and "sort" but also "appearance" and "seeing" (*Profanations* 56). In order to find his identity, man had to make a distinction between his appearance (Latin *species*) and those of other beings. Species is the image used to create a separation between humans and nonhumans, through which man could recognize himself. But this process of differentiating and categorizing used to define humanity comes with a decisive consequence. In Agamben's words, "The transformation of the species into a principle of identity and classification is the original sin of our culture, its most implacable apparatus. Something is personalized—is referred to as an identity—at the cost of sacrificing its specialness" (*Profanations* 59). Here "apparatus" clearly refers to the anthropological machine: finding his identity by establishing differences and separations from animals, man also started the process of speciesism and the consequent use of human animalization for political means. This is man's "original sin": his search for an identity resulted in a classification that now justifies violent acts against not only animals but also fellow humans. In *The Open*, Agamben tries to detail a description of this "original sin" in the process of separation from other animals. Subsequently, he suggests a possible reconciliation between men and animals, a step toward the halt of the anthropological machine. He begins by advocating that philosophical discourse should pay closer attention to the processes of separation at work inside man: "What is man, if he is always the place—and, at the same time, the result of ceaseless divisions and caesurae? It is more urgent to work on these divisions, to ask in what way—within man—has man been separated from non-man, and the animal from the human, than it is to take positions on the great issues, on so-called human rights and values. And perhaps even the most luminous sphere of our relations with the divine depends, in some way, on the darker one which separates us from the animal" (*Open* 16).

In pointing to the inner divisions that define what it means to be human, and in noticing the connection between the natural and divine spheres, Agamben is moving on a path similar to the one already walked by Luzi. What in Luzi's poetry was called "shadow" is here defined as "ceaseless caesurae," and the ecumenical biocentrism described by Luzi would be one of the possible results of Agamben's enquiry on the relationship between animality and spirituality within man. The Italian philosopher is also aware that any articulation of biocentrism, or of any other alternative system to current anthropocentrism, would face the problem of language. The attempt to solve or collapse the human–animal divide would result in something "for which we seem to lack even a name" (*Open* 22). Here Agamben shows doubt about the possibility of walking the path toward biocentrism, fearing, perhaps, that eroding the human–animal divide carries with it the risk of moving toward the animalization of man typical of the same mechanism it is trying to jam. Biocentrism could be misinterpreted and become a tool used to sustain the anthropological machine.

At this point, Luzi's poetry could come to Agamben's aid—as he had already faced the problem of defining a world where no separation exists between human, nature, and the spiritual world—in avoiding the aporia of a biocentrism that would animalize humans again. However, Agamben prefers a different outcome: not biocentrism, but a world determined by a "Shabbat," a suspension of the status of both animal and man that would solve the human–animal divide, making the anthropological machine inoperative. In order to halt the working of the machine, he provocatively argues that we should recognize the central emptiness of the human–animal division within man and, consequently, reach a status of *otium*, or inactivity. He uses a visual example to exemplify this end point: a painting by Titian titled *Nymph and Shepherd* representing two human figures in the foreground (the nymph and the shepherd of the title, considered "lovers") and an animal—presumably a goat—in the background. Agamben's interpretation of this painting is as follows: "In their fulfillment, the lovers learn something of each other that they should not have known—they have lost their mystery—and yet have not become any less impenetrable. But in this mutual disenchantment from their secret, they enter [. . .] a new and more blessed life, one that is neither animal nor human. It is not nature that is reached in their fulfillment, but rather (as symbolized by the animal that rears up the Tree of Life and Knowledge) a higher stage beyond both nature and knowledge, beyond concealment and disconcealment" (*Open* 87).

For Agamben, the couple depicted are lovers who have fulfilled their pleasure and who, for this reason, have lost each other's mystery. They have been mutually disenchanted, since they now know one another's secrets, and have just entered a life that is neither animal nor human. As Agamben points out, they let themselves be outside of being. In order to maintain this status, Agamben argues radically at the end of *The Open* that they must remain in a state of "*inoperosità*"—inactivity, a workless condition. This translates into the allegory of a mankind that does not set the anthropological machine into action because it has suspended any development of previous historical and political tasks and has reached a posthuman condition—an alternative status in which the human–animal divide is left behind by the fulfillment of being inactive. This conclusion is quite different from Luzi's, who has overtaken the human–animal divide by actively showing the inadequacy of this differentiation and by suggesting that the human animal must pursue a partnership with the "dark animal eternity / which moans inside us" ("And the Wolf," *Tutte* 249). Luzi's biocentrism derives from an active process, which also requires great effort to maintain, since the opposite forces of anthropocentrism are constantly active. However, it seems that for Agamben the way to fight these forces is not through a vigorous opposition; instead, he suggests making these forces ineffective by defrauding them of the subject and origin of their power: the current human being and his *bíos*. While for Luzi man has to embrace being an animal born "under human species," for Agamben he has to go beyond his current status—even the one of being a human animal—by suspending his activities, in a posthuman dimension where the human–animal divide would be idle.

Agamben elaborates on this aspect of his philosophy on three more occasions: in the essays "Heidegger and Nazism" and "Man's Work" and in the book *Nudities*.[6] In these texts, Agamben explains that being inoperative, embracing *otium*, does not mean refusing any action. It means, instead, ceasing all activities typical of biopolitics: those actions whose only goal is to influence and control bare life. According to Agamben, political activity has to be reconfigured completely so that its goal would be to make men reach happiness by maintaining the original status of being human—that is, the status of a being that does not perceive any particular purpose (*Potenza* 330). Without any further purpose to achieve, there is no historical mission, no fundamental task, no *zoē* to dominate that would distract man from the happiness of rest and ease. The trajectory of these philosophical considerations reaches its end in *Nudities*. Here Agamben underlines that man has to free himself from the imaginary assumption that his well-being depends on reaching something unknown and almost unattainable in his future. Comparing this behavior to ancient feasts, he points out that man still thinks that somewhere there are gods to propitiate in order to achieve prosperity. In continuing in this way, there will never be something to really celebrate: "We continue to squander and destroy—even, and increasingly often, life itself—though we are no longer able to reach *menuchah*, the simple, but for us impracticable, inoperativity that could alone restore meaning to the feast" (*Nudities* 106). Idleness would thus eventually evolve into festiveness: being inoperative would free man to enjoy and celebrate life, instead of destroying it. This festiveness emerging from inoperativity would deter humans from setting into motion the anthropological machine, consequently avoiding speciesism and the crimes of biopolitics.

There is a problem, however, with the idea of *otium* and *menuchah* proposed by Agamben: a risk of transforming his theories into a form of biopolitical "weak thought," as the solution he suggests does not encourage individuals to act but is instead based on the premise that cessation of activity is productive. In other words, it seems that Agamben gives a sense of agency to the concept of inoperativity. Finding a solution in idleness and considering it an antidote for the negative aspect of human interspecies violence opens the door to justifying a failure to take responsibility and appears a dangerous opportunity for the proliferation of a laissez-faire philosophy. This idea emerges, in particular, from the use of the concept of "feast," which makes explicit the importance of abstaining from political action and instead focusing only on distractions and playfulness. Even more threatening is that this inoperativity can allow those in power to seize control over the feast, with the goal of manipulating the humans that are now distracted and docile. Even if this inoperativity weakens the mechanisms of the anthropological machine, it runs the risk of putting more dangerous and more disguised mechanisms into motion, making it easier for biopolitical powers to control subjects who have become indifferent to the process.

Since the functioning of the anthropological machine depends on the efficacy of speciesism, then the best way to block this functioning is not by inoperativity but by active struggle against this prejudice. As suggested by Marco Maurizi, antispeciesism would become not only a way to free the animal but also the key to free humanity from the oppression of the biopolitical mechanism that animalizes humans in order to dominate them (9–29). This should become the historical mission of the human animal: to negate speciesism and make the anthropological machine inoperable. In practice, this can be achieved by developing a different relationship with animals and showing humanity how to identify itself in this relationship. It is necessary to build empathy with the animal sphere, to understand our historical and biological relationship, and to see how this relationship continues to define our humanity (Marchesini 111–20), so that the human animal can embrace the historical duty of preserving this empathetic relationship. I would suggest, following Marchesini's and Luzi's take on the human–animal divide, that if a "caretaking" of the animal were to become the historical destiny of humanity, this would also reconfigure an interspecies "caretaking" that would make the mechanisms of the anthropological machine not only inefficient but also unthinkable.

The animalization of human life made possible by the modern anthropological machine and put into practice by biopolitical powers in order to achieve control over man's *bíos* would be less effective if the ecumenical biocentrism proposed by Luzi and the posthuman idleness suggested by Agamben were in place. Here I will not argue for the possibility of putting into practice such philosophical and ethical positions, which, from a certain perspective, could be easily condemned as idealistic and utopian. It is instead important to underline the consequences produced by Luzi's and Agamben's interpretations of the human–animal divide. Luzi's approach to the issue seems particularly enlightening. From his perspective, since humans and animals belong to the same natural reality, with no difference in rank, using categories like "superiority" or "inferiority" typical of speciesism would not have any effect. Luzi's biocentric interpretation of the world, by making speciesism innocuous, would consequently jam Agamben's anthropological machine. In addition, by reading Luzi's use of theriomorphisms through the lens of Agamben's observations on the state of exception, it can be argued that a shift in the linguistic use of animal images could have consequences for the paradigm of animalization that justifies injustice and violence over human beings. Ending the practice of reducing animals to symbols and metaphors means making those negative aspects of words such as *animal*, *beast*, *rat*, and *louse* disappear. By restoring the animal to its biological existence, biopower no longer possesses the rhetorical tools necessary to marginalize, colonize, or eliminate humans by animalizing them. By putting Luzi's poetry in dialogue with Agamben's philosophy, it is evident that freeing the animal from the cage of metaphor would have important repercussions for human biological and political life.

Notes

1. All translations of Marchesini are my own.
2. Many studies have focused on the theme of faith and the symbolism of light and fire in Luzi's poetry. Particularly inspiring in the interpretation of this passage have been Giorgio Cavallini, *La vita nasce alla vita* (2000), 73–84; Vitaliano Tiberia, ed., *Fede e poesia* (1999); and Gaetano Mariani, *Il lungo viaggio verso la luce* (1982).
3. Due to the relative scarcity of published translations, when not otherwise indicated, poetic translations are by Matteo Gilebbi and Elizabeth Tremmel.
4. In place of the English "binary," the Italian original uses the adjective "*ancipite*," literally "double-headed." This seems to confirm that Luzi is referring in this poem to imaginary dragons and not to those reptiles sometimes commonly referred to as "dragons" ("*draghi*") in Italian.
5. He elaborates: "[N]on-man is produced by the humanization of an animal: the man-ape, the *enfant sauvage* or *Homo ferus*, but also and above all the slave, the barbarian, and the foreigner, as figures of an animal in human form" (Agamben, *Open* 37). Agamben does further clarify his interpretation of this premodern anthropological machine. It could, however, be argued that slaves and barbarians could also have been victims of the second mechanism (i.e., the animalization of human beings) and not only of the humanization of animals.
6. "Heidegger and Nazism" ("*Heidegger e il nazismo*") and "Man's Work" ("*L'opera dell'uomo*") appear in Agamben, *La potenza del pensiero. Saggi e conferenze* (2005), 321–32; 365–76.

Works Cited

Agamben, Giorgio. *Homo Sacer: Sovereign Power and Bare Life*. Trans. Daniel Heller-Roazen. Stanford: Stanford UP, 1998.
———. *Nudities*. Trans. David Kishik and Stefan Pedatella. Stanford: Stanford UP, 2011.
———. *The Open: Man and Animal*. Trans. Kevin Attell. Stanford: Stanford UP, 2004.
———. *La potenza del pensiero. Saggi e conferenze*. Vicenza: Neri Pozza, 2005.
———. *Profanations*. Trans. Jeff Fort. New York: Zone, 2007.
———. *State of Exception*. Trans. Kevin Attell. Chicago: U of Chicago P, 2005.
Cavallini, Giorgio. *La vita nasce alla vita*. Rome: Studium, 2000.
Derrida, Jacques. *The Animal That Therefore I Am*. Ed. Marie-Louise Mallet. Trans. David Wills. New York: Fordham UP, 2008.
Foucault, Michel. *The Birth of Biopolitics: Lectures at the Collège de France, 1978—1979*. Basingstoke: Palgrave Macmillan, 2008.
Lippit, Akira Mizuta. *Electric Animal: Toward a Rhetoric of Wildlife*. Minneapolis: U of Minnesota P, 2000.
Luzi, Mario. *Dottrina dell'estremo principiante*. Milan: Garzanti, 2004.
———. *Earthly and Heavenly Journey of Simone Martini*. Trans. Luigi Bonaffini. Copenhagen: Green Integer, 2003.
———. *For the Baptism of Our Fragments*. Trans. Luigi Bonaffini. Montreal: Guernica, 1992.
———. *Tutte le poesie*. Milan: Garzanti, 1998.
Manghetti, Gloria. *Sul primo Luzi*. Milan: Scheiwiller, 2000.
Marchesini, Roberto. *Post-Human: Verso nuovi modelli di esistenza*. Turin: Bollati Boringhieri, 2002.
Mariani, Gaetano. *Il lungo viaggio verso la luce: Itinerario poetico di Mario Luzi*. Padua: Liviana, 1982.
Maurizi, Marco. *Al di là della natura. Gli animali, il capitale e la libertà*. Aprilia: Novalogos, 2011.
Rizzoli, Lisa, and Giorgio C. Morelli. *Mario Luzi*. Milan: Mursia, 1992.
Tiberia, Vitaliano, ed. *Fede e poesia. Omaggio a Mario Luzi*. Todi: Ediart, 1999.

Part 2

Biopolitics and Historical Crisis

6

Creatureliness and Posthumanism in Liliana Cavani's *The Night Porter* and Pier Paolo Pasolini's *Salò*

Alexandra Hills

With this essay, I wish to offer a reading of two films occupying an infamous space in the Italian cinematic canon of the 1970s, Liliana Cavani's *The Night Porter* (*Il portiere di notte*, 1974) and Pier Paolo Pasolini's *Salò* (1975), arguing that they contribute to the theoretical debate surrounding the posthuman through their portrayal of the relationship between embodiment and history.[1] While the films are often analyzed together for their sexualized portrayal of fascism, the important and interlocking themes of the materiality of historical influence on the body and the body's subsequent metamorphosis and animalization have hitherto been neglected by scholars. Thus this paper builds on Kriss Ravetto's reading of a body of Italian cinematographic works that, in Ravetto's words, "refus[e] to disengage Nazism and moral humanism" by exposing the "rhetoric of violence at the heart of bourgeois humanism" (227).[2] First, *Salò* and *The Night Porter* engage with humanism in the sense of the Romantic notion of humanist art that revealed man's true essence. As Margaret Atwood explains, "[W]hat man wrote [...] was self-expression—the expression of the self, of a man's whole being" (52). But along with staging humanism as the artistic expression of man, I argue that Cavani and Pasolini are responding to a renewed investment in the notion of "humanity." This term, privileged in Italian postwar cultural production, was used to explain the urgency of assessing fascism and the crimes against humanity perpetrated during the Second World War, in the name of salvaging a notion of "the human," which was felt to be still redeemable in the aftermath of almost three decades of fascist rule, Nazi occupation, and global war. As Robert Gordon argues, "[I]nterrogating the 'humanist' and partly Christianising topos of Man as a part of a response to the Holocaust is a telling feature of this postwar moment more widely" (53).[3] My essay argues that the films expose continuity between moral humanism and the cultural traditions it engendered, showing that, for Pasolini and Cavani, the logical outcome of these same traditions was the aberration of fascism. Thus the notion of the "human" is cast under suspicion in the aftermath of the war and the Holocaust, which represent, for Gordon, "a perfectly rational and *inhuman* end, pursued through the 'means' of millions of men, with extreme violence and pure reason producing immense suffering and [. . .] paradoxically vast reserves of residual humanity" (114, emphasis mine).

In *Salò* and *The Night Porter*, humanistic values and culture that center on the notion of man in control of the universe and its representation are responsible for ontological and bodily fissures in the physical and psychic makeup of mankind—the inverse of the self-presentation that Atwood posits. *Salò* and *The Night Porter* both thematize the violence of fascism as inherent to the dominant artistic practices of Western Europe (including opera, ballet, and literature) and its bodily effects. For both directors, the body is a site of cultural, social, and aesthetic investment: as Myra Seaman notes, embodiment "troubles the human 'person,' and is a highly slippery entity despite its concrete givenness, due to the porosity of the mind to the vicissitudes of the body and vice versa" (247). Thus manifold forces exert themselves on the body and subject, where creatureliness and rationality compete to define the status of human beings. These beings exist at the frontiers between an idealized rationality and affect, and the bodily forces that constantly resketch the status of mankind. Indeed, as Andrew Benjamin observes, "the body is the continual register of human animality" (23). Notions of porosity and limits play a major role in my analysis of the two films: how is the limit between human and animal historically conditioned? What is the particularity of human animality as depicted in *Salò* and *The Night Porter*? How does the exposure to historical and physical violence transform, or animalize, one's humanity? Depicting subjects undergoing experiences that are, to borrow Aaron Kerner's phrase, "at the outer limits of our subjective and cultural capacities" (6), *Salò* and *The Night Porter* take place in the "after," the "post" of the fascist catastrophe, and envisage the physical and psychological consequences of life in the throes of tremendous political upheavals.

In *The Night Porter*, Lucia, a concentration camp inmate, is reunited in postwar Vienna with her former lover and tormentor, the *Sturmbahnführer* Max. Their memories and fantasies are replayed against Mozart's *The Magic Flute*, and Viennese imperial architecture serves as a backdrop to a relationship that ends in the couple's death at the hands of Max's fellow former Nazi officers. The film relies on the nexus of architecture and embodiment, sensuality and memory to retrace the repressed history of Austria's involvement in the Holocaust. In *Salò*, Pasolini depicts a catastrophic, even apocalyptic, undoing of the joyful optimism for the body he portrayed in his cinematic *Trilogy of Life* (*Trilogia di Vita*): *The Decameron* (1971), *The Canterbury Tales* (1972), and *Arabian Nights* (1974). Scenes of torture, rape, and coprophagia feature in *Salò*'s dramatization of Italy's double capitulation: first, to historical fascism, emblematized in Pasolini's chosen setting of Marzabotto for the opening sequences of *Salò*,[4] and second, to what Pasolini called the "new," "structural" fascism of postwar neocapitalism. Through a combination of the historical legacy of Italian fascism and the "new" fascism of consumer capitalism, Pasolini claimed that humanity was entering a new era whose manifestations were primarily traceable at a bodily level. In the "Repudiation of the *Trilogy of Life*" ("Abiura della *Trilogia di vita*"), Pasolini notes—in a statement that could also apply to *The Night Porter*—that this nefarious combination has meant that "even the 'reality' of innocent bodies has been manipulated, manhandled by consumerist power: indeed, such violence to human bodies has become the most macroscopic fact of the *new human epoch*" (*Lettere* 71–72, emphasis mine).[5] Here Pasolini claims that mankind is entering a posthuman era, in the sense that "innocent bodies" are being refigured through the violence and coercion of economic and political power—namely, the "new fascism" that has evolved from the historical event depicted in *Salò*. Together *Salò* and *The Night Porter* interrogate the consequences of the porosity of biology and politics and thereby portray humans undergoing the physically distorting force of power, complemented by modes of embodiment caused by what Anat Pick has called "the permutations of necessity and materiality that condition and shape human life, the inhuman side of culture" (5). These films debunk the notion that "human essence *is freedom from the wills of others*" (Macpherson 3, emphasis mine) and pose questions as to the remainders of humanity in the aftermath of violent historical catastrophe. Thus, within this essay, I will expand Pasolini's observation about the innocent bodies of the *Trilogia di vita* by asking whether this "new human" is actually posthuman, and what vision of history is implied by its advent.

Posthumanism and the Creaturely

Posthumanism is often seen as an optimistic theory, thanks to important contributions by Katherine Hayles, Myra Seaman, and Cary Wolfe that aspire to empower human beings as liberated, "prosthetic creature[s] that ha[ve] coevolved with technology and material" (Wolfe xxv). Yet Jeff Wallace's more somber exploration of the "posthuman" will inform my investigation; he notes that "the 'posthuman' tends to combine connotations of evolutionary development with those of transgression and loss. A notion of some integrally 'human' condition is confronted with its demise" (26). I suggest that Pasolini and Cavani sketch the loss of an integrally important part of human nature—namely, its ability to invite compassion and an affective response from the other—a loss embodied in the depiction of "creaturely" bodies in both films.

The notion of "creatureliness" indicates a spectrum of physical disturbances that crystallizes both directors' engagement with fascism and the aftermath of humanism, thus shedding light on the intertwining of animality, culture, and history. The term *creatureliness* condenses the liminality of man and animal as well as the tension between man as part of God's creation (the word *creature* is linked etymologically to that of *creation*) and as an abject being that can be instrumentalized, provoking disgust and fear. Indeed, the OED defines *creature* first as "a created thing or being" and second as "a human person or being, an individual" who can be described either with "a modifying word indicating the type of person, and esp. expressing admiration, affection, compassion or commiseration," or as "a reprehensible or despicable person." Third, *creature* stands for "a living or animate being; an animal, often distinct from a person." Finally, *creature* is subservient in that it can be defined as "a person who is willing to do someone else's bidding." Etymologically speaking, *creature* generates four productive lines of enquiry for this essay: the creature as (1) created by forces external to it; (2) interpreted as human, in which case inviting a particular kind of affective response, positive or negative; (3) animal or human; and (4) subservient, echoing the first definition of the creature as "created" or "creation," owing its existence to something external to itself.

The first intensive reflections on the issue of "creatureliness" in the twentieth century appear in the journal *Die Kreatur* (*The Creature*, 1927–30), which posited an editorial stance that all worldly beings were united by their having been created and by their shared vulnerability: "This publication wishes to speak of the world—of all beings, things and all the elements that compose today's world—so that their creatureliness [*Geschöpflichkeit*] may be recognised" (Buber, von Weizsäcker, and Wittig 2).[6] One essay in particular emphasizes the creature's vulnerability, as well as man's tendency to exclude himself from the spectrum of creatureliness and thereby ignore the violence done to other creatures in the name of the (false) superiority of man: "Mankind has promoted itself so high above the rest of creation [. . .]. [M]ankind has dreamed and philosophised itself so deeply into a supracreaturely intellectual world that the distance between man and creature has become very great. [. . .] When the new power [Wittig is speaking of religious faith here] by means of which we will inherit the earth, becomes strong enough, then the creature will be freed from the physical causality into which we have built our own violence" (Wittig 138).

In 1930, Wittig's concept of creatureliness offers a possibility of redemption, since the creature is a religious creation, while it also collapses animality and humanity as hierarchical categories and promises renewed hope in compassionate affect beyond species and power relations. However, in light of the historical violence that lay just around the corner, new inflections of "creatureliness" were necessary. Eric L. Santner's recent study *On*

Creaturely Life (2006) adapts the redemptive, religious idea of the creaturely while retaining the ethical impact of the concept. His concept of creatureliness also hinges on the biopolitical aspect of the notion, defined as follows: "The essential 'disruption' that renders man 'creaturely' has a distinctly political—or better *biopolitical*—aspect; it names the threshold where life becomes a matter of politics and politics comes to inform the very matter and materiality of life" (Santner 12). Here, the creaturely moves from the optimistic guarantor of the unity of God's creation to the symptom of a traumatizing entrapment in the political that defines and molds man's physicality, suggesting once more the previous definitions and their notions of the creaturely passivity of the person "doing someone else's bidding." A consideration of Karl Schoonover's *Brutal Vision: The Neorealist Body in Italian Cinema* (2012) may help clarify by contrast. Arguing that the neorealist portrayal of the "brutalized body" grounded a "global empathy in cinematic corporeality" (xv), Schoonover identifies a visual politics of "brutal humanism" that invokes an imagined spectator who, at the sight of the suffering body, "is overcome with political pathos, cosmopolitan goodwill, liberal guilt and charitable imperatives" (xvii). By contrast, in *Salò* and *The Night Porter*, suffering, rather than absorbing the spectator into affective compassion for the victims, alienates the viewer, who does not recognize a common humanity in the sufferer. Rather, viewers are faced with an uncanny and discomfiting creatureliness that underscores the precariousness of humanism as an ethical mode of engagement with others and complicates the notion of suffering as redemptive.

Surfaces of Consumerism

Both Pasolini and Cavani problematize their position as filmmakers and intellectuals within a European humanist legacy. However, neither director seeks to establish a valid moral code to counter this humanist political and cultural inheritance. Rather, Pasolini and Cavani work to show how this humanist tradition has been turned into its opposite: an inhumane exchange of images and visual pleasures at the expense of a human being that has been commodified (Ravetto 8).

Cavani's film exposes the violence inherent in humanist cultural production. A significant scene is set in the darkened Vienna opera house where the protagonists watch a scene from Mozart's *Magic Flute*, an opera describing the pleasures of married life and directed by Lucia's American husband. Max and Lucia exchange glances, each look followed by an image of their relationship in the concentration camp where Max was a guard and Lucia an inmate. Their gazes are complicated by the fact that, first, the opera in no way reflects Lucia's marriage to her rich but uninterested spouse and, second, the performance offers hints that Max and Lucia's relationship is more authentic due to its physical, noneconomically consumerist basis. Furthermore, Lucia's husband is actually conducting the scene of the opera, which shows the coextensiveness of the culture industry and the marriage economy in the film. But the reverse-angle shots jump between Pamina's light melodies on married life and scenes of a sadistic and sexual nature from the concentration camp; violent sexuality and Nazi symbolism intertwine to provide a counternarrative to Lucia and Max's current existences. Hence Lucia's past as sexually abused inmate acts as a point of resistance to the conformist narrative she now subscribes to as the wife of a successful conductor.[7] While the scene shows the collusion of high art with consumerism through the figure of the American conductor/husband (a cipher for Western wealth and consumption), the opera also stands for sexual consumption within the fascist economy of desire for power through the *mise en abyme* of the opera scene and concentration camp flashbacks. Thus this episode shows the highly problematic status of humanist culture that is literally in bed with a contaminated historical legacy and the consumerist economy that it both represents and sustains.

Max and Lucia's visions of the camp, while being a salient portrayal of physical abuse, rely on what has become a standard iconography of the Holocaust. The inmates' striped pajamas, the SS guards' black leather gloves and uniforms, and the showy SS banners are well-known features of material archiving the Holocaust. Furthermore, the horrifying stereotypes of the camp doctor (also emblematized in Lina Wertmüller's *Pasqualino Settebellezze* [1975]) and the music-loving SS guards demanding that the inmates entertain them (Bert, the ballet dancer, performs for the guards seminude, further demonstrating the consumption of the body at a cultural, political, and economic level) contribute to a stock image that replaces a sense of suffering in the reality of the camp. Despite the lack of color filter that adds rawness to the images of the camp, the setting of the *Lager* is unarguably kitsch in the sense proposed by Tomas Kúlka: "[K]itsch does not appeal to individual idiosyncracies [...] [S]ince its purpose is to please the greatest number of people, it always plays on the most common denominators" (27). The heavily stylized "Holocaust" scenes invite the audience to delight in their capacity to be moved while indulging in the visual pleasure of well-circulated, familiar, and impacting images. Kúlka borrows Milan Kundera's definition of kitsch emotion to elucidate this: "Kitsch causes two tears [. . .] [T]he second tear says, how nice to be moved, together with all of mankind" (27). Thus Cavani problematizes the ways in which human emotion is commodified as an instrument of pleasure through the self-conscious deployment of kitsch images, suggesting that like Mozart, images signifying the Holocaust belong to an equally consumable cultural economy. In *The Night Porter*, human vulnerability is absorbed into a logic of capitalism, voyeurism, and exchange, as bodies and emotions are conditioned by structural powers.

In *Salò*, human vulnerability and suffering are coopted into the libertine's regulated system of exploitation and consumption, which overrides any affective humanist responses to the suffering body. Pasolini's film emphasizes the nexus of victimhood and sexual pleasure by staging beautiful, classically proportioned bodies chosen by the libertines for their perfection (for instance, one girl is rejected due to a blackened tooth). Furthermore, Pasolini's adaptation of Sade's hyperviolent novel *The 120 Days of Sodom* (1785) to a fascist-era context underscores his condemnation of the complicity between humanist culture and dehumanizing violence. *Salò* shows, beyond the accusations of grossly equating Nazism and Sadism, how the lust for the spectacle of violence is embedded within European culture at the same time that it highlights Pasolini's own position within that very culture.[8] This provokes a transition between the body as a means of experiencing reality in the *Trilogy of Life* to the body as rigid, frozen image in *Salò*. One need only think of the symmetry and coldness of the architecture matching that of the eight male and eight female victims and their thin, pale bodies, whose movement obeys the libertines' orders and desires. In his review of *Salò*, Barthes writes that Pasolini's "stubborn" adaptation of Sade's text resulted in a purely descriptive form of figuration: "Pasolini has shot his scenes to the letter, the way that they had been *décrites* [described] (I do not say "*écrites*" [written]) by Sade; hence these scenes have the sad, frozen and rigorous beauty of large encyclopedic sheets" (100). Yet the ossified brutality that Barthes sees as the consequence of "describing" the Sadean text, for Pasolini is the figure of the contemporary bourgeoisie. It is, in other words, the driving force and product of the exploitative structures of capitalism as "creators of a new type of civilization," which "could not help but arrive at the de-realization of the body" (Pasolini, "Tetis" 246). The human body of *Salò* is the interface on which various modes of signification and exploitation have inscribed themselves, a mere virtual surface. As Ravetto notes, Pasolini's obsession with cultural "layering" (his quotations of Sade, Klossowski, Nietzsche, to cite but a few) "culminates in the disappearance of notions of depth" (128). Suffering and eroticism are removed from the realm of affect to that of the image in *Salò*, as for instance when the young victim Renata's suffering at the death of her mother is displayed to the libertines as she sobs beneath a painting of Maria, *mater dolorosa*. Yet in *Salò* the collusion of affect and eroticism into the libidinal and consumerist economy of the libertines means that rather than being a guarantor against the exploitation of others as Joseph Wittig would have it, emotional vulnerability and an appeal to shared bodily vulnerability only entrench the libertines' power over their victims, stripping the latter of their dignity as unique human sufferers.

Cavani and Pasolini thus represent the body in the throes of the historical violence represented by "fascism-substance," defined by Barthes *not* as the precise historical phenomenon of fascism but as "one of the modes in which political 'reason' happens to color the death drive which, in Freud's words, can never be seen, unless tainted with some kind of phantasmagoria" (102). In this sense, Pasolini's and Cavani's characters are remainders, in that historical violence becomes imprinted on the psyche and its bodily manifestation, and the repetition of the *Gestus* replaces the vitality of the act, a theme to which I will return later. Thus Pasolini and Cavani shatter Nietzsche's optimism that art ultimately furnishes man with the capacity to see himself joyously from the outside, to experience himself as an "aesthetic phenomenon" (104). Instead, in both films, a redeeming perspective becomes impossible, as all modes of signification are inscribed into the heavily referential, thus closed, representational economy. In other words, a concern for aesthetics amounts to being coopted by the system that causes the devaluation of the human, reduced to a knot of economic, cultural, and political influences: art, politics, ideology, and consumption are all equally contaminated. But how is this cooption of corporeality into the political worked out in *Salò* and *The Night Porter*?

Creaturely Embodiment in the New Human Epoch

Both Pasolini and Cavani dramatize the modes of human embodiment brought about by the intimacy of the political and the physical. I would suggest that the exposure of the human body to the vicissitudes of the political brings about new "creaturely" forms of embodiment in *The Night Porter* and *Salò*. Santner states that a creaturely body manifests the "uncanny proximity between human and animal" (146); it is one that has begun to exist in ways that are precarious, liminal, and subject to collapse as a result of exposure to the political and its practices of exclusion. In Santner's words, "Creatureliness will thus signify less a dimension that traverses the boundaries of human and nonhuman forms of life, than a specifically human way of finding oneself caught in the midst of antagonisms in and of the political field" (xix). Thus the creaturely is the bodily medium whereby the traumas of historical and political violence are inscribed on and expressed by the human body, whose lack of corporeal and affective depth is compensated by a continuing, animal, animated energy. Whereas Santner sees the "creature" as an ethical and redemptive figure that elicits compassion and attentiveness in the name of rescuing humanity from the instrumentalization of reason, Cavani and Pasolini foreclose an ethical response to the "creatures" they depict in order to complicate the viewer's ethical framework. New posthumanist configurations of the human body emerge in these films, configurations that reflect the concept of creatureliness and recall Seaman's observation: "Posthumanism observes that there has never been one unified, cohesive 'human,' a title that was granted by and to those with the material and cultural luxury to bestow upon themselves the faculties of reason, autonomous agency and the privileges of 'being human'" (247).

An exemplary character in *Salò* highlights the collapse of the boundary between the animal and the human. Renata, one of the victims whose mother died trying to save her, is petted and given food by the Duc—a situation that mirrors Signora Vaccari's story of sharing food with her tormentor's dogs. Renata's humiliation is first expressed in animal terms. Armando Maggi perceptively links the persistent reference to the mother's sobs and death to the following scene where she is forced to eat feces kneeling down; her retching body echoes the mother's sobs (267). As Maggi illustrates, the Freudian overtones in this episode are clear. First, in *Civilization and Its Discontents*, Freud situates the advent of humanity at the moment when human beings begin to revile excrement, thus separating themselves from the animality of their bodies (99). Second, Renata's crouched posture undermines what Freud would have considered the civilizing force of man's upright gait.[9] Thus her grief for her mother as well as her humiliation are turned into bodily abjections, which due to the spectator's lack of access to Renata's interiority obfuscate the psychic malaise at their root. The conversion of the psychic into the bodily resonates with the conversion of traumatic memories (the death of the mother) into bodily symptoms, which Santner describes as "creaturely" due to "a traumatic kernel around which the 'ego life' of the other has, at some level, been (dis)organized" (xii). Thus the traumas that stem from a toxic history are reenacted as a physical symptom. Furthermore, in *Salò*, Pasolini exchanges the sexual dynamism of the promiscuous bodies of *Decameron* for a closed and static body, which in all its physical beauty is sterile and lifeless. The victims of sexual violence are most often portrayed crouching or sitting down (think of the disturbing scene in which some of them kneel in a vat of excrement), and in one striking scene, they are leashed up and forced to walk about on all fours like dogs, suggesting the dehumanization effect of subjection to another's will.

As Pasolini does not dwell on the affective states of the victims but includes them in an overall economy of desire and consumption, the viewer feels no compassion or excitement at their plight. The cringed postures and animalistic behavior of the victims dehumanize them to the extent that they inhabit the uncanny margin between animality and humanity, and the violence of this positioning is registered on the body. While Renata is a victim of an intolerable situation, which may otherwise evoke pity or compassion in the viewer's response, her dilating rib cage and her submission to her torturers' will provokes revulsion in the spectator. Blangis even addresses the young prisoners as "creatures" before reading them "the rules that will govern your life," signifying their submission to the will and rules of others: "[W]eak enchained creatures, destined for our pleasure, I hope you have not deluded yourself that you will find here the ridiculous freedom conceded by the outside world."

The Night Porter further thematizes the creaturely in-betweenness provoked by the traumatic exposure to history. Like predators honing in on their prey, the gang of ex-Nazis stalks Lucia and Max as the couple begins to starve in Max's apartment until they are forced to surrender by leaving the flat. Despite their starvation and imminent death, Max and Lucia's relationship evidently fulfills their desires, which makes the scenes in the apartment some of the most disturbing in the film. Their relationship to the tight, confined space of the apartment that provides safety from external predators underscores the physical dehumanization caused by a toxic past.[10] Their subjection to the predators who are stalking them transforms them physically. Indeed, once they move into the apartment, Max and Lucia almost stop speaking altogether and their movements revolve around making love, touching each other, fighting physically for food or sexual dominance, and crouching and crawling under tables. When Max cuts his foot on a piece of broken glass, Lucia licks his wound in an animal-like way. As food becomes scarcer, they break a jam jar and cut their mouths, tongues, and faces trying to lick its contents. Furthermore, when Max leaves the apartment in search of food, he chains Lucia to the bed; from then on, until the final scene on the bridge, we do not see Lucia without her chain, which animalizes her further. As their bodies become more and more crouched from hunger, confinement, and pain, the couple not only collapses the victim–perpetrator binary (she as postwar Europe's archetype of the "victim," and he as a Nazi guard, the archetypal "perpetrator") that society imposes but also blurs the boundaries between human and animal through their gestures and silence. Their relationship cannot be integrated into a political system where the past is systematically denied. This results in their physical transformation into an uncanny amalgam of animal-like physicality, rendering them creaturely. According to Santner, "[Creatureliness] is an excess of pressure—really a kind of life in excess both of our merely biological life and of our life in the space of meaning" (34). Their liminal, creaturely bodies mirror this as symptoms of "caesuras in the space of meaning" that cannot be recuperated into the social order (Santner xv). To quote Agamben, "the non speaking man is a bridge from the animal to the human" (35), and it is precisely from their suspension between these two poles that Max and Lucia's creatureliness springs.

Furthermore, since *Salò* and *The Night Porter* dramatize subjection to systemic modes of embodiment that transform the legibility of the body as human from without, both films engage with Agamben's concept of "bare life," which defines the breakdown of boundaries between the human and animal. In Agamben's words, "[E]xperiments in totalitarianism involve the 'bare life' of human beings which collapses the biological and the political" (46)—that is, the human being under totalitarianism is "separated and excluded from itself" (76). Agamben contends that man can only exist historically by policing his animality, and that the role of culture and society has been to ultimately separate human agency from its animal bodiliness. *Salò* and *The Night Porter* portray the re-encroachment of animality into the historical life of man, denoting that the human being is the product of a historical disaster that undermines the Hegelian notion of history as progress. Thus in light of Pasolini's and Cavani's portrayal of human embodiment after the onset of an "inhumane" regime, we may ask, via Agamben, "What becomes of the animality of man in posthistory?" (12). According to Agamben, man is "a field of dialectical tensions. [...] Man exists historically only in this tension; he can be human only to the degree that he transcends and transforms the anthropophorous animal which supports him, and only because, through the action of negation, he is capable of mastering and, eventually, destroying his own animality" (12).

Salò and The Night Porter disclose an opposite process to this; man cannot be confidently distinguished from the animal, because the body's dehumanization at the hands of historical and structural fascism undermine man's historical agency. Without an anthropocentric definition of man, the usefulness of a concept and practice of history starts to erode, to the extent that the blurring of boundaries between man and animal shift humanity into a posthistorical framework. Thus through the demands made on the human body by the dehumanizing forces of historical violence, man and animal draw closer in this postcatastrophic zero hour of Pasolini's "new human epoch." The inviolability of man has been corrupted by the instrumentalization of his animality for the pleasure of the libertines in Salò and by his exposure to the aftershocks of historical violence in The Night Porter. The film apparatus is complicit in this process that undoes the autonomy of Agamben's posthistorical subject described thus: "[P]osthistorical man no longer preserves his own animality as undisclosable, but rather seeks to take it on and govern it by means of technology" (80). Pasolini's and Cavani's figures are "creatures" in the sense of "creations" of a system who also willingly comply with it; they have lost all potential for self-governance due to the manipulation of their animality.

Nonproductive Sexuality and Homeostasis

The sexual relationship has been one of the battlegrounds on which recent theorizing of the posthuman has taken place. As Slavoj Žižek imagines, "[T]he end of sexuality in the much celebrated 'posthuman' self-cloning entity expected to emerge soon [. . .] will simultaneously signal the end of what is traditionally designated as the uniquely human spiritual transcendence." Sexuality is generally seen as uniquely human; however, what becomes of sexuality when it is relegated to the aforementioned "surface phenomena"? An exploration of the depiction of sexuality as nongenerative and nonaffective in these two films shows that sexual relations and bodily intimacy cannot be sites of resistance but are instead coopted into the system of exchange and capital.

Salò has been referred to as "the death of sex" (Musatti qtd. in Boarini et al. 131) as well as "the funeral dirge of eroticism" (Chapier qtd. in Greene 116). In his essay "Tetis," Pasolini expressed disillusionment with the joy of the popular body, now reshaped by the new fascism of consumerism. The essay illustrates how Pasolini realized that the relaxation of censorship in Italy actually contributed to making the human body part of a capitalist machine of sexual freedom. The new sexual permissivity was determined, according to Pasolini, by "a new hedonistic and completely (if stupidly) secular ideology. [. . .] Eros is in the area of such permissiveness. It is both source and object of consumption" ("Tetis" 246).

Indeed, *Salò* follows a logic of symmetry and repetition, fundamentally contrary to that of excitation and titillation based on concealment and surprise. Also significant are the villa's symmetrical hall of mirrors as the setting of the farcical wedding: four libertines and four female narrators line up eight male and eight female victims amid the gelid lines of the decor. The windows are too high to see out of and as such only provide lighting for the perverse spectacle, with the mirrors echoing the closedness of the system. The libertine fascination with sodomy and the abjuration of female genitalia emphasizes this closedness and nonproductivity. In a much analyzed sequence, the duke states that sodomy is "the most absolute gesture, for all the fatal significance it contains for the human species, and the most ambiguous because it accepts social norms in order to break them." The act of sodomy sterilizes sexuality by recuperating it into a mechanics of repetition: "It's the most gratuitous, and thus most expressive of the infinite repetition of the act of love, and at the same time the most mechanical" (Bachmann 44). Furthermore, the repetitiveness of sodomy betrays the libertines' unquenchable lust for consumption: "[T]he gesture of the sodomite has the advantage of being able to be repeated thousands of times."

Sodomy (and to some extent, excrement) also contributes to the abolishment of sexual difference in *Salò*. Pasolini had previously expressed political hope in the idea of unrecognizability, claiming that intellectuals must make themselves "continuously unrecognizable [. . .]: they must scandalize, disturb" (*Lettere* 125). However, for Rinaldo Rinaldi, the collapse of difference in accordance with a politics of "unrecognizability" culminates in universal sameness and bourgeois hypostasis: "This equivalence is the perfect schema of the new world" (184). Žižek poses a pertinent question: "What if sexual difference is not simply a biological fact, but the Real of an antagonism that defines humanity, so that once sexual difference is abolished, a human being effectively becomes indistinguishable from a machine?" A vision emerges of bodies of imperialist capitalism transformed into automata due to their absorption into the economic system of pleasure production. *The Night Porter* and *Salò* show the physical outcome of political manipulations: the body is caught in the sphere of the biopolitical and rendered creaturely and sterile. Indeed, Maggi restructures *Salò* as the perverse genesis of a nonproductive, apocalyptic social order through a sodomitic negation of sexual intercourse and maternity (330). Sodomy is coupled with excrement in this new, static world: "In *Salò* shit is the sign of the new perennial decadence, the sign of a perverted, albeit static and enduring system" (Maggi 302). It is no coincidence that at the libertines' wedding banquet, excrement is served.

While Pasolini's victims are doubtlessly subjugated, Joan Copjec suggests that the source of the libertine's excitement is "that of the other's choosing to stop rising above the pain, to which he has up until now been subjected, and deciding instead to submerge himself in it" (223). Recalling the OED's definition of the creature as the "despicable person," subject to the wills of others, the libertine takes delight in "the other's free decision to identify himself with the obscene, unutilisable facticity of his pain" (Copjec 223). Thus the victims themselves are complicit in this system of consumption and repetition, which forecloses the possibility of feeling compassion. In *Salò*, the lack of psychological depth accorded to the victims encourages the viewer to objectify them, and consequently, as Greene writes, "unable to feel for the victims as fellow human beings, we become uneasy, unsure about the extent of our own humanness" (199). The violated body does not elicit a compassionate, "human" response, and so the validity of ethical thought and affect is thrown into disarray. Pasolini's diagnosis of modern Italy is that historical fascism is coextensive with economic exploitation. In a critique of modern Italy, which proclaimed itself to be radically antifascist after the 1948 elections, Pasolini unmasks the false dichotomy of the Italy of *Salò* and the Italy of the economic boom. Pasolini's reflections in *Salò* provide an allusion to Marx, who diagnoses the progress of modern capitalism as reliant on the enslavement of its subjects in *Capital*: "It squanders human being, living labour, more readily than does any other mode of production, squandering not only flesh and blood, but nerves and brain as well. In fact it is only through the most tremendous waste of individual development that the development of humanity in general is secured and pursued, in that epoch of history that directly precedes the conscious reconstruction of human society" (182). Thus Pasolini's *Salò* exhausts any possible redemption for Italy and its bodies.

The Night Porter also dramatizes how the body compulsively repeats the past and forecloses any avenues for progress or transformation. In the final scenes of the film, Max and Lucia dress up in their concentration camp uniforms. This once again points to the disturbing idea that the pair see their camp experience as the only true locus of their desire. For Cavani, "The war is only a detonator: it expands the field of possibility and expression, takes off the brakes, opens the floodgates. My protagonists have removed all restrictions and live their roles lucidly" (x). However, it is difficult to see the resistance or lucidity that Cavani discerns in the plot, as there is nothing liberating about this relationship. Max and Lucia are unable to live under the conditions of everyday life due to their fixation on their past, which they compulsively repeat. Their performance is inflexible and conditioned by the clichéd repetition of the past to which they finally succumb; in this sense, one may be able to describe them as always already *undead*, a condition which Santner describes as a creaturely "stuckness" between "real and symbolic death" (xx).

Conclusion: Spectating the Creature at the End of History

In Cavani's and Pasolini's worlds, the possibility of resistance or dissent is completely foreclosed, and any hope for historical change disabled; the creaturely, subjected bodies undermine the possibility of historical agency and intervention, underlining the films' posthistorical framework. In *Salò*, when one of the victims is denounced and executed for a genuine act of sexual intercourse with a fellow prisoner, his last gesture—a communist salute—is followed by a gunshot wound to the head. Thus sexuality and left-wing politics are undermined as strategies of resistance by the collaborators, and by extension, by the viewers, who are forced to adopt the gunman's perspective. This shot is taken from the subjective point of view of one collaborator, which is sutured onto that of the viewer. In the closing scenes of *The Night Porter*, the couple's car is followed by another, from whose position the camera follows the couple in a long tracking shot: the camera, and by extension the spectator, alternate between shots of Max and Lucia and their pursuers, not only heightening the tension of the chase, but making the viewer occupy the unsettling position of both pursuer and pursued. As Marguerite Waller affirms, "[T]he camera's restless comparison of every position to every other is among the film's most powerful and most disturbing strategies" (216). They are filmed from a distance, a formal choice that problematizes the destructive and ambivalent modes of vision as well as the pervasiveness of the Nazi past that radically ossifies the body in postwar European culture. Thus Max and Lucia are punished for their relationship, which brings the history of the camp back to the foreground of contemporary society as well as to the foreground of the screen image; they are also shot in the back, from a camera position that is simultaneously that of the executioner and spectator. The way the spectator is forced to watch the scenes in both films suggests an unconscious complicity in the actions taken against the characters on screen.[11] As Copjec argues, "[T]he lens that produces objectivity is not in front of but *behind* the spectator" (202, emphasis mine). Thus the directors suggest the viewer's implication in the societal processes that disable an affective response to the suffering human body: we become "creatures" of the camera.

The films end with a disturbing interrogation of the conditions of postwar spectatorship that enable us to challenge the scopic relations on which humanism and ethics are based. After collecting material for her first documentary about the history of the Third Reich aired on RAI Television in 1961 and 1962, Cavani stated in an interview how the archival footage revealed a disturbing thirst for images that challenged the limits of spectators' experiences: "The Germans loved to record every event on film, and they did it well. My editor and I saw rolls upon rolls on the *Lager* and the Russian campaign. [...] Clearly there has been a progress in cruelty, a true escalation. For whom did those cameramen think they were leaving these images? For monsters?" (qtd. in Marrone 84). Perhaps it was for the new "creatures" of the postfascist, posthuman era depicted in *Salò* and *The Night Porter*.

Notes

1. I would like to thank the Arts and Humanities Research Council for providing the funding to make the research for this publication possible.
2. These are works that Marcus Stiglegger calls *sadiconazista*, which he defines as a genre of films featuring a combination of the following: (1) they make assumptions about fascism as a system; (2) they use fascism as a screen for individual obsessions; and (3) they use the historical backdrop as an excuse for sadomasochistic excess and pornography (31).
3. Gordon references Primo Levi's *If This Is a Man* (*Se questo è un uomo*, 1946), Natalia Ginzburg's essay "The Child of Man" ("*Il figlio dell'uomo*," 1946), and Alberto Moravia's *Man as End* (*L'uomo come fine*, 1954) as examples of this preoccupation with "man" as a problematic, yet ultimately redemptive, notion in Italy. Wider European studies of this discourse include Levinas's *Humanism of the Other* (1972), which investigates the possibility of humanism after the Holocaust, and Hannah Arendt's *The Human Condition* (1958).
4. Marzabotto was the location of a large scale massacre of civilians in the final days of Mussolini's puppet republic in 1944.
5. Unless otherwise indicated, translations in this essay are mine.
6. The journal was edited by Buber, Viktor von Weizsäcker, and Wittig, respectively Jewish, Catholic, and Protestant, and it was chiefly preoccupied with religious and philosophical concerns.
7. Indeed, Lucia later claims to her husband that, while he goes to conduct in Frankfurt, she wants to stay behind in Vienna because of "all that shopping [she] wanted to do," thus conforming to feminine and capitalist clichés.
8. Roland Barthes notes that "it is eventually not Pasolini's world that is bared, but our glance: our glance stripped naked, such is the effect of the letter" (100).
9. Freud writes that man's newfound ability to walk caused "a deterioration of man's olfactory stimuli" which in turn led to the urge for cleanliness based on a newfound repugnance for excrement. The

transition to an upright posture leads to a disavowal of man's animality: "The fateful process of civilization," writes Freud, "would thus have set in with man's adoption of an erect posture" (99).
10. The apartment becomes a sort of den: both an animal dwelling place and a place of refuge that buffers the couple from exposure to their habitat. In their exploration of dens and nests, Paul Farley and Michael Symmons ascertain that "there is always an element of danger as if the nest-like space is all the more secure for having some darkness and threat it needs to keep out" (42). Gaetana Marrone reveals that the apartment was reconstructed in Rome's Cinecittà studios with mobile walls to enhance the enclosure of the protagonists under siege. She describes the close-up, squared shots as "tight, confining" (87).
11. Millicent Marcus identifies this uncomfortable complicity underscored in *The Night Porter*: "in the malevolent activities of the ex-Nazi officers who seek to exorcise the couple's threat to their post-war normalization we cannot help but recognize our own complicity" (55).

Works Cited

Agamben, Giorgio. *The Open: Man and Animal*. Trans. Kevin Attell. Stanford: Stanford UP, 2004.
Atwood, Margaret. *Negotiating with the Dead: A Writer on Writing*. Toronto: Doubleday, 2003.
Bachmann, Gideon. "Pasolini on de Sade: An Interview during the Filming of 'The 120 Days of Sodom.'" *Film Quarterly* 29.2 (1975–76): 39–45.
Barthes, Roland. "The Poetics of Heresy" [1976]. Trans. Verena Conley. *Stanford Italian Review* 2.2 (1982): 100–102.
Benjamin, Andrew. *Of Jews and Animals*. Edinburgh: Edinburgh UP, 2010.
Boarini, Vittorio, Pietro Bonfiglioli, and Giorgio Cremonini, eds. *Da Accattone a Salò: 120 scritti sul cinema di Pier Paolo Pasolini*. Bologna: Tip. Compositori, 1992.
Buber, Martin, Viktor von Weizsäcker, and Joseph Wittig, eds. *Die Kreatur: Eine Zeitschrift*. Berlin: Verlag Lambert Schneider, 1927–28.
Cavani, Liliana. *Il portiere di notte*. Turin: Einaudi, 1974.
Copjec, Joan. *Imagine There's No Woman: Ethics and Sublimation*. Cambridge, MA: MIT Press, 2002.
Farley, Paul, and Michael Symmons. *Edgelands*. London: Jonathan Cape, 2011.
Freud, Sigmund. *Civilisation and Its Discontents*. Trans. James Strachey. *The Standard Edition of the Complete Psychological Works*, vol. 21. London: Vintage, 2001.

Gordon, Robert S. C. *The Holocaust in Italian Culture 1944–2010*. Stanford: Stanford UP, 2012.
Greene, Naomi. *Pier Paolo Pasolini: Cinema as Heresy*. Princeton: Princeton UP, 1990.
Kerner, Aaron. *Representing the Catastrophic*. Lewiston: Edwin Meller, 2007.
Kúlka, Tomás. *Kitsch and Art*. Philadelphia: Pennsylvania State UP, 1996.
Macpherson, C. B. *The Political Theory of Possessive Individualism: Hobbes to Locke*. Oxford: Oxford UP, 2011.
Maggi, Armando. *The Resurrection of the Body: Pier Paolo Pasolini from St Paul to Sade*. Chicago: Chicago UP, 2009.
Marcus, Millicent. *Italian Film in the Shadow of Auschwitz*. Toronto: Toronto UP, 2007.
Marrone, Gaetana. *The Gaze and the Labyrinth: The Cinema of Liliana Cavani*. Princeton: Princeton UP, 2000.
Marx, Karl. *Capital*. Vol. 3. Harmondworth: Penguin, 1991.
Nietzsche, Friedrich. *The Gay Science*. Ed. Bernard Williams. Trans. Josephine Nauckhoff. Cambridge: Cambridge UP, 2001.
Pasolini, Pier Paolo. "Abiura della *Trilogia di vita*." In *Lettere luterane*, 71–76. Turin: Einaudi, 1976.
———. "Tetis." In *Pier Paolo Pasolini—Contemporary Perspectives*, trans. Patrick Rumble, ed. Patrick Rumble and Bart Testa, 243–49. Toronto: Toronto UP, 1994.
Pick, Anat. *Creaturely Poetics: Animality and Vulnerability in Literature and Film*. New York: Columbia UP, 2011.
Ravetto, Kriss. *The Unmaking of Fascist Aesthetics*. Minneapolis: U of Minnesota P, 2001.
Rinaldi, Rinaldo. *L'irriconoscibile Pasolini*. Venice: Mursia, 1980.
Santner, Eric L. *On Creaturely Life: Rilke—Benjamin—Sebald*. Chicago: Chicago UP, 2006.
Schoonover, Karl. *Brutal Vision: The Neorealist Body in Italian Cinema*. Minneapolis: U of Minnesota P, 2012.
Seaman, Myra J. "Becoming More (than) Human: Affective Posthumanisms Past and Future." *The Journal of Narrative Theory* 37.2 (2007): 246–75.
Stiglegger, Marcus. "Cinema beyond Good and Evil? Nazi Exploitation in the Cinema of the 1970s and Its Heritage." In *Nazisploitation! The Image of the Nazi in Low-Brow Cinema and Culture*, ed. Daniel H. Magilow, Elizabeth Bridges, and Kirstin T. Van Der Lugt, 22–37. London: Continuum, 2012.
Wallace, Jeff. *D.H. Lawrence, Science and the Posthuman*. Basingstoke: Palgrave Macmillan, 2005.
Waller, Marguerite. "Signifying the Holocaust: Liliana Cavani's Portiere di Notte." In *Feminisms in the Cinema*, ed. Laura Pietropaolo and Ada Testaferri, 259–72. Bloomington: Indiana UP, 1995.

Wittig, Joseph. "Der Weg zur Kreatur." In *Die Kreatur: Eine Zeitschrift*, ed. Martin Buber, Viktor von Weizsäcker, and Joseph Wittig, 137–55. Berlin: Verlag Lambert Schneider, 1929–30.
Wolfe, Cary. *What Is Posthumanism?* Minneapolis: U of Minnesota P, 2010.
Žižek, Slavoj. "No Sex Please We're Post-Human." http://www.lacan.com/nosex.htm.

7

Elsa Morante at the Biopolitical Turn

Becoming-Woman, Becoming-Animal, Becoming-Imperceptible

Giuseppina Mecchia

Few Italian writers of the twentieth century have had a stronger sense of the connection between the human and the animal than Elsa Morante. In the following pages, I will consider this enduring concern as part and parcel of a narrative and philosophical project that resonates with the ones elaborated by the most innovative of her contemporaries. It is often the case that a writer expresses, through fictional characterization and plot creation, "truths" that can also be found outside of his or her specific narrative works. This has nothing to do with the "reality" of the facts narrated but with the sense that they are given through discursive strategies and procedures. Deeply connected to the social, political, and cultural dimensions of their historical backdrops—although not reducible to them because of the difference introduced by artistic mediation—these truths give us an image of humanity that is both temporal and eternal in its ability to resonate with readers long past the time of a work's creation. This is why we cannot be surprised when, at a certain point in time, the creations of writers, critical thinkers, and philosophers seem to converge around a common point of interest, modulated differently according to the conventions of a specific discursive genre. Differences notwithstanding, something appears whose contours are similar to the "complicated network of similarities overlapping and criss-crossing: sometimes overall similarities, sometimes similarities of detail," that Ludwig Wittgenstein characterizes as "'family resemblances'" (32). Indeed, we feel that we are listening to variations of the same tune; we recognize the melody, even though, sadly, we might not be able to sing along or to express precisely what makes the resemblance possible.

In the following pages, I will retrace some of the melodies recurring in the "tune" played by Elsa Morante, proposing a discussion about the surprisingly understudied nature of the resemblances between her aesthetic project and the philosophical work that was being conducted by Michel Foucault, Gilles Deleuze and Félix Guattari, and, in an Italian context, Giorgio Agamben. In particular, I will tie Foucault's and Agamben's work on biopolitics and biopower to the conceptualization of becomings articulated by Deleuze and Guattari in the early 1970s, in an attempt to show how Morante's aesthetic and ethical vision could, at times, surpass Foucault's stark stoicism and Agamben's apocalyptic morality, reaching a more poetic, fully Deleuzian involvement with the forces of the cosmos.

My goal is not so much to pursue the direct "influences" that have tied Morante to these thinkers, although in the case of Agamben some details concerning their long friendship will necessarily be brought into the picture. Instead, I seek to acknowledge that the "truths" contained in Morante's works go beyond the idiosyncratic, trauma-related, and politically controversial specificity of her poetic creation. In the 1970s, against the grain of the dominant cultural and political forces active in the Italian landscape—which on the left were still tied to the activist, polemical positions of the Italian Communist Party and its strictly ideological doctrines—Morante was involved in a wholly different project. In a philosophical formulation related to what Deleuze and Guattari considered to be the common ground of all artistic, scientific, and philosophical endeavors, she furthered a dialogue with the inhuman forces of life and death, with the chaos that surrounds us in infinite ways but whose articulation, perception, and reception is highly dependent on historical circumstance—that is, the space left to us by the violence of the dominant ideologies restricting our field of vision. In the discourse of philosophy, such articulations can take the shape of *concepts*: "A concept always has the truth that falls to it as a function of the conditions of its creation [...] Of course, new concepts must relate to our history, and, above all, to our becomings. But what does it mean for a concept to be of our time, or of any time? Concepts are not eternal, but does it mean that they are temporal?" (Deleuze and Guattari, *Philosophy* 27).

Of course, Morante was not, strictly speaking, a philosopher, but she did create what Deleuze and Guattari call *percepts* and *affects*: the "stuff" of art. These creations populate the "plane of immanence"—the intellectual and aesthetic ground, so to speak—that, although always singular, each artist imagines in a way that can indeed "resemble" concepts created in another field of discursive engagement (while evolving quite independently). Following these resemblances, I hope to show that Morante's vision was politically controversial because it refused the restrictions that were still imposed on the notion of the writer's political engagement in the 1970s: recalcitrant and even hostile to the leftist slogans and the feminist demands of her time,

Morante looked in another direction, one that resonates with the concepts of biopolitics, of bare life, of woman and animal becomings, and ultimately the utterly inhuman forces of chaos calling for the disintegration of historical subjectivity in a space of impersonal contemplation and joy.

The realpolitik enacted by the forces of the Left, be it the Italian Communist Party or the liberal-progressive Radical Party, against the reactionary drift of Italian government forces did not know what to do with Morante, a writer whom they repeatedly tried to reduce to the hysterical/mystical halo of her "feminine" side. Even today, most critical works on Morante try to answer the question of her relation to the feminist movement while simply naming her politics "anarchist." Morante's rejection of feminism is perhaps best addressed in an essay by Adalgisa Giorgio, who says that Morante has been accused of "essentialism," since her women are supposedly tied to a valorization of nature over culture, thereby perpetuating all sorts of stereotypes. However, for Morante, what really matters is the process of *becoming*-woman—and the related movement of becoming-animal. Most important, as I will show, both becomings can also be undergone by male or animal protagonists.

Morante's understanding of politics was less anchored in the extraparliamentary and governmental forces visible respectively in the Italian streets and halls of Parliament in the 1970s, as she was instead engaged in a reflection *on the conditions* of political life, which could not find a collective representation in the ideological confrontations typical of those years. In this respect, she was intellectually closer to her friends Pier Paolo Pasolini and Natalia Ginzburg, who also often found themselves at odds with the orthodoxy of the Italian Left. As for Pasolini and Ginzburg, Morante's ambitious and stern ethical-political engagement is hard to classify, especially in the context of Italian women's writing. In step with the expectations attached to women's writing, Morante, like Ginzburg, confronts issues of maternity, affective bonds, loss, and utter disempowerment in the face of violence. However, the greater horizon on which these issues are played out tends to remain unseen. Tethered to the "woman question," Morante and Ginzburg are denied a fuller reception, and even without turning to what remains a very real critical sexism, this also happens because the creation of truths is a difficult business. When "we head for the horizon, [. . .] we return with bloodshot eyes, yet they are the eyes of the mind" (Deleuze and Guattari, *Philosophy* 41).

From *Biopolitics* to *Bare Life*

The invention of the term *biopolitics* famously rests with Michel Foucault and the lectures he delivered at the Collège de France in the mid- to late 1970s. While a detailed account of this notion is beyond the scope of this essay, I would like to underscore those aspects of Foucault's thought that are most readily recognized in the works authored by Morante from the late 1960s until her death. These years saw a turn in her poetics, as her focus on family secrets and childhood erotic development—which we find at the center of *House of Liars* (*Menzogna e sortilegio*, 1948) and *Arturo's Island* (*L'isola di Arturo*, 1951)—opens onto larger social and historical issues in a thoroughly Pasolinian vein, starting with the poems of *Il mondo salvato dai ragazzini* (1969; *The World Saved by Children*, not translated into English).[1]

A few quotes from Foucault's lectures help set up a critical framework for the understudied relation between the French philosopher and Morante and more precisely for the very nature of the historical project in which Foucault was engaged, which also appears in Morante's 1974 novel *History* (*La Storia*). As for Agamben and Deleuze and Guattari, the Italian writer shared many of Foucault's concerns, though her contribution to the critical field remains unacknowledged.

The title of Morante's masterpiece helps us connect her with Foucault's project in their common relation to "history" as disciplinary discourse. First of all, Foucault underscores how his is not a historicist project, since "historicism starts from the universal, and it passes it, so to speak, through the sieve of history" (5). Instead, he is interested in the "opposite problem," since he believes that "universals" are invented by the modern, governance-oriented state, whose version of concepts such as "nature," "madness," "criminality," "sexuality," and the like articulate "that which does not exist" in such a way that "it becomes something" (21). We are made to understand that *history* itself does not exist but takes the place of reality in our discursive systems. Historicism thus creates the history of unreal universals that have taken the place of something else: a natural life that is now rendered all but invisible. This replacement of reality with abstractions is the trace left by the negation of the unexpressed history of what modern forms of politics could not think: "Violence, excess, abuse, yes maybe, but at the bottom, these excesses, violences and abuses cannot be attributed to the sovereign's mean spirit. The real issue, that which explains all these things, is that when the government violates the laws of nature it is, in fact, misunderstanding them. And it misunderstands them because it ignores their existence, their mechanisms, and their effects" (19).

Foucault remains stoically impassible in the face of the "misjudgments" of modern governments, which systematically destroy what exists in order to establish that which does not exist, the distinctions and separations that make the smooth functioning of social rules possible. We would have a hard time finding in his texts the gut-wrenching pathos of Morante's *History*, whose protagonists are immolated on the altar of Nothingness despite their vivid, corporeal reality, or the cries of distress of *Aracoeli*'s protagonist, faced with his disabling incapacity to belong to his own sociopolitical environment. But in the lucid, often ironic essayistic voice that accompanies the narrative vicissitudes of Iduzza, her children, her dog Bella, and the other unforgettable characters of *History* at the beginning of every year of their lives, we find a strikingly similar assessment of the historical mechanisms of oppression: "Though always in menacing and armed competition among themselves, the Powers from time to time join in blocs, for common defense of their interests (which are also [...] the interests of the 'powerful.' For [...] those [...] who have no share of the gain but still must serve such interests are presented in terms of ideal abstractions, varying with the variations of the advertising methods)" (*History* 4). These "ideal abstractions" are also "what takes the place of the real" in Foucault's assessment of the state's betrayal of the realities that it governs but is unable to value in themselves. The "violences and abuses" that result from this process constitute, of course, the very matter of the narrative chapters of *History*.

The double voice of the novel also parallels, to a certain extent, the two kinds of works that Foucault authored during his lifetime, although perhaps in inverted proportion: he mostly wrote great historic-theoretical frescoes, such as *History of Madness* (1964) or *Discipline and Punish* (1971). His less widely studied accounts of singular cases of existential or artistic engagements and real cases of mental strife and violence—such as the 1963 monograph on the French fantastic writer Raymond Roussel or the historical account of the lives of the parricide Pierre Rivière and the transgendered Herculine Barbin—are a relatively smaller part of his oeuvre, while of course the account of individual cases is the hallmark of Morante's legacy. The more didactic tone in some of the poems of *The World Saved by Children* and *History* is certainly a minor part in Morante's work. We can still see, though, how similar Morante's wider understanding of historical dynamics is to one of the most innovative intellectuals of her time.[2]

Like Morante, Foucault was not particularly appreciated by the leftist parties of his time, but his analyses were ultimately part of a profound renewal of the forms of intellectual engagement that were to emerge after the fall of the European communist parties. Foucault's denunciation of the mechanisms of oppression tied to the modern Western states, from massive incarceration to colonization, fascism and other forms of exclusion and extermination, and the economic exploitation brought about by late capitalism, prompted a reflection on what remained of the very notion of humanity. Modern values and practices appeared once again as dangerous, empty "abstractions," which masked the complex forms of servitude and neglect bestowed by political power on its subjects. Whether "human" or not, and despite the ethical value arguably still present in the term, we come to acknowledge that the subject of political power is not intrinsically endowed with the dignity and assigned the respect that it assumes in juridical or philosophical discourse. "Human rights" and "human nature," to mention some of the terms associated with modern, public notions of humanity, are historically inactive unless they are positively caught in great waves of political struggle. Foucault showed repeatedly how different discursive webs create "abstracted" signifiers, such as *madness, punishment,* or *sexuality*, that determine the way in which subjects—and not unqualified human beings—evolve in the public sphere.

In Italy, it is with Agamben that the concept of *biopolitics*, understood as modern governments' hold on the physical lives of their subjects, evolved in a way that most resembles Morante's vision. Agamben, of course, modifies Foucault's categories. Most significant to our argument, the theological dimension of the concept of sovereignty makes it impossible to maintain the Foucauldian assertion that power does not have a center and is diffused throughout the social body. Agamben, following in the steps of Hannah Arendt, is very attentive to the machinations of the legal bodies that sanction certain forms of exclusion and oppression, and he gives less agency to the common people as perpetrators of injustice. In this difference, Morante would probably agree with Agamben, since for her there exist, at any historical juncture, true innocents, completely foreign to the machinations of power.

This convergence is not surprising: it is a little-known fact that Agamben met Morante in Rome in 1963 when he was a 21-year-old philosophy student, and that they remained very close friends until Morante's death in 1987. In an essay published right after Morante's death, Agamben details his passionate friendship with the older writer, who was fond of establishing relations with younger men, preferably poets and revolutionaries. After describing how the Argentinian poet Juan Rodolfo Wilcock had introduced them on the Rome-Viterbo train, Agamben recalls, "From that day on, our intense, almost feverish friendship began. We saw each other every day, sometimes from morning till evening [. . .]. In addition to younger friends, Pier Paolo Pasolini, Sandro Penna, Natalia and Gabriele Baldini, and Cesare Garboli were also often present. [. . .] I will never forget the support—capricious but incomparable—that Elsa's friendship gave me" (*End* 130–31).³ The motley cast of characters in this episode reveals a daring, committed group of writers and critics who all reconsidered the issue of what Agamben would later call bare life, mostly as it articulated itself in the bodies of women, children, prostitutes, drug addicts, and sexual minorities. They all shared with Morante a long-standing friendship and numerous professional connections. It is surprising that the gratitude and the admiration expressed by Agamben do not become a critical assessment of influence or even of philosophical proximity. Instead, Agamben's essay limits itself to a statement of filial devotion, only citing the maternal "support"—which he furthermore characterizes as "capricious"—that Morante gave him in his youth.

I also find it telling that another of Agamben's critical essays devoted to Morante's narrative work is on *Arturo's Island*, originally published in 1957, long before their encounter. Even in the previously cited text, he only mentions the poems that Morante published in *Alibi*, a collection that came out in 1958. Is this glossing over of her influence due to the fact that Morante was a "novelist" and her work could therefore not be read on the same plane as that of Foucault, Heidegger, or Benjamin? Is it because only someone like Hannah Arendt, a woman whose philosophical credentials were unassailable and who furthermore never gave in to the "feminine" genre of melodramatic fiction, could be invoked when it came to elaborating the concept of bare life? These might be unfair questions,[4] but it is striking to see how the famous *incipit* of *Homo Sacer* reminds us of the basic distinctions that are at the very core of the characterization of Morante's protagonists, especially in *History*: "The Greeks had no single term to express what we mean by the word 'life.' They used to two terms [...] semantically and morphologically distinct: *zoē*, which expressed the simple fact of living common to all living beings (animals, men or gods), and *bíos*, which indicated the form or way of living proper to an individual or a group" (Agamben, *Homo Sacer* 1). Agamben specifies that politics are referred to as *bíos politikos*, and that the simple fact of being alive does not create a subject of, or even *for*, political action or historical relevance. Modernity, according to Agamben, inserts the bare life of all human beings into the political scene only in a negative manner, as that which can be taken away, an innovation best exemplified by the massacres of the two World Wars and the Holocaust. A similarly apocalyptic view is, of course, the theoretical backdrop for the events narrated in *History*—entirely set during World War II in Rome—which exemplify the relentless crushing of bare life by a new and terrible approach to political power. Only by ignoring those beings who are not or cannot become political subjects—that is, according to ancient law and until very recently, women, children, and animals—can power modulate itself in always new but profoundly analogous forms: "In Western politics, bare life has the peculiar privilege of being that whose exclusion founds the city of men" (Agamben, *Homo Sacer* 7).

In *History*, several characters eventually come to be seen as bare life: without rights, social status, or political representation. Even the German soldier who rapes Ida at the beginning of the novel, whose behavior apparently conforms to the retrospective historical judgment given on the Nazis, is too simple and "innocent" a creature to be considered truly complicit with the legal and national framework bestowed on him by his military uniform: "In contrast with his martial stride, he had a desperate expression in his eyes. His face betrayed an incredible immaturity, although he was six foot tall, more or less. And his uniform—a really comical thing for a soldier of the Reich [...]—though new and fitting his body tightly, was short at the waist and in the sleeves, exposing his thick wrists, rough and innocent, like a worker's or peasant's" (*History* 13). The young Gunther, although an assailant from the perspective of the hapless Ida, is still only a child, whose body had outgrown his uniform in just a few months, and who comes from the village of Dachau completely unaware of what had been going on there. Under the uniform, his "bare" bodily features also betray his humble, peasant stock. His description is the perfect counterpart to the one given of his "victim" just a few pages later. Although she is a 38-year-old widow, mother, and teacher,

> Ida had remained basically a little girl [...] and in her great dark almond eyes there was the passive sweetness of a very profound and incurable barbarism [...] [T]he strangeness of those eyes recalled the mysterious idiocy of animals, who, not with their mind, but with a sense in their vulnerable bodies, "know" the past and the future of every destiny. I would call that sense—which is common in them, a part of the other bodily senses—the sense of the sacred: meaning by sacred [...] the universal power that can devour them and annihilate them. (*History* 21)

The last lines of this quote bear a startling resemblance to Agamben's notion of the *homo sacer*, the figure in Roman law that designates a human being stripped of all legal and juridical attributes in such a way that it can be killed outside of any legal or ritual proceedings. This is the sacred then: the appearance of a life that deserves no humanistic or even human qualification; a life similar to the one of nonhuman animals. In *The Origins of Totalitarianism* (1951), Hannah Arendt detailed the juridical decrees that progressively reduced the German Jews to this condition during the Nazi era, and Agamben quotes her repeatedly in *Homo Sacer*. It is remarkable that Morante, whom Agamben knew personally, never appears in his bibliographical archive, which encompasses Plato and Schmitt, Arendt and Kafka.

Although killed by crushing powers, Gunther, Ida, and many other characters in *History* never gain a "human"—that is, rational and controlled—sense of their situation. Even when the 1938 racial laws suddenly attribute a political meaning to Ida's maternal Jewish descent, she reacts paradoxically. Instead of hiding her ancestry or falsifying her papers, the widowed mother tries to reconnect with her family like an "orphaned stray puppy," "preferring the confines of the Roman Ghetto," stopping to talk to some maternal "neighborhood woman, who, encouraged perhaps by Ida's Semitic eyes, would chat with her in passing" (*History* 62). By the time she meets Gunther, Ida is thoroughly terrified of the Nazis and their anti-Semitic policies, and when she sees a man in a German uniform, she is paralyzed with fear. Gunther, on the other hand, is drunk and has no inkling of Ida's Jewishness, nor does he really intend to take her by force. The "boy," as Morante refers to the young German soldier most of the time, tries to communicate with Ida—although in German—before and after the rape, and he does not depart without leaving her a gift and telling her that he would remember her "for all [his] life" (*History* 79). However, that "life" is dramatically reduced, as Gunther is killed only three days later on his way to Africa. Both Ida and Gunther play the parts imposed on them by the biopowers of their time: a defenseless half-Jewish widow is raped by a German soldier. In their childish and animalistic innocence and largely instinctual life, they are not responsible for a *history* that they neither understand nor influence in any way. Their vital energies are absorbed in a struggle for basic happiness and affective connections.

Becoming-Woman, Becoming-Child, Becoming-Animal

Ida's reactions to the pregnancy resulting from Gunther's rape are telling of Morante's attitude toward the life of the body. Socially established if legally forbidden expedients do not even cross her mind, as "the idea of procuring an abortion never even entered her imagination" (*History* 93). Her body seems to react on its own, and her second pregnancy continues Ida's evolving feminization, a physical and psychological "becoming-woman" that started in puberty and continued in unenthusiastic but regular heterosexual relations with her husband and her first maternity.

Morante details the physical changes that accompany these socially expected mutations, which nonetheless take place in Ida's mind and body in a silent, largely unconscious way. Politically excluded from citizenship, first as a woman and then as a Jew, Ida is left to her minoritarian becomings, which are feminine and animal in nature. Deleuze and Guattari specify that a minority is not defined by percentage but by a process of becoming that constitutes it as such: "Why are there so many becomings of man, but no becoming man? First because man is majoritarian par excellence, whereas becomings are minoritarian [. . .]. It is not a question of knowing whether there are more mosquitoes or flies than men, but of knowing how 'man' constitutes a standard [. . .]. In this sense women, children, but also animals, plants, and molecules, are minoritarian" (*Thousand* 291). Minoritarian becomings, however, are not limited to women, and Morante's narratives always remind us of that: *Aracoeli*'s Manuele, whose journal we follow starting from the entry dated November 1, 1975, recreates in his mind his mother's (whose name gives the novel its title) "becomings" in a startling process of hallucinatory identification that leaves him profoundly doubtful of his own gendered and human status. The narration, mainly focused on Aracoeli's womanhood and her two ill-fated pregnancies, significantly starts at the time of the Italian feminist struggles for the decriminalization of abortion. While this particular issue is not directly mentioned in the novel, its impact pervades the narration, as Manuele is fixated on reconnecting with his dead mother in a visceral, uterine manner—a fixation that renders him utterly unable to understand not only the political aspect of the abortion issue but *any* political struggle at all.[5] For instance, on the day of his departure for his mother's village, Manuele reacts viscerally to the slogans chanted by some young demonstrators, whose words seem to target his incapacity to claim the social or political subjectivity of the working class (or any class):

"This is the time, this is the hour! Those who toil must have the power!"—one of their favorite slogans. And again this morning [...] the squads of the Youth Revolution [...] insisted on howling it in chorus, like an open accusation against me. In fact, I have never really worked in my life. And, unfit for Toil, I would be equally unfit to their famous Power, which this young crowd seems to consider the Supreme Blessing [...]. At this point, automatically, I took off my eyeglasses, as I customarily do when there is nothing I care to see. (*Aracoeli* 17)

Here, Morante's characters are unable to recognize the social structures that modulate the biopolitical hold of "Power" on its subjects: they choose to stick closer to a biological understanding of their bodily memories and instincts, even refusing, in the case of Manuele, to try to fully perceive their surroundings, let alone analyze them: "I have been nearsighted—and astigmatic—since I was a little boy, and with adulthood, some years ago, I have grown farsighted as well [...]. Nor do eyeglasses always help me, because in my poverty and indolence I continue to use old glasses, long out-of-date. And so I wander around, derelict" (*Aracoeli* 19). When we meet him, Manuele has long left what Agamben called "the city of men" (*Homo Sacer* 7). Abandoned by his sick mother even before her death, alienated from his traumatized father, he progressively undergoes a physical disintegration that leaves him unfit for any socially acceptable role. Manuele is an overweight, balding, middle-aged gay man, whose love for younger men is portrayed as a reenactment of a traumatically interrupted maternal relationship, and he alternately plays both child and mother. Now that he no longer believes that he can be truly loved by anyone, all sex reenacts the same ritual: "The maximum grace they could grant me was to let themselves be sucked by me. For money. They like regal statues. I, kneeling at their feet as if they were the statues of saints. And my eye, while I drank their sperm, became veiled, in that adoring and sleepy gaze of an infant nursed by his mother" (*Aracoeli* 91).[6]

Manuele, then, transforms himself from *man*, the majoritarian bearer of sexual and social power, into either a powerless and unaware *child* or an equally adoring and self-effacing *mother-woman*. Accordingly, after Aracoeli's death, Manuele feels a passionate affection for two younger men. One, Sandro, was a younger pupil at the boarding school where Manuele spent several unhappy years; the other, Mariuccio, is a very young, drug-addicted drifter that Manuele deeply loves as an adult. In both cases, Manuele's relation with them is described in maternal terms. When little Sandro shares his bed at the boarding school, Manuele says that "from that pygmy body that sought refuge in my larger body [...] I received a sensation of calm cheer [...] Maternity, there is no other term for that odd feeling of mine. I was a mother with her own little child" (*Aracoeli* 86). When, many years later, 33-year-old Manuele falls in unrequited love with the 18-year-old Mariuccio, the older man describes the boy who rejects him and disappears thus: "He was a rejected puppy, the kind that are eliminated from the litter [...]. I never heard anything of him again. And I wonder if he's still alive. He did not seem fated to survive long" (*Aracoeli* 48). Manuele, in his final becoming-*bitch*, wants nothing more than to adopt the stray puppy, but he is frustrated in his attempts by the nomadic nature of the young drifter.

Throughout the novel, Manuele disassembles his masculine identity bit by bit, in a process that gains from being considered a "becoming" in the terms described by Deleuze and Guattari. In fact, the concept of "becoming" allows us to take this otherwise sad destiny beyond what could have easily slipped into melodrama, and it helps us gauge the true political and philosophical impact of Morante's characterization of her protagonist and his relation to history: "It is perhaps the special situation of women in relation to the man-standard that accounts for the fact that becomings, becoming minoritarian, always pass through a becoming-woman [....]. Unlike history, becoming cannot be conceptualized in terms of past and future [...]. Every becoming is a block of coexistence" (Deleuze and Guattari, *Thousand* 291–92).

Manuele's life, as a "block" of becomings, cannot be conceived historically, nor does he conceive of himself in that way. In a similar manner, Ida, in *History*, progressively becomes a woman, then a Jew, and to a certain extent an animal when she is willing to entrust her only remaining son to a bitch, Bella, who helps her in providing for their only remaining puppy. The political reasons for her suffering do not enter her mind, just like Manuele never wonders about the politics of gendered identities. Ida and Manuele stick so close to their everyday existence that any historical understanding of their circumstances is unthinkable. However, Deleuze and Guattari affirm the anarchist thrust of these asignifying living blocks when they say that "through becomings-woman, -child, -animal, or -molecular, nature opposes its power, and the power of music, to the machines of human beings, the roar of factories and bombers" (*Thousand* 309).

Manuele's animal drift is clearly affirmed in *Aracoeli* when he summarizes his relation to the structures of human organization. As a child, he was proud of his maternal uncle Manuel—after whom he was named—an anarchist who had been killed while fighting against Franco during the Spanish Civil War. Now, though, the adult Manuele—far from enjoying his socially privileged status in terms of both class and gender—cannot sustain that heroic masculine identification, and he thinks of himself in terms that could be embraced by many of Morante's proletarian, female, and animal characters: "My nature rejects politics and history; my attempts to overcome this failing have been wretched and vain. I am an animal whose back is crushed by a huge stone. With desperate paws I scrape the ground, and I discern, half-blind, only some blue mists above. I don't know why I am glued to the earth. I don't know the substance of those mists. I don't know who hurled the stone on me. I don't know what animal I am" (*Aracoeli*

134). In this stunningly lucid, Kafkaesque quote, we see a desperate answer to the question of the meaning of human life, and indeed of life in general: once we come to be outside the mechanisms of history and power, we don't know anything anymore, and not only are we no longer "human"; we don't even know what kind of animal we are.

Some of Morante's characters, like the aforementioned Spanish republican fighter Manuel in *Aracoeli* or, in *History*, the anarchist Davide Segre and Ida's older son, Ninuzzu, who both become antifascist partisan combatants during the German occupation, do embrace, at a certain point, the necessity of involving themselves in political struggles for freedom and power. But their choices, no matter how politically "correct," will not save them from a death that brings them closer to a dehumanized common destiny. In this respect, it is significant that both Davide Segre and Ninuzzu survive the horrors and the struggles of World War II and the German occupation only to die in a much less dignified manner. Neither of them dies "like a man," rifle in hand: Davide, right after the war, becomes a heroin addict and dies of an overdose in a shack near the Tiber river; Ninuzzu is killed in an accident while riding on a truck on the Via Appia. Morante describes Nino's final expression in a way that reminds us of Manuele's words: "The last expression which has remained on his face is an animal, hesitant ingenuousness, which seems to be asking, filled with amazement: 'What's happening to me?! I feel something I have never felt before. Something strange, I don't understand'" (*History* 523). Manuele, of course, acknowledges his own incomprehension in a spirit of despair and self-loathing. Davide Segre is also thoroughly beaten by his dark descent into the madness of addiction and dies an angry and embittered man.

Nino, however, is the most lively and joyous of Morante's characters, and while he dies before his twenty-first birthday not knowing that he is a father, he has ensured the continuity of life through the little girl that he conceived with his girlfriend Patrizia. The possibility of this outcome of heterosexual encounters pleased Nino a good deal, and he wishes the same for his little brother. After having had sex with Patrizia, he addresses his little brother thus: "'Come here Useppe, show Patrizia what a nice little cock you have too!' and spontaneously, as if it were nothing, Useppe came forward and showed it. 'When you're bigger,' Nino said to him merrily, 'you'll screw with this, too, and you'll make some *Useppolini*'" (*History* 455). Useppe, of course, won't do anything of the sort, but the gaiety accompanying the mere anticipation of creating new lives remains extraordinarily vivid in Nino's words and makes Useppe's worsening illness and shattering death after an epileptic seizure all the more tragic.

Morante, however, does not completely share the desperation displayed by Manuele in his confrontation with the meaningless of nonhuman, minoritarian, and thus historically marginal life—and death. While introducing the narration of the last two days in Useppe's life, the narrator gives us the following insight: "Some may think it is now useless to narrate the rest of Useppe's life, which lasted a little over two days more, since the end is already known. But it doesn't seem useless to me. All lives, really have the same end: and two days, in the brief passion of a kid like Useppe, are not worth less than years" (*History* 701). Yes, all lives end in the same way, in meaningless suffering and death; however, the time of life, whether two days or many years—as in the case of Manuele or the crazy Ida after the death of both her sons—is never worthless. On the contrary, the "passion"—alluding to the last few days in the life of Christ—might be the one story worth telling, since it follows a less obvious path than the one narrated by the writers of history.

From the Creature to the Cosmos

Although, as stated before, Agamben did not comment publicly on the last two novels of his friend and early protector, he did write Morante a long and sympathetic letter at the time of *History*'s publication, when the novel created a controversial stir among contemporary critics and excited admiring astonishment among Italian readers. Agamben, in his letter, already seems to be thinking about what will soon become the core of his philosophical thought: "If your book is unique and miraculous, it is because it shows a descent into the world of creatures that is unparalleled in the literature of this century [...]. But this is just why this miracle makes of your book something like a closed city, a sort of lost paradise that it's hard to enter without having the feeling of surrendering to an illusion [...] I call creature all that is, naturally and effortlessly in God [...]. Well, I think that this dimension has been taken away from us because we have destroyed it" ("Letter" 516). Maybe now we can approach the issue of why Agamben does not retrace Morante's legacy as anticipating his own intellectual trajectory. Taking a cue from Agamben himself, it is clear that for Morante the processes of becoming-woman and becoming-animal in her late narratives are strongly dependent on the medieval understanding of the world as creature: what emanates from God "without effort," the natural unfolding of the Divine. This is what Morante calls the sense of the sacred. In this respect, she is different from both Foucault and, albeit to a lesser extent, Deleuze, who relies on a Spinozian, rationalist interpretation of *Deus sive natura*.

However, Morante's closer, although by no means absolute, "resemblance" to Deleuze becomes clearer once we consider that Agamben, in a later essay, reflects further on Morante's portrayal of the world, starting from the fact that he was in possession of Morante's copy of Spinoza's *Ethics*, with all her marginal markings and annotations. He notices, in particular, that she marked some passages of Spinoza in decisive strokes, specifically the ones concerning his thesis that "particular things are nothing but affections and attributes of God; that is, modes wherein the attributes of God find expression in a definite and determinate way" (Agamben, *End* 102). There is a point in her copy of the *Ethics* where Morante expressed her disagreement with the philosopher, however: when Spinoza establishes a clear separation between animals and humans, since according to him we do not share the same emotions and our essences differ. In the margins, Agamben tells us, Morante wrote, "Oh Baruch! I feel very sorry for you, but here you did not UNDERSTAND" (Agamben, *End* 103).

In accordance with his own grounding in medieval theology, Agamben interprets this disagreement with the Dutch philosopher with the help of a little-known poem by Morante dating to 1950, titled "The Garden of Eden" ("*Paradiso Terrestre*"), in which she writes that God's mercifulness was shown in his leaving to men the opportunity to live with animals, "who had not eaten from the tree of knowledge as he had" (qtd. in Agamben, *End* 105). Agamben, though, seems to repeat the same move that had caused Morante to distance herself from Spinoza, by establishing the clear separation between men and the other earthly creatures that, as we have seen, Morante denies repeatedly. Her human characters are involved in processes of becoming-animal, while her animals—like Bella in *History*, who is loved by Nino as a girlfriend and speaks with little Useppe in fully articulated dialogues—are constantly put on a par with their human companions, with whom they form what Deleuze and Guattari call *blocks of becoming*, "traversing human beings and sweeping them away, affecting the animal no less than the human" (*Thousand* 237).

Such "blocks" recur in Morante's novels, as a sign not only of creatural dispossession and biopolitical oppression but also of the joyous potentialities of living. The components of the most unforgettable of these instances of relational becoming, the dog Bella and the little "idiot" Useppe, before encountering their tragic, common death, share many glorious days in the outskirts of Rome—and on the margins of history. In their aimless wanderings, they seem able to escape along a "line of flight" that connects their otherwise pathetic beings to a much larger, truly cosmic plane of immanence involving both animate and inanimate beings. Useppe's poem, which he recites to Davide during one of their meetings, perfectly expresses the sense of wonder that can, in the creature, replace the scared, helpless lamentation of Manuele. The opening of the poem revolves around heavenly bodies compared with more terrestrial elements including inanimate stairways and the animate Bella: "Stars like trees and rustle like trees. / The sun on the ground like a handful of little chains and rings. / The sun all like lots of feathers a hundred a thousand feathers. / The sun up in the air like lots of steps of buildings. / The moon like a stairway and at the top Bella looks out and hides." The child's poem then addresses a variety of natural elements, including rivers, trees, and nonhuman animals, all connected in a network of comparisons: "Sleep canaries folded up like two roses. / The ttars like swallows saying hello to each other. And in the trees. / The river like pretty hair. And the pretty hair. / The fish like canaries. And they fly away. / And the leaves like wings. And they fly away. / And the horse like a flag. / And he flies away" (*History* 588).

Davide Segre, a figure that reminds us of Morante's young friends in the 1970s, not only has studied philosophy and been a partisan combatant but is also a poet himself, and he immediately glosses Useppe's improvised poem in explicitly Spinozian terms, emphasizing, though, the profound connection—and not the separation—of all things: "The only true God is recognized through the resemblances of all things [...] For a religious mind, the universe represents a process where, from one testimony to another, all in agreement, you arrive to a point of truth ... And the most reliable witnesses, obviously, are not clergy, but atheists. And it's not with institutions, or with metaphysics that you testify: *God, that is nature*" (*History* 589). From the poetic resemblance of things that can best be perceived by those minds that are marginalized and oppressed by the historical violence of their time, we can maybe, if only for a few precious moments, leave behind our status of creatural victims to recognize our belonging to a universe of life that provides us with its own affections and joy. From the dark truth of biopolitical power, Morante was able to proceed to the positive affirmation of life itself—a *bare* life to be sure, but one that can still clothe itself in poetic language.

Notes

1. It would be impossible to retrace in full the reciprocal influence exerted by one writer on the other, although their common appreciation of what Pasolini called a form of "desperate vitality" is strikingly similar. As their recently published correspondence clearly shows, starting in 1958, the date of Pasolini's introduction into Moravia and Morante's circle, the two remained extremely close until Pasolini's death, which would play a notable role in Morante's own career. See the letters to Pasolini published in *L'amata. Lettere di e a Elsa Morante*, ed. Daniele Morante e Giuliana Zagra.
2. It is difficult to ascertain whether Morante knew Foucault's work and even more difficult to hypothesize about her knowledge of Deleuze and Guattari. However, it is not unthinkable to imagine that she had a certain familiarity with these texts, given her friendship with Agamben and other younger intellectuals in the 1970s, such as Adriano Sofri and Goffredo Fofi, who might have introduced them to their inquisitive older friend.
3. Natalia Ginzburg (born Levi) is referred to, somewhat surprisingly, with the name of her second husband, Gabriele Baldini, an English literature professor at the University of Rome. While she did change her legal name after the wedding, she generally remains known under the name of her first husband, Leone Ginzburg.

4. Agamben does in fact acknowledge in another text that "Elsa's relation to philosophy [. . .] is anything but settled," but he immediately adds, "this is not the project I wish to pursue" (*End* 102).
5. November 1, 1975, the date of the first journal entry, was the last day in the life of Pasolini. Like Morante, Pasolini opposed the legalization of abortion, in a controversial move that was however consistent with both writers' attachment to maternal imbrications in the creation of life and affectivity. However, it would be mistaken to consider them "reactionary": as Lucia Re explains in the case of Morante, they embrace a minoritarian position, and both writers articulate "a relational or strategic way of positioning the writer's discourse to address the question of history, gender, and their narrative representation. Furthermore, it is a voice that takes 'woman' not only as a representative of herself as historical being but also as a sign of everything that is traditionally marginalized" (361).
6. I have changed Weaver's translation, which contains a highly unusual mistake in an otherwise impeccable, poetic rendition. The Italian original reads, "*E la mia pupilla, al berli, si velava,*" but Weaver translates, "And my eye, **at their taunts**, became veiled," probably mistaking "*berli*" with "*burle*." This is a small but important detail.

Works Cited

Agamben, Giorgio. *The End of the Poem: Studies in Poetics*. Stanford: Stanford UP, 1999.

———. *Homo Sacer: Sovereign Power and Bare Life*. Trans. Daniel Heller-Roazen. Stanford: Stanford UP, 1998.

———. "Letter to Elsa Morante of October 1 1974." In *L'Amata: Lettere di e a Elsa Morante*, ed. Daniele Morante, 515–16. Turin: Einaudi, 2012.

Deleuze, Gilles, and Félix Guattari. *A Thousand Plateaus: Capitalism and Schizophrenia*. Minneapolis: U of Minnesota P, 1987.

———. *What Is Philosophy?* Trans. Hugh Tomlinson and Graham Burchell. New York: Columbia UP, 1994.

Foucault, Michel. *Naissance de la Biopolitique. Cours au Collège de France 1978–1979*. Paris: Seuil-Gallimard, 2004.

Giorgio, Adalgisa. "Nature vs Culture: Repression, Rebellion and Madness in Elsa Morante's *Aracoeli*." *MLN* 109 (1994): 93–116.

Morante, Elsa. *Aracoeli*. Trans. William Weaver. Rochester: Open Letter Editions, 2009.

———. *History*. Trans. William Weaver. Hanover: Steerforth, 2007.

Re, Lucia. "Utopian Longing and the Constraints of Racial and Sexual Difference in Elsa Morante's *La Storia*." *Italica* 70.3 (1993): 361–75.

Wittgenstein, Ludwig. *Philosophical Investigations*. Trans. G. E. M. Anscombe. Oxford: Blackwell, 1998.

8

Foreshadowing the Posthuman

Hybridization, Apocalypse, and Renewal in Paolo Volponi

Daniele Fioretti

Pushing beyond Anthropocentrism

The crisis of humanism poses new questions to scholars, compelling them to redefine the category of "human" and consequently to reevaluate the epistemology that places man at the center of the entire gnoseological experience, as described in Michel Foucault's *The Order of Things* (22). One of the most important contributions to the discussion comes from Giorgio Agamben's book *The Open: Man and Animal*. Starting from Linnaeus's definition of the human being in his *Systema* (1735), Agamben claims that "*Homo sapiens* [. . .] is neither a clearly defined species nor a substance; it is, rather, a machine or device for producing recognition of the human. [. . . .] *Homo* is a constitutively 'anthropomorphous' animal (that is, 'resembling man,' according to the term that Linnaeus constantly uses until the tenth edition of the *Systema*), who must recognize himself in a non-man in order to be human" (26–27). In other words, for this Italian philosopher, the distinction between animal and human life is a kind of mobile frontier that is, above all, internal to man. This approach subverts the traditional logic of humanism and poses the question of the relationship between human and nonhuman beings in a new way.

Another important contribution comes from Jacques Derrida's essay *The Animal That Therefore I Am*. Stating that *animal* "is a word that men have given themselves the right to give," Derrida addresses the same matter, but from a linguistic point of view (32). In fact, what does an ant have in common with a whale, if not the characteristic of being a nonhuman, nonvegetable living being? So "animal" becomes the category to which all nonhumans are relegated—a category defined, it should be no surprise, from the perspective of mankind. This categorization, of course, is not ideologically innocent. As Marianne Dekoven highlights, "*Nonwhite, non-European,* and *non-Western* are parallel to *nonhuman* and reveal what is at stake in using it" (363, italics in original). Dekoven's point of view implicitly links the category of the human with anthropocentrism, the belief that human beings are the most important entities in the world. Moreover, Dekoven underscores the double risk of anthropocentrism: both marginalizing human others and insisting on the primacy of human experience over that of other species.[1] Humanism as such implies, as its first and most important consequence, that the whole world is seen and interpreted only in terms of human experience and values: every nonhuman entity exists only to be used and exploited by mankind.[2]

Studies such as those by Agamben and Derrida are rapidly changing our vision of what is human and what is nonhuman. In fact, according to Roberto Marchesini, after Darwin the opposition of human and nonhuman exists only as an anthropocentric prejudice (*Post-Human* 134). My aim here is to demonstrate that this epistemic shift, which is now evident, was foreseen and expressed in the literary works of Paolo Volponi, especially in the novels he wrote in the 1970s. This epistemic question seems to be intimately connected with Volponi's poetry itself, stemming from the poet's keen awareness of the relationship between human beings and nature, in which the animal is a kind of "agent" of nature. This awareness is consistently evident in his poetry, even in his first book, *The Green Lizard* (*Il ramarro*, 1948). In the poem "Cousin Fox" ("*Cugina volpe*"), published in the collection *The Old Coin* (*L'antica moneta*, 1954), the poet manifests his strong relationship with nature; he claims he has in his own body "the metallic structure of balm-crickets" and that the turtledove is his sister, and he identifies the grass snake, the swallow, and the fox as his mothers: "My mother is also the grass snake, / the lustful one that waggles / on the shores under the sun / and sets enchanted ambushes / and the chirping swallow / the fox, / the frightened one / the fleeing, the helpless one / who screams / only one time in her life" (*Poesie* 7).[3]

This is only one of many possible examples of the relationship between the poetic self and nonhuman entities in Volponi's poetry. But the focus of this essay is not on poetic but rather on narrative production; I will examine in particular two novels written by Volponi: *Corporeal* (*Corporale*, 1974) and *The Irritable Planet* (*Il pianeta irritabile*, 1978). In fact, starting with *Corporeal*, the redefinition of the category of the human through a different relationship with animality becomes a fundamental concern. In this novel, even if only potentially, we witness for the first time the narrative intermingling and hybridization of the categories of "human" and "animal." It is not by chance that, in the first draft, one of the possible titles of the book was *The Animal* (*L'animale*).[4]

Animality and the Apocalyptic Imagination

Volponi began work on the new novel in the summer of 1965; just three months later, the first draft of the manuscript was already five hundred pages long. But this first draft was very different from the final text published in 1974 and titled *Corporeal*. The novel was initially written in a "traditional" style, like Volponi's first two published novels, *My Troubles Began* (*Memoriale*, 1962) and *The World-Wide Machine* (*La macchina mondiale*, 1965), the latter the winner of the prestigious Italian literary award "Premio Strega." During the long process of revision, Volponi decided to radically change the structure of the novel, introducing some experimental innovations partially inspired by the narrative strategies of the Italian *neoavanguardia* (neoavantgarde), like, for example, the critique of the traditional autobiographical subject (staged by a repeated shift in the perspective of narration from the first to the third person) and the deliberate confusion between reality and hallucination in the plot, which produces an explosive mixture in the text's structure. As Volponi said in an interview, the novel "exploded" in his hands while he was writing it: "It was the middle of the 1960s. A lot of things were collapsing around us; we realized that our Country did not exist as a historical unity, as a social vocation. Working in a factory allowed me to understand and see countless phenomena, tensions, dramas. [...] All these things contributed to widening the subject of the book" ("Questo pazzo").

During this process of revision there was a sudden change not only in the structure but also in the plot and in the meaning of the novel—a change that perhaps facilitated Volponi's turn to a much deeper philosophical engagement with animality. The main concerns in *Corporeal*, together with the personal and ideological crisis of the protagonist, are the atomic bomb and the threat of global destruction. These, of course, were not concerns exclusive to Volponi. For example, Theodor W. Adorno was probably one of the first philosophers to realize that the world (and culture) would never be the same after World War II: "The idea that after this war life will continue 'normally' or even that culture might be 'rebuilt'—as if the rebuilding of culture were not already its negation—is idiotic" (55). In fact, after the Holocaust and the unprecedented scale of this technological conflict ended with the explosion of the most frightening weapon ever built (i.e., the atomic bomb), the world was radically different from the past, so literature had to change as well, in order to adapt to this new situation. In his essay *The Lion's Marrow* (*Il midollo del leone*), Italo Calvino stated that writers had to confront what he called "the acute conscience of the negative": "[T]his conscience of living in the lowest and most tragic moment in history, of living between Buchenwald and the H bomb, is the starting point of our every fantasy, of our every thought" (22). Volponi, in complete accord with Calvino about the fact that the world was irrevocably changed, decided to start writing a novel on the "fear of the bomb" that gradually became a book on the fear for society at large.[5] Very important for Volponi was the influence of his friend Elsa Morante, who in her essay *For or Against the Atomic Bomb* (*Pro o contro la bomba atomica*, quoted at the beginning of *Corporeal*) establishes a close connection between capitalist society and the nuclear threat. According to Morante, the bomb is a sign of the times, the apotheosis of aggressive and colonialist imperialism, its natural consequence: "[O]ur bomb is the flower, in other words the natural expression of our contemporary society, like Plato's dialogues are the expression of the Greek city; the Coliseum of the imperial Romans; the Madonnas painted by Raffaello of Italian humanism; [. . .] and the extermination camps of the bureaucratic petit-bourgeois culture, already infected by a rage of atomic suicide" (99).

Volponi agreed with Morante's point of view and puts this concern at the center of *Corporeal*.[6] He starts from this position of critique, but instead of resigning himself to the inevitable decline of our civilization, he decides to overturn it by means of the nuclear catastrophe, which, in his literary universe, is not exclusively a deadly threat but also an opportunity to envision a revitalized mankind. Gerolamo Aspri, the protagonist of *Corporeal*, decides in the third part of the novel to build a bomb shelter, called "*arcatana*," in order to survive a nuclear catastrophe and to rise again (Volponi uses purposefully the verb "*risorgere*," replete with its religious meanings) with a new body, transformed by radiation. The subject is no longer human but hybridized—animalized. As Volponi writes,

> *Arkburrow*: ark, burrow, arch . . . natural, used to cover with appropriate excavations and devices and tools a man-animal-emerald willing to rise again [. . .], to resurface different, encrusted, thinned, reduced to half, faded, one-eyed, bat-like because of the dark, lizard-like because of the soil, eel-like because of the mud, with only one foot, coelenterate, with or without fur, dumb, feathered, carnivorous, omnivorous, bacteria, blue algae, moss, sponge, fungus, mold, jellyfish [. . .] multicellular, able or not to perform photosynthesis, as long as I am alive, alive, alive, and therefore capable, in a certain way, to think, to grow, to breed, and different, different, different, from the current cowardly creature, naked and bandaged [. . .] sedentary and stercorary, with the brain, the nose, the cock in search of services to give or to get. (*Romanzi* 1:883–84)

As we can see here, Volponi is interested in the entire spectrum of organic life; his delirious protagonist dreams of hybridizing himself not only with animals but also with plants and microorganisms. In fact, Gerolamo's only care is to be totally different from, and hopefully better than, the horrible creature that man has become. It is important to note that the transformation into life forms like viruses or bacteria, morphologically simpler than humans, does not imply in Volponi the idea of biological regression. On the contrary, with a surprising inversion of the chain of being, Volponi contests the paradigm of anthropocentrism. It is well known, in fact, that traditionally the comparison between man and animal was (and sometimes still is) used as a metaphor for the regression of the human being, because anthropocentric thought considers humanity as a progressive distancing from the animal level. In fact, according to the anthropocentric tradition, being "human" is not only a biological question; in order to be completely human, man must avoid any contamination with the animal condition. As Marchesini writes, "In the anthropocentric tradition, in fact, to become human means to take distance from the animal condition, which therefore acquires the characteristics of a dangerous path of contamination or involution, a threshold where man does not have to stand because, when he does, he puts in jeopardy his own distinctive qualities" (*Tramonto* 41).

But how is it possible that man can run this risk of regression to animality if he is the so-called center of gravity of the whole world? The answer comes from the material part of human experience. Western culture, starting from the ancient Greeks, had a particular concept of materiality and of the body, which is already evident in the distinction between *zoē* and *bíos*. As Giorgio Agamben pointed out in the introduction to *Homo Sacer* (1995), both these words mean "life" in Greek, but *zoē* expresses the simple fact of living (common to animals and men), while *bíos* indicates political life, the way of living of an individual or of a community (1). In other words, *bíos* is a "superior" form of life that is characteristic of human beings. But man, among all the other beings, is the result of the union of these two different natures: the body, the material part that is ruled by *zoē*, and the mind (or spirit) related to *bíos*. From this distinction comes the traditional idea of the body as something inferior: a necessary support for the mind but nothing more than a vessel. Consequently, if the body is something separated from the spirit, it is also what man has in common with the animal, and every aspect connected to the materiality of the body, especially bodily functions and fluids, is disregarded and considered inferior, sometimes even disgusting. It is evident even from the title of the novel, *Corporale*, that the position of Volponi diverges from the anthropocentric tradition. He wrote his novel two decades before Agamben's *Homo Sacer* and years before Foucault's *Birth of Biopolitics*,[7] but he is determined to challenge and even to invert the hierarchy, giving priority to the body over the mind. *Corporeal*'s Gerolamo Aspri experiences the world through his corporeality. There are countless references in the novel to blood, sperm, feces, and urine; moreover, these bodily products acquire a positive valence. This is evident when the protagonist is eating cantaloupes in a field with his children:

> My children started to defecate where the garden is thicker, right in the labyrinth of the plants as a gift to the farmer; at the same time I was drinking from his flask. Then I drank again at every fountain and when I couldn't take it anymore I plunged my face and my hands. I drank two cokes and

two lemonades and then a fernet that finally made me throw up, while I was already feverish, with a bluish tinge, while the cars were running endlessly on the Adriatica, making the asphalt tremble under my feet. (*Romanzi* 1:424)

The positive implication of the reference to bodily functions is fairly evident. The vomit helps the protagonist to cure his indigestion, and the mention of the feces as a gift to the farmer is not sarcastic, because dung is a natural fertilizer and is precious for agriculture. Here Volponi, who was an enthusiastic reader of Rabelais, is also probably influenced by Mikhail Bakhtin's *Rabelais and his World* (1965). In fact, in his analysis of *Gargantua and Pantagruel*, Bakhtin insists on the ambiguity of feces in Renaissance popular culture; it can be seen as waste but also as something related to life and regeneration: "[T]he lower stratum is [...] the area of the genital organs, the *fertilizing and generating stratum*. Therefore, in the images of urine and excrement is preserved the essential link with *birth, fertility, renewal, welfare*. This *positive* element was still fully alive and clearly realized in the time of Rabelais" (148, my italics). So in spite of the fact that these bodily substances might at a first glance look distasteful to the reader, they are used with a clear positive emphasis in Volponi.

Another crucial element in *Corporeal*, also related to Bakhtin's reading of Rabelais, is the centrality of the belly, which is evidently much more important than the mind throughout the entire novel but particularly in its first part. The belly is connected with emotions and love (also parental love); for this reason, Gerolamo wants to have his children on his belly: "[T]he children were on my belly because I wanted them to be there" (*Romanzi* 1:424). Emotions and feelings have an immediate effect on Gerolamo's belly: "I was dispirited; I really was, inside my belly" (426). But the most interesting point is when the protagonist makes a comparison between the human body and a star when he is explaining to his son the birth of a star: "The star warms up, like us. When its center, now my belly, reaches the celestial temperature, around 15 million Celsius degrees, the nuclear reactions start to release energy and the contraction of the star stops" (425). This description is not a reenacting of the anthropocentric centrality of man, but it clearly shows how, for the protagonist, every idea and concept is, first and foremost, filtered through the body and the perception of the senses, with a definite predominance of the sense of touch, taste, and smell. At a certain point in the book, it becomes clear that close contact with his own body coincides, for the protagonist, with critical thought and with his perception of society: "Midway through the journey ... the contact with one's body is complete as well as watchful: it follows every small event, fixed to all the folds and repercussions on all the fibers and on every hem, until the formulation and then to the evidence of a critical thought and then of a story and of a diagnosis even about the smallest event, like a hiccup" (420).

In other words, throughout the novel (and especially in the first part) we see a revaluation of the corporeal aspects of human life as a way to experience the world. Paradoxically, for Volponi, man is more "human" when he is "corporeal," or in other words, when he is deeply in touch with his body and totally aware of his animality. This revaluation is closely connected to animality and to the hybridization of the human being. The destruction of the world as we know it, for Volponi, foreshadows a new beginning for humanity: a metamorphosis brought about by the deus ex machina of nuclear radiation, which will provide new, animal features for the protagonist. As Gerolamo says, "I like to draw myself, at least in the essential features, at least those which now I see as essentials: a beak, a longer retractable neck, scaled? Four hands plus six fins? The head, as narrow as a coin or divided in four like a blackberry? Everyone with one eye? It is absurd to foresee it: it will be the result of the microevolution of this environment, contaminated with many R's and following combinations: sequential microevolution, divergent speciation; divergent macroevolution (adaptive diversification and diffusion), megaevolution" (*Romanzi* 1:890).

It is not clear what Volponi means by the term "megaevolution"; what is certain is that he is not looking at the hybridization man-animal as something regressive, an involution (like the anthropocentric thinkers). On the contrary, he seems to look at this event with confidence, as something that could help human beings to adapt better to the environment. Unexpectedly, here Volponi anticipates some of the positions expressed by Marchesini about the concept of hybridization. Marchesini, of course, does not talk of a biological hybridization but of a cultural one;[8] only through a continual repositioning of the threshold of the human and the consequent partnership with the animal can what we call "human" maintain its character of an open ontogenetic process.[9] The corporeal metamorphosis of Gerolamo is really a metaphor for the transition to a new model of rationality and culture that, according to Volponi, reconciles humanity with nature, and the relationship with the animal can help man to reach that goal. The writer himself makes this concept explicit in an interview with Gian Carlo Ferretti: "This novel (*Corporeal*) can be read as the search for a new relationship between intelligence or reason/rationality and feelings, between conscience and body; a search, in other words, for a new, authentic rationality, and for a new, authentic culture" (Ferretti 3).[10]

Corporeal, in its first draft, ended with a nuclear catastrophe and the actual metamorphosis of the main character into a new, animalized being. But in the final version of the novel, Volponi refuses such a "positive" ending. No bomb explodes in *Corporeal*, and Gerolamo is not even able to build his atomic shelter. In other words, no regeneration through the human-animal hybridization seems to be possible for humanity. The novel ends with the escape of his protagonist, who leaves behind only the diary written by his *alter ego*, the outlaw and revolutionary Joaquin Murieta.[11] When Corboli, one of the characters in the novel, goes in search of Gerolamo, he finds the diary in a drawer: "a school notebook. And yet it exhaled that fluid which is contained in closed books that contain some truth. He opened the notebook and recognized Aspri's handwriting on the first page, in the middle" (*Romanzi* 1:1007). So the final outcome of Gerolamo's experience is a text, a book like *Corporeal* and, more important, a text that contains truth. Here Volponi evidently reaffirms his confidence in literature as a way to discover the truth or at least to know and describe a social and historical crisis. Thanks to this book, all the efforts of the protagonist nonetheless have value, in spite of the final defeat.

Capitalism and Theriomorphosis

This situation changes radically in *The Irritable Planet* (1978), which reads like a dystopian science-fiction novel. The story is set in 2293 after a huge nuclear catastrophe. The Earth's surface has been turned, for the most part, into a desert of radioactive dust; there are no more seasons, and the surviving, wretched humans wander like plague-stricken people in scattered groups without a purpose or a goal. This is the context in which the dwarf Mamerte, protagonist of this novel, carries out his Bildung, following the scheme of one of the most important genres of modernity, the "novel of education."[12] But if the typical protagonist of this genre has to face trials and adversities in order to achieve the status of an adult and learn how to deal with social rules, Mamerte's goal is precisely the opposite: his Bildung consists of losing his characterization as a human being through a process of physical theriomorphosis (Papini 76). Mamerte is not alone in this picaresque adventure. His companions are three animals: Roboamo the elephant, Plan Calcule the goose, and Epistola the monkey, all of whom worked in a circus before the catastrophe. What saved Mamerte from the terrible fate of other humans in the first place was his marginalized status; because of his deformed body, Mamerte was not considered entirely human by other men. He was treated like an animal, and this is one of the reasons (but not the most important one) he can be saved from the general destruction of humanity. Mamerte, then, is saved not only because of his deformity, which marks his diversity from the other men, but because he (unconsciously) did the right thing, joining the group of animals against what is left of the human race. As the elephant says to the dwarf: "It's not enough to be just a little different, in order to not become a man; it is necessary to want it and, also, to put your will into effect with a lot of strength and with great wisdom. Otherwise you wouldn't have been saved" (*Romanzi* 2:428).

The Irritable Planet is an allegorical novel, a fact evident from the opening anecdote of the tree. This story brings us back to 1623, when a Venetian consul comes back from Poland to Italy with a holm seed hidden in his underwear. Together with the seed, he brings the plague to Italy. The consul is ultimately killed and thrown into the sea by his traveling companions after they discover a bubo on his skin, but the contagion spreads anyway. A sailor refuses to throw away all the Venetian's possessions, and, greedy for money, he keeps the consul's apparently valuable chest so that "the plague could land in Venice and stay there, amused, for many months" (*Romanzi* 2:285). The author's decision to link the plague to the greed of men parallels Volponi's association of the nuclear threat with capitalism. Immoderate greed and ambition are then the results of a perversion of what Volponi considers "real" human nature, not alienated by capitalism. But before his untimely death, the ambassador had sexual intercourse in Pesaro with a countess and left her the holm seed. The lady also died from the plague, but before dying she threw the seed in a deep hole in the garden; from that seed grew a holm that lived more than 670 years, surviving 84 strikes of lightning up to the nuclear catastrophe. The wound inflicted on the tree by the lightning also created a cavity, in which Mamerte took refuge during the atomic explosions. The image of this tree, then, seems to underline Volponi's deep faith in nature, as well as his condemnation of contemporary human society. The tree represents biological life that, even if wounded, is still alive; nature is able to regenerate itself.

Just like the tree, the animals in this novel have allegorical meanings. The elephant and the monkey in particular can be seen as anthropomorphic figures, in accordance with the tradition that uses animals as symbols of human virtues and vices, starting at least from Aesop's fables. The elephant Roboamo can talk and represents wisdom and long-lasting memory, while the monkey Epistola imitates the worst of human behavior, assuming leadership of the group and treating the other members of the party cruelly. The goose, on the other end, has no particular characterization and seems to offer comic relief. It is important that Mamerte, the human being, is chained and beaten by an animal, the monkey. But in order to proceed to a new definition of humanity, the party must get rid of Epistola's grotesque attempt to reenact the old violent hierarchy through a patent imitation of human violent behavior. No regeneration, no new definition of mankind is possible if the old model is not completely destroyed. The climax of the novel occurs during the battle between the party led by Epistola and the submarine commander named Moneta by the animals. This name also reveals an evident allegoric intention. Moneta (coin) is the hateful money, the source of the catastrophe, and it must be destroyed: "'If you think about it, the right name is Coin. [...] The governor is Coin. And like a coin, disembarking, it will roll.' 'So Coin it will be! We will call him by this name! But only for a short time, because soon we'll have to spend it.' 'No, we will not spend it,—Roboamo remarked,—we will melt it! Liquefy it!'" (*Romanzi* 2:428–29).

During the final duel with Epistola, Moneta claims that he, "homo sapiens et scientificus" (*Romanzi* 2:436), cannot be defeated by a vulgar animal. But as Mamerte (also called "Zuppa") answers, the governor is not what he claims to be: "'You are not a man, true or false; you are only the man at the end of mankind,' burst out Zuppa, nauseated [...]. 'The man who perverted and left mankind is you. Therefore you are a piece of shit, only a piece of shit!'" (*Romanzi* 2:437–38). Moneta is only "man at the end of mankind," the man who craves money and power more than anything else and who, having betrayed his nature and his origins,[13] is now bound to disappear.[14] Both Epistola and Moneta must die; in fact, if the governor represents the old society, the image of the monkey seems to foreshadow a possible resurgence of a social order tainted by the same mistakes made by humans. There is no place for them on this "irritable planet." Mamerte, on the other hand, abandons the remains of his humanity during his travels and becomes more and more similar to the nonhuman animals, implying the possibility of a new society in which humans can live together with animals. Is it possible to consider this outcome as a successful ending of an education, like in a Bildungsroman? As stated previously, the transition from man to animal in Western culture is usually considered an involution; this, as Cary Wolfe underlines, is one of the reasons why the reduction of the human to the animal is one of the most frequently used rhetorical strategies to dehumanize an enemy (567). Volponi does exactly the opposite; he sees the metamorphosis from human to animal as an improvement, a way to restore contact with the nonalienated, real human nature.

After the defeat of Moneta, Mamerte comes to the end of his quest. The protagonist who had to endure such a difficult process of distancing from the human society as we know it (quite the opposite of the socialization in the Bildungsroman) finally seems to lose every human attribute, until he becomes exactly like an animal. His very hands are almost transformed into hooves, with his fingers bent and stuck into the palms of his hands. The final step of this process takes place when Mamerte rips a sheet of rice paper on which a Chinese nun had written a poem (a gift for him) and eats it with his companions. Here, the nihilistic denial of human heritage seems to reach its highest point; if in *Corporeal* the written text (the diary of Murieta) is still viewed as of value, in *The Irritable Planet* we see an apparent refusal not only of literature but of human language itself. This is paradoxical, because it seems to represent Volponi's intention to demolish the value of his own artistic work. But as noted by Maria Carla Papini, this final act is a sort of nonreligious Eucharistic ceremony; the nun's poem is destroyed, but only in order to be shared and assimilated. Only in this "corporeal" way can poetry become part of the flesh of these creators of the new society (90).

Can we speak of Volponi as a posthuman author? He clearly wrote his novels years before the remarks made by Agamben and Derrida on animality and before the formulation of posthuman theory. We must remember the allegoric intention of *The Irritable Planet* and also the "traditional" use Volponi makes of animals like the elephant and the monkey, extending to them a model of human subjectivity. Nonetheless, Volponi certainly foresaw the main point of the contemporary debate on animality: the idea that human beings are not something separate from animals. The idea that humans are "incomplete"—that is, they have no predetermined nature like the other animals—has been present in Western culture since the myth of Prometheus told by Hesiod. This idea, reinforced by Pico della Mirandola in his *Oratio de homini dignitate*, has been recently challenged by posthuman scholars like Roberto Marchesini who focus attention on the cognitive specialization of the human being.[15] In other words, it is not true that man has no specialization; the volume and the complexity of the human brain clearly state the opposite. The real ability of humans, then, is to use their brains to adapt themselves to the environment through a complex range of cultural hybridizations with the animal kingdom.[16] Man is, therefore, not an "incomplete" system but an open one that changes continually, thanks to cultural hybridization with the animal; man can learn from other species, and he uses this characteristic to his advantage (Marchesini, *Post-human* 113). This concept of hybridization is also present in Paolo Volponi, who considers the hybridization of man and animal and the renunciation of what is traditionally considered "human" (especially in *The Irritable Planet*) as the only possible cure for our ill society. I would argue, therefore, that the "man as an open system" described by Agamben and Marchesini, this subject who continually repositions the threshold of what can be considered human, was accurately foreshadowed in the narrative of Paolo Volponi.

Notes

1. This connection between the human and anthropocentrism is even more explicit in Rosi Braidotti's article "Animals, Anomalies and Inorganic Others": "The animal has ceased to be one of the privileged terms that indexes the European subject's relation to otherness. The metaphysics of otherness rested on an assumed political anatomy, implicitly modeled on ideals of whiteness, masculinity, normality, youth, and health. All other models of embodiment, in the sense of both dialectical otherness (nonwhite, non-masculine, non-normal, non-young, non-healthy) and categorical otherness (zoomorphic, disabled, or malformed), were pathologized and cast on the other side of normality—that is, viewed as anomalous, deviant, and monstrous. This morphological normativity was inherently anthropocentric, gendered, and racialized" (526).
2. Roberto Marchesini qualifies posthumanism as the end of a cultural perspective named "humanism" characterized by these five elements: disjunctivity (man is a separate entity from the world); anthropocentrism (man is the "center of gravity" of the world; all nonhuman entities exist only because they are instrumental to man); autopoiesis (man is self-sufficient, so he is also the demiurge of his own dimension); tendency to subsume (man is the sum of every being; he is able to contain the world and, at the same time, he is the unit of

measurement of the world); and virtuality (absence of limitation; the human being is seen as an *apeiron*; *Tramonto* 5–8).
3. Translations in this essay are my own unless otherwise indicated.
4. Other possible titles were *Signals from the Animal* (*Segnali dall'animale*), *To Free the Animal* (*Liberare l'animale*), and *The Trace of the Animal* (*La traccia dell'animale*; *Romanzi* 1:1137). A reference to the title *L'animale* also appears in a letter that Volponi wrote to Pier Paolo Pasolini in 1965 (Volponi, *Scrivo* 154).
5. This is what Volponi wrote in a note found by Emanuele Zinato among the author's papers and quoted in the critical apparatus accompanying *Romanzi* 1:1132.
6. Many years later, in 1994, in the book interview he wrote with Francesco Leonetti a few months before his death (*The Lion and the Fox* [*Il leone e la volpe*]), Volponi's condemnation of society remained unchanged, and the relationship between the nuclear bomb and capitalism persisted as one of the central topics of his thought. But this time Volponi condemned not only Western capitalism but also the already dead Soviet Union. In fact, he declares that the twisted logic of the nuclear threat influenced both capitalism and socialism: the consequence of this logic is the creation of a globalized society without any alternative: "The planet is dominated by the atomic bomb, this is the real dominator. It influenced both the capitalistic and the socialistic systems making them practically the same, because both existed only to produce the same thing: the bomb [...] I refuse this logic. The bomb is oppressing, no matter what its trademark is; and it does not guarantee anything but catastrophe" (Volponi and Leonetti 107).
7. Foucault's course of lectures *Naissance de la biopolitique* (1977–78) were published in French in 2004 and in English, with the title *The Birth of Biopolitics*, in 2008.
8. A clear example of cultural hybridization is, for Marchesini, the relationship between man and dog. See Marchesini, *Post-human* 44–45.
9. According to Marchesini, the open system (the fact that man is open to the cultural hybridization with the animal), with its constant disequilibrium, makes possible human cultural and scientific development: "[I]t is the very openness of the 'man system' that creates the instability of the human being. In other words the capacity to imagine new goals, which inevitably become new expectations that can never be completely satisfied. To set up a system in non-equilibrium means to create a continual shift of the expectations that transforms the perception of expertise from an element of homeostasis to a dynamic factor, and this makes every perception of competency something temporary" (*Post-human* 65).
10. It is also worth acknowledging the vagueness of terms like "authentic rationality and culture." Volponi in fact did not have a clear picture of what the new utopian society he dreamed would be like, but he

clearly understood what it was that he opposed—namely, the false logic of the industrial neocapitalist society.
11. One of the most problematic aspects of *Corporeal* is the continual shift from first person to third person narration. The first part of the novel is narrated by Gerolamo Aspri himself; the second part has Joaquin Murieta as the protagonist and is narrated in third person. The change is rather shocking; only later do we discover that the protagonist is still Aspri, but he changed his name and became an outlaw in order to raise enough money to incite a revolution, though the plan fails. In the third part the narrative goes back to the first person and the name of the protagonist is once again Gerolamo Aspri.
12. As noted by Franco Moretti, the Bildungsroman or novel of education is a novel in which the protagonist (usually a young man) endures several trials in order to achieve a moral and psychological maturation. Moretti calls this process "socialization," a process that implies the acceptance of the rules on which the social environment of the protagonist is founded (45).
13. According to Volponi's "utopian" conception, human nature is intrinsically good when it is not ruined by the negative influence of society.
14. In this case the reference to feces has no value of regeneration, as in *Corporeal*; in fact here it does not represent the outcome of a natural cycle but a metaphor of money (and capitalism). Mamerte states it clearly: "You are shit and you will remain shit. But not the good shit, the honest dung of a body: satisfaction and refuse of a gratified existence, day after day, even defecating and fertilizing: giving and not only taking and eating. You are by no means the shit of a natural cycle; but the pile, the treasured turd of a forced circulation. Like in the unnatural you take the gold for shit, and not the gold useful metal for the teeth and the useful shit for the fertilizer; but the gold money of the shit money!" (*Romanzi* 2:438).
15. About Pico's *De hominis dignitate*, Marchesini states, "While every existing reality has its own nature, man is not determined nor forced by any essence, in other words man has no condition but one; freedom, or the responsibility to choose his own destiny, for better or for worse" (*Post-human* 18).
16. Marchesini clarifies this point: "[I]t is not true that the human being is not a specialist in the biological world. The volume alone of the encephalon, hypertrophic organ, plus the metabolic price to make it work, provides testimony of the opposite" (*Post-human* 19).

Works Cited

Adorno, Theodor W. *Minima Moralia: Reflections from Damaged Life*. Trans. E. F. N. Jephcott. London: NLB, 1974 [1951].

Agamben, Giorgio. *Homo Sacer: Sovereign Power and Bare Life*. Trans. Daniel Heller-Roazen. Stanford: Stanford UP, 1998.
———. *The Open: Man and Animal*. Trans. Kevin Attell. Stanford: Stanford UP, 2004.
Bakhtin, Mikhail. *Rabelais and His World*. Trans. Hélène Iswolsky. Bloomington: Indiana UP, 1984.
Braidotti, Rosi. "Animals, Anomalies, and Inorganic Others." *PMLA* 124.2 (2009): 526–32.
Calvino, Italo. *Saggi 1945–1985*. Ed. Mario Barenghi. Milan: Mondadori, 1995.
Dekoven, Marianne. "Why Animals Now?" *PMLA* 124.2 (2009): 361–69.
Derrida, Jacques. *The Animal That Therefore I Am*. Ed. Marie-Louise Mallet. Trans. David Wills. New York: Fordham UP, 2008.
Ferretti, Gian Carlo. *Volponi*. Florence: La Nuova Italia, 1972.
Foucault, Michel. *The Order of Things: An Archeology of the Human Sciences*. New York: Pantheon, 1971.
Marchesini, Roberto. *Post-human: Verso nuovi modelli di esistenza*. Turin: Bollati Boringhieri, 2002.
———. *Il tramonto dell'uomo: La prospettiva post-umanista*. Bari: Dedalo, 2009.
Morante, Elsa. *Pro o contro la bomba atomica e altri scritti*. Milan: Adelphi, 1985.
Moretti, Franco. *Il romanzo di formazione*. Milan: Garzanti, 1986.
Papini, Maria Carla. *Paolo Volponi. Il potere, la storia, il linguaggio*. Florence: Le Lettere, 1997.
Volponi, Paolo. *Poesie 1946–1994*. Ed. Emanuele Zinato. Turin: Einaudi, 2001.
———. "Questo pazzo signor Aspri" (interview with Corrado Stajano). *Il Giorno*, February 21, 1974.
———. *Romanzi e prose*. Ed. Emanuele Zinato. 3 vols. Turin: Einaudi, 2002.
———. *Scrivo a te come guardandomi allo specchio. Lettere a Pasolini 1954–1975*. Ed. Daniele Fioretti. Florence: Polistampa, 2009.
Volponi, Paolo, and Francesco Leonetti. *Il leone e la volpe*. Turin: Einaudi, 1994.
Wolfe, Cary. "Human, All Too Human: 'Animal Studies' and the Humanities." *PMLA* 124.2 (2009): 564–75.

9

The Postapocalyptic Cookbook

Animality, Posthumanism, and Meat in Laura Pugno and Wu Ming

Valentina Fulginiti

Future Histories, Present Fictions

Reviewing Nicoletta Vallorani's novel *Eva* (2002), Salvatore Proietti identifies an emerging dystopianism in Italian fiction: "The dystopian setting is the common trait identifying a major line of recent Italian science fiction, a line that is definitively taking shape only now. The names could include Catani, Valerio Evangelisti, Carlo Formenti, Francesco Grasso, Riccardo Pedrini, Enrica Zunic."[1] More than ten years later, these claims have been confirmed: in fact, if anything, Proietti's list is too short, failing to include the names of Tullio Avoledo, Alessandro Bertante, Tommaso Pincio, Davide Longo, Laura Pugno, Paolo Zanotti, and the Wu Ming collective. Indeed, it is hard to deny that a dystopian tide is rising in Italian fiction. What appeared in the early 2000s to be a subgenre of science fiction is now a minor but persistent vein of Italian narrative, with a growing number of works published every year. Rosi Braidotti's claim that minor and marginal genres such as science fiction and cyberpunk provide a more honest cultural illustration of society than "more self-consciously representational" genres seems now to be proven also in Italy (*Metamorphoses* 182). Writing novels about the future is no longer an exclusive commitment to a genre, nor does it cast anathema on its authors.[2] Writers such as Davide Longo and Wu Ming provide evidence of the current fortunes of these genres and of the fact that writing science fiction does not limit an author's generic choices. Pugno, equally versed in lyric poetry and science fiction, and Pincio, whom Franco Cordelli credits with being one of the most stylistically gifted contemporary Italian authors (36), are luminous examples of the new respectability of dystopian genres.[3]

The concerns of the dystopian and postapocalyptic imagination have also productively entered the thinking of literary critics and philosophers. Carla Benedetti, for instance, opens the door to literary ecology, advocating for a posthuman gaze against the hubris of anthropocentrism. In her *Inhuman Letters* (*Disumane lettere*, 2011), the quest for a "nonhuman" ideal of literature coincides with an antianthropocentric plea: "[T]he *human letters*, as we once used to call them in Italy, that is to say humanistic knowledge, based for centuries on the guiding idea of 'man as an end,' are now facing for the first time the possibility of the end of the human, at least in its current form" (4).[4] Benedetti's claim goes further: she suggests that "realist" narratives, with their implicit anthropomorphism, represent an act of violence toward the living, a category that comprehends all animal and vegetal creatures (99).

Benedetti is not the first Italian to make an attempt at "greening the humanities." Wu Ming 1 offers similar thoughts in "New Italian Epic: Memorandum 1993–2008," a text charting tendencies of Italian narrative. Here, Wu Ming 1 suggests that anthropocentrism is the product of a gaze that forgets that Earth was here long before us. Literature is therefore left with a crucial task: it should embody nonhuman perspectives; it should keep us aware of the *longue durée* of astronomical, geological and evolutionary time. The "Memorandum" encourages science fiction to adopt nonhuman perspectives on the future: "The fact that we no longer have an idea of the future is not helping. We are overwhelmed by our inability to put things into perspective; even science fiction [. . .] has mostly given up any attempt to narrate 'future histories,' opting for *atemporal* settings, faraway distant epochs or even a near future—so near that it is already our present. [. . .] Similarly important, and increasingly so, is the ability to render extra-human gazes in literary terms [. . .]. Extra-human, non-human, non-identifiable gazes: such experiments help us to exit from ourselves" (58).[5] To some extent, this passage echoes David Ketterer's classification of science fiction into three broad categories: one based on "the future consequences of present circumstances," one based on "the consequences of a modification to the present circumstances," and one that "that puts humanity in a radically new perspective" (16–17). The last category, which Ketterer considers the most philosophical form of science fiction (17), roughly corresponds to Wu Ming 1's ideal of narrating "future histories" from the perspective of "extra-human gazes."

A new concern for the future is haunting Italian literature: a future from which humanity as a species might be absent. This concern will be at the center of this essay, which examines the changing notion of humanity and its relation to animalism and monstrosity in Laura Pugno's *Sirens* (*Sirene*, 2007) and Wu Ming 5's *Free Karma Food* (2006), two works that effectively represent the tragic ultimatum offered to future humanities: evolve or face extinction. Both novels question the boundaries between the human and the animal through a multiplicity of figurations. In my analysis, I first engage with the variety of "monstrous" regimes put in place by the authors. Mythological creatures, chimeras, or genetically engineered hybrids—these "monstrous" labels could be applied to the posthuman creatures featured in these novels, challenging and broadening our current understanding of "humanity." At the same time, a deeper challenge to humanism is posited by cannibalism, the second issue I address. Pugno and Wu Ming 5 speculate over the future of our current industrial meat production, producing two full-fledged alimentary dystopias; more important, they present a variety of extreme modes of meat consumption, varying from the eating of domesticated, traditionally nonedible species to full-fledged anthropophagy. As I argue, these two notions (posthumanism and cannibalism) are deeply interlaced, within the common frame of a collapsing social order: they represent two opposite yet converging ways toward a narrative discourse of the *nonhuman*.

Contagion, Degeneration, Evolution

In recent Italian postapocalyptic fiction, the body emerges as a privileged site of discourse. Though postmodern tropes of immateriality had condemned the realities of the physical body to silence, the body now returns deformed by pain and disease, refusing the neutralizing silence of the postmodern: it is a body made monstrous. "Monsters are coming back, monsters and lepers," warns Pugno in the opening pages of *Sirens* (7). In fact, Italian dystopian novels swarm with "monsters" of all different kinds—the undead, chimeras, the infected, and other potential subjects of "unworthy life" (Agamben 142).[6] Monsters are the hopeless men we see in these tales, capable of doing horrible things to their own kind and to their *cognate species*—a label that ultimately encompasses all species, since all earthlings are cognate in relation to their native planet. Monstrous are the futures that these stories foresee for the human species. Monstrous are the postapocalyptic settings, marked by radiation-induced mutations, the looming threat of extinction, or the collapse of our most fundamental taboos. Monstrous are some of the "animals" portrayed, bearers of a murderous instinct resulting from artificial mutations. Importantly, many of these animals are not existing biological species: they are the result of either technological manipulation or fantasies that rewrite modern and ancient mythologies. They are fantastic creatures, monstrous hybrids of human and animal. Monstrous also is the tone of these stories: a tone that Daniele Giglioli has recently described with the label "extreme narration"—a shocking language that emphasizes the abnormal and the grotesque (14–15). Finally, these stories can be inscribed in the monstrous through their deliberately problematic use of literary genres, recombined into abnormal discursive formations.

Monstrosity, however, is an ambivalent paradigm. Although it aptly describes the omnipresence of decay, it is also charged with the positive values of excess and vital proliferation in the work of authors who challenge the human from feminist, antianthropocentric, or nomadic perspectives. This is especially the case for Donna Haraway and Rosi Braidotti, who investigate the productive synergies of women, machines, and the animal. In particular, Braidotti advocates for the study of monsters, or, as she defines it, a new teratology: "What we witness in popular culture is almost a Bakhtinian ritual of transgression. The fascination for the monstrous, the freaky body-double, is directly proportional to the suppression of images of both ugliness and disease in contemporary post-industrial society. It is as if what we are chasing out the front door—the spectacle of the poor, fat, homeless, homosexual, black, ageing, decaying, leaky body—were actually creeping in through the back window. The monstrous marks the 'return of the repressed' of techno-culture and as such it is intrinsic to it" (*Metamorphoses* 200). Teratology serves multiple functions in her conceptual architecture. First and foremost, it provides a heuristic frame that subverts the power balance of "classic" teratology (i.e., the medical study of monsters popular in the eighteenth century). From this point of view, Braidotti's teratology accounts for the hybrid formulations of our culture—an economy of masks, practices, and identities that can be worn and changed at one's pleasure. The current fascination with the "freak" is therefore another incarnation of a teratology à la Braidotti: "The social imaginary of the late urbanized Western postmodernity is in the grip of teratological or monstrous others. The monstrous, the grotesque, the mutant and the downright freakish have gained widespread currency in urban post-industrialist cultures also known as 'postmodern Gothic'" (*Metamorphoses* 177–78).

Second, studying monsters authorizes the scholar to speak from a subversive location. Teratology thus emerges as an alternative to the dominant perspective of male, white, able bodies. Such a perspective is, in fact, the device generating the other as a monster, constantly reading all difference in terms of a deviant, abnormal subjectivity: "In the metaphysics of substance, the bodily equivalent of the 'power of reason' is the notion of Man as 'rational animal' which is expected to inhabit a perfectly functional physical body. All other modes of embodiment, being zoomorphic, disabled, malformed or ill-functioning, are pathologized and classified on the other side of normality, that is to say monstrosity. This process is inherently racialized in that it upholds aesthetic and moral ideas based on white European civilization" (*Metamorphoses* 123). This point is particularly important in order to understand the subversive nature of monsters, both today and historically. Precisely because of their forced identification with the other, monsters often fall prey to rape and racism (as we will see in *Sirens* and *Free Karma Food*). For the same reason, the study of monsters enables thinkers to problematize the status of difference in Western philosophy, as Braidotti makes clear (*Madri* 81).

Third, monsters provide a potential location for antianthropocentrism. In this respect, monstrosity is a discourse based on proliferation and excess: its economy relies on what Braidotti has dubbed "the unholy marriage of *bios* and *zoe* with *technos*" (*Metamorphoses* 170). The maternal (a site of new fears in late capitalism) here meets the animal and the mechanical, producing new bodily regimes that overtly challenge the self-proclaimed sovereignty of mankind over the universe. But if the monstrous is an excessive and proliferating interaction between the human, the animal, and the mechanical, what is, precisely, the space of the animal in such a discourse? And to what extent does the symbolic domain of monsters challenge the anthropocentric violence of our society?

When the Animal Looks Back

Pandemics do not threaten our species alone: animal pandemics also loom, as a result of mass pollution and ongoing "earthicide." The common genealogy of apocalyptic imagination and "earthicide" was first addressed with clarity in Martin Jay's *Force Fields* (1993). In a chapter devoted to the apocalyptic "tone" of philosophy and popular culture in the 1980s, Jay associates the phenomenon with the loss of a maternal object that might coincide with our world. More precisely, it coincides with that "earthliness" with which humanity has severed ties: "It is thus tempting to interpret the apocalyptic moment [. . .] as a convoluted expression of distress at the matricidal underpinning of the modernist project, indeed of the entire human attempt to uproot itself from its origins in something we might call mother nature" (96).

Matricide and earthicide clearly overlap in the environmental dystopia *Sirens*, whose plot is marked by metaphors of maternal fluids (blood, milk, and water), by a succession of female generations, and by violence against bodies gendered female. Pugno imagines the last days of mankind, threatened by environmental collapse, the unstopped flow of solar radiation, and a new strain of skin cancer: the "black cancer." This fictional cancer appears to be contagious and attacks the human population with various degrees of intensity, depending on their skin phototypes. In the chaos, old state formations give way to new powers, such as organized crime; powerful yakuza run the West Coast and what is now known as "Nu.Ba.Ca," New California Bay. As humanity vanishes, divided between the happy few who inhabit the sea floor and the hoi polloi dying in the millions, a new species emerges from the depth of the ocean: mermaids, or sirens, immune to the devastating pandemics. The rise of mermaids is directly linked to the threat of human extinction. According to environmental activists and followers of new cults, black cancer is a divine punishment for what men have done to mermaids, first hunted almost to extinction and later farmed in special plants run by yakuza. While male mermaids have no commercial value, female ones are precious; they represent a status symbol, both as a culinary delicacy and as a sexual obsession.

The main character, Samuel, is young and desperate: originally trained to become a yakuza boss, he now works as a superintendent on an illegal mermaid farm. His personality is structured around the double trauma of his father's premature death and the loss of his lover, Sadako: his gaze is posthumous by definition, the gaze of a survivor. Samuel eventually gives in to his underlying death drive, neglecting all prevention and developing black cancer. At the same time, he begins having intercourse with mermaids, eventually fathering a human-mermaid hybrid, Mia. Despite having a complete human phonatory apparatus, Mia is seemingly incapable of articulating words; as soon as her ability to pronounce her father's name is discovered, she becomes strategic for the yakuza, who see the new hybrid as a potential source of genetic material and therefore a key to a treatment for the black cancer. Just before dying, Samuel finds the strength for a single act of rebellion: he releases himself and his daughter into the ocean. After Samuel's death, the book ends with the image of Mia breaking free on the ocean floor, a member of an entirely new, posthuman species, completely forgetful of humans and their consciousness. Meanwhile, the yakuza have discovered a new way of making profit: the skin of African Bushmen, seemingly immune to the disease, will provide a new cancer treatment. As the narration seems to imply, Mia is destined to live, but her success will most likely coincide with the demise of humanity—either replaced by a new, posthuman species incapable of formulating thought as we know it or turned into gruesome monsters, literally ready to rip the skin off their own kind.

As indicated before, the maternal element is central to the plot: humans control the breeding cycle of mermaids, manipulating their hormonal cycles, inducing their mating, and selecting their offspring. The reference to motherhood is both explicit and implicit, appearing in the descriptive section of the novel and reinforced by many lexical and rhetorical choices. The mermaid's milk, for instance, is described as "that substance as fat as human breast milk" (9). Similarly, in the novel's ending, Samuel's final dive into the ocean contains a reference to amniotic fluids: "The ocean on his skin, the taste, the flavor, the soft consistency of water, as thick as a placenta" (117).

Sirens represents a bodily politics of obscenity that resonates with the paradigm of monstrosity presented earlier in this essay. In particular, the violence against the maternal takes the double form of cannibalism (or quasicannibalism) and rape: "Mermaid meat was in high demand. There were mermaid brothels too. [...] Mermaids were the new sexual sport, the new Beluga caviar" (6–7). Mermaids and female humans are almost interchangeable under the sign of masculine violence, making it evident that mermaids, with their mixture of species, question the boundaries between the animal and the human. Furthermore, the identification between animal and human meat looms in the narration, implacably carried out by the logic of metaphorical replacement. The urban legends circulating in the dystopian society of Underwater bear evidence of this: "The half-albino mermaids, with their white, silvery skin, slightly softer than average, were the closest to the female of the sapiens species. Rumors circulated about a yakuza who used to let his wife have sex with a half-albino, filmed her and sold the videos. Whether the woman consented or not, the rumor did not tell" (29). While the male protagonist perceives the gravity of raping women, he fails to read the same violence when it is not perpetrated against a human being. Indeed, as Robert Rushing has noted, one might really wonder if the men represented by Pugno are, after all, deserving of a future (12).

From the first pages of the novel, Samuel indulges in fantasies of ritualistic cannibalism, building on the same law of symbolic replacement that often brings him to recognize his lost love in the mermaids he feeds, brutalizes, and slaughters. While his sexual fantasies involving mermaids are often dominated by the memory of Sadako, he also fantasizes about ritual cannibalism as a way to exorcise his irrevocable loss: "[W]hen Sadako died, Samuel thought about devouring her body, before they cremated it. Eating her flesh meant having her inside forever, or at the very least until the end of the meal and of the digestive cycle of his body. Something would pass, though, from the blood to his own body" (65). Ironically, it is Mia, not Samuel, who performs the only true act of ritual cannibalism in the book, by feeding on the body of her biological father to survive at the novel's end (142).

In Pugno's fiction, the only human legacy remaining lies in the taste for blood, since the carnivore instinct is one of the strongest features that the hybrid Mia inherits from her human father. Unlike her fellow mermaids, naturally inclined to appreciate only the taste of plankton and seaweed, Mia enjoys hunting and savoring smaller fish. Mia thus becomes something close to the "chimeras" that already populate our laboratories, with their frightening mixture of human and animal genomes (Mehlman 81). Mankind will be most likely wiped out, either turning into a monstrous, unempathic species or simply being exterminated by solar radiation, but mankind's murderous drive will survive, transformed into a genetic marker for the new humanoid species.

If *Sirens* blends environmental catastrophe, disease, and human extinction in a compelling narrative, the same elements also intertwine in the postapocalyptic world of *Free Karma Food* (2006). Despite their stylistic and thematic differences, these two novels share several important traits. First, they both represent the emergence of posthumanism in a globalized setting. Their represented culture blends elements of the "American" way of life with Asian culture—Japanese in *Sirens*, Chinese and Indian in

Free Karma Food. Different cultures are presented through linguistic patches of color, artificially recreating the condition of writing in a permanent "state of translation" typical of our globalized world.[7] Finally, both present humanity as a global mixture of interchangeable lifestyles, masks, and performances, seemingly proving Perniola's claim that "[o]n the one hand, we witness the emergence of tribal behavior in big cities, on the other the profound impact of technological and economic rationality in underdeveloped areas. All this gives way to an unusual and surprising blending of archaic and modern, of past and future, which our ordinary categories are entirely inadequate to comprehend" (44).

In the fictional universe depicted by Wu Ming 5, humanity has been torn apart by a global war between India, China, and Pakistan that ended with a nuclear bombing. Meanwhile, a viral pandemic has wiped out all the traditional meat animals. Ironically, while the most common meat animals are exterminated in a desperate attempt to save humanity, the final outcome of such an action is the destruction of humanity at a deeper level. In a proteic frenzy, the food industry turns to kinds of meat previously overlooked, like rats, dogs, and cats. Eventually, the consumption of human meat is legalized in certain circumstances. Productive members of society are apparently safe; however, outcasts, addicts, and the homeless can be legally hunted and slaughtered by certified "meat-procurers." The license to kill is also extended to those responsible for violent crimes, whose summary execution is left in the hands of ruthless bounty hunters. Once again, the mass extinction of animal and vegetal species affects mankind, shifting the boundaries of what is currently considered "humanity": cannibalism, or the reduction of the human body to its edible nature, represents the ultimate outcome of a world from which nature as such has been expelled.[8]

Both Pugno and Wu Ming 5 challenge our current idea of interspecific relations, echoing the question often posed by animal-rights activists: why do we eat pigs and love dogs? Further, why would the slaughtering of a mermaid substantially differ from that of a dolphin or a shark? In other words, these fictions question the notion of "companion species," a definition that includes domestic species like cats and dogs but could also suit a cognate species like that of the mermaid. As Donna Haraway indicates, companion species are not to be mistaken for "companion animals"—our common pets such as dogs, cats, and hamsters. Although in practice these two categories often overlap, the notion of "companion species" is not a rigid grouping of species but rather an operative notion, a new mode of understanding the animal. Its implicit reference to "an ongoing 'becoming with'" makes it a more productive and fertile category than "posthumanism" itself, Haraway claims (*Species* 16–17).

In *Free Karma Food*, men begin their degeneration by slaughtering their former "best friends": cats and dogs. Initially, they still maintain a façade: while the practice is nominally prohibited in America, it is outsourced to Central America and East Asia, far from the "oversensitive" eyes of the public: "Intensive farming of cats and dogs: sidewinder dogs, teaser-dogs, slaughtering hooks, slaughtering guns, slaughterers of dogs and cats. This was all illegal here, on US territory. But gigantic cat slaughterhouses were being built in Honduras. Dog slaughterhouses were being built in Taiwan, Ho Chi Min Ville, in Guangzhou" (97). However, no such euphemism is applied to the hunting, killing, and consuming of human flesh, which is perfectly legal in the United States by the mid-twenty-first century as Wu Ming 5 imagines it. In *Sirens*, Pugno resorts to the definition of "commensal species"—a close etymological relative of "companion species"—which she applies to the gender distinction within species, that of mermaids: "Some scientists had argued that it was not unique, but two different species, mysteriously hybridized in a third one. The female would be the form of the mermaid, while the so-called 'males' would simply be a commensal species" (5–6). The word *commensal*, like *companion*, contains in its roots a reference to the sharing of food, an ancient sign of intimacy and solidarity. Such a reference, however, acquires a sinister resonance in the new postapocalyptic society of Underwater: "A bad ending, for a commensal" (6), jests the narrator cynically in describing the short life cycle of all mermaids, male and female alike.

Pugno's reference to "commensal species" is particularly interesting for two different reasons. On the one hand, Pugno reminds us of the arbitrariness of distinctions between domesticated, companion animals and all the rest, which are considered a legitimate source of food. If even male and female individuals of a species can be seen as members of two different, unrelated, species, humanity is one step away from cannibalism; indeed, the mermaids are often depicted as "quasihuman" species throughout the novel. Mermaids could therefore be an example of the "uncanny valley," the feeling of revulsion and sudden recognition experienced by human beings when faced with artificial creatures that are almost, but not completely, identical to them.[9] For instance, in the restaurants of Underwater, chefs prepare "newborn sashimi" (29) without further specification; to the Italian reader, the word "newborn" ["*neonata*"] immediately evokes horrific visions of human infants. Another example of the porous boundary between human and nonhuman is when Samuel selects a victim to rape. Among all mermaids, he chooses the one with "an almost human mug" (76); subsequently, Samuel lauds the "almost human" facial features of the chosen victim in a murderous fantasy: "She would have looked great, with her own quasi-human facial features and her white, silvery skin, embalmed and placed on a desk" (77). The specter of recognition, of the One and the Same, is therefore the nightmare haunting this fiction, which cautions us to recognize the murderous drive at the base of anthropocentrism, if not of *humanity* itself.

On the other hand, by defining males and females as members of two different species, the author suggests a pattern of pseudospeciation, or what Joseph Meeker might term "the adoption of interspecific behavioral patterns of aggression inappropriately applied to a conspecific" (70). As its first theorist Erik Erikson has suggested, pseudospeciation is a specifically human behavior and a powerful enabler of murder, war, and genocide (213–17). Notable examples include the depiction of Jews as rats, pigs, or dogs under the Nazi persecutions and the comparison of Vietnamese children to cattle during the Vietnam War. Pseudospeciation is therefore a product of culture, yet it entails the reading of phenotypal variation as a specific variation, or the "naturalization" of cultural difference (including ethnicity, gender, or age); it is, in short, a powerful instance of "naturalization," or another way to reduce humanity to its presumed biological essence. The link to racism is particularly evident in *Sirens*, which is pervaded by hints at a segregated world. For instance, the Japanese see themselves as the dominant ethnicity in New California Bay, which leads to racist resentment of the Japanese assistant Ken'nosuke on the part of Samuel. As indicated earlier, the contagious cancer attacks different phototypes with varying degrees of virulence, and the novel ends with a reference to using the immune skin of African Bushmen as a new medical treatment—quite literally profiting from their skin. Similarly, the cannibalistic violence in *Free Karma Food* assumes racist overtones in claims such as "We prefer young Caucasian women in their twenties, but these are tastes, and as we all know, tastes can vary greatly," assimilating the phenotypal variation among human beings to different cuts of meat (242).

Yet one should be careful not to mistake the apparent "naturalization" of cannibalism for the elimination of culture *tout court*: while the fictions of pseudospeciation allow men to slaughter their out-group of choice, they still belong to a societal pattern. As Baudrillard makes clear, cannibalism is not the abolition of society but rather the defining ground of a *different* society: "Cannibals themselves do not claim to live in a state of nature, nor in accordance with their desire at all; they quite simply claim, through their cannibalism, to live in a society, the most interesting case being a society that eats its own dead" (138). In both *Free Karma Food* and *Sirens*, normative mechanisms regulate the desire for human meat, which is simultaneously an addiction, a status symbol, and a commodity of strategic importance. Both the quasicannibalism of *Sirens* and the full-fledged cannibalism of *Free Karma Food* rest on industrial mechanisms, with specific sites of production and consumption. In *Free Karma Food*, we have norms regulating these practices and even associations like the Human Meat Restaurants Association, whereas in *Sirens*, mermaid meat is one of the most profitable businesses of the yakuza. Moreover, the dystopian societies represented by Pugno and Wu Ming 5 normalize the drive for a formerly prohibited food by linking it to an ancient, and secretive, culinary tradition. Wu Ming 5, for instance, throws fictional hints at Asian cultures, citing legends of the Tartar domination (162–63). Similarly, Pugno imagines a link between the taste of mermaid meat and umami, an existing flavor in traditional Japanese cuisine: "What drove the eaters of mermaid meat to madness was, as the Yakuza knew too well, the umami taste. The fifth flavor. Known and unknown at the same time. Suddenly, it was so popular that it became a drug. The Yakuza craved it too" (103).

In both dystopias, cannibalism and the eating of companion and/ or cognate species are seen as the ultimate realization of mankind. In *Sirens*, the meat of mermaids is the preferred meal of the alpha males, the powerful members of the yakuza who constitute a separate caste in the postapocalyptic Underwater. Similarly, attending the mermaid brothels is, more than a status symbol, a social obligation for the recently promoted yakuza boss Ken'nosuke (130–31). Ironically, none of the human characters is really destined to prevail: some will survive longer than others, but they all are doomed to an early death, whether by cancer or at the hands of other men. In fact, the only "alpha" individual bound to prevail in the story is not a human. Mia, the genetic hybrid born to a mermaid and a human, is the "alpha female" who will have the privilege of mating with the fittest male of her school: "The school was small, and she was the alpha. In the next mating season, she would surely choose the best male, his green skin so dark that it would seem almost black, she would have him mount her in open water, and then she would kill him, as was written in her DNA" (144).

The theme of evolution is referenced more directly in *Free Karma Food*, where anthropophagy is presented as the culminating moment of human history: "Oh, the shining proteic future of the human species! Every human being could finally feed him or herself—that is, build and rebuild their own tissues—with the meat of their own fellow species, the only food really suitable for the animal on top of the food chain" (98). According to Wu Ming 5's self-proclaimed alpha males, evolution is driven by the same primal drive to destruction, homicide, and violence. Cannibalism is thus the ultimate consequence of instrumentalism and might be the only food available after the mindless destruction of our planet. The characters' banter confirms this view of the strategic importance of meat: "All I am saying is that human intelligence—the origin of intelligence, do you get me?—is related to the acquisition of meat in the human diet, through the evolution of the cognitive skills necessary to share meat strategically among the members of the clan. That was the recipe leading to the expansion of the human brain: meat. Do you get it?" (125). Yet Wu Ming 5 is not revealing anything new: these fictional voices of twenty-first-century America closely resonate with the "hunting hypothesis" promoted by evolutionary biology from the 1920s to the 1940s, a view that Haraway criticizes as instrumental in legitimizing patriarchy on evolutionary grounds and that works to reduce "humanism" to its presumed "natural essence" (*Simians* 11, 22).

In his analysis of *Sirens*, Rushing highlights the role played by posthumous perspectives in the narration, claiming that the impersonal viewpoint adopted by Pugno at the novel's conclusion fully enables her to represent a posthuman condition. At the same time, Rushing argues, Pugno's operation is less utopian than the final liberation of Mia might superficially suggest: Pugno represents a fully apocalyptic gaze, an ending nobody will ever represent or narrate with human words. Conversely, *Free Karma Food* concludes with a fictional appendix, titled "The Hairless Goat: A Practical Guide to the Slaughtering of Human Corpses." In accordance with its gruesome title, the appendix provides advice on how to slaughter a human in a manner consistent with best culinary practice. On the one hand, this appendix is consistent with the ideal of "narrating future histories" mentioned at the beginning of this essay, by virtue of its pseudodocumentary and metafictional quality. On the other hand, such appendices are a common device of dystopia and closely related genres.[10] As Margaret Atwood claims in *In Other Worlds*, such narrative devices might document their authors' "faith in the resilience of the human spirit" (146).[11] Yet Wu Ming 5's "Practical Guide" could be credited with a deeply dystopian aim: instead of representing a *better* future, the appendix confirms and amplifies the horror, showing a complete acquiescence to the new order of cannibalism. The "Practical Guide" is written in the present tense, carries no date, and presents no deictic distance from the events it references. If anything, it is our taboo against cannibalism that is regarded with suspicion: "Man, known in the history of culinary art with the name of 'long swine' or 'hairless goat,' has not always been considered an adequate source of protein. Religious and superstitious reasons opposed its consumption, or at least its overt consumption" (241).

Ultimately, Wu Ming 5's bleak vision of the world of tomorrow suggests that our future history might be one where human bodies are instrumentalized in a manner identical to the current treatment of nonhuman animal bodies. In this respect, the two novels enact opposite linguistic strategies. As I have suggested, the language of *Sirens* constantly hints at the quasihuman nature of its "cognate species"; on the contrary, Wu Ming 5 emphasizes the "animal" nature of the human species, in particular in the appendix. The author describes human bodies with an apparently neutral language, including the acronym "H meat" and expressions such as "the individual," "the subject," "the specimen," or even "the animal." The fact that we are indeed talking about the *human animal* is explicitly noted only in two strategic places of the "Practical Guide": the title and the conclusion.

In their opposite strategies, however, both novels achieve a similar effect—namely, that uncanny recognition considered earlier. Whether they humanize the animal (*Sirens*) or animalize the human (*Free Karma Food*'s appendix), both authors effectively equate the two terms. Their world is thus governed by duplicity, recognition, and symbolic replacement. In both of these fictions, animals are clearly staring back, and their eyes reflect a quite unflattering image of our humanity. Most important, mankind is seen in terms of its nature as meat. Inverting the commandment of another famous Orwellian dystopia, we might say that in these fictions all animals are equal, but this time no animal is more equal than others. Yet as both authors show, such equality can only come at the price of a generalized politics of horror.

By challenging the hierarchies that govern our interspecific relations, both novelists subtly question the core of humanity. Returning to Haraway, we find that the notion of "companion species," originally designating the historical, "co-constitutive" relation between dogs and humans, is characterized by three main elements: an *ethics* of relation (where the animal species is not merely passive but is also an active participant), a *cultural history* of such a bond of affection, and finally a *technology* of interspecies bond, which the author defines as "the webbed bio-social-technical apparatuses of humans, animals, artifacts, and institutions in which particular ways of being emerge and are sustained" (*Species* 134). These three elements—ethics, cultural history, and technology—play a prominent role in the analyzed fictions. By slaughtering its companion species (dogs or mermaids), the men in these fictions definitively leave behind their humanity, their history, or, as Haraway has it, their own "becoming with."

At the same time, the bond with our animal companions suggests a possible way beyond a culture imbued with the ideologies of supremacy and violence. If we look beyond the apparent oxymoron of the expression *companion species* (the bonding element of *companionship* as opposed to the divisive drive of *species*), this notion also recalls the idea of *respecere*, or looking back. Haraway's original interpretation of *companionship* thus highlights the responsive nature of such relation, one that requires a double perspective and, from the human side, the ability to recognize the other's gaze:

> I have tried to live inside the many tones of regard/respect/seeing each other/looking back at/meeting/optic–haptic encounter. Species and respect are in optic/haptic/affective/cognitive touch: they are at table together; they are messmates, companions, in company, *cum panis*. I also love the oxymoron inherent in "species"—always both logical type and relentlessly particular, always tied to *specere* and yearning/looking toward *respecere*. "Species" includes animal and human as categories, and much more besides; and we would be ill advised to assume which categories are in play and shaping one another in flesh and logic in constitutive encounterings. (*Species* 164)

Two radicalized versions of our present-day anthropocentrism, the future humanities imagined by Pugno and Wu Ming 5 lack what should be their defining trait: empathy. Both authors seem to suggest that a possible salvation lies in the ability to enter into dialogue with the animal—to return the animal's gaze, to cite Derrida's formulation. In other words, our survival as a species might not depend on our ability to prevail but rather on our ability to sustain *polyphony*, a fundamental model for literary ecology.[12]

Exit: Of Men, Animals, and Monsters

By no means isolated in the context of current Italian narrative production, *Free Karma Food* and *Sirens* stand out because they expand on scabrous themes that other novels simply mention in passing. These fictions blend together the themes of contagion, disease, and degeneration in order to offer a dreadful vision of future societies based on a generalized economy of cannibalism and rape. Most important, they question the boundaries of humanity through a discussion of anthropocentric violence against animals. Both authors suggest that the difference between eating cognate species and full-fledged cannibalism is merely one of degree and not one of essence. If instrumentalism, with its murderous consequences, is the fundamental nature of humans, we might come to regard posthumanism as a way of salvation. Finally, these tales effectively represent the paradox humanity will have to face unless it abandons its current path of anthropocentrism. Whether it is through an evolution into something different (becoming posthuman) or by accepting ruthless atrocity as our new law (becoming inhuman) does not matter; either way, we are losing our residual "humanity."

No matter how extreme these fictions might appear, it is worth noting that they are rooted in our current society. In 2006, Braidotti warned us about the cannibalistic turn taken by biotechnologies: "If people in war-torn lands like Afghanistan are reduced to eating grass in order to survive [...], the former herbivore bovine animals [...] have turned carnivore. Our agricultural bio-technical sector has taken an unexpected cannibalistic turn by fattening cows, sheeps and chickens on animal feed" (*Transpositions* 97–98). Men forced to eat grass and cannibalistic cows could be easily sold as science-fictional inventions. Consider Atwood's fictional Crakers in *Oryx and Crake* (2003), a humanoid species genetically engineered to eat grass: once again, the solution to human overconsumption and environmental collapse comes at the cost of humanity itself. The mad cow epidemic that raged across Europe in the 1990s and the 2000s, masterfully described by Italian narrator Helena Janaczek in *Mad Cow* (2012), has nothing to envy in the fictional epidemics discussed here. As Braidotti claims, these "fictions" are already part of our landscape. In this respect, one might question the radicalism of these dystopias. Are the authors merely emphasizing the grotesque and monstrous excesses of our current times? Still, these cautionary tales suggest a paradigm shift by looking creatively at humanity through the eyes of victimized animals. They suggest that in order to survive, we must be ready to criticize, challenge, and even overcome our humanity. By depicting the horrors of our present, the novels remind us of our future choice, and in this respect, they do provide alternatives. They give a voice, and a face, to the monsters of our worst nightmares, but in so doing, they urge us to ensure that monstrosity never becomes our fate.

Notes

1. Unless otherwise indicated, all translations in this essay are my own.
2. Canonical Italian authors have toyed with apocalyptic imaginings—especially in the nuclear age. Carlo Cassola and Paolo Volponi experimented with science fiction in *The Survivor* (*Il superstite*, 1978) and *The Irritable Planet* (*Il pianeta irritabile*, 1978), respectively. Italo Calvino's *Cosmicomics* (*Le cosmicomiche*, 1965) is also an example of canonical culture's fascination with science fiction. For further consideration, see Pierpaolo Antonello, "La nascita della fantascienza in Italia: il caso Urania" (2008), and Renato Giovannoli, "Montale e la Fantascienza" and "Manzoni e Pierre Menard" (2013).
3. This is not, however, to suggest that the critical establishment has unanimously welcomed the dystopian tide. Many accounts of the 2000s convey a bleak perspective of the future of Italian literature. Such a perspective is made evident by the many titles containing negative judgments: *Without Trauma* (*Senza trauma*), *Without Shame* (*Senza vergogna*), *Throwaway Writing* (*Scritture a perdere*), *Don't Encourage the Novel* (*Non incoraggiate il romanzo*), to mention a handful of works published in the last years.
4. It is worth noting that the mention of "man as an end" is a reference to Alberto Moravia's book of the same title.
5. Building on these reflections, Wu Ming 1 questioned the limits of historical, anthropocentric time in several essays and talks, often citing masters of science fiction such as William Gibson and Jacques Spitz. See in particular the essay "L'occhio del purgatorio: i tempi della rivolta e dell'utopia."
6. Agamben here becomes a key point of reference. His definition of "bare life" starts from a figure of Roman law, that of homo sacer, "who *may be killed and yet not sacrificed*" (8, emphasis in original): bare life is the place where politics and life are so interlaced they are no longer distinct. A crucial feature of bare life in my analysis is the blurring of the line between human and animal, "a threshold of indistinction and of passage between animal and man, *physis* and *nomos*, exclusion and inclusion: the life of the bandit is the life of the *loup garou*, the werewolf, who is precisely *neither man nor beast*, and who dwells paradoxically within both while belonging to neither" (Agamben 105, emphasis in original).
7. Both novels allude to a globalized twenty-first-century culture, citing proper nouns and idioms in different languages or presenting instances of direct discourse described as happening in different languages. Rushing highlights this aspect: "We have Africa, South America, the Caribbean, America, and Asia. Already we see that what this 'what if' future history seems to lack is Europe" (8). In particular, Rushing frames this "linguistic cosmopolitanism" (7) within

Wu Ming's category of "New Italian Epic" (NIE), in which Pugno is included. The multilingualism has been a major bone of contention between those who have accused NIE works of being dominated by Anglo-American models and those who sided with Wu Ming 1 and his claim of a "subtle subversion." Fellow NIE writer Girolamo De Michele argues that NIE authors strive to reproduce today's linguistic complexities, although in a "translative," subtle, implicit way.

8. In this respect, *Free Karma Food* (together with *Sirens*) fits in the family of "alimentary" dystopias, which includes films such as *Soylent Green* (1973) and novels like Thomas Disch's *The Genocides* (1965), Paolo Bacigalupi's *The Windup Girl* (2009), and Margaret Atwood's MaddAdam Trilogy, including *Oryx and Crake* (2003), *The Year of the Flood* (2009), and *MaddAdam* (2013).

9. Coined by Masahiro Mori in the field of robotics, this term is not valid exclusively for humanoid robots; its original explanation includes corpses, traditional puppets, and even zombies.

10. Notable examples include "The Principles of Newspeak," George Orwell's famous appendix to *Nineteen Eighty-Four* (1948), and the fictional essay which concludes Margaret Atwood's *The Handmaid's Tale* (1985).

11. Here Atwood suggests that such fictional appendices are meant to undermine the pervasiveness of the dystopian imagination, leaving the door open to hope: "The essay on Newspeak is written in standard English, in the third person, and in the past tense, which can only mean that the regime has fallen, and that language and individuality have survived" (145–46).

12. My use of *polyphony* draws on Meeker's use of the term as necessary to a productive ecosystem. This he opposes to an anthropocentric monologism characterized by a fear of diversity and a tendency to the oversimplification of polar thinking (32).

Works Cited

Agamben, Giorgio. *Homo Sacer: Sovereign Power and Bare Life*. Trans. Daniel Heller-Roazen. Stanford: Stanford UP, 1998.

Antonello, Pierpaolo. "La nascita della fantascienza in Italia: il caso Urania." In *Italiamerica. Le origini dell'americanismo in Italia*, ed. Scarpellini, Emanuela and Jeffrey Schnapp, 99–123. Milan: Il Saggiatore / Fondazione Alberto e Arnoldo Mondadori, 2008.

Atwood, Margaret. *Oryx and Crake*. New York: Anchor, 2004 [2003].

———. *In Other Worlds: SF and the Human Imagination*. Toronto: McClelland and Stewart, 2011.

Baudrillard, Jean. *Symbolic Exchange and Death*. Trans. Iain Hamilton Grant. London: Sage, 1993 [1977].

Benedetti, Carla. *Disumane lettere*. Rome: Laterza, 2011.
Braidotti, Rosi. *Madri mostri e macchine*. Rome: Il manifesto, 2004.
———. *Metamorphoses: Towards a Materialist Theory of Becoming*. Malden: Polity, 2002.
———. *Transpositions: On Nomadic Ethics*. Malden: Polity, 2006.
Cordelli, Franco. "Pincio, ovvero la svista di Giglioli." *Corriere della Sera* (Milan), July 10, 2011, 36. http://archiviostorico.corriere.it/2011/luglio/10/Pincio_ovvero_svista_Giglioli_co_9_110710863.shtml.
De Michele, Girolamo. "'Neorealismo' ed epica. Una risposta ai critici letterari (e agli altri)." *Carmilla*, June 23, 2008. http://www.carmillaonline.com/archives/2008/06/002676.html#002676.
Derrida, Jacques. *L'animal que donc je suis*. Paris: Gallimard, 2006.
Erikson, Erik. "Pseudospeciation in the Nuclear Age." *Political Psychology* 6.2, Special Issue: A Notebook on the Psychology of the U.S.-Soviet Relationship (1985): 213–17.
Giglioli, Daniele. *Senza trauma. Scrittura dell'estremo e narrativa del nuovo millennio*. Macerata: Quodlibet, 2011.
Giovannoli, Renato. "Manzoni e Pierre Menard. L'influenza di Borges sulla letteratura italiana intorno al 1960 e il *Diario minimo*." In *Tra Eco e Calvino: Relazioni Rizomatiche*, ed. Rocco Capozzi, 221–50. Milan: EncycloMedia, 2013.
———. "Montale e la Fantascienza." *Cartevive* 47 (2011): 126–37.
Haraway, Donna J. *Simians, Women, Cyborgs: The Reinvention of Nature*. New York: Routledge, 1991.
———. *When Species Meet*. Minneapolis: U of Minneapolis P, 2008.
Janaczek, Helena. *Mad Cow*. Milan: Il Saggiatore, 2012.
Jay, Martin. *Force Fields: Between Intellectual History and Cultural Critique*. New York: Routledge, 1993.
Ketterer, David. *New Worlds for Old: The Apocalyptic Imagination, Science Fiction, and American Literature*. Garden City, NY: Anchor, 1974.
Meeker, Joseph W. *The Comedy of Survival: Studies in Literary Ecology*. New York: Scribner, 1974.
Mehlman, Maxwell J. *Transhumanist Dreams and Dystopian Nightmares: The Promise and Peril of Genetic Engineering*. Baltimore: Johns Hopkins UP, 2012.
Mori, Masahiro. "The Uncanny Valley." Trans. Karl F. MacDorman and Takashi Minato. *Energy* 7.4 (1978): 33–35. (Now in *Android Science*: http://www.androidscience.com/theuncannyvalley/proceedings2005/uncannyvalley.html.)
Perniola, Mario. *Ritual Thinking: Sexuality, Death, World*. Trans. Massimo Verdicchio. Amherst, NY: Prometheus, 2001.
Proietti, Salvatore. "Ripensando a *Eva*." *Intercom*, 2002. http://www.intercom.publinet.it/ic14/ripenseva.htm.
Pugno, Laura. *Sirene*. Turin: Einaudi, 2007.

Rushing, Robert. "Sirens without Us: The Future of Humanity." *California Italian Studies Journal* 2.1 (2011): http://escholarship.org/uc/item/0cc3b56b.

Wu Ming 1. "New Italian Epic: Memorandum 1993–2008." Revised and expanded version in *New Italian Epic: Letteratura, sguardo obliquo, ritorno al futuro*, ed. Wu Ming, 5–61. Turin: Einaudi, 2009.

——. "L'occhio del purgatorio: i tempi della rivolta e dell'utopia." Talk delivered at Siena University, June 1, 2011. (Podcast: http://www.wumingfoundation.com/giap/?p=4353.)

Wu Ming 5. *Free Karma Food*. Milan: Rizzoli, 2006.

Part 3

Ecologies and Hybridizations

10

The Monstrous Meal

Flesh Consumption and Resistance in the European Gothic

David Del Principe

Vegetarian Monstrosity

In nineteenth-century Gothic literature, allegories of flesh consumption and *procr-eat-ive* aberrance, a resistance to both procreating and eating, mark the monster's transhuman body as a key site of articulation for the construction of species and national identity. In this essay, I employ an ecogothic approach to examine how the Creature in Mary Shelley's *Frankenstein; or, The Modern Prometheus* (1818) and the Count in Bram Stoker's *Dracula* (1898) exhibit an alimentary economy that frames (non) consumption as a construct of monstrosity, setting the benchmark for a transnational discourse articulated in the monstrously troped protagonists of Ugo Tarchetti's *Fosca* (1869) and Carlo Collodi's *The Adventures of Pinocchio* (1883).[1] In these works a recurrent thematics of inappetence coincides with one of procreative stasis: the Creature and the puppet are the products of a procreative collapse, while the Count and Fosca foster one. The Creature's vegetarian decree to eat food that is "not that of man" (Shelley 99) and the Count's habit of not eating animal flesh or, as Van Helsing observes, "not as others" (Stoker, *Dracula* 244) may be seen as a roadmap of counterconsumption, part of a broader trend in Gothic literature to navigate ideologies of nation with the fork. Whether of a human/nonhuman constitution like the Creature, zoomorphic like the Count, a transhuman, arboreal mutant like Pinocchio, or *un*human like Fosca, the monster's body is encoded with a herbivorous form of protest—an alimentary iconoclasm that might be summed up as a politics of "eating (against the) grain." Inscribed with a counterimperialistic ideology, the monstrous body contests the national body's colonizing impulse to consume, challenging the nutritional, evolutionary, and ontological constructs of industrialized society. Such a contestation harbors a Malthusian anxiety over the food supply and population and points to intersecting androcentric and anthropocentric discourses—the demonization, animalization, and feminization of the marginalized Other.

In a society undergoing seismic industrial and evolutionary upheaval, monster figures are cast in the role of contesting conventional food, sex, and species paradigms. With the advent of mechanization and Darwin's theories of evolution, monstrosity became a signifier for radically shifting bodily paradigms—an erosion of distinctions between the species and the sexes that is encoded on the monster's body in the form of allegories of flesh consumption. Nineteenth-century nutritional theory reinstated the dominion of humans over animals and promoted a dissociation between the species that would culminate in institutionalized slaughter and the creation of the modern "food animal"—livestock that is born to die, an abject figure that becomes a fertile source of allegories of monstrosity in Gothic literature.[2] For example, physician George Beard, in *Sexual Neurasthenia* (1898), emphasizes eating high on the food chain—a diet consisting of an "increase [in] the quantity of animal food" and few vegetables—a nutritional decree that can be seen as promoting the modern, institutionalized methods of food production and consumption that the deviantly eating monster rejects (272).[3] As Beard states, in a testimonial to the role that alimentary mores and species hierarchies played in the construction of the protomodern (national) body, "If we know what a nation eats, we know what a nation is or may become," a nutritional dictum that crops up repeatedly in allegories of consumption and monstrosity in Stoker's works and throughout Gothic narrative (282).[4]

Nutritional theory in nineteenth-century Europe was based on principles that upheld the superiority of meat eating and white men. As a result, eating became a powerful site of articulation of species, gender, and racial marginalization. As Carol J. Adams summarizes, "[I]f the meat supply is limited, white people should get it; but if meat is plentiful all should eat it" (40), a racial bias that extends to the construction of gender and nation—feeding men meat before women (and children), especially to enhance military and imperialistic authority. Mothers, in a provocative conflation of alimentary and imperialist rhetoric, were urged "to feed their sons meat daily in order for them to be 'healthy, strong, and courageous,' because 'all courageous animals are carnivorous, and greater courage is to be expected in a people, such as the English, whose food is strong and hearty, than in the half-starved communality of other countries'" (Health Advisor Pye Henry Chavasse qtd. in Vrettos 166). *Frankenstein*, *Pinocchio*, *Dracula*, and *Fosca* reject the imposition of a dominant, meat-eating ideology—dispelling the myths on which military and national hegemony are constructed, especially the association between nutritional, physical, and national aggression—and thus function as a persuasive index of (counter) imperialist sentiment.

The Creature and the puppet eat dissentingly low on the food chain, abstaining from eating (meat) and demonstrating an alimentary resistance that is tied to their reproductive circumstances—their aberrant, motherless births and nonhuman constitution. Their self-imposed hunger and, moreover, rejection of animal-based food underscores a shared past of flesh consumption and an inherently transhuman nature. The Creature is stitched together from both human and nonhuman body parts, the result of meat eating and medical dissection, while Pinocchio is a wooden, arboreal mutant born of mutilating hatchet blows. Both figures are born into an alive/dead state that portrays animal slaughter, butchery, sentience, and fluctuating species boundaries within a multilayered, allegorical framework. The Creature's body, with its highly charged but suppressed history of slaughter, dissection, and bodily disenfranchisement, anticipates the modern slaughterhouse and the "institutionalized [...] industrial compartmentalization of a particular segment of the animal kingdom" (Lee, "Introduction" 2). The Creature's body is, of course, also entrenched in a nineteenth-century discourse about grave robbing that led to the 1832 Anatomy Act and a transformation in medical dissection and education: the replacement of hanged murderers with "the bodies of paupers dying in workhouses and hospitals, too poor to pay for their own funerals" (Richardson xv).

Motherless Parturition

Both the Creature and Pinocchio's bodies and births are presented in a highly allusive way. Laden with carnal innuendo and an air of secretiveness, they summon the anonymity of animal slaughter, serving as allegorical and ideological mediations on the metaphor of meat. Although the Creature does not initially know what he is made of, his musings suggest, especially in the slippage from "who" to "what," a suspicion about his nonhuman origins: "And what was I? Of my creation and creator I was absolutely ignorant; [...] I was not even of the same nature as man [...] My person was hideous, and my stature gigantic: What did this mean? Who was I? What was I? Whence did I come? What was my destination?" (80, 86). While reading Victor's laboratory journal, the Creature makes a crucial discovery, one that enlarges his moral sphere and culminates in the espousal of an ethic of vegetarianism and peace: "You minutely described in these papers every step you took in the progress of your work, this history was mingled with accounts of domestic occurrences [...] 'Cursed creator! Why did you form a monster so hideous that even you turned from me in disgust? God in pity made man beautiful and alluring, after his own image; but my form is a filthy type of yours, more horrid from its very resemblance'" (87–88).

The discovery of his "accursed origin" as part meat is a turning point in the novel in two related ways. It not only causes the Creature to embrace his own alterity and vegetarianism, but it projects Shelley's use of the cloak of fiction to broach a tabooed subject—the animal suffering caused by meat eating—and to pry open the doors of the slaughterhouse.[5] The Creature is, of course, the progeny of a motherless birth, a key factor in the construction of gender subjectivity in *Frankenstein* that, if read through the animal-sensitive, vegetarian frame of Shelley's life, also bears significant implications for the construction of species subjectivity. As Stephanie Rowe points out, "Growing up in the (at times) vegetarian household of William Godwin, whose circle included the chief writers on vegetarianism of the day, and madly in love with Percy Shelley, also a vegetarian, at the time the novel was composed, Mary Wollstonecraft Godwin Shelley was hardly unaware of animal suffering in the world around her, or of the consequences of meat-eating for human health and social justice. Her father had adopted a vegetarian diet around 1804, when Mary was seven" (139).[6]

The key to understanding the role that Shelley's vegetarian experience plays in the formation of the Creature's identity lies in his predeceased past. Because the Creature is composed of dead nonhuman as well as dead human parts resulting from animal slaughter and medical dissection, his birth is, in fact, a unique act of rebirth, reuniting the once-killed bodies of dispossessed communities of animals and humans and raising anthropocentric implications for Victor's androcentric appropriation of female reproductive authority. By identifying the erasure of the womb with the corpses of two species, *Frankenstein* tropes Victor's generative act as both androcentrically and anthropocentrically disenfranchising, a double bind of oppression by which women are figuratively disembodied and non-humans are literally disembodied, designating the Creature's body as an intensely necrophagous site—the point at which flesh consumption and procreation merge with death. As Rowe states, "The materials collected from the slaughterhouse are those of animals other than humans, most likely cows, sheep, pigs, birds, or horses; those collected from the dissecting room might be the remnants of pigs, rabbits, birds, dogs, cats, or apes and other primates including humans—given the Creature's generally hominid form, this last certainly must have been included in its composition" (137).

By creating the "spark of life" from slaughterhouse parts, Victor horrifyingly resuscitates the carnivorous meal whose tabooed specter he, as a carnivore acting on an unspoken, fetishistic desire to both dismember and re-member, finds both intriguing and repulsive. One reason for Victor's unremitting persecution of a being who is, by nature, peaceful is that, as the embodiment of unconsumed, nonhuman corpses, the Creature symbolizes an indictment of the carnivorous act, a threat that necessitates both the silencing of his past—its consignment to Victor's journal—and the eradication of his future. By destroying the Creature's mate and trying to kill the Creature, Victor elevates his penchant for consumption to an act of carnal, double indemnity, killing/consuming what has already been killed—animals as meat—in order to subdue the haunting specter of their living bodies. Victor, confronting the face behind the anonymous, carnivorous meal, fails to kill the part-nonhuman Creature because to do so would cast a symbolic light of complicity on his own carnivorous impulses and nonhuman constitution and thus imply snuffing out the human *and* nonhuman sparks of life that constitute his own body.

Victor's wish to kill a being that is both human and nonhuman infuses his fantasized act of infanticide with meaning on the higher, symbolic order of species and nation. As a composite of slaughtered, nonhuman bodies, the Creature's propagation would not only imply the supplanting of humankind with a "race of devils" but erect a symbolic memorial to a practice whose widespread repercussions are denied a public voice: the institutionalized commodification of animal flesh. Thus Victor, in a moment of apocalyptic panic that bears a chilling resemblance to Jonathan Harker's concern that the Count's transferal to London would unleash an "ever-widening circle of semi-demons" (Stoker, *Dracula* 74), takes on the role of imperial agent, raising his fear of monstrous propagation on the social ladder from family to species to the rung of "world-historical importance" (McLane 981). As Victor insists, "Even if they were to leave Europe, and inhabit the deserts of the new world, yet one of the first results of those sympathies for which the daemon thirsted would be children, and a race of devils would be propagated upon the earth, who might make the very existence of the species of man a condition precarious and full of terror" (Shelley 114).

In order to safeguard the human race from potential annihilation, Victor destroys the Creature's mate, causing the Creature to launch a counterattack formulated in a rhetoric of food and human consumption: "You can blast my other passions; but revenge remains—revenge, henceforth dearer than light or food! I may die; but first you, my tyrant and tormentor, shall curse the sun that gazes on your misery [. . .] Man, you shall repent of the injustices you inflict" (116). The Creature chooses food as a symbolic vehicle for revenge not only because, like light, it is necessary for survival but because the Creature *is* food; he is the carnivorous meal come back to haunt Victor and thus constitutes the battleground on which the struggle between humans and nonhumans takes place.

By creating an innately peaceful offspring, Victor harbors a potentially redeeming quality, one that can be traced to two overlapping experiences with death in Shelley's life—of humans dying in childbirth and of nonhumans dying to make meat—casting *Frankenstein* as her attempt to mourn this loss by eliding two life-affirming experiences, an unmedicalized "maternity" and a vegetarian awareness, onto the body of the Creature. Victor's reproductive ministrations not only erase the womb and the mother from the reproductive equation in *Frankenstein*; they also adumbrate a wish to transform human and nonhuman death into life by begetting, even if inadvertently, a vegetarian creature. As Adams states, "The Creature's vegetarianism serves to make it a more sympathetic being, one who considers how it exploits others. By including animals within its moral circle the Creature provides an emblem for what it hoped for and needed—but failed to receive—from human society" (122). If Victor's actions express a curiosity or "apologetics" for speciesism that originated in Shelley's own experience, his "spark of life" may be seen as establishing a covenant of peace so terrifyingly monstrous to him and his fellow humans that it can only be understood in demonizing terms as an "un-human" creation, a "daemon."

While Collodi's intention may not have been to question flesh consumption through an explicit, ideological consciousness, his transhuman puppet nonetheless follows a similar trajectory to that of Shelley's Creature, exhibiting a nutritional resistance that stresses hunger and cross-species bodily consumption—a reflection of the growing rift between humans and nonhumans caused by the commodification of flesh and the mechanization of food production. Pinocchio either eats low on the food chain—sugar, vetch, candy, cauliflower, straw, and hay (Collodi, *Adventures* 201, 263, 279, 391)—or simply refuses to eat, for example, a walnut and bread (167), adopting a diet distinctly at odds with the dominant, meat-eating ideology.[7]

The puppet's unborn nature and mutability reinscribe the matrophobic, reproductive terms of Shelley's human-animal hybrid, proposing Geppetto as an Italian Victor Frankenstein, an heir to his positivist desire to create life from a nonhuman source. As a nonhuman carved violently from an anonymous, lifeless piece of wood that allusively may contain "someone [...] hidden inside it," the puppet vividly evokes the anonymity of animal slaughter (87). His patrilineal descent, alive/dead state, muted past, and unanatomical construction cast his carved body as mimicking the synecdochal elision that an animal's body undergoes when reduced to a piece of meat. If a butchered animal is a living being made into an anonymous piece of dead meat, Pinocchio is a (half-)dead, anonymous piece of wood "butchered" into a live being. And as an animal is dismembered, defaced, and disfigured to be made palatable for consumption, Pinocchio is a nonhuman that is re-membered, reembodied, and refigured to be made palatably human. In this light, Geppetto and Victor, in their ardent desire to create human from nonhuman life, may be seen as banishing two related fears—the fear of species otherness, of all that is disturbingly non/trans/un-human, and, by eschewing Pinocchio and the Creature's cross-species identities, the atavistic fear of species sameness.

Geppetto and Master Cherry's violent carving of a lifeless, unanatomical, and *dis*figured nonhuman body that is destined, like digested meat, to mutate into human form allegorically casts them as butchers and Pinocchio as a block of *re*figured wood/meat; his monstrous birth, like the Creature's, results in a state of human-directed vengeance and perpetual hunger. While in actual slaughter an animal's voice is silenced, Cherry's carving restores, although in mitigatingly supernatural terms, the puppet's subjectivity and nonhuman voice, instilling it with a spirit of defiance and retribution aimed at his human aggressors: "[H]e quickly grasped his sharpened hatchet so as to begin to remove the bark and whittle the wood down. But just as he was about to strike the first blow he stopped, with his arm raised high, because he heard a thin little voice say pleadingly: 'Don't hit me so hard!' [...] And taking up the hatchet again, he came down with a powerful blow on the piece of wood. 'Ouch! You've hurt me!' The same little voice cried out, complainingly" (83–85).

Cherry's violent use of a hatchet to "deliver" the puppet suggests both a butcher's knife and a forceps, casting him in a dual, symbolic role, as a butcher and a male midwife; he consumes the flesh of the meat/child he symbolically carves up and experiences symptoms of trauma for his complicity in a violent act of slaughter/childbearing: "Master Cherry was petrified, and he stood there with his eyes bulging out of his head with fright, his mouth wide open [...]. His face seemed disfigured, and even the tip of his nose, which was almost always purplish, had turned blue with fright" (85–87). By presumably troping the instrument-based carving as acts of animal slaughter and childbearing, *Pinocchio* constructs a gender/species hierarchy that, as Andrea Henderson points out, draws on androcentric and anthropocentric representations of flesh consumption: "[I]f human flesh starts to look like animal meat in late eighteenth-century [medical] texts [...], it is because men, instrumentarian by nature, have brought their hacking and chopping tendencies to a traditionally female domain" (113).[8] While *Pinocchio* and *Frankenstein*, by hacking or evoking the act, cast maternal and nonhuman bodies as absent or butchered, they also remember their consumed presences, by either stitching together or carving back to life the fleshly reminders of their absence.

The allegory of animal slaughter invites a closer examination of the puppet's transspecies nature. Cherry wonders about his enigmatic past: "But where could that little voice that said 'Ouch!' have come from? [...] I mean, there's not a living soul here [...] I can't believe it. This piece of wood—look at it here. It's a piece of firewood like any other [...] So then? [...] Could someone be hidden inside it?" (87). Cherry's suspicions about the piece of wood foreshadow the unveiling of Pinocchio's hybrid nature and cross-species mutations when, for example, suggestively covered by "donkey bark [...] from head to foot," he is rescued by fish sent by the Fairy to eat away the donkey bark but who, upon coming "to the bone, or rather to the wood [...] [which] wasn't meat for their teeth," become disgusted by "indigestible food" and leave (413–15). This episode of carnal innuendo brings food hierarchies and Pinocchio's transspecies nature, for which his surface bark is a thinly veiled disguise, into congress. As Pinocchio's outer layer is eaten off, a clearer picture of his mutating, tripartite body and pattern of consumption comes into focus. Hidden beneath a surface of bark, Pinocchio's true nature may be bone as well as wood, a glimpse into the puppet's flesh-and-blood identity that the novel pulls in irreconcilable directions—toward plant, animal, mammal, and ultimately human form. In this way *Pinocchio* serves as a testimonial to Collodi's engagement with evolutionary and nutritional thought and, in particular, to his fascination for the role that plants, animals, and humans played in a cycle of consumption driven by the impulse to (not) eat / be eaten. Such an exploration of cyclicality and consumption is reflected in the "horrified" reaction to cross-species consumption that Pinocchio's buyer experiences here, swearing to "never taste fish again" (413) for fear of consuming Pinocchio's body. By questioning what a body destined for consumption really is—"open[ing] a red mullet or a fried hake and find[ing] a donkey tail inside"—the buyer calls attention to taboos on flesh eating, in particular to the question of whose flesh is acceptable to humans (413). By repeatedly subjecting the puppet to carnal and species mutations, *Pinocchio* fractures the tenuous, classificatory borders between the species, disrupting conventional notions of consumption and casting carnivorism and cannibalism as perilously interchangeable on the food chain.

Cannibal Ethics

A similar, *procr-eat-ive* carnal tension, but with a more explicitly cannibalistic design, characterizes *Dracula* and *Fosca*. The Count forsakes the animal flesh that the Victorians eat but consumes human blood, while Fosca's anorexic abstention from eating (meat) leads to a form of displaced cannibalism and the vampiric possession of Giorgio's body. By abstaining from eating meat, while paradoxically cannibalizing humans, the Count carries the Creature's promise of noncarnivorous consumption to a panicked, dystopian extreme, threatening to conflate carnivorism and cannibalism and explode the well-policed, flesh-mediated borders of species identity.[9] While in *Dracula*, Harker eats paprika *hendl*, forcemeat, robber steak, and a roast chicken, the Count eats "not as others," a peculiar habit for which Harker expresses alarm: "It is strange that as yet I have not seen the Count eat or drink. He must be a very peculiar man!" (50). Similarly, an alarmed Van Helsing says, "Even friend Jonathan, who lived with him for weeks, did never see him to eat, never!" (244). While these passages are generally read as an allusion to what the Count does consume, human blood, they may also be read as a commentary on what, or whom, the part-nonhuman Count does *not* consume: the flesh of other nonhumans.[10] By not eating (meat), the Count, like the Creature and Pinocchio, resists indoctrination into the dominant, meat-eating hierarchy, an act of countercultural opposition that threatens to dissolve the carnal borderline between the species and dismantle the alimentary codes that govern the Victorians' lives. By eating in human form as a cannibal but not a carnivore, the Count gains the upper hand in a flesh-based confrontation with Harker (who, with his own flesh on the line at the castle, becomes indifferent to the pleasure of eating) by launching the threat of escalating *intra*species consumption. By casting a light on the tabooed border between carnivorism and cannibalism, the Count poses one of the novel's most potent threats: that carnivorism is suppressed cannibalism or, alternately, that cannibalism is unrestrained carnivorism. Stoker's short story "The Dualitists, or, The Death Doom of the Double Born" (1887) has even stronger, apocalyptic connotations, as suggested when the narrator, relating Tommy and Harry's carnage of animals and humans, provocatively asks, "How was it all to end?" (83). The Count's potential to extinguish humanity by begetting an "ever-widening circle of semi-demons" relates, as in *Frankenstein*, the monstrous extinction of the human species by cannibalism to the human extinction of the nonhuman species by carnivorism—in an industrial society capable of providing a seemingly unlimited supply of meat. Stoker's narrative perilously underscores the contiguity of human and nonhuman flesh, exploding orthodox concepts of species identity by threatening a reversion to the Darwinian, primal state of species sameness that nineteenth-century anthropocentric authority sought so vigorously to suppress.

The vampire's procreative habits constitute a similar act of counterconsumption and threat to the human race. Whether understood as the fruitless union of two vampire parents or of one vampire parent and one offspring, vampire procreation means the conversion of the existing population and thus a state of fixity, negating the creation of a third body and inducing populational stasis. Vampires, by eliding eating, reproduction, and death into one oral act, express a *procr-eat-ive* deviance that invites a comparison to similar forms of resistance as inscribed, for example, on the inappetent, unlaboring body of Tarchetti's Fosca. Fosca is an iconoclastic woman and figurative vampire who does not eat or procreate but who instead takes physical possession of Giorgio's body, engaging in a dual act of counterconsumption that, like vampires, is freighted with cannibalistic overtones. Although her gestation is normal, Fosca experiences an occluded pregnancy, remaining mystifyingly unpartitive: "My child lived but I could not become a mother" (Tarchetti, *Tutte* 347). With no medical explanation for her condition, Fosca's horizontally terminating pregnancy evokes the synecdochal erasure and populational fixity characteristic of vampires, a correlation that is reinforced by the mysterious yet transformative illness that, leaving her bedridden for a year, bears a strong resemblance to vampire conversion: "I miraculously escaped certain death, but now, one year later, I am a corpse, consumed by this illness" (qtd. in Del Principe 94).[11] By remaining permanently indivisible, Fosca's pregnancy terminates statically rather than leading to species propagation and population growth. By not giving birth and, further, aggressively pursuing a carnal, unmarital relationship with Giorgio, Fosca effectively resists bourgeois notions of femininity and maternity, acting in opposition to the dominant constructs of gender in nineteenth-century, patriarchal society.

As with other monster figures, Fosca eats lower than men on the food chain, exhibiting eating habits that contest bourgeois mores. While men share meat-based meals such as turkey and partridge, avoiding the "particularly demoralized vegetables," Giorgio's lover Clara eats "herb stalks" and "musk peaches," and Fosca, accused by the colonel of "never [having] eaten an entire [cutlet] in [her] life," survives "only on coffee" (270, 259, 350, 399, 358). Although Fosca is repeatedly reviled as ugly, there is compelling evidence that her "ugliness," product of the misogynistic, male gaze, may serve to disguise symptoms of hysteria and, moreover, anorexia. As Grazia Menechella points out, "In *Fosca*, as in medical texts of the day, anorexia is one of the symptoms of hysteria; Fosca does not ingest food, nor does she sit at the table to eat but instead 'devours' books and 'devours' Giorgio" (377). She thus engages in suppressed acts of consumption that are transferentially diffused to Giorgio in her vampire-like cannibalization of his body. While men in the novel stigmatize Fosca by associating her mysterious illness with her "hideous ugliness," Giorgio, sensitive to her ostracization, associates her ugliness with her "excessive thinness" (277–78), casting her refusal to eat as an act of self-awareness devised to manipulate the alimentary-gender codes on which "healthy, bourgeois values and rules" such as femininity are constructed (Menechella 377). Indeed, Fosca's skeletal body stands in sharp contrast to conventional representations of the female body that, in Tarchetti's era, was often perceived as having "maternal destiny written all over it, down to [a woman's] skeleton [. . .] [and] ribcage [. . .] more flexible to allow her to breathe better throughout her pregnancy" (Mazzoni 27).

By refusing to eat (meat), Fosca resists the food and gender hierarchies in bourgeois society, rejecting participation in a meat-eating order that conspires to oppress both women and animals. In nineteenth-century Europe, such mutually reinforcing ideologies were constituted by men eating at the top of the food hierarchy, while women were prevented from eating beef and other meats because, as Elaine Showalter explains, meat eating implies a sexual threat: a "carnivorous diet was associated with sexual precocity, especially with an abundant menstrual flow, and even with nymphomania" (129). Showalter's correlation between meat eating and gender ideologies also bears connotations for the development of nationhood, underscoring two interrelated constituents of the patriarchal power structure, violence directed at women and animals that stirs aggression at a national level, and imperialist ferment. Moreover, as indicated before, meat, connoting both physical and social power, was generally reserved for men in a patriarchal order—a policy reflected, for example, in Beard's nutritional recommendation to make "meat the food of choice for white middle-class men, while vegetables and grains, lowest on the meat hierarchy, were left for women and non-white races" (Stavick 25). And as Adams states, meat and vegetables constitute gender-defined food categories: "Meat is king; this noun describing meat is a noun denoting male power. Vegetables, a generic term meat eaters use for all foods that are not meat, have become as associated with women as meat is with men, recalling on a subconscious level the days of Woman the Gatherer. Since women have been made subsidiary in a male-dominated, meat-eating world, so has our food" (43–44).

By rejecting the carnivorous meal and bourgeois codes of maternal behavior, Fosca resists the consumption and commodification of both the nonhuman and female body, contesting the androcentric and anthropocentric hierarchies on which the marginalized body is constructed. As in the case of the Count, Fosca's politics of counterconsumption plays out in the form of carnal displacement—the psychic and physical transference of her "illness" onto Giorgio. Rather than eat the nonhuman other, a reflection of her own objectified, *un*human, or "demonized" self, Fosca takes possession of Giorgio's body in a vampirizing and even cannibalizing act that serves to reverse both the male colonization of her body and, on a broader scale, the patriarchal colonization of the female body. As the Count challenges the flesh-mediated borders between carnivorism and cannibalism, so Fosca crosses the carnal lines separating the sexes, casting her vampiric disembodiment of Giorgio as an act of countercolonization directed against the patriarchal body:

> I cannot say what came over me at that moment. My breathing stopped and I thought my veins and heart would burst. A black shade passed before my eyes and my muscles contracted in a hideous spasm. I fumbled for a moment trying to grab hold of something and then erupted in a piercing, agonizing cry of desperation, the kind unknown to human ears except Fosca's and collapsed into the arms of the doctor who rushed to my side. In that instant I was possessed by the illness that had horrified me for so long: Fosca's disease had been transmitted to me. I finally beheld the pitiful error of my ways and of my love. (qtd. in Del Principe 107)

Fosca's predatory nature is repeatedly couched in a mutually stigmatizing, androcentric, and anthropocentric rhetoric. Trapped in a double bind of oppression targeting both women and animals, Giorgio casts her in a state of gender and species disenfranchisement, as an unhuman or nonhuman "being" and "monster" that culminates in her animalizing transformation into "that wild Creature" (409, 421). Like Lucy Westenra in *Dracula*, Fosca is the victim of a mutually objectifying, speciesistic, and misogynistic male gaze that fetishistically elides the animalization of women with the demonization of animals.[12] Yet *Fosca*, like *Dracula*, mediates in such objectification by employing an iconography of aberrant flesh consumption, cutting across flesh-demarcated, species, and gender lines to broach tabooed subjects about who—men, women, or animals—consumes and who is consumed.

Demographic Resistance

The *procr-eat-ive* deviance inscribed on the monstrous, transhuman bodies in *Frankenstein*, *Pinocchio*, *Dracula*, and *Fosca* can be traced to the influence of Malthusian discourse on nineteenth-century narrative: his fundamental theory that population growth will outstrip the food supply.[13] Whether depicted as vegetarianism or as allegories conveying their authors' convictions about social issues such as population, malnourishment, hunger, and famine, these works portray crises over reproduction and nourishment that reconvene the terms of Malthus's theory by reframing it in the form of dystopian allegories of consumption.

The Creature's body and birth, laced with the threats of an unregulated population and a dwindling food supply, project Shelley's experience with family death and, through carnivorism, animal death, staging an intriguing reenactment of the Malthusian drama.[14] By denying the Creature a mother, *Frankenstein*, like *Pinocchio*, raises Malthus's concerns regarding population within a dialectic of under/overpopulation, restating it as a *de*populating collapse of the bourgeois family and, in Victor's perceived threat of the propagation of a "race of devils," the threat of *over*population. While the Creature's amalgam of bodies tropes Malthus's unchecked population, his herbivorous diet harbors, conversely, a solution for a depleted food supply—tillage rather than pasturage—echoing a model of food production that Malthus treated in considerable depth in *An Essay on the Principle of Population* (1798). In their narrative-long quest to eat plant-centered diets, *Frankenstein* and *Pinocchio* subtly elide the dwindling food supply that Malthus predicted and, especially in the case of the Creature, the specter of modern, institutionalized animal slaughter.

Similarly, the Count and Fosca, by not eating and procreating, recast the Malthusian drama as a crisis of over/underpopulation and over/undernourishment. Fosca's pregnancy terminates, like vampiric gestation, in populational stasis and underpopulation rather than expansion and thus restricts multiplication to a finite pool of subjects and opposes a utopian conceptualization of the healthy, propagating social body. The Count and Fosca's procreative fixity and refusal to eat may be read as a perverse abridgment of Malthus's principle of population, replacing an increasing rate of 1, 2, 4, 8 with a horrifyingly arrested one of 1, 1, 1, 1, treating both horns of the Malthusian dilemma in very different ways. On one hand, their act of counterconsumption unleashes an apocalyptic fear about an imploding population—the eclipse of the human race by a monstrously unhuman or nonhuman one and its subsequent extinction—and on another, it alludes, paradoxically, to the agricultural and social benefits of a plant-based diet in combatting world hunger.

Like the vegetarian Creature, the Count's abstemious consumption and unfecund nature punctuate a Malthusian discourse with populational, nutritional, and agricultural implications of a contrastingly dystopian and utopian nature. By associating the Count's diet and procreative fixity with the desire for immortality, *Dracula* not only stirs up Malthusian anxieties but momentarily lifts the monster's veil to reveal alternatives to social ills, casting the vampire, incongruously, as an emissary of nutritional, contraceptive, and populational messages. Despite such an association, the vampire's primary debt to utopian thought is as a rejection of Godwinian concepts such as biological perfectibility and, furthermore, representations of immortality characterized not by a utopian vision but by starvation, degeneration and, in a nefarious twist on a Swiftean solution for surplus population, eternal cannibalism.[15]

The engagement that the authors in this study had with Malthusian issues either stems from personal experience with issues such as vegetarianism and famine, as with Shelley and Stoker, or, as is the case with Collodi and Tarchetti, is evident in their underexamined, theoretical writings on topics such as hunger and social welfare. Tarchetti's little-known exposé "Hunger" ("*La fame*," 1868) may be seen in this light, serving as a persuasive testimonial of how the author was influenced by Malthusian discourse. Written during the same period in which he wrote *Fosca*, "Hunger" positions Tarchetti as a social theorist deeply engaged in social debate over issues such as nourishment, agriculture, population, war, government intervention, and especially hunger, what he calls "the question of the *utmost importance in Europe*" (297, emphasis in original).[16] Despite its critical neglect, the exposé is particularly important, as it sheds light on the central role that Tarchetti's social convictions played in his intellectual formation and, in turn, in the construction of nutritional allegories in his narrative: "Isn't it painful to think that amidst the agonizing cries of the masses there are people who are concerned solely with armament and future battles? Instead shouldn't all nations and governments join together to declare war on *poverty and hunger*? [. . .] [I]n some of the most populous cities and richest capitals people are dying of hunger [. . .] [W]hile populations await government stimuli, poverty is rampant and the poor classes are decimated by cold and starvation" ("Fame" 297–98, emphasis in original).

Similarly, Collodi, in his equally unexamined work "Bread and Books" ("*Pane e libri*"), demonstrates the high value he placed on the role of nourishment in fostering the well-being of the individual and the social body. Collodi urges Italians to address social and political malaise through a biological valorization of freedom and education, a process that he reasons can only be accomplished with a "nourished stomach" ("Pane" 187). Drawing on a fundamental, utopian concept, the "homological relationship between individual and social organisms" (Gallagher 84), Collodi asserts that that "before all else, man must eat and drink," accusing positivist culture of "reordering the social body"—that is, neglecting the crucial role that sustenance plays in the formation of body and mind: "Nature—positivist par excellence—teaches us that newborn children eat: then they feel and think" (186, 188–89). Collodi's belief that his society has "addressed man's moral and intellectual needs before his most urgent physical ones" testifies to the importance he placed on nourishment and explains the dominant, physical, and "uncerebral" nature of his puppet (186). Collodi reiterates the importance of nourishment in fostering education: "Let's pay a little more attention to the stomach and see if we can introduce human dignity into the bloodstream with bread faster than we can into the mind with compulsory education and books" (189–90). By casting his puppet as constantly famished but nevertheless eating very little and low on the food chain, Collodi rouses Malthus's concerns over the agricultural, economic, and ideological factors that determine the availability of food and the well-being of society. *Dracula*, too, is set against a backdrop of hunger and starvation: the Irish potato blight and famine of the 1840s, a national tragedy that left its mark on Stoker's childhood and narrative. As Sarah Goss states, "Dracula is reminiscent of a survivor of Ireland's Great Hunger. In his refusal to die and stay buried, in his 'persistence' and 'endurance' [...] he can be seen as an image of the Famine's dead, forcing a reluctant memory from the Old pre-industrialized world on the modern New [...] Born in the year the Famine was at its worst—'Black '47'—Stoker grew up in the immediate aftermath of Ireland's shattering trauma. He could not have failed to be influenced by it" (79). Indeed, the sharp contrast between who eats and is eaten or not in *Dracula* can be read as a sobering, Malthusian-inflected reflection on famine and, moreover, its greatest irony: "that it is not about a lack of food [...] [but] about who has access to food" (Campbell Bertoletti 55).

In nineteenth-century Gothic literature, the monster's body challenges newly forming anthropocentric and androcentric hierarchies and epistemologies of commodification, collapsing the carnal borders between the species and causing what Kelly Hurley calls a "radical destabilization of what had formerly been a fixed boundary between man and animal" (56). By engaging in bodily acts of abstention, depopulation, and contraction rather than consumption, reproduction, and expansion, the monster issues a challenge to hegemonic and imperialistic constructions of the national body, establishing a policy of counterconsumption that contests dominant speciesistic and patriarchal models. By eating food that is "not that of man," the Creature, Pinocchio, the Count, and Fosca propose an alternative to the dominant ideology of flesh consumption in modern society, setting a place for the monster and a meal of resistance at humanity's dinner table.

Notes

1. My ecogothic approach applies Ecofeminist, Vegetarian, and Monster Theory to the fields of Animal and Food Studies to examine monstrosity and the construction of species, especially in the

industrializing nineteenth century, when questions of human and nonhuman identity reach a critical crossroads. In this essay I will, at times, use *nonhuman* in place of *animal* to underscore a contrast with the terms *unhuman* and *human*.

2. Chris Otter notes that nineteenth-century Britain's public abattoir radically shifted the methods and apparatus employed for slaughtering animals (90). A breach between the species can be attributed to the displacement of the site of death from urban butchers to more remote locations and, in the twentieth and twenty-first centuries, to the banishment of slaughterhouses to the outskirts of the city. See also Massimo Montanari, *The Culture of Food*, 155.

3. As Montanari notes about evolving eating habits in Europe during industrialization, "[T]he greatest change [. . .] was quantitative: for the first time in many centuries the nutritional role of grains began to decline, while that of other foods, especially meat, increased" (153). Chris Otter states that British consumption of meat "rose from around 80 pounds per person in the 1840s to around 132 pounds per person by the early twentieth century" (89).

4. Athena Vrettos points out that Stoker demonstrated Beard's nutritional dictum by "linking the attainment of perfect health to practical questions of diet—however fantastically" (167).

5. Paula Young Lee addresses the slaughterhouse's forbidden nature: "[I]t deliberately evades the gaze, because for others to witness its activities implies responsibility for the killing, tethering the consumption of mass-produced meat to a collective cultural guilt" (47).

6. *Frankenstein* deterritorializes the anthropocentrically constructed body, a transgressive act that can be traced to Shelley's intense experience with the death of family members—both her newborn child and her mother, Mary Wollstonecraft, who died days after giving birth to her. *Frankenstein*, then, harbors a wish, as Victor says, to "bestow animation upon lifeless matter" (30).

7. With the exception of *Pinocchio*, translations from Italian are my own or are taken from Del Principe, *Rebellion, Death, and Aesthetics in Italy: The Demons of Scapigliatura*.

8. Henderson explains how male midwives replaced female ones in the eighteenth and nineteenth centuries by "undermining public confidence in the midwife's capacities," a phenomenon that contributed to fostering "mechanistic accounts of fetal development and childbirth" and bringing childbearing into "ever-closer alliance with economic modes of production" (100–102). Pinocchio epitomizes such a mechanistic account of childbearing and is an image of the "doll machine," a wooden statue that served as a model of instruction for male students of midwifery (104).

9. Monsters, as Jeffrey Jerome Cohen states, are "disturbing hybrids [...] that threaten to smash distinctions" and who refuse "to participate in the classificatory 'order of things'" (6).
10. The Count becomes a bat and a wolf, but his intuitive contact with animals also implies that, if not by actual transmogrification, he may also be, as Van Helsing intimates, part horse, dog, rat, owl, moth, and fox.
11. As Elena Coda points out, Fosca is cast as having "unhealthy reproductive organs," drawing on the Lombrosian typology of the criminal woman, a stigmatization characteristic of medical portrayals of women in Tarchetti's day (448). Fosca's impaired reproductive system and nulliparous body are associated with animals—for example, in her self-confessed identification with a bird whose nest, like her body, "contained no egg."
12. Such an elision is an example of the recurring, literal demonization of women and animals in Gothic literature, representations that can be traced to Cesare Lombroso's influential work *La donna delinquente* (*Criminal Woman, the Prostitute, and the Normal Woman*, 1893). In this work, he depicts, for example, how "[a]nimalization, or women as cows and mares, combined [...] with anthropomorphization, or animals as nymphomaniacs, in order to homogenize femaleness in the entire animal world" (Mazzoni 171).
13. In *An Essay on the Principle of Population* (1798), Malthus postulated that population increases at a faster rate than its food supplies and, more precisely, that unchecked population increases in a "geometrical" ratio (1, 2, 4, 8, 16, 32, etc.), while subsistence increases only in an "arithmetical" ratio (1, 2, 3, 4, 5, 6, etc.), leading to an inevitable state of misery (Malthus 19–23). While often seen by his contemporaries as a doomsday prophet, Malthus's theories were intended to be ameliorative, recommending policies to improve agriculture, land reform, human labor, and food production, and they remain the benchmark of social policy on hunger.
14. Shelley had firsthand knowledge of Malthus's theories through a prominent debate with her father, in which Malthus countered Godwin's utopian argument for "the link between healthy individual and social bodies" and "biological perfectibility" with the polemical notion that "the unleashed power of population, the reproducing body [...] will eventually destroy the very prosperity that made it fecund, replacing health and innocence with misery and vice" (Gallagher 83–84).
15. Jonathan Swift raises populational issues in "A Modest Proposal," where he satirically proposes offering children as food to address surplus population and poverty in Ireland; Stoker projects many of the traumatic aspects of the famine and starvation experienced by the Irish during his childhood. For a discussion of the Malthusian dilemma in Swift, see Sussman's "The Colonial Afterlife of Political Arithmetic: Swift, Demography, and Mobile Populations."

16. Originally published in the periodical *L'emporio pittoresco* but not included in Ghidetti's two-volume collection of Tarchetti's works, *Tutte le opere*, "Hunger" is a virtually unknown work that was reprinted in a chapter edited by Franco Contorbia in the volume *Convegno Nazionale su Igino Ugo Tarchetti e la Scapigliatura*.

Works Cited

Adams, Carol J. *The Sexual Politics of Meat: A Feminist-Vegetarian Critical Theory*. Tenth Anniversary Edition. New York: Continuum, 2004.
Beard, George M. *Sexual Neurasthenia [Nervous Exhaustion]: Its Hygiene, Causes, Symptoms and Treatment, with a Chapter on Diet for the Nervous*. New York: Arno, 1972 [1898].
Campbell Bertoletti, Susan. *Black Potatoes: The Story of the Great Irish Famine, 1845–1850*. New York: Houghton Mifflin, 2001.
Coda, Elena. "La cultura medica ottocentesca nella *Fosca* di Igino Ugo Tarchetti." *Lettere Italiane* 52.3 (2000): 438–54.
Cohen, Jeffrey Jerome. "Monster Culture: Seven Theses." In *Monster Theory: Reading Culture*, ed. Jeffrey Jerome Cohen, 3–25. Minneapolis: U of Minnesota P, 1996.
Collodi, Carlo. *The Adventures of Pinocchio: Story of a Puppet*. Trans. and ed. Nicolas J. Perella. Berkeley: U of California P, 2005.
———. "Pane e libri." In *Note Gaie*, ed. Giuseppe Rigutini, 185–90. Florence: R. Bemporad and Figlio, 1893.
Del Principe, David. *Rebellion, Death, and Aesthetics in Italy: The Demons of Scapigliatura*. Madison: Fairleigh Dickinson UP, 1996.
Gallagher, Catherine. "The Body versus the Social Body in the Works of Thomas Malthus and Henry Mayhew." In *The Making of the Modern Body: Sexuality and Society in the Nineteenth Century*, ed. Catherine Gallagher and Thomas Laqueur, 83–106. Berkeley: U of California P, 1987.
Goss, Sarah. "Dracula and the Spectre of Famine." In *Hungry Words: Images of Famine in the Irish Canon*, ed. George Cusack and Sarah Goss, 77–107. Dublin: Irish Academic, 2006.
Gregory, James. *Of Victorians and Vegetarians: The Vegetarian Movement in Nineteenth-Century Britain*. London: Tauris Academic Studies, 2007.
Henderson, Andrea. "Doll-Machines and Butcher-Shop Meat: Models of Childbirth in the Early Stages of Industrial Capitalism." *Genders* 12 (1991): 100–119.
Hurley, Kelly. *The Gothic Body: Sexuality, Materialism, and Degeneration at the Fin de Siècle*. Cambridge: Cambridge UP, 1996.
Lee, Paula Young. "Introduction: Housing Slaughter." In *Meat, Modernity, and the Rise of the Slaughterhouse*, ed. Paula Young Lee, 1–9. Durham: U of New Hampshire P, 2008.

———. "Siting the Slaughterhouse: From Shed to Factory." In *Meat, Modernity, and the Rise of the Slaughterhouse*, ed. Paula Young Lee, 46–70. Durham: U of New Hampshire P, 2008.

Malthus, Thomas. *An Essay on the Principle of Population*. Ed. Philip Appleman. New York: W. W. Norton, 2004.

Mazzoni, Cristina. *Maternal Impressions: Pregnancy and Childbirth in Literature and Theory*. Ithaca: Cornell UP, 2002.

McLane, Maureen Noelle. "Literate Species: Population, 'Humanities,' and *Frankenstein*." *English Literary History* 63.4 (1996): 959–88.

Menechella, Grazia. "Scrittrici e lettrici 'malate di nervi' nell'800 e nell'900." *Forum Italicum* 34.2 (2000): 372–401.

Montanari, Massimo. *The Culture of Food*. Oxford: Blackwell, 1994.

Otter, Chris. "Civilizing Slaughter: The Development of the British Public Abattoir, 1850–1910." In *Meat, Modernity, and the Rise of the Slaughterhouse*, ed. Paula Young Lee, 89–106. Durham: U of New Hampshire P, 2008.

Richardson, Ruth. Introduction. *Death, Dissection and the Destitute*. 2nd ed. Chicago: U of Chicago P, 2000.

Rowe, Stephanie. "'Listen to Me': Frankenstein as an Appeal to Mercy and Justice, on Behalf of the Persecuted Animals." In *Humans and Other Animals in Eighteenth-Century British Culture: Representation, Hybridity, Ethics*, ed. Frank Palmeri, 137–52. Hampshire: Ashgate, 2006.

Shelley, Mary. *Frankenstein; or, The Modern Prometheus*. Ed. J. Paul Hunter. New York: W. W. Norton, 1996.

Showalter, Elaine. *The Female Malady: Women, Madness, and English Culture, 1830–1980*. New York: Pantheon, 1985.

Stavick, J. E. D. "Love at First Beet: Vegetarian Critical Theory Meats *Dracula*." *The Victorian Newsletter* 1.89 (1996): 23–29.

Stoker, Bram. *Dracula: Case Studies in Contemporary Criticism*. Ed. John Paul Riquelme. New York: Bedford/St. Martin's, 2002.

———. "The Dualists or the Death Doom of the Double Born." In *Best Ghost and Horror Stories*, ed. Richard Dalby, Stefan Dziemianowicz, and S. T. Joshi, 73–87. Mineola: Dover, 1997.

Sussman, Charlotte. "The Colonial Afterlife of Political Arithmetic: Swift, Demography, and Mobile Populations." *Cultural Critique* 56 (2004): 96–126.

Tarchetti, Igino Ugo. "La fame." In *Convegno Nazionale su Igino Ugo Tarchetti e la Scapigliatura*, 297–300. San Salvatore Monferrato: Il Comune e la Cassa di Risparmio di Alessandria, 1976.

———. *Tutte le opere*. Ed. Enrico Ghidetti. Vol. 2. Bologna: Cappelli, 1967.

Vrettos, Athena. *Somatic Fictions: Imagining Illness in Victorian Culture*. Stanford: Stanford UP, 1995.

11

Contemporaneità and Ecological Thinking in Carlo Levi's Writing

Giovanna Faleschini Lerner

Coexistence and Time

At the core of Carlo Levi's 1950 novel *The Watch* (*L'Orologio*) lies the narrative and theoretical principle of *contemporaneità*, or temporal coexistence, which Levi presents as a corrective to the abstract notion of mechanically measured time. Levi first introduces this concept in a discussion about the realist novel and its impossibility after the historical tragedies of the twentieth century. As the character, Casorin, provocatively asks, "What sort of novel do you want after Auschwitz and Buchenwald?" (*Watch* 56). The Nazi extermination camps are, for Casorin, the inevitable endpoint of the processes of modernity, which isolate the individual from the world and turn him into an object: "A piece of soap that is the body and soul of a man" (56). The story of this soap no longer fits in the orderly world of the realist novel, which has dissolved into the fragments of modernist prose. *The Watch*'s meandering structure, which defies linear temporality, represents Levi's challenge to the possibility of an all-encompassing rational account of human experience.[1] Casorin opposes to the realm of the isolated and abstract individual[2] the more authentic awareness of the connection between humanity and its environment, described through an analogy with the forest as complex ecosystem: "There isn't just one blade of grass in a meadow, there is not one tree but a forest where all the trees stay together, not one in front of the other but merged, big and small, along with mushrooms, bushes and rocks, dry leaves, strawberries, myrtle berries, birds, wild animals, and perhaps fairies and nymphs and boars and poachers, and wanderers who have lost their way, and who knows how many more things. There is the forest" (57). Here, the rhetorical device of the catalogue emphasizes inclusiveness, while the coordinating conjunctions *but* and *and* show how, in the forest of *contemporaneità*, animals, plants, humans, and even sprites coexist in a nexus of relationships that includes predators as well as symbiotic units, outside any hierarchical (and romanticized) organization of the natural world.

The origins of *contemporaneità* can be traced back to *Christ Stopped at Eboli* (*Cristo si è fermato a Eboli*, 1945) and Levi's encounter with peasant philosophy during his southern exile. In a letter to his American publisher, Roger Straus, Levi reminisces about the process of writing *Christ Stopped at Eboli* several years after his stay in Lucania, and he describes the workings of his memory as the unearthing of "the infinite, poetic contemporaneity of all time and every destiny" (*Christ* ix). He explains that the agrarian civilization of Lucania introduced him to "a contemporaneousness that is inexhaustible, existence which is coexistence" (xi). According to the mentality of the southern peasant, "there is no wall between the world of men and the world of animals and spirits, between the leaves of the trees above and the roots below" (77). In this respect, the peasants of Lucania situate themselves in a premodern cultural space, where, as Giorgio Agamben argues, there is no fixed distinction between human, animal, or vegetal world (24). *Christ Stopped at Eboli* describes Levi's fascination with this culture, which has not severed its connection with nature, and he presents it as the essence of all his subsequent work.

Levi's approach to peasant civilization [*civiltà contadina*] is farsighted in anticipating many current ecocritical concerns. I am thinking in particular about Serenella Iovino's definition of nonanthropocentric humanism, an intellectual and critical position that, by "[e]mbedding humanism in an ecological paradigm, [gives] humans not simply the feeling of their intellectual independence from dogma and authorities but, most of all, the awareness of their ecological interdependence" (32–33). Such an approach, Hubert Zapf claims, allows for the breaking up of "dogmatic world views [. . .] in favour of plural perspectives, multiple meanings and dynamic interrelationships" (56). In this respect, an ecocritical stance embraces eccentric and marginalized social experiences (Iovino 37). Levi's writings about the Italian South share this preoccupation with marginalized subjects—whether socially or ontologically excluded from hegemonic intellectual and political discourses. At the same time, an unresolved tension exists between Levi's rootedness in the humanist intellectual tradition and his broader ecological concerns.[3] In this essay, I propose a critical reconsideration of Levi's ecological thinking that both problematizes it and recognizes its contribution to the Italian intellectual, political, and environmental discourse on the South.

My analysis is structured into two parts: in the first I trace the development of Levi's ecological thought from *Fear of Freedom* (*Paura della libertà*, 1946) to *Christ Stopped at Eboli*, whereas the second part touches on a series of essays on animal life that Levi wrote in the 1950s. I argue, in agreement with Franco Cassano's reading of these essays, that Levi's writings on animals constitute the logical point of arrival of the intellectual journey he began during his southern exile. I further propose that the encounter with the peasant civilization of Lucania provoked a radical reconsideration of human existence that, in turn, led Levi to a repositioning of the human in a more complex, less anthropocentric interrelationship with the world. My reading is also informed both by current trends in ecocriticism, specifically Matthew Calarco's and Serenella Iovino's work, and by broader philosophical considerations on the animal in Jacques Derrida's *The Animal That Therefore I Am*.

Rethinking Modernity in Exile: *Fear of Freedom*

Levi's meditation on agrarian culture as an alternative to the abstraction of modern political discourses, developed fully in *Christ Stopped at Eboli*, actually first begins in *Fear of Freedom*, an essay of political and historical philosophy written during his French exile in 1939. In this text, Levi examines the causes of totalitarianism through the notion of the mass, which has a dual meaning. First, mass is—as in physics or chemistry—the indeterminate matter from which all things originate. Within each human being a trace of this original mass remains, "hidden in a depth far deeper than conscience and memory" (*Fear* 72). When, as in the alienating landscape of the modern metropolis, the individual is uprooted from familiar human connections and is incapable of generating new ones, he becomes lost in the mass as "infinite repetition, infinite uniformity, infinite impossibility of correlation" (75). In this experience of modernity emerges, then, the second meaning of mass as crowd. According to Levi, the fear of becoming lost in this indistinct chaos generates the idolatry of the state typical of totalitarianism: "[I]dol-states need the crowd, and create the crowd, and tend, in conformity with their nature, to suppress every personality and every relationship" (75). In both of these notions of mass, Levi laments the loss of individuality, which he opposes to both the indistinction of primal matter and the anonymity of the crowd. According to Levi, the individual is "a work of art: the place of all possible relations" (94). Human life finds meaning in creativity, which coincides with "the identification of man with the world, of every relation as an act of love" (94). Thus the necessary process of individuation must not dissolve the web of natural relationships that constitutes the self. The price of withdrawal from the connectedness of all living beings is abstraction, in its etymological meaning of withdrawal from the material world (131). It is also anonymity, which Levi defines literally as the incapacity to name oneself, the inability to identify oneself as distinct from others and from things, and therefore to speak. Language—and poetic language in particular, with its affective openness to ambiguity—in the crowd of totalitarian regimes is replaced by ritual expressions and symbols, like uniforms, badges, and medals, whose meaning is arbitrary and univocally determined by the structures of power (111).

Nothing could be more different from the linguistic wasteland of the autocratic state than the landscape of Eden, where Adam was invested with the power of naming things, using each word as "poetry, identical with its object and of absolute value" (*Fear* 84). While in the mass-state the relationship between words and their meaning is arbitrary, in the terrestrial paradise words and objects coincided fully and were, thus, poetical.[4] Adam lived in the Garden with woman, animals, trees, stars, and planets: "[H]e was not alone, for he was not separated from them; although an *autonomous being*, he was at one with all; and because he was not alone, not separated, neither he nor they knew death" (84, my italics). His immortality, continues Levi, should be understood not as a continuous temporal flow but rather as *contemporaneità* with living and nonliving things, as being "entirely one with the earth of which he had been formed" (84).

Levi's language here anticipates the discussion of peasant poetry later developed in his lecture called "The Peasant and the Watch" ("*Il contadino e l'orologio*," 1950). For Levi, the rural civilization of Southern Italy has not severed its link with original chaos but exists on the verge of indeterminacy and indistinctiveness from nature. In this vertiginous position, each word pronounced or image evoked is an act of freedom that distinguishes the individual from the undifferentiation of nature ("Contadino" 27). This act of self-distinction, which asserts the existence of the individual and her experience of herself and the world as engaged in a productive and affective relationship, coincides, in Levi's words, with poetry, in its etymological sense of *poiein*—making, creative activity ("Invenzione" 54). Words and images are fully referential in peasant civilization, but if the coincidence between sign and referent makes peasant language Edenic, it also raises issues of power and authority both in regard to animals, who, in Genesis as in Levi's account, are silent and subjected to man's naming, and in regard to Levi's human *others*.

The question of man's authority over animals is central to Jacques Derrida's gloss of Genesis in *The Animal That Therefore I Am*, which offers a productive counterpoint to Levi's theory of Adamitic language. Derrida emphasizes that God "has created man in his likeness *so that* man will *subject, tame, dominate, train*, or *domesticate* the animals born before him and assert his authority over them" (16). Adam names the animals without letting them do the same—a gesture that, in Derrida's reading, asserts both "his sovereignty and his loneliness" (17). Man is alone in naming, because in this version of the creation story he does not yet have woman as a companion and because he sets himself apart from animals. But his is also an act of sovereignty insofar as God does not interfere with his naming but watches as if to be surprised by Adam's creative word. Derrida, like Levi, associates Adam's language with poetry; poetry is tantamount to "God's exposure to surprise," God's openness to hearing Adam's names and even to the possibility of hearing his own name, a sign of both God's omnipotence and his finitude (17). The element of creative surprise excludes the animal, who remains subjected to Adam's despotic rule (18). This rule generates in nature an aphasic sadness, "a foreshadowing of mourning," as Walter Benjamin interprets it (Derrida 20). Derrida reads Benjamin's notion of the sadness of nature not as "a muteness and the experience of a powerlessness, an inability ever to name; it is, in the first place, the fact of *receiving one's own name*" (19–20). Adam's naming, thus, is revealed to imply a violence that renders the animal mute.

Representation, Naming, and *Christ Stopped at Eboli*

Unlike Derrida, Levi does not problematize Adam's naming gesture in relation to animals. *Christ Stopped at Eboli*, however, does bring to the fore his representation of the peasants and their existence as the equivalent of Adam's naming. If in Genesis the animals do not resist Adam's God-given authority, in Levi's memoir the peasants' deep awareness of the imbalance of power inherent in language and representation motivates them to resist being portrayed in Levi's painting—to refuse being "named" and represented, so to speak, in another form of poetic language.[5] In his memoir, Levi describes how his housekeeper, Giulia, systematically refuses to pose for a portrait. According to Giulia, Levi writes, "[a] portrait takes something away from the sitter—to be exact, an image of herself. By this means the painter acquires complete power over anyone who poses for him" (154). I have discussed elsewhere, drawing on Wendy Steiner's study of the role of models in art, how the gendering of the painter as male and the sitter as female is not casual but is an important part of the power relations at work in Giulia's resistance to modeling. The painter's brush becomes a phallic symbol of male dominance over the woman's body, literally objectified in the work of art.[6] Indeed, Giulia's challenge to male creativity is ultimately "corrected" by the threat of physical violence, which restores Levi's authority and finally leads Giulia to sit for him. By including this detail, Levi problematizes the power relationships between artist and subject, which, in *Christ Stopped at Eboli*, can be read in political terms as a metonymy for the relationship between the Northern intellectual and the rural underclass of Southern Italy. Levi frequently grapples with the difference between his own rationalism, rooted in the Enlightenment tradition, and the mentality of Lucanian peasants, connected to ancient cultural forms: "Giulia, who lived in a world ruled by magic, was afraid of my painting her, not so much because I might use the portrait as a waxen image and cast an evil spell upon her, but rather on account of the tangible sway I should exercise over her" (154).

Giulia resists being portrayed because, in her culture, any form of representation asserts the artist's power over his subject. But Giulia's fears also concern her community as a whole. In her view, Levi's painting allows him to exercise power over the entire landscape of her experience, "over the people and things and trees and villages that were the subjects of my painting" (154). In alluding to the artist's authority, Levi again points out the inequality inherent in Adam's naming of animals, expanding his reflection on representation and power to include nonhuman beings. By painting Giulia, the trees, and the villages, Levi objectifies them, even while creating the opportunity for them to emerge to the consciousness of the world beyond Eboli. Indeed, the first meaning of the term *representation* coincides with speaking on behalf of someone, as in a political system of democratic representation of citizens.

Levi's ambitious project in *Christ Stopped at Eboli* is precisely to give voice to the peasants and the landscapes in his paintings in the artistic and the political arena. As Marxist critic Carlo Muscetta famously wrote at the time of the publication of *Christ Stopped at Eboli*, however, Levi remains a Northern intellectual, who, in describing the South, inevitably reduces its reality to his own terms.[7] Levi reflects on this conundrum during a train trip back to Lucania after a leave due to a death in the family. As he reminisces on his conversations over the few days spent among friends and family, Levi recognizes their fundamental estrangement from his experiences in the South. Although politically engaged and passionate about justice and equality, Levi's Turinese friends lack a real understanding of the South. They advance elaborate plans for the resolution of the "problem of the South," which had preoccupied the Italian political élites since Unification, but the solutions they propose, and the language they adopt to describe them, are alien to the reality of Southern Italian peasants. According to Levi, the main issue is the fact that "[t]he State [. . .] cannot solve the problem of the South, because the problem which we call by this name is none other than the problem of the State itself" (250). The solutions that his Turinese associates put forth are based on their transcendent "worship of the State": "Whether it was tyrannical or paternalistic, dictatorial or democratic, it remained to them monolithic, centralized, and remote" (249). Accordingly, "[a]ll of them agreed that the State should do something about [the South], something concretely useful, and beneficent, and miraculous" (250). In Levi's analysis, however, "[t]here will always be an abyss between the State and the peasants, whether the State be Fascist, Liberal, Socialist or take on some new form" (250).

To bridge this abyss, Levi calls for a radical "reversal of the concept of political life"—one that places at its center the individual as "a link, a meeting place of relationships" and as the building block of the State (253). The peasants' notion of the individual as connected to all other living beings is clearly at the core of Levi's idea and the only way out of the fascist (and antifascist) worship of the State (223). He thus highlights how peasant culture offers a productive alternative to fascist state absolutism, and he legitimizes the South as an autonomous agent of change in the Italian political arena. While criticizing the political leadership for not understanding the peasant classes, however, he reasserts his own power as a Northern intellectual and a member of the same political élite he deprecates: "[T]he political leaders and *my* peasants could never understand one another" (249, my emphasis). With the possessive "my," Levi implicitly situates himself in a position of authority, emphasizing the tensions inherent in his own sympathetic approach toward the Southern peasant classes.[8]

In his exploration of Lucanian rural civilization, Levi tries an alternative to Western rationalism in order to gain access to what he calls the peasants' "magical thinking." Upon arriving in Gagliano, the hamlet where he spent two years in exile, Levi is warned that he should guard himself from women's love potions; Giulia is widely considered a witch: "She knew herbs and the power of talismans; she could cure illness with the repetition of spells and she could even bring about the death of anyone she chose by uttering terrible incantations" (107). Even the village air is filled with spirits and divine presences that, in peasant mentality, often become embodied in animals. Animals appear frequently in *Christ Stopped at Eboli*, where they have a very material, as well as symbolic, presence. The ubiquitous goat is, for example, a source of practical financial concern, since the central government imposed a heavy tax on this animal based on its imagined omnivorous threat to agriculture. On another level, the goat is demoniacal: "a living satyr, lean and hungry, with curling horns, a crooked nose, and pendulous teats or male organ; a poor, hairy, brotherly, wild satyr" (66). The animal's "brotherly" quality points to another fundamental aspect of Levi's understanding of peasant culture: its sense of a common earthly existence encompassing human as well as nonhuman and botanical life forms. The recognition of this commonality brings to the fore the mysterious power of this relationship, which—as Levi's description of the goat as satyr shows—shares something of the divine.

Since "there is no definite boundary line between the world of human beings and that of animals or even monsters" (*Christ* 112), there is nothing strange in the fact that certain creatures have a dual nature, being at the same time fully human and fully animal. As Agamben writes, in this premodern culture there exist "zones of indifference in which it [is] not possible to assign certain identities" (24). A woman from Gagliano, for example, is known as having both a human and a bovine mother (*Christ* 98); Giulia instructs Levi on how to respond if a werewolf comes knocking (99); Levi's own dog is named Barone, and the villagers recognize in him both leonine, and human characteristics (102). This duality is particularly evident in Levi's description of his first encounter with Giulia. Her body, he notices, breathed "an animal vigor" (105) and moved with "the nimble agility of a goat" (107). Her eyes "had whites with blue and brown veins in them like those of dogs" (105). When she laughs, her lips uncover "sparkling, wolf-like teeth" (105, translation modified). She has a "the small, black head of a serpent" (106). Giulia belongs, in other words, to a human society that has not broken its connection with animality but, on the contrary, recognizes the symbiotic unity of all living things. Giulia's magical powers and wisdom, connected to the earth and its rhythms, are directly contrasted with the rationalism of the "mathematical countryside of Romagna" (268, my translation). The orderly vineyards of the Piedmontese hills and the checkerboard regularity of the fields of the Po Valley are, in Levi's view, the product of modernity, with its rationalist, exploitative mentality.

If, upon his arrival in Gagliano, Levi saw himself as a representative of modern rationalism and considered peasant culture as fundamentally foreign, *Christ Stopped at Eboli* records the development of a radically different attitude. His familiarity with Giulia leads Levi to reformulate his definition of knowledge to include folkloric wisdom. Incorporating in his own writing the local beliefs in the power of magic, Levi writes, "Magic can cure almost any ill, and usually by the mere pronouncement of a spell or incantation" (237). Here Levi does *not* adopt a Verghian form of impersonality, which would appropriate the language of the people through free indirect discourse. The voice describing the ability of magic to cure is unequivocally Levi's own, and the Turinese intellectual seems to embrace the folkloric mentality: "I respected the amulets, paying tribute to their ancient origin and mysterious simplicity, and preferring to be their ally rather than their enemy" (238). His respect goes further. The sick hide their amulets when he visits them, aware that, as a man of science, he might scoff at their superstition. Levi criticizes Northern condescension, however: "This is all very well where reason and science can take over the role of magic, but in this remote region they are not yet, and perhaps never may be, deities which enjoy popular worship and adoration" (238). Here Levi challenges the modern dismissal of folkloric thinking as superstition by suggesting the equivalence between the belief in magic and the belief in science and reason. Although fundamentally different in method, Levi implies that both rationalism and magical thinking tend to assert themselves as absolutes that leave no space for the incongruities of human experience. To accept modern medicine while still relying on amulets seems to indicate a third cultural space, in which scientific thought and magic coexist. The peasants' embrace of the mysterious complexity of life—of which their valorization of the dual nature of animals and humans is an additional example—seems to reflect a greater wisdom than the rationalistic rejection of that which cannot be explained in scientific terms.

Southern Thinking

In the peasants' way of life, then, Levi finds a liberating approach to human existence, an alternative to the strictures of rationalist modernity. Franco Cassano, the theorist of Mediterranean thought, recognizes in Levi's writings about Lucania a view of the South akin to his own. Both he and Levi conceive the "Southern thinking" as a critical position from which to observe the hegemonic North-West axis. As we have seen, in *Fear of Freedom* Levi clearly draws a connection between modernity and the ascent of the totalitarian regimes responsible for the tragedies of the twentieth century. As Levi argues in another essay, "Fear of Painting" (*"Paura della Pittura"*), modernist art reflects the alienation brought about by industrial modernity. For Levi, even Picasso's work, exemplified by *Guernica* as a gesture of resistance to the destructive powers of totalitarianism, ultimately mirrors fascism's destruction of the human. Picasso's gesture of protest is empty, uprooted from reality, as abstract as the individual itself, lost in the chaotic uniformity of the mass (132–33). In the peasants' visceral attachment to the land, their profound grounding in their secular rural traditions, Levi recognizes a corrective to the existential deracination of modern man. Seen from this perspective, *Christ Stopped at Eboli* is much more than an ethnographic account of Lucanian folklore; it is an argument for preserving the culture of the rural South, in all its radical difference, as a form of resistance in the face of Northern dominance.

Levi's analysis is, then, deeply connected to the political and historical reality of his time. Beginning with his analysis of totalitarianism in *Fear of Freedom*, in fact, he suggests a fundamental equivalence between modernity and the fascist state. Indeed, Mussolini's fascism accelerated Italian entry into modern Europe through a series of national campaigns that were meant to place Italy on the same level as Northern European nations. The grand land reclamation projects, the electrification of the railroad network, and the push toward a strong national industry were all part of Mussolini's vision of a truly modernized nation. As Ruth Ben-Ghiat has argued, "[F]ascism appealed to many Italian intellectuals as a new model of modernity that would resolve both the contemporary European crisis and long-standing problems of the national past" (2). The futurist allegiance to fascism is connected to the modern ideals the fascist regime seemed to advance; rationalist architecture, too, was embraced by fascism, as the Casa del Popolo in Como or the EUR in Rome still testify.[9] It seems, then, only natural that the antifascist Levi, upon encountering a civilization that defied the state-imposed drive toward modernity, would see it as a form of cultural and political resistance to fascism.

For both Cassano and Levi, at the core of this resistance lies the temporal dimension. Cassano emphasizes the value of *lentezza*, or slowness, as the Southern temporality, and he discusses it in terms of plurality of time. Levi's *contemporaneità*, too, describes a complex, nonlinear notion of time, in which different temporal planes coexist. In *Modernizing Makes You Tired* (*Modernizzare stanca*, 2001), Cassano offers a critique of modernity's alienating emphasis on the ideal of the *"homo currens"* ("running man"), which is merely "an appendix of the production machine that he built" (Bouchard and Ferme xxvii). He argues for the need to embrace a slower pace of living to recover the fullness of human experience. One of his proposed practical strategies is *passeggiare* (strolling), which may mean "having a dog as a friend, or a friend that is as free as a dog, with whom you can talk about anything, someone who will listen to you and feels like wasting time with you" (*Modernizzare* 149).

The reference to human–animal friendship is not casual here. Cassano traces the origin of his Mediterranean thought to early experiments with the experiences of others—whether individuals of other gender, of different ethnic and national origins, or even nonhuman animals (Fogu and Cassano). He devotes one section of *Approximation: Exercises in the Experience of the Other* (*Approssimazione: Esercizi di esperienza dell'altro*, 2003) to an exploration of animal perception, written to challenge the teleological anthropocentrism implied in the evolutionary perspective (13). By structuring his investigation around the five senses, he shows how animal perception reveals a wide spectrum of experiences that escape human consciousness, reminding us, as Italo Calvino observes in *Mr. Palomar*, that "the world of man is not eternal and is not unique" (86). But Cassano also explicitly questions the legitimacy of using human intelligence as a criterion to adjudicate the superiority of one life form over the other, rejecting the rationalist view of "problem solving" as an ontological standard (46). He thus firmly situates himself within a postmodern reassessment of Enlightenment reason and its limitations and opens up new ecological, posthuman dimensions of thought.[10]

In particular, Cassano's thinking echoes Derrida's meditations in *The Animal That Therefore I Am* when the philosopher invites his audience to contemplate the active animal gaze, for, "as with the eyes of the other, the gaze called 'animal' offers to my sight the abyssal limit of the human" (12). According to Derrida, the limit of philosophy consists precisely in its disavowal of the animal's ability to see, a disavowal that masks a profound anxiety about what is properly human (14). In dealing with the animal, thus, philosophy has either tended toward anthropomorphism or deprived the animal experience of any power of manifestation (18). Heidegger's understanding of the animal as "poor in world" evokes a lack—specifically, the aforementioned sadness at the inability to name oneself and instead having been named (19).[11]

As we have seen, Derrida's preoccupation with the human power of naming the animal univocally, which he sees as a logocentric form of violence, resonates deeply with Levi's own ethical and political concerns in *Christ Stopped at Eboli*. After his encounter with the otherness of Lucania, Levi becomes persuaded, like Derrida, that rationalist humanism ultimately constitutes a betrayal "of repressed human possibilities, of other powers of reason, of a more comprehensive logic of argument" (Derrida 105). *Christ Stopped at Eboli* thus chronicles Levi's attempt to embrace the "more comprehensive logic" of the Lucanian peasants, who refuse binary thinking within the multiplicity of living, without denying the "abyss" that separates different forms of life. Indeed Levi, in tune with Cassano, recognizes the impossibility of completely letting go of one's historically determined perspective. As Cassano observes, any exercise in "approximation" must acknowledge that "ultimately, precisely our respect of the radical otherness of the other will show that even the most fantastic and generous effort is only a station within ourselves" ("Approssimazione" 7, my translation). Cassano recognizes, then, the unbridgeable gap between self and other, the "absolute transcendence of the other," which both inspires Levi's search for an original expressive code through which to recount his encounter with alterity and remains as an unresolved tension in *Christ Stopped at Eboli*.

Animal Life and Coexistence: *The Reasons of the Mice*

Cassano's ecological preoccupation with an integrated, holistic approach to human and nonhuman experience—in turn influenced by Derrida's thinking about the animal—also helps illuminate the series of texts in which Levi directly deals with animality, published posthumously as *The Reasons of the Mice* (*Le ragioni dei topi*, 2004). Most of the pieces are autobiographical sketches published in the late 1950s and early 1960s in *La Nuova Stampa* (later *La Stampa*), the Turin-based daily. All have the animal world as their subject. In his introduction to the volume, Cassano recognizes that Levi's writings on animal life can be read as the point of arrival of his intellectual journey in the South and reflect his ecological concern, absorbed during his exile, with the interconnectedness of all living beings ("Compresenza" xv–xvi). The impact of the peasants' philosophy of complexity and ambivalence can indeed be recognized in the stories collected in the volume, in which Levi portrays sea monsters, magical birds, and archetypal reptiles that are both real and mythical, ancient and modern. The animals' dual nature echoes the peasant's understanding of the nature of all things in *Christ Stopped at Eboli*, thus establishing the roots of Levi's approach to animal life in his southern exile.

Particularly important in the texts of *The Reasons of the Mice* is the notion, which first emerged in *Christ Stopped at Eboli* and was later elaborated in *The Watch*, of *contemporaneità*, or temporal coexistence. Levi opens the story "The Owl" ("*Il gufo*") by reexamining the mythical status of nocturnal birds in classical times and Romantic literature, from the Athenian owl to Ossian's funereal bird (*Ragioni* 5). From here springs his own emblematic use of the owl as an archetypal symbol of time, a witness to its eternity: the owl is a symbol "of the origin of time, because of its infinite antiquity, and that of the end of time, for its character as the final judge" (5).[12] For this reason, the figure of the owl dominates the pages of *The Watch*, set in Rome as the "Eternal City" (7). Levi thus institutes a direct connection between the stories collected in *The Reasons of the Mice* and *The Watch*. The texts' common preoccupation with *contemporaneità* can be traced to the fact that Levi's animal stories all take place in the "secretly sylvan" Rome, populated by a hidden fauna of "crickets, scorpions, geckos, snakes, butterflies, dragonflies, bees, ticks, cockroaches, beetles, reptiles and birds of all kinds, and marble elephants and lions" (*Ragioni* 27). These animals live in Rome as in a space defined by "the synchronicity and the juxtaposition of times and individual destinies," as he writes in a 1960 essay, "The Roman People" ("*Il popolo di Roma*"), now published in *Fleeting Rome* (*Roma fuggitiva*, 2002; 17).

Thus in "The Life of the Little Ones" ("*La vita dei piccoli*"), a story in which Levi recounts his misadventures with the mice, turtles, and ducks cohabitating in his Roman villa, the duck's assault on Levi's housekeeper is recast in mythical terms as a new version of Leda's encounter with the divine swan: "While she was bringing, as she did every morning, their feed to the mute ducks that lived in the garden, the big male duck, with his gleaming metal black-green feathers and his eye framed in flaming red, all of a sudden attacked her, certainly moved by an animal sort of mythological love [. . .] This new Leda had experienced something of the ancient fear, the awesome presence of a god" (*Ragioni* 33). This passage perhaps seems to fall into the trap of fabulization, which Derrida describes as "an anthropomorphic taming, a moralizing subjection, a domestication" of the animal, entirely designed for and subjected to man (32). Yet in the stories and essays collected in *The Reasons of the Mice*, Levi in fact resists anthropomorphization, highlighting instead the "heterogeneous multiplicity of the living" (Derrida 31). Animals are cast as concrete reminders of the interrelatedness of human and nonhuman experiences, but they are also material beings engaged in the specificity of their own existence.

In an exemplary episode, a lizard on the wall of St. Agnes church in Piazza Navona in the tepid heat of a January sun is "an animal of time" (*Ragioni* 28). Contemplating the lizard, Levi is reminded of his own childhood garden hunts, of the poet Giacomo Leopardi's first winter in Rome, and of a nineteenth-century naturalist's account of the first seasonal appearance of lizards in the Roman piazzas, where, in Levi's words, "they delight in eternity" (29). For Levi, the lizard, as a primitive reptile, is a symbol of time that advances but never arrives and defines Rome as a palimpsest of different epochs and civilizations (29). Levi, adopting the lizard's temporality as a model, depicts a Piazza Navona where time is dilated into an entirely subjective dimension, occupied by memories, desires, and oneiric visions, defying the forward movement of history. These spaces and these animals become reminders of the coexistence of the prerational dimension—the remnants of primordial chaos—and reason within us. They are spaces, in other words, of *contemporaneità*.

From the perspective of *contemporaneità*, perhaps the most compelling text in the collection is "Dawn in the Garden" ("*L'alba sul giardino*"). The story's main character is the garden of Levi's Roman residence, Villa Strohl-Fern, near Piazza del Popolo. At dawn, the garden awakens, repeating the miracle of creation when the first heroic bird bursts into song. It is a space of wholeness and inclusion, in which one can find "[h]olm oaks, pine trees, poplars, and a great Lebanon cedar [standing out] against the sky, and oleanders, and ivy on the hedge, and a medlar tree, and grass; [...] roses, tall sunflowers, and vegetables: lettuce, tomatoes, flavorful herbs, basil, rosemary, and garlic and onions mixed up with irises and pansies, with splendid sage and fuchsias, dahlias, hydrangeas" (*Ragioni* 77). It is, in other words, a terrestrial "paradise of trees and birds, a green oasis, guarded by gatekeeping angels, and closed off by the four rivers" (73).

This paradise is, however, threatened by the intrusion of a worker ordered to cut down the grove of rare bamboo edging the garden. This urban Eden is but an ephemeral illusion, destined to end when the rational forces of modernity enter its space. The desire—epitomized in Adam's authoritarian naming of animals—to impose human rule on the natural world is destined to destroy the garden and, with it, the possibility of a wholeness with nature. Levi's text thus explores the philosophical and existential implications of the experience of "exile, the loss of the golden paradise that precedes birth, and of the green paradises of childhood" (91). His Edenic loss is the equivalent of Pier Paolo Pasolini's lament over the disappearance of fire flies, a symbol of the lost purity of preindustrial eras.[13] At the same time, though, the loss of the bamboo is represented as an ill omen connected—in the temporality of *contemporaneità*—to what happens outside the garden, for "the trees, too, carry the burden of a common destiny" (81). The French testing of nuclear warheads in the Algerian Sahara and the vote of confidence for the new government led by the conservative Christian Democrat Fernando Tambroni in 1960 are two events that, in Levi's account, the cutting of the bamboo anticipates. The strange behavior of the garden animals, from the rats that invade his house only to suddenly disappear, to Pasqua, the tortoise that used to follow him everywhere and is suddenly gone, signals "a sense of loss, uncertainty, and death" in Levi's paradise (89). In Levi's garden, the concurrence and correspondence of all things, private, existential, and public, are potentially preserved, maintained intact from the "awakening of screeching or deep sirens, screams, mechanical noises of engines, drain pipes, flushes, elevators, automobiles and tramways, dead objects, pop art, commonplaces, collective jailers, plaster triangles" (73). Yet his garden is under siege by the forces of modernity and ultimately destined to fall.

It is the ability to recognize and maintain the connections among individuals, epochs, and species that Levi admired in Lucanian civilization. Indeed, as Cassano makes clear in his introduction to *The Reasons of the Mice*, Levi's lament for the way that modernity frayed the fabric of social relationships and destroyed the connection between humans and animals does not coincide with a desire for regression to a mythical harmony with nature (xxii). On the contrary, Levi's attention to the natural world is motivated by its ability to offer a richer form of culture that welcomes "the entire complexity of the world, the multiplicity of its life forms, the richness of its rhythms" (xxii). While the values of technological progress are narrowly defined in ethno- and anthropocentric terms, "The coexistence of different times," writes Cassano, "designates a completely different perspective, based on a Goethian complicity and friendship with the world and all of its expressions" (xxii).

Levi's interest in the animals that share his space is thus a natural result of his work as a "witness of the presence of another time within our time, [...] the ambassador of another world within our own" (my translation), as Calvino wrote in an article for the journal *Galleria*, now regularly included in the Italian edition of *Christ Stopped at Eboli* (x). In "The Life of the Little Ones," Levi quotes Rocco Scotellaro's poem in which the subaltern classes of Southern Italy are compared to mice, which nobody believes have eyes and a will of their own: "They do not believe, and that small and crooked man, / that mice can be silent in the light of day: / they would like to light the lamps, / to poison their pasta!" (qtd. in *Ragioni* 32). Through Scotellaro's words, Levi invites his reader to look through the eyes of the mice, not to repress that *other* "ancient heart, / solemn mouse that does not come out / and cannot express itself." For Levi, as for Derrida, the openness to the diversity of animal experiences is inextricably connected to the experience of difference *tout court* and a condition for a fully ethical engagement with this otherness.

But for Levi, as we have seen, the otherness of rural Southern civilization is associated not only metaphorically but also concretely with animal life. The Lucanian peasants are closely tied to the animals that accompany their daily labor and to the seasonal rhythms of the earth that sustains them. Unlike the industrial North, their culture has not turned against its own soil in the rational exploitation made possible by technology. Their temporality is one of "coexistence of different temporalities and the eternity of myths" (*Ragioni* 33), where, as Levi writes in *A Face That Resembles Us* (*Un volto che ci somiglia*, 1960), "the archaic is very close and familiar, everything remains without wasting itself, [...] centuries overlap, [...] and contradictions become identity" (23, my translation). In this sense of *contemporaneità*, Levi recognizes the basis for social and ecological solidarity, the awareness of a common belonging that invests both human and nonhuman beings and that is the only possible form of resistance to any fundamentalism.

Levi's ecological thought is fraught with the tension between the rationalist impulses of (human) language and the emergence of other categories of experience that language cannot apprehend. The disparity between his authority as writer and artist and Giulia's power of resistance in the face of his desire to represent her remains unresolved, both in *Christ Stopped at Eboli* and in other texts about the South, where this tension assumes broader political connotations in the context of North–South relations.[14] Yet Levi is not afraid of confronting these contradictions in his writings, where he explicitly thematizes and explores them. Thus, far from being regressively nostalgic, Levi's discussion of peasant civilization anticipates by several decades the concerns that have become the focus of ecocritical and ethical approaches to the arts and proves a crucial contribution to the formation and development of these critical positions in the Italian cultural landscape.

Notes

1. *The Watch* begins when Carlo, the first person narrator, sets out to find a place to repair his broken watch. His wanderings around Rome offer constant narrative shifts between past and present, memories and dreams, descriptions and digressions, subverting realist structural logic.
2. Levi first uses the term "abstract" in *Fear of Freedom* (*Paura della libertà*) to refer to the absence of meaning and the fear of engagement with the world that he attributes to modernity (105–6).
3. This tension is perhaps inherent in the definition of a nonanthropocentric humanism and its positioning within the humanist tradition but beyond the split between human and nature (Iovino 47).
4. This is one of the many contradictions that emerge in Levi's ecological thinking: although language is entangled with the material world, seemingly anticipating positions theorized by material ecocriticism, Levi's discussion of Adam's Edenic naming power is manifestly anthropocentric, as it entirely ignores the "entangled agencies" of animals and world (Iovino and Oppermann 466).
5. Levi uses the term *poetry* to encompass all forms of human creativity, so that "every mark, every sign, [is] painting" (*Fear* 94).
6. For a more detailed discussion of gender and authority in portraiture, see Steiner, *The Real Real Thing*, 15ff; and Lerner, *The Painter as Writer*, 30ff.
7. For more on Muscetta's and other critical reactions to *Christ Stopped at Eboli*, see Gigliola De Donato and Sergio D'Amaro, *Un torinese del sud*, 178.
8. His own failure to become a truly organic intellectual in the Gramscian tradition is, perhaps, what prompted him to champion Rocco Scotellaro, a Lucanian poet and activist, who became for Levi the symbol of the potential for radical reform in the South.
9. In addition to Ben-Ghiat's book *Fascist Modernities*, other recent scholarly accounts of fascist modernity are Claudia Lazzaro and Roger J. Crum's *Donatello among the Blackshirts* and Emilio Gentile's *The Struggle for Modernity*.
10. On the need to reconsider the ontological primacy of human reason, see Iovino and Oppermann, "Material Ecocriticism: Materiality, Agency, and Models of Narrativity."

11. Calarco complicates Derrida's reading of Heidegger, stating that his "reflections on the human/animal distinction present [...] an effective challenge to metaphysical *humanism* on the one hand [...] but an extremely problematic reinforcement of metaphysical *anthropocentrism* on the other" ("Heidegger" 29). Calarco's understanding of Heidegger's position reveals the same tension that underlies Levi's concept of poetry. In discussing Edenic language, Levi advocates a use of language that embraces materiality while positing language as indispensable to self-consciousness and thus excluding animals and other material beings from agency. This inconsistency results from Levi's attempt to reconcile his desire to give voice to marginalized forms of existence with a deeply rooted humanism.
12. All translations from *The Reasons of the Mice* are mine.
13. See Pasolini, "La scomparsa delle lucciole."
14. See, for example, *Le parole sono pietre* or *Tutto il miele è finito*.

Works Cited

Agamben, Giorgio. *The Open: Man and Animal*. Trans. Kevin Attell. Stanford, CA: Stanford UP, 2003.

Ben-Ghiat, Ruth. *Fascist Modernities: Italy 1922–1945*. Berkeley: U of California P, 2001.

Bouchard, Norma, and Valerio Ferme. "Preface to the English-language Edition." In *Southern Thought and Other Essays on the Mediterranean*, by Franco Cassano, ed. and trans. Norma Bouchard and Valerio Ferme, xxvii–xxxii. New York: Fordham UP, 2012.

Calarco, Matthew. "Heidegger's Zoontology." In *Animal Philosophy: Essential Readings in Continental Thought*, ed. Matthew Calarco and Peter Atterton, 18–30. New York: Continuum, 2004.

———. *Zoographies: The Question of the Animal from Heidegger to Derrida*. New York: Columbia UP, 2008.

Calvino, Italo. "Adam, One Afternoon." In *Difficult Loves*, trans. William Weaver, Archibald Colquhoun, and Peggy Wright, 3–15. San Diego: Harcourt Brace Jovanovich, 1984.

———. *Mr. Palomar*. Trans. William Weaver. San Diego: Harcourt Brace Jovanovich, 1985.

Cassano, Franco. *Approssimazione. Esercizi di esperienza dell'altro*. Bologna: Il Mulino, 2003.

———. "La compresenza dei tempi. Introduzione." In *Le ragioni dei topi. Storie di animali*, by Carlo Levi, ed. Gigliola De Donato and Luisa Montevecchi, xiii–xxv. Rome: Donzelli, 2004.

———. *Modernizzare stanca. Perdere tempo, guadagnare tempo*. Bologna: Il Mulino, 2001.

———. *Southern Thought and Other Essays on the Mediterranean*. Eds. and trans. Norma Bouchard and Valerio Ferme. New York: Fordham UP, 2012.
De Donato, Gigliola, and Sergio D'Amaro. *Un torinese del sud: Carlo Levi*. Milan: Baldini and Castoldi, 2001.
De Donato, Gigliola, and Luisa Montevecchi. "Presentazione." In *Le ragioni dei topi. Storie di animali*, by Carlo Levi, ed. Gigliola De Donato and Luisa Montevecchi, ix–xii. Rome: Donzelli, 2004.
Derrida, Jacques. *The Animal That Therefore I Am*. Ed. Marie-Louise Mallet. Trans. David Wills. New York: Fordham UP, 2008.
Fogu, Claudio, and Francesco Cassano. "Il pensiero meridiano oggi: Intervista e Dialoghi con Franco Cassano." *California Italian Studies* 1.1 (2010): http://escholarship.org/uc/item/2qf1598v#.
Gentile, Emilio. *The Struggle for Modernity: Nationalism, Futurism, and Fascism*. Westport, CT: Praeger, 2003.
Iovino, Serenella. "Ecocriticism and a Non-Anthropocentric Humanism." In *Local Natures, Global Resposibilities: Ecocritical Perspectives on the New English Literatures*, ASNEL Papers 15, ed. Laurenz Volkmann, Nancy Grimm, Ines Detmers, and Katrin Thomson, 29–53. Amsterdam: Rodopi, 2010.
Iovino, Serenella, and Serpil Oppermann. "Material Ecocriticism: Materiality, Agency, and Models of Narrativity." *Ecozon@* 3.1 (2012): 75–91.
Lazzaro, Claudia, and Roger J. Crum, eds. *Donatello among the Blackshirts: History and Modernity in the Visual Culture of Fascist Italy*. Ithaca: Cornell UP, 2005.
Lerner, Giovanna Faleschini. *The Painter as Writer: Carlo Levi's Visual Poetics*. New York: Palgrave Macmillan, 2012.
Levi, Carlo. "L'arte luigina e l'arte contadina." In *Prima e dopo le parole. Scritti e discorsi sulla letteratura*, ed. Gigliola De Donato and Rosalba Galvagno, 37–50. Rome: Donzelli, 2001.
———. *Christ Stopped at Eboli*. Trans. Frances Frenaye. New York: Farrar, Straus and Giroux, 1974 [1947].
———. "Il contadino e l'orologio." In *Prima e dopo le parole. Scritti e discorsi sulla letteratura*, ed. Gigliola De Donato and Rosalba Galvagno, 17–35. Rome: Donzelli, 2001.
———. *Fear of Freedom. With the Essay "Fear of Painting."* Trans. Adolphe Gourevitch. Ed. Stanislao Pugliese. New York: Columbia UP, 2008.
———. *Fleeting Rome*. Trans. Anthony Shugaar. Chichester, West Sussex: John Wiley and Sons, 2005.
———. "L'invenzione della verità." In *Prima e dopo le parole. Scritti e discorsi sulla letteratura*, ed. Gigliola De Donato and Rosalba Galvagno, 51–54. Rome: Donzelli, 2001.
———. *Le parole sono pietre*. Turin: Einaudi, 1955.
———. *Le ragioni dei topi*. Ed. Gigliola De Donato and Luisa Montevecchi. Rome: Donzelli, 2004.

———. *Roma fuggitiva. Una città e i suoi dintorni.* Ed. Gigliola De Donato. Rome: Donzelli, 2002.

———. *Tutto il miele è finito.* Turin: Einaudi, 1964.

———. *Un volto che ci somiglia. Ritratto dell'Italia.* Turin: Einaudi, 1960.

———. *The Watch.* Trans. Mrs Arnold Gifford and John Farrar. South Royalton, VT: Steerforth, 1999 [1951].

Pasolini, Pier Paolo. "La scomparsa delle lucciole." In *Scritti corsari*, 160–61. Milan: Garzanti, 1975.

Steiner, Wendy. *The Real Real Thing: The Model in the Mirror of Art.* Chicago: U of Chicago P, 2010.

Zapf, Hubert. "The State of Ecocriticism and the Status of Literature as Cultural Ecology." In *Nature in Literary and Cultural Studies: Transatlantic Conversations on Ecocriticism*, ed. Catrin Gersdof and Sylvia Mayer, 49–70. Amsterdam: Rodopi, 2006.

12

Hybriditales

Posthumanizing Calvino

Serenella Iovino

Cages and Thresholds

In her essay "On Singularity and the Symbolic," Carrie Rohman analyzes the way Italo Calvino's character Mr. Palomar muses, in silent conversations, about the boundaries that separate humans from other animals. Confronted with the enigmatic singularity of an albino gorilla named Snowflake, or with the neat classification of iguanas in a Parisian reptile house, Palomar searches for "an eternal or permanent system, structure, or taxonomy of meaning" (Rohman 73), a recognizable order whose validity would also extend outside cages and boxes. As though challenging the Darwinian evidence of biological continuity with the implicit evocation of a *Linnaeus redivivus*, Palomar dreams of a nostalgic taxonomy of "fixed" forms able to "resist the flux that undoes them and mixes and reshapes [them]"—forms "separated forever from the others, as here in a row of glass case-cages of the zoo" (*Palomar* 86). Calvino is well aware that this dream is an artful delusion: were species separated like cages in a zoo, the order of discourse would prevail over the complexity of nature and its ongoing metamorphosis (Rohman 73). Rohman writes, "[Palomar's] description [of the zoo] points out the exaggerated and ultimately fantastic idea that species are eternally distinct, that species barriers represent some permanent and reliable mode of differentiation. Rather, this passage implicitly exposes the *human* investment in inviolable and discreet [sic] life-forms. [...] Palomar longs for species barriers that are clear and unassailable, but [...] such longings are more akin to humanist wish-structures than anything else" (73).

The search for taxonomies is a concern that Calvino shares with two authors with whom he is often associated. Jorge Luis Borges's famous "Celestial Emporium of Benevolent Knowledges," a (seemingly fictitious) ancient Chinese encyclopedia, contains a curious taxonomy that pigeonholes living beings into 14 categories, including "(d) suckling pigs, (e) mermaids, (f) fabulous ones, (g) stray dogs, (h) those that are included in this classification, (i) those that tremble as if they were mad, [. . .] (n) those that resemble flies from a distance" (*Other Inquisitions* 108). Years later, Borges insists that the experience of the animal realm is as "bewildering" as a cognitive phenomenology of ever-emerging things: "[T]o discover the camel is itself no stranger than to discover a mirror or water or a staircase" (*Imaginary Beings* 13). In Borges, like in Calvino, the emphasis falls on the ironic and de facto culturally arbitrary character of classification systems. Another author, biographically closer to Calvino, the French *oulipiste* Georges Perec, describes the search for order as an extravagant occupation to which Mr. Bartlebooth, the Palomar-like protagonist of *Life: A User's Manual* (1978), unsuccessfully devotes his existence: "Let us imagine a man [. . .] of exceptional arrogance who wishes to fix, to describe, and to exhaust not the whole world [. . .] but a constituted fragment of the world: in the face of the inextricable incoherence of things, he will set out to execute a (necessarily limited) program right the way through, in all its irreducible, intact entirety" (117).

In all these cases, the attempt to define "orders of things" (Michel Foucault's reference to Borges's "Celestial Emporium" is commonplace here; see Foucault, *The Order of Things*, xvi) and to map the fault lines between species and beings is at the very least problematic. If in Borges it is a cultural construction, in Perec it is a hobby for wealthy male adults. In Calvino, irony and epistemology go together. To sketch separations between life forms, in fact, is a way to counterbalance the inconsistency of the subject, which is in turn always permeable, always exposed to a world full of other and full of others.

But considered more closely, the question underlying Palomar's solitary observations is not solely about a classification of living forms. Palomar focuses on thresholds, including the "threshold of the human," as Rohman evinces, but his zoological adventures are just another occasion for Calvino to explore—taking irony as a heuristic strategy—the way thresholds can be blurred, betrayed, deconstructed, hybridized, and remanipulated in narrative forms. In this essay, I will examine this tendency and crisscross Calvino's works via the posthumanist lens of a "relational ontology" (Oppermann), maybe the most apt tool for reading through his universe of hybrids, evanescent thresholds, and "queer critters," where the human world is a haphazard emergence on a "turbulent, immanent field in which various and variable materialities collide, congeal, morph, evolve, and disintegrate" (Bennett ix).

In the stories of Palomar, Qfwfq, Priscilla, and his many "critters," Calvino shows how, as Latour puts it, "It is possible, to have our cake and eat it too—to be monists and make distinctions" (214). Calvino the monist—like Perec, and certainly like Borges—cuts his posthuman cake by tracing ironical distinctions. But, along with his reader, he is well aware that these lines are marked only in order to reinforce the narrative of connections in a universe of things that are, as Deleuze would say, "ontologically one, but formally diverse" (*Expressionism* 67). Through an *ars combinatoria* made of segments of potential natures and unstable material-semiotic orders, layers of history and layers of biology intermingle and interfere, spreading out a playful complexity of stories and beings, where literature becomes a form of cosmic knowledge and imagination a vibrant extension of reality.

Past the Human

Where do the boundaries of the human lie? Are there boundaries (literally) *de-fining* the division between the human and its other, and where do these borders lie? Or, more properly, where does the human's "other" lie?[1] To answer these questions, a belief in an essentialist vision about the human would certainly help. The human, according to this vision, would be an ontoepistemological category that doggedly emerged from the evolutionary struggle in order to stay fixed in its purity, simultaneously a being, an essence, and a theory. But is it really so? "I firmly believe that we have never been human," Donna Haraway writes in "A Kinship of Feminist Figurations": "There is no border where evolution ends and history begins, where genes stop and environment takes up, where culture rules and nature submits, or vice versa. Instead, there are turtles and turtles of naturecultures all the way down. Every being that matters is a congeries of its formative histories" (2). Our existence, the existence of our species and its cognitive evolution, is far from being pure and confined within secure margins. From the mitochondria all the way up, the human is constantly mixed with the nonhuman. It reveals itself by way of hybridizations. For this reason, a perfectly consequent atlas of human biology would be a treatise on xenobiology. A compelling example is that of the bacteria colonies that constitute our microbiome. Even though they do not have anything "human" in their genetic code, they are an integral part of our body and our health. As Jane Bennett observes, "My 'own' body is material, and yet this materiality is not fully or exclusively human. My flesh is populated and constituted by different swarms of foreigners" (112).[2] But let us also think of the way pollutants, medicines, and humanly made substances—xenobiotics—become our resident aliens, interacting with our bodies "in unpredictable, uncontrollable ways" (Alaimo 24). Forms of environmental illness, for example multiple chemical sensitivity (MCS), speak clearly about the way "human bodies are coextensive with the natural, unnatural, and hybridized material world" (167).[3]

The cyborg is also a hybridization of the human: a mingled creature made of humanly built mechanisms and of "ourselves and other organic creatures in our unchosen 'high-technological' guise as information systems, texts, and ergonomically controlled labouring, desiring, and reproducing systems" (Haraway, *Simians* 1). Against dualistic assumptions, humanity belongs "in the crossover" of agencies and presences, and like our everyday life, "our very body, is composed to a great extent of sociotechnical negotiations and artifacts" (Latour 214). If we keep these examples in mind next time we hydrate our skin, take an antibiotic, or see an advertisement for ear implants, the fact that humans are assemblages of organic and inorganic matter, and therefore blended with alien presences, will become suddenly clearer. In this light, our bodies are congregational entities always reminding us of "the very radical character of the (fractious) kinship between the human and the nonhuman" (Bennett 112).

Calvino's literary imagination is pervaded by this idea, and much of his narrative undertaking consists in mapping potential otherness within and around the human, in both its ontological and social categories. It is interesting how this vision emerges even in occasional writings, like "The Sky, Man, the Elephant" ("*Il cielo, l'uomo, l'elefante*"), a preface to Pliny the Elder's *Natural History*, published in 1982 and included in *Why Read the Classics?* (*Perché leggere i classici*, 1991). In this treatise of things natural and of cultural anthropology *avant la lettre*, Calvino discovers humankind to be located in a pervious zone of forms and matters, precarious in its destiny of unpredictable metamorphoses. "Human beings form an area of the living world which must be defined by carefully drawing its boundaries," he remarks (*Why Read* 42). However, these boundaries are negotiable, and not only in the case of the unsuspected family ties that "spiritually" connect the human with the "*reliqua animalia*, [...] the other animated beings" (45). The human is also a technological hybrid of things and products, in a dimension that Latour would call a "collective" of humans and nonhumans. Calvino comments, in fact, that "[a]nticipating those modern anthropologists who maintain that there is a continuity between biological evolution and technological development, from palaeolithic tools to electronics, Pliny implicitly admits that the additions made by man to nature become an integral part themselves of [human] nature" (44).[4] Here, the adverb "implicitly" tells us how Calvino thought about the structural hybridity of the human, where biological evolution and technological development are an open horizon of substantial transitions and oscillations. Against such a horizon, it is possible that future layers of existence will ironically reproduce the previous ones by turning their allegedly immovable order upside down. Think of the human-car-petrol symbiosis described in "The Petrol Pump" ("*La pompa di benzina*"), a short story written by Calvino in 1974: "The day the earth's crust reabsorbs the cities, this plankton sediment that was humankind will be covered by geological layers of asphalt and cement until in millions of years' time it thickens into oily deposits, on whose behalf we do not know" (*Numbers* 175).

Open to transformations, the human is materially and historically permeable to other natures, other matters, and other cultural agents. To be properly human is therefore, in a certain sense, to go past the boundaries of human "nature." This is the meaning of posthumanism, as theorists such as Donna Haraway, Karen Barad, Roberto Marchesini, Bruno Latour, Andrew Pickering, Rosi Braidotti, or Cary Wolfe conceptualize it. For these authors, posthumanism is a vision of reality according to which the human and the nonhuman are confluent, coemergent, and defining each other in mutual relations. More precisely, a posthumanist vision rejects the essentialist separation between the human and the nonhuman and, quite like Calvino's narratives, emphasizes their hybridizations and their active interplay. Such a vision pictures a world whose ontological categories are performed rather than given, where mixing with "anotherness" is the dynamic destination of being, and where the human is itself the result of intersecting agencies and meanings. Its very meaning is that of a material-discursive consociability, built "through the pleasurable connection with the other, with the different, with whatever is able to produce new states of instability, thus reinforcing the human endeavor to conjugate with the world" (Marchesini 70).[5] Against the posthumanist horizon, different forms of agency and materiality feed each other. There is communication within every fragment of existing materiality, and therefore our relationship with the world is of conjoined determination: "The world makes us in one and the same process in which we make the world" (Pickering 26). In this performative account of being and knowing, human experience depends on and produces hybridizations. Not only are our bodies materially entangled with other bodies, but culture and every form of knowledge are discursive processes of coupling with others: "[E]very culture is the outcome of a process of hybridization with an otherness" (Marchesini 15). In tune with Calvino's vision of a world full of human aliens, posthumanism implies therefore a picture according to which, both in discursive and material terms, "otherness saturates the human structure [. . .] [H]umanity oozes with the nonhuman" (Marchesini 70).

But as Calvino will emphasize, the human is not alone in the crossover. A whole world of hybrids, collectives, and "critters" shares with us a horizon on which material forces concur with meanings in the process of hybridization that shapes our existence(s). Existence is composed of the "force of collective life" (Wheeler, *Whole* 30), and this force is expressive: if culture is an ongoing process of hybridization with nature, a continuous formation of "naturecultures," to use Haraway's vivid coinage, the force of life is also a force of signs and information, a semiotic force. It is a potential of stories inbuilt into matter. This world is not only a world of material emergences but also a world that becomes meaningful because meaning coemerges with matter, as research in the field of biosemiotics shows.[6] The narrative landscape of posthumanism is a landscape of encounters, where "the organism-environment coupling is a form of conversation" (Wheeler, *Whole* 126), and where the human is constitutionally responsive to "a universe which is—and perhaps always has been—'perfused with signs'" (155).

In the paragraphs that follow, I will trace the way these issues are developed in Calvino's narratives. After an overview of works where such topics are most visible, I will concentrate on *Mr. Palomar* (*Palomar*, 1983) and *Cosmicomics* (*Le Cosmicomiche*, 1965). These are, I would suggest, the main expressions of Calvino's attempt to build stories that move the narrative focus and strategy "past the human," and where the tangle of matters, forms, and signs shapes "hybriditales"—stories in which reality itself is a continuous flow of crossings.

A World of Hybrids, Collectives, and Critters: Literature outside the Self

The human world emerging from Calvino's posthumanist "hybriditales" is a combination of substances and meanings: as we have seen, only a game of proportions separates the human from the nonhuman, defining them as dif-*ferents*, as bearers of an internal split. For Calvino this split is profoundly problematic and requires deconstruction. In his narratives, the entanglements with an otherness come often from within—from within the cells, like in *Cosmicomics* or *t zero* (*T con zero*, 1967), or from within the mind, the body, and their social categorization, like in *The Watcher* (*La giornata di uno scrutatore*, 1963). This short novel, in particular, is a reflection on the "borders of humanity," where the very idea of being human, "essentially" enlightened by reason, is confronted with its own "odd" side: mental and physical illness. One of the most philosophically challenging among Calvino's novels, *The Watcher* is the story of two days spent by an election watcher in Turin's Cottolengo, a hospital for the mentally and physically disabled during the elections of 1953. Here, while the protagonist intensely meditates on "the boundary line between the Cottolengo humans and the healthy" (*The Watcher* 36), the very concept of "humanity" is overcome by its internal alterity, and the human becomes a human alien, an anthropological form of wilderness.[7]

But hybridity and enmeshment with alterity are features that Calvino bestows also on other early characters, in works where the realism and conceptual depths of *The Watcher* are superseded by fantasy and ironic lightness. The trilogy *Our Ancestors* (*I nostri antenati*) is an interesting case in point: in *The Baron in the Trees* (*Il barone rampante*, 1957), as a deliberate consequence of his *hubristic* refusal to eat snail soup, Cosimo Piovasco di Rondò turns into an "arboreal" man who will never touch the ground again, becoming part of Europe's landscape of disappearing forests; *The*

Cloven Viscount (*Il visconte dimezzato*, 1952) is a moral hybrid of good and evil; *The Nonexistent Knight* (*Il cavaliere inesistente*, 1959) is a hybrid of matter and void, a presence-absence, alive only thanks to his armor (he is, we could say, a human-metal-crafted assemblage). In *Marcovaldo* (1963), nature is an ironic hybrid of "urban nature," which is "mischievous, counterfeit, compromised with artificial life" (Calvino, "Presentazione" 1233). This nature is visible through its absence and its paradoxical appearances: mushrooms near a tram station, municipal pigeons, billboards mistaken for trees by kids who have never seen a forest, the pale light of the moon competing with the neon signs of a cognac brand. In *Cosmicomics* (and in the sequels, *t zero*, *The Memory of the World*, *Cosmicomics Old and New*)[8] the hybridization is extended to the entire universe, mediated through and concentrated in the indefinable Qfwfq, a "queer critter" who embodies the entire range of natural forms, possibility, and stories.[9]

Marcovaldo's hybridized nature becomes *Mr. Palomar*'s landscape of naturecultures, a landscape of cheese, stones, gardens, tortoises, butcher shops, stars, geckoes, zoos, slippers, sand, and eyes. Here hybridity takes more explicitly the literal form of *post*humanism, of a movement aimed to cross the boundaries of the human and to locate processes—whether cognitive or formative—in a wider horizon of mutually dependent phenomena. Palomar's mind, in fact, is always strained between the "in-side" and the "out-side," like a consciously permeable membrane connecting (and separating) the self and the world. Stretching the human beyond itself in space and in time, this coevolutionary gaze is an essential component of Calvino's relational ontology. Palomar's fluctuations between subjectivism ("All this is happening not on the sea, not in the sun, [...] but inside my head. [...] I am swimming in my mind" [15]) and objectivism ("If I see and think and swim the reflection, it is because at the other extreme there is the sun, which casts its rays. [...] All the rest is reflection among reflections, me included" [15]) are—if not overcome—conciliated in a geoevolutionary vision in which experiences and presences are occasional coemergences. Humans, too, are episodes in the world's self-shaping:

> Mr. Palomar thinks of the world without him: that endless world before his birth, and that far more obscure world after his death; he tries to imagine the world before eyes, any eyes; and a world that tomorrow, through catastrophe or slow corrosion, will be left blind. What happens (happened, will happen) in that world? Promptly an arrow of light sets out from the sun, is reflected in the calm sea, sparkles in the tremolo of the water; and then matter becomes receptive to light, is differentiated into living tissues, and all of a sudden an eye, a multitude of eyes, burgeons, or reburgeons. (18)

This passage is the typical example of the human's material and historical porosity, of its contiguity with other natures and agents. Like all other physical systems, humans do not exist a priori or separately; the scale of their existence is participatory and relational. In the dicey process of evolutionary causality, humans "happen" in a world of spontaneously concurring phenomena, outside any preexisting order or harmony. The "before-and-after" sequence taking place in Palomar's mind is therefore not a way to delimit the human as a chronological or ontological watershed. It is rather an instant movie that recapitulates evolutionary pathways tracing them back to the unpredictable ways nature's "agentic force [...] interacts with and changes the [...] elements in the mix, including the human" (Alaimo and Hekman 7). Far from ruling the world in its ongoing evolution, order and harmony are only a misleading human projection, a vague aspiration. In fact, as Palomar says, between humankind and world, "there is a sense of possible harmony, as if between two nonhomogeneous harmonies: that of the nonhuman in a balance of forces that seems not to correspond to any pattern, and that of human structures, which aspires to the rationality of a geometrical or musical composition, never definitive" (94).

This structural impermanence justifies and spawns the observational attitude displayed by Mr. Palomar, whose name recalls an astronomic observatory in California. While using this quality, Calvino is perfectly aware that objectivity is a mere regulative ideal, in the first place because the human eye is conditioned by biocultural factors. Nonetheless, the eyes of a human can be open to a world in which all things inexhaustibly emerge and converge. This explains a narrative and linguistic strategy that, in almost all Calvino's late works, becomes more and more antimetaphysical and antisubjective: only if the human self recedes can the world be visible and eloquent. Here, instead of a knowledge based on depth, and therefore on hierarchy, whether of objectivity or subjectivity, Calvino privileges a nonhierarchical way of looking, knowing, and describing phenomena. This both inverts and enlarges our cognitive patterns: "It is only after you have come to know the surface of things [...] that you can venture to seek what is underneath. But the surface of things is inexhaustible" (55). Only in a perceptive and conceptual horizon made of silence, of hearing, of observing, can humans acquire familiarity with the world in which they *occur*: a world both *before* and *after* the human one, inhabited by things and beings proving that "the world of man is not eternal and is not unique" (*Palomar* 86).

If the world is narratable only through the silence of the ego, literature mirrors this paradox, this ambivalence between silence and narration. Sustained by a vision of imagination as a creative force, a "means to attain a knowledge that is outside the individual, outside the subjective" (Calvino, *Six Memos* 91), literature can explore how the world progressively *opens* to itself. In this openness, Calvino situates Palomar's attempt to mingle his existence and perspective with the existence of other beings, whether geckoes, grasses, slippers, tortoises, or birds. For example, as Palomar assumes the perspective of a bird flying over the rooftops, the categories of experience are moved "past the human" again, and the self is outspread:

> Nothing of this can be seen by one who moves on his feet or his wheels over the city pavements. And, inversely, from up here you have the impression that the true crust of the earth is this, uneven but compact, [...] and it never occurs to you to wonder what is hidden [...]. This is how birds think, or at least is how Mr. Palomar thinks, imagining himself a bird. "It is only after you have come to know the surface of things," he concludes, "that you can venture to seek what is underneath. But the surface of things is inexhaustible." (*Palomar* 54–55)

Palomar is an extended ego, a self "outside the subjective." He is the intersection of city, birds, plants, roofs, things, and himself as a human individual who tries to "escape subjectivity" (38), not so much in order to reach a supposed objectivity, but rather to embrace a wider portion of the never-ending surface of things. Here, while the posthuman finds the form of an urban-animal-architectonic-cultural-vegetable assemblage, Rome, the city's experiences and bodies, the humans, and the birds form a collective. In this collective, unexpectedly, the human finds itself in a relationship of communication based on sharing a landscape of materiality and signs, a situation that can be addressed using the words of the ecophenomenologist David Abram:

> It is the reticence, the inexhaustible otherness of things, that enables them to hold my gaze, to sustain themselves in my awareness. I can never plumb all the secrets of even a single blade of grass [...] or the totality of the relations that it sustains [...] because I am not a disembodied mind [...], because, that is, I myself am a body, a material being of weight and density like this tree or that stone [...]. Because, finally, I am a thing myself, and hence have only a finite access to the things around me. (43)[10]

The human is a finite being among other finite beings, and this finitude is the horizon for the ontological crossover in which humans, nonhumans, and their stories belong. Likewise, Calvino's reflections on the human-bovine's coimplication also emphasize the hybridity of the human and of its "naturecultural" reality: "[T]he man-beef symbiosis [...] has guaranteed the flourishing of what is called human civilization, which at least in part should be called human-bovine" (*Palomar* 77–78).

Calvino highlights the need to describe the story (and nature) of human civilization in the perspective of its intersection with the stories (and natures) of others. But these stories could also be inverted, or written from perspectives that are not necessarily human-centered. After all, humans, too, are parts of the metabolic cycles of nature's economy: if we incorporate "the world's flesh" into our own "it can only be so because we, too, are edible. Because we, too, are food" (Abram 62). Thus Calvino radically ushers in a narrative microcosmology, enunciated in "Being Stone" ("*Essere pietra*"), a two-page monologue "in Palomar's style" written in 1981 for an exhibit of sculptures by Alberto Magnelli. Here a stone speaks and reflects on the entanglement of agencies and elements that characterizes the temporality and stories of impersonal matter:

> [T]he stones' time is concentrated in our interior, where ages thicken and sediment [. . .]. But our story lies also upon us, it is carved on our dented and broken and whittled surface [. . .]. And I am not talking only of a mineral story of rocks, which are subjected to slides, exfoliations, erosions, slow flows or sudden cataclysms. I am talking of a story marked by human tools, too: by the helical band of the electric saw that, sliding, cleaves its groove in the hard cohesion of molecules; by the well-aimed chisel stroke; by the crack-opening wedge that has been struck by the hammer; by the frenzied explosion of the mine. ("Essere pietra" 420)

As Manuel De Landa put it, "[I]n a nonlinear world in which the same processes of self-organization take place in the mineral, organic, and cultural spheres, perhaps rocks hold some of the keys to understanding [. . .] humanity [. . .] and all [its] mixtures" (70).[11] While advancing along the paths of the human's structural "mixtures," we are accompanied in a migration outside the human, and thus *ipso facto* outside the subject, in a process through which the very category of identity is reconfigured. In *Mr. Palomar*'s closing chapter this issue is a matter of very intense scrutiny:

> [H]ow can you look at something and set your own ego aside? Whose eyes are doing the looking? As a role, you think of the ego as one who is peering out of your own eyes as if leaning on a window sill, looking at the world stretching out before him in all its immensity. So, then: a window looks out on the world. The world is out there; and here, what do we have? The world, still—what else could there be? [. . .] perhaps the "I," the ego, is simply the window through which the world looks at the world. To look at itself the world needs the eyes (and the eyeglasses) of Mr. Palomar. (114)

These words, published in 1982,[12] obey the logic Calvino expressed in a 1967 interview, where he declared, "I believe that the world exists independently from the human; it existed before the human and will exist after it, and the human is only an opportunity that the world has to organize some information about itself. Therefore literature is for me a number of attempts to know and organize information about the world" (*Romanzi e racconti II* 1347). In Calvino's mind, literature has both creative and cognitive functions, which can extend our experience "outside the individual and outside the subjective" but also explore the realm of potentialities that lies "out there." Again in *Six Memos*, hybridity emerges as a realization of a nonsubjective imagination and of the interconnected potentialities of more-than-human existence: "Think what it would be to have a work conceived from outside the *self*, a work that would let us escape the limited perspective of the individual ego, [. . .] give speech to that which has no language, to the bird perching on the edge of the gutter, to the tree in spring and the tree in the fall, to stone, to cement, to plastic" (124).

The literature "outside the self" that Calvino describes is a creative apprehension of things that includes the self only as long as its consciousness is not superimposed on the totality of phenomena. Quoting Carlo Emilio Gadda, in fact, Calvino emphasizes that, while modern novels are a way to know and recreate the complexity of the world, "to know is to insert something into what is real, and hence to distort reality" (*Six Memos* 108). In this process, the self profoundly interferes with the world, changing it irremediably: consciousness, as Haraway says, "changes the geography of all previous categories; it denatures them as heat denatures a fragile protein" ("Manifesto" 16). The object of a literature "from outside" escapes the borders of definitive morphologies and converges instead in processes of mixing and becoming. In so doing, this literature contemplates not "life" generally taken but rather the pure asubjective stream of vitality of what Gilles Deleuze would call "a life"—that is, "an immanent life carrying with it the events or singularities that are merely actualized in subjects and objects" (*Immanence* 29). These asubjective narratives draw attention "not to a world of human design or their accidental, accumulated effects, but to an interstitial field of non-personal ahuman forces, flows, tendencies, and trajectories" (Bennett 61).

Going past the human and finding the narrative pathways of its hybridizations with other beings is what a posthumanist literature par excellence does. In this framework, the *Cosmicomics* are an important station on the way toward *Mr. Palomar*'s postsubjectivity. In the infinite forms and matters assumed by Qfwfq, Calvino expresses both the contingency of the human as a cosmic actor and the expansive asubjective and aindividual narrativity of things in their evolutionary becoming, from atoms to planetary forces. The *Cosmicomics* are the history of a hybridizing universe. Scientific hypotheses give Calvino the cue for imagining stories whose main character is the unpronounceable Qfwfq, an unstoppable flow of material-semiotic stages that speaks, plays, and evolves using the human as a form of representative mimicry. Qfwfq is everything: a nebula, a simple cluster of primordial matter, a dinosaur on the verge of becoming extinct, a mammal just emerged from its previous evolutionary stage of pulmonate fish. Qfwfq is the universe in its synchronic and diachronic metamorphoses, the whole presenting itself in different fragments. In its very narrative strategy, this book is based on a stylistic-cognitive hybridization: scientific hypotheses and theories are first quoted in an opening paragraph and then ironically anthropomorphized and disguised as the settings for everyday situations. The result is a cosmological Darwinism, a collective evolutionary biography of the world in which Qfwfq is and becomes a huge number of things, reminding us of the permeability and continuity of every being.

Moving from subatomic particles to dinosaurs, from empty space to chaos, Qfwfq's identity is asubjective, open, and relational. It is an ecological and hybridized identity, based on the osmotic-semiotic exchange between the self and the other, the inside and the outside. In "Identity" ("*Identità*"), a short autobiographic essay of 1977, Calvino wrote that "my personal identity is crisscrossed by the genetic continuity that gets splintered and meshed in apparently separated individuals" (2825); "the most solid and self-confident identity is nothing but a sort of bag or hosepipe full of swirling heterogeneous stuff" (2825–27). Every form of identity, whether individual or social, is definable and understandable only through the relationship it has with the "outside": "[I]t is the outside that defines the inside, in the horizon of space, as well as in the vertical dimension of time" (2827). Similarly, Qfwfq's identity is transitive and transitional; it is made of "swirling heterogeneous stuff." In spite of the anthropomorphism of the narrative, here the human is not simply leveled out but restructured in terms of complexity.

In its hybridizing flows, Qfwfq points at the "other" (others) that is (are) present within the human and, at the same time, at a human that is present in its "other." In its material indifference to forms and states, to being individual or collective, Qfwfq is the typical example of what posthumanist thought calls a "critter," a being/thing that is "material, specific, non-self-identical, and semiotically active" (Haraway, *When Species* 250). Critters are, exactly like Qfwfq, animate beings "where the line between 'animate' and 'inanimate' is taken as given, rather than an effect of particular boundary-drawing practices" (Barad, "Nature's Queer" 127). These boundaries are, in fact, always kept open, and for this very reason, a critter "is already internally queer, having contrary associations as a term defined both in contrast to or as distinct from humans (as in its reference to animate nonhumans), and, in relation to humans (e.g., as a term of reprobation or contempt, but also sometimes as term of affection or tenderness)." In an important sense, therefore, critters—like Qfwfq—"do not have inherently determinate identities, by definition" (ibid.).

"The Spiral" ("*La spirale*") exemplifies Calvino's representation of this "internally queer" world of associations and its blurred boundaries of space-time-matter. Here Qfwfq is a marine organism that, out of love, produces its shell and recognizes it as a nucleus of further development and determination. This organism prompts the emergence of a spiraling constellation that encompasses, "five hundred million years" later, a congeries of beings: pyramids and Egyptian airlines, Spinoza and the "Spinoza" entry in a Dutch encyclopedia, a Neolithic mattock buried in a field and the mattock of the peasant that unburies it, Herodotus and those who read him in bilingual editions, a cloud of bees, coal, horoscopes, Cleopatra, and films about Cleopatra (*Cosmicomics* 147–48). Identity, like reality, is here a process of mutual determination of interconnected phenomena, not a property of individuals. It is "diffracted through itself" (Barad, "Nature's Queer" 126) and open to multiplicity.

In the *Cosmicomics* and their sequels, the striving toward becoming multiple—and toward multiple becomings—is represented as intrinsic to an agentic universe that uses itself as a partner and as a language. One of the most significant examples of this dynamic is "Priscilla," a tale from *t zero* in which Calvino describes the phenomenology of a vibrantly active matter busy organizing itself and moved by love, perception, imagination, consciousness, and memory. In this journey of self-organization, Qfwfq, a "loving/desiring" cell, produces other beings and meanings, marked by the emergence of plurality within the nucleus: "[M]y state of desire, my state-motion-desire of motion-desire-love moved me to say, and since the only thing I had to say was myself, I was moved to say myself, to express myself. [. . .] [A]ll this me was a place where there was everything except me: what I mean is, I had the sense of being inhabited, no, of inhabiting myself. No, of inhabiting a me inhabited by others" (68–69). This plurality is our immanent destiny. Generation by generation, it is inscribed in our cells and becomes a future-producing memory in which every move appears like a recapitulation of the past: "[O]nce we've established that what I call 'I' consists of a certain number of amino acids which line up in a certain way, it's logical that inside these molecules all possible relations are foreseen" (*Cosmicomics* 79).

Here Calvino, with one of his tranquil *coups de théâtre*, moves us to another landscape, one derived from the transformation of cells, their loves, and their combinations:

> All we can say is that in certain points and moments that interval of void which is our individual presence is grazed by the wave which continues to renew the combinations of molecules [. . .] and this is enough to give us the certitude that somebody is 'I' and somebody is 'Priscilla' in the temporal and spatial distribution of the living cells [. . .]. This is in itself enough, Priscilla, to cheer me, when I bend my outstretched neck over yours and I give you a little nip on your yellow fur and you dilate your nostrils, bare your teeth and kneel on the sand, lowering your hump to the level of my breast so that I can lean on it and press you from behind bearing down on my rear legs. (85–86)

In this vorticous horizon in which language and consciousness, memory and love, pop up from bubbling oceans of matter, it does not matter whether a human voice is used to let a cell speak of its (our) semiotic desire or is lent to a camel to recall his (our) mating joy.

"Priscilla"—like Calvino's numerous "hybriditales" on biological themes—is theoretically mirrored in a passage from *A Thousand Plateaus*: "[A]ll becomings are already molecular. [. . .] Starting from the forms one has, the subject one is, the organs one has, or the functions one fulfills, becoming is to extract particles between which one establishes the relations of movement and rest [. . .]. This is the sense in which becoming is the process of desire. [. . .] It indicates [. . .] a *zone of proximity or copresence.*" (Deleuze and Guattari 300–301). And like Deleuze's and Guattari's, Calvino's subjects are nomadic subjects distributed in a space without enclosures or boundaries. Embracing multiple perspectives of subjectivity and identity, Calvino's narrative technique, especially in *Mr. Palomar* and *Cosmicomics*, is also nomadic and deterritorialized. By tracing the genealogy of life back to the universe's genealogy, Calvino rewrites human history in a more inclusive way, enacting a "creative sort of becoming" and staging a "performative metaphor that allows for otherwise unlikely encounters and unsuspected sources of interaction, experience, and knowledge" (Braidotti 38).

Blurring Boundaries without Burning Bridges: Conclusions

In her essay "Otherworldly Conversations, Terran Topics, Local Terms," Haraway reflects on the "stunning narrative [. . .] of structural-functional complexity" in which all living forms are "bound together in the ultrastructural tissues of our being" (163). She writes, "We must engage in forms of life with the nonhumans [. . .]. Refiguring conversations with those who are not 'us' must be part of that project" (174). A posthumanist vision based on pathways of hybridization and on dynamic entanglements where "mind, body and environment [form] a processual continuum" (Wheeler, *Whole* 22) does not deny the human as such but rather covers the distance between us and "those who are not 'us,'" "blurring boundaries without burning bridges" (Braidotti 26). This vision aims to relocate the human—and the nonhuman—in a (non-Platonic) horizon in which "being" is not synonymous with "essence" or "nature." In this monist horizon, distinctions define and connect phenomena, which are not "facts" but coemergences of concurring agencies. Posthumanism is also a more "humane" form of humanism—a humanism more inclusive of human others and aware of the (inner and outer) exposure, openness, and vulnerability that characterize the human. As *Mr. Palomar, Cosmicomics,* and also *The Watcher* show, if the human has thresholds and boundaries, these are so subtle that they can be eluded and taken as a chance to reshape our categories of experience, opening borders for reconjunctions.

Calvino's critters, their "hybriditales," give relevant instructions about how to restore the conversation with "those who are not 'us.'" To ask what the world looks like where there are no eyes to see it, or to lend human voice to cells, camels, atoms, and stars, is an exercise in restructuring "otherworldy conversations." It implies a welcoming dimension for a human so mature that it can find itself by going past itself. And maybe, after "posthumanizing" Calvino, we could do the same with another classic: Henry David

Thoreau. We could start with this famous passage from *Walden*: "Not until we are lost [...] do we begin to find ourselves, and realize where we are and the infinite extent of our relations" (459). Here, clearly and unmistakably, cognitively and ontologically, the human's hybridizing nature shines in the luminous form of a declaration of interdependence.

Notes

1. For a development of this question in biosemiotic terms, see Timo Maran, "Where Do Your Borders Lie? Reflections on the Semiotical Ethics of Nature."
2. Analyzing this issue more closely, Bennett discusses the crook of the human elbow, "a special ecosystem, a bountiful home to no fewer than six tribes of bacteria," noting that the "bacteria in the human microbiome collectively possess at least 100 times as many genes as the mere 20,000 or so in the human genome" (citation from Nicholas Wade, "Bacteria Thrive in Crook of Elbow, Lending a Hand," *New York Times*, May 23, 2008; see Bennett, *Vibrant Matter* 112).
3. On this coextensivity, Alaimo articulates her notion of transcorporeality, a "movement across bodies" that reveals "the interchanges and interconnections between various bodily natures" (2).
4. In the English version, the last crucial adjective ("human") has been mistakenly omitted.
5. Unless otherwise indicated, translations are my own.
6. First developed in the works of Charles Sanders Peirce and Jakob von Uexküll, biosemiotics is "the study of signs and significance in all living things" (Wheeler, *Whole* 19). As Timo Maran puts it, "[S]ign processes take place not only in human culture but also everywhere in nature [. . .] Meaning is the organising principle of nature" (455, 461). Therefore "all living things—from the humblest forms of single-cell life upward—[...] are engaged in sign relations" (Wheeler, "Biosemiotic Turn" 271).
7. I have analyzed this novel in my essay "The Wilderness of the Human Other."
8. The original Italian titles of these last two books are *La memoria del mondo e altre storie cosmicomiche* (1968) and *Cosmicomiche vecchie e nuove* (1984). *Cosmicomics*, a collection of 12 short stories on the life of the universe, first appeared in 1965. During the following twenty years, Calvino wrote several other "cosmicomics" books and several scattered tales. Most of these "cosmicomic stories," in English translation, are collected in *The Complete Cosmicomics* (2011).
9. For an ecocritical interpretation of *Cosmicomics*, see Iovino "Quanto scommettiamo? Ecologia letteraria, educazione ambientale e *Le Cosmicomiche* di Italo Calvino." On "queer critters" as beings that "do

not have inherently determinate identities, by definition" (127) see Barad, "Nature's Queer Performativity."
10. Abram actually used *Mr. Palomar* as a source of inspiration for his "earthly cosmology," as he himself declares (285).
11. For considerations about stone and posthumanism, see Jeffrey J. Cohen, "Stories of Stone," and the intriguing ecocritical development proposed by Cohen in *Animal, Vegetal, Mineral: Ethics and Objects*.
12. Before being incorporated into *Mr. Palomar*, the text of this chapter appeared in French (translated by Jacques Roubaud) in the July–August 1982 issue of the *Cnac Magazine*, the journal of the *Centre national d'art et de culture Georges Pompidou*.

Works Cited

Abram, David. *Becoming Animal: An Earthly Cosmology*. New York: Pantheon, 2010.

Alaimo, Stacy. *Bodily Natures: Science, Environment, and the Material Self*. Bloomington: Indiana UP, 2010.

Alaimo, Stacy, and Susan Hekman. "Introduction: Emerging Models of Materiality in Feminist Theory." In *Material Feminisms*, ed. Stacy Alaimo and Susan Hekman, 1–19. Bloomington: Indiana UP, 2008.

Barad, Karen. *Meeting the Universe Halfway: Quantum Physics and the Entanglement of Matter and Meaning*. Durham: Duke UP, 2007.

———. "Nature's Queer Performativity." *Qui Parle* 19.2 (2011): 121–58.

Bennett, Jane. *Vibrant Matter: A Political Ecology of Things*. Durham: Duke UP, 2010.

Borges, Jorge Luis. *The Book of Imaginary Beings*. Trans. Jorge Borges and Norman Thomas di Giovanni. London: Vintage, 2002.

———. *Other Inquisitions 1937–1952*. Trans. Ruth L. C. Simms. New York: Washington Square, 1966.

Braidotti, Rosi. *Nomadic Subjects: Embodiment and Sexual Difference in Contemporary Feminist Theory*. 2nd ed. New York: Columbia UP, 2011.

Calvino, Italo. *Cosmicomics*. Trans. William Weaver. San Diego: Harcourt Brace, 1976.

———. "Dialogo con una tartaruga." In *Romanzi e racconti*, ed. Mario Barenghi and Bruno Falcetto, vol. 3, 1155–58. Milan: Mondadori, 2004.

———. "Essere pietra." *Romanzi e racconti*, ed. Mario Barenghi and Bruno Falcetto, vol. 3, 419–21. Milan: Mondadori, 2004.

———. "Identità." In *Saggi 1945–1985*, ed. Mario Barenghi, vol. 2, 2823–27. Milan: Mondadori, 2001.

———. *Mr. Palomar*. Trans. William Weaver. San Diego: Harcourt Brace Jovanovich, 1985.

———. *Numbers in the Dark*. Trans. Tim Parks. London: Penguin, 2009.

———. "Presentazione 1966 all'edizione scolastica di *Marcovaldo*." In *Romanzi e racconti*, ed. Claudio Milanini, vol. 1, 1233–39. Milan: Mondadori, 2003.

———. *Romanzi e racconti*. 3 vols. Ed. Mario Barenghi and Bruno Falcetto. Milan: Mondadori, 2004.

———. *Six Memos for the Next Millennium*. Trans. Patrick Creagh. London: Penguin, 2009.

———. *t zero*. Trans. William Weaver. San Diego: Harcourt Brace, 1969.

———. *The Watcher and Other Stories*. Trans. William Weaver. San Diego: Hartcourt Brace, 1971.

———. *Why Read the Classics?* Trans. Martin MacLaughlin. London: Penguin, 2009. (Original edition: *Perché leggere i classici*. Milan: Arnoldo Mondadori Editore, 1991.)

Cohen, Jeffrey Jerome, ed. *Animal, Vegetal, Mineral: Ethics and Objects*. Washington, DC: Oliphaunt, 2012.

———. "Stories of Stone." *Postmedieval: A Journal of Medieval Cultural Studies* 1 (2010): 56–63.

De Landa, Manuel. *A Thousand Years of Nonlinear History*. New York: Zone, 1997.

Deleuze, Gilles. *Expressionism in Philosophy: Spinoza*. Trans. Martin Joughin. New York: Zone, 1992.

———. *Pure Immanence: Essays on A Life*. Trans. Anne Boyman. New York: Zone, 2001.

Deleuze, Gilles, and Félix Guattari. *A Thousand Plateaus: Capitalism and Schizophrenia*. Trans. Brian Massumi. London: Continuum, 2004.

Foucault, Michel. *The Order of Things: An Archaeology of the Human Sciences*. Trans. Alan Sheridan. London: Routledge, 1989.

Haraway, Donna J. *The Companion Species Manifesto: Dogs, People, and Significant Otherness*. Chicago: Prickly Paradigm, 2003.

———. "A Kinship of Feminist Figurations." In *The Haraway Reader*, 1–6. New York: Routledge, 2004.

———. "A Manifesto for Cyborgs: Science, Technology, and Socialist Feminism in the 1980s." In *The Haraway Reader*, 7–45. New York: Routledge, 2004. (First published in *Socialist Review* 80 [1985]: 65–108.)

———. "Otherworldly Conversations, Terran Topics, Local Terms." In *Material Feminisms*, ed. Stacy Alaimo and Susan Hekman, 157–87. Bloomington: Indiana UP, 2008.

———. *Simians, Cyborgs, and Women: The Reinvention of Nature*. New York: Routledge, 1991.

———. *When Species Meet*. Minneapolis: U of Minnesota P, 2008.

Iovino, Serenella. "Quanto scommettiamo? Ecologia letteraria, educazione ambientale e *Le Cosmicomiche* di Italo Calvino." *Compar(a)ison* 2 (2010): 107–23.

———. "The Wilderness of the Human Other: Italo Calvino's *The Watcher* and a Reflection on the Future of Ecocriticism." In *The Future of Ecocrit-*

icism: New Horizons, ed. Serpil Oppermann, Ufuk Özdag, Nevin Özkan, and Scott Slovic, 65–81. Newcastle upon Tyne: Cambridge Scholars, 2011.

Latour, Bruno. *Pandora's Hope: Essays on the Reality of Science Studies*. Cambridge: Harvard UP, 1999.

Maran, Timo. "Where Do Your Borders Lie? Reflections on the Semiotical Ethics of Nature." In *Nature in Literary and Cultural Studies: Transatlantic Conversations on Ecocriticism*, ed. Catrin Gersdorf and Sylvia Mayer, 455–76. Amsterdam: Rodopi, 2006.

Marchesini, Roberto. *Post-Human: Verso nuovi modelli di esistenza*. Turin: Bollati Boringhieri, 2002.

Oppermann, Serpil. "Feminist Ecocriticism: A Posthumanist Direction in Ecocritical Trajectory." In *International Perspectives in Feminist Ecocriticism*, ed. Greta Gaard, Simon C. Estok, and Serpil Oppermann, 19–36. London: Routledge, 2013.

Perec, George. *Life: A User's Manual*. Trans. David Bellos. London: Vintage, 2008.

Pickering, Andrew. *The Mangle of Practice: Time, Agency, and Science*. Chicago: U of Chicago P, 1995.

Rohman, Carrie. "On Singularity and the Symbolic. The Threshold of the Human in Calvino's *Mr. Palomar*." *Criticism* 51.1 (2009): 63–78.

Thoreau, Henry David. *A Week on the Concord and Merrimack Rivers, Walden, The Main Woods, Cape Cod*. New York: Library of America, 1989.

Wheeler, Wendy. "The Biosemiotic Turn." In *Ecocritical Theory: New European Perspectives*, ed. Axel Goodbody and Kate Rigby, 270–82. Charlottesville: U of Virginia P, 2012.

———. *The Whole Creature: Complexity, Biosemiotics and the Evolution of Culture*. London: Lawrence and Wishart, 2006.

13

(Re)membering Kinship

Living with Goats in *The Wind Blows Round* and *Le quattro volte*

Elena Past

Landscapes and Copresence

The Wind Blows Round (*E l'aura fai son vir*, 2005, dir. Giorgio Diritti) opens with a visual introduction to its setting, curving along an Alpine road through tunnels in a series of bumpy handheld shots. Although urban eyes might be accustomed to thinking of rocky mountain slopes as wild, uncultivated places, the Italian Alps, like all Italy, bear deep material traces of the complex relationships linking humans, nonhumans, environment, and *technē*.[1] As early as the 1500s, the Dominican historian Leandro Alberti remarked, "Since men have multiplied so notably in Italy, and there are not enough flat places, and customary for cultivation to produce the things necessary to live, it has been necessary to cultivate the high and wild mountains" (qtd. in Pratesi 104). Alberti's tall, wild sixteenth-century mountains, however, had themselves already been traversed, deforested, and inhabited by humans for centuries, as Fulco Pratesi's *Storia della natura d'Italia* demonstrates.[2] Landscape, as Serenella Iovino argues, is never mere scenery but rather "a balance of nature and culture stratified through centuries of mutual adaptation. It is a 'warehouse' of common memories to humanity and nature, in which human and natural life are dialectically interlaced in the form of a *co-presence*" ("Ecocriticism" 31, original emphasis).

In and through the Italian Alps, infinite stories of conflict and copresence might be told: stories of nomadic communities and hermits, stories of Alpine crossings and avalanches, stories of world wars and antiglobalization protests. These stories are written not just in history books but also in the geologic layers, biotic communities, and cultural traditions that characterize and constitute the mountain landscapes. Told in this way, they are the kinds of stories recounted by the emerging field of material ecocriticism, which argues that "stories, bodies, landscapes, bacteria, assemblages, quantum entanglements, waste dumps, animal testing, cyborgs, cheese, nuclear sites, art, time, nature" are all part of a posthuman performativity at work (Iovino, "Material" 58).

This chapter focuses on the interwoven stories of Italian mountains, humans, dogs, and goats in two films—*The Wind Blows Round* and *Le quattro volte* (*The Four Times*, 2011, dir. Michelangelo Frammartino)[3]—set at the two extreme ends of Italy, geographically speaking. The former film is set in the Valle Maira, a valley in the Occitan Alps, not far from Turin and on the border with France, in a liminal space where the local dialect is Provençal. It is perhaps the only film ever made in the *Lingua d'Oc*. *Le quattro volte*, on the other hand, is set at the extreme end of the Apennine Mountains in Calabria, where people certainly speak dialect, but human language is absent from this film, which has almost no audible (human) dialogue (and no subtitles). In cultural, linguistic, and geographic ways, the films' settings are spaces for what Iovino calls "'peripheral' narratives," narratives that she argues are key factors in an "ecological" or "non-anthropocentric" humanism (alternative terms for what contemporary criticism identifies as "posthumanism"). In spite of the breathtaking verticality of the mountains in the frames, the films are in fact narrative spaces that participate in the kind of horizontality characteristic of posthuman thought, a horizontality that helps bridge the gap—both literally and discursively—between humans and the nonhuman (Iovino, "Material" 58–59).[4] They remind us, as Rosi Braidotti has suggested, that "the bond between us is a vital connection based on sharing this territory or environment on terms that are no longer hierarchical or self-evident. They are fast-evolving and need to be renegotiated accordingly" (528).

In revisions of auteur theory, which reads cinema as an emanation primarily of the intentions and vision of the central figure of the director, recent scholarship has focused attention on viewing and interpreting film as a collective enterprise, the result of teams (thus far usually considered to be teams of humans) working together to create the spectacle.[5] Following the double cues of postauteurist and posthumanist scholarship, I posit that the collective of humans working in the film industry collaborates with, depends on, and is shaped by a complementary collective of environmental, technological, and other nonhuman forces.[6] Furthermore, a deliberately liminal cinema, like that of Diritti and Frammartino, draws our eyes to a cinematic construction of what Iovino describes as a "sphere of existence which does not belong solely to humans" ("Ecocriticism" 38) and to the nonhuman actors that feature importantly in the films, in particular to mountains, dogs, and goats. Such cinema reminds us, as Neel Ahuja argues, that "visual culture is also a multispecies domain" (560).

The two films tell dramatically different stories of cohabitation. Diritti's tale follows a goatherd and cheese maker who moves his family to a small village in Italy, where they and the goats quickly encounter the limits of the villagers' hospitality. Frammartino's film tells four interwoven stories, first of a goatherd, then a young goat, next a tree, and finally carbon, in a poetic meditation on cycles of interrelated lives. While Diritti's story cautions against utopian visions of agrarian pasts or globalized agrarian presents, Frammartino's film realizes in visual terms—and without nostalgia—what Braidotti refers to as posthumanism's "bioegalitarian turn," a shift that radically repositions the human subject in a horizontal space of non-species-specific collectivity (526). In narrative and material ways, both films create what Donna Haraway calls "situated histories," showing that "all the actors become who they are *in the dance of relating*, not from scratch, not ex nihilo, but full of the patterns of their sometimes-joined, sometimes-separate heritages both before and lateral to *this* encounter" (*When Species* 25, original emphasis).

Crisis in Cohabitation

The website for the Valle Maira claims that the region is "wild and uncontaminated, where nature is the undisputed queen" ("Natura"). Yet while the entrancing mountains often exceed the frame in their enormity, Diritti's film consistently captures pieces of landscape that betray human presence: a road, a steeple, a stone wall. In the rural mountain village of Chersogno, human spaces and animal spaces overlap architecturally and otherwise, with homes and stalls blending seamlessly into one another. The human protagonist is Philippe Heraud (Thierry Toscan), a French cheese maker and former professor of philosophy who decides to relocate his family from the Pyrenees to the Alps because a nuclear power facility is being constructed near their home. The small Alpine town he chooses as their destination is, like many Italian villages, almost devoid of human inhabitants except in the summer, when people flock in for country vacations. A quarrelsome town council ultimately decides to help Philippe in his relocation, and the fluid boundaries of the European Union initially open to accept this new community member.

Implicit in *The Wind*'s story of "otherness"—linguistic otherness, cultural otherness—we also find an account of what Haraway terms "significant otherness"—that is, the story of cohabitation of species. The film begins with a short prologue and then flashes back to the beginning of the story of the Heraud family in Chersogno, nine months before, a time frame that approximately corresponds, of course, to the human gestation period. When pressed by the mayor, who helps facilitate the move, to say when he wants to relocate his family of five to the small village in the Valle Maira, Philippe responds that he needs to do so as soon as possible, "before the kids are born," referring to the time when the baby goats will enter the world. The film's framework establishes its temporal space as biological time, following the life cycles of human and nonhuman animals.[7] While human linguistic polyphony dominates the soundtrack, featuring Occitan, French, and Italian often spoken interchangeably, other kinds of language also proliferate: squawking, bleating, barking, snorting, mooing, and crowing, courtesy of the many animals that exist around the film's borders. Life in Chersogno has long been a matter of partnership of species, a partnership that Haraway argues has long formed us "in flesh and sign" (*Companion* 25).

Reinforcing the multispecies focus of the film, when Philippe first arrives in the village, he is greeted by a dog, who barks and wags his tail. Emerging from his car, Philippe glances around the yard of a rural home, his eyes scanning its balconies, but no one is home. No humans are home, that is. In a series of shots, he exchanges gazes with the tail-wagging black dog, whose gaze is actually the first we see, before the camera cuts to Philippe's frank eyes, and eventually back to the amiable, barking canine. This exchange becomes more significant when the French protagonist at last meets a few of the town's human inhabitants a few shots later, in the local bar. Their furtive, suspicious glares at the foreigner lend immediate evidence of the hesitant, if not hostile, human welcome for newcomers. By contrast, then, and in retrospect, the dog represents a fleeting alternative present throughout the film, an ethical possibility of cohabitation inscribed in the fabric of the Alps but forgotten by the region's human inhabitants.

In a canonical essay titled "Why Look at Animals?" John Berger reminds us that when we look at animals, they look back: when man "is *being seen* by the animal, he is being seen as his surroundings are seen by him" (5). For Berger, many contemporary representations of animals, including Disney films but more incisively wildlife documentaries, are guilty of forgetting the important exchange of gazes possible when nonhuman animals are the subject. In these kinds of films, he argues, "animals are always the observed. The fact that they can observe us has lost all significance. They are the objects of our ever-extending knowledge. What we know about them is an index of our power [. . .]. The more we know, the further away they are" (16). A one-way gaze on the animal world encloses man in what Roberto Marchesini identifies as an "autonomous cage that does not allow him to dialogue with an other, whatever this other may be" (*Post-human* 12). When Philippe and the tail-wagging dog exchange, thanks to the technological capacities of film editing, a steady, level gaze, the potential of the two-way, inclusive vision that also allows animals to observe humans has been restored, and the hierarchies and borders separating human from canine subjects are momentarily suspended.

This conspiratorial gaze has deep material significance in the evolutionary history of men and dogs. According to Haraway, recent studies of dogs' mitochondrial DNA have demonstrated their emergence from wolves earlier than had previously been thought possible—perhaps 15,000 to 50,000 years ago, making them extremely long-term companions for the human animal; scientists note that "human life ways changed significantly in association with" them (*Companion* 28–29). Domestication, far from being a one-way bending of the animal will to the needs of the human, is a complex process of "co-habiting," where minds, bodies, and cultures of both humans and dogs coevolve so that we coexist in relationships that are "multiform, [...] unfinished, consequential" (Haraway, *Companion* 30).

In the thickly layered spaces of the film, however, discordance and the encounters between communities, both biotic and cultural, are at the heart of the story. When the people of Chersogno initially decide to work together to welcome the extended Heraud family to their village, their preparations include painting the rustic kitchen and, significantly, burning lavender in the stalls where the animals will be housed: hospitality extends to the nonhuman guests. When the family arrives in town, the goats are immediately led to their new quarters, and then human interactions—words of welcome, a communal meal—begin. At first, it seems that the residents of Chersogno will recall, as their mayor urges them to, that these new inhabitants reanimate an integral part of the town's agricultural past. But the period of amity is short-lived. After a few sequences depicting rambles on spectacular mountainsides, sunny church picnics, and rousing community festivals, the town begins to regard the French family's "otherness" not as "significant" but as threatening. Allegations are leveled in particular against the goats, accused of straying from their designated pastures when residents begin to police the borders of their often-unfenced land in the mountains. Using binoculars, peering from doorways, and generally instating a reign of surveillance, the Chersognesi patrol the invisible boundaries that are supposed to pen in the Heraud family and their goats. "*Here* people pay close attention to their *own*," explains one meddlesome resident. *Your* goats, *my* land, the residents complain; possessive pronouns become the means to demarcate ownership and exclusion. But while residents are concerned about what is *theirs*, affirming private property, Philippe points out that they are not actually "attentive" to their property—they do not take care of it. The grass rots in the fields, he argues, actually making it inhospitable to the animals that used to graze there. Through neglect, owners fail to realize a collective stewardship of their environment, substituting the interests of private ownership for a true "attention" to the land.

The problem, thus, is in part one of (re)membering a material past, recalling a history written on the goats and the residents, on the mountains and in the relationships linking them, and in part one of embodying, in contemporary practice, a relationship that honors this memory. The relationship between humans and goats is a long one: according to David E. MacHugh and Daniel G. Bradley, "[A]ccumulating archaeological evidence indicates that goats, in the form of their wild progenitor—the bezoar (*Capra aegagrus*), were the first wild herbivores to be domesticated" (5382).

Used by humans for meat, milk, skins, and fiber, goats have long been key players in the human exploitation of the animal world (they are described in a particularly utilitarian formulation by MacHugh and Bradley as perhaps "the first 'walking larders'" [5382]). Classified as a minor ruminant, the domestic goat is adaptable and sure-footed, able to live in harsh climates and traverse rough terrain; goats can climb trees and graze close to the ground, allowing them to navigate pastures that other animals cannot (De Rancourt et al. 176). Their grazing can help, as Philippe suggested, maintain the land by minimizing the fire risk (De Rancourt et al. 176). Yet because of their agility and their eclectic, efficient dietary habits, goats have also historically caused human conflict. In their guide to raising goats, Roberto Di Natale and Delia Solazzo warn, "These are goats, not other herbivores who might 'steal' a bit of grass, but universal devourers of all that is vegetable, including vineyards, orchards, gardens, flowers, tree bark, and so on" (33). In Italy, goats have been agents of environmental change, as intensive grazing contributed to deforestation as early as the Renaissance (Pratesi 110). They have also been subjects of the law, as shifting Italian states alternately legislated in favor of nomadic grazing, allowing herds of goats, sheep, and cattle to move freely up and down mountain slopes, or instead against it, asserting private property rights and allowing for fences.[8] Both agents and instruments of cultural and environmental history, goats to some degree allow Alpine villages like Chersogno to come into existence, and they shape its boundaries. As Philippe, a former teacher, sarcastically schools his goats to read maps, we are reminded of the arbitrary nature of boundaries, geographical and between species, in a world where spaces and beings evolved together. What the goats perform, and what the Chersognesi seem to have forgotten, is that, as Catriona Mortimer-Sandilands argues, "*all meaning* includes a perceptual dimension and that perception itself is a quality of the relationship between body and world, necessarily a dynamic product of relationship, experience, influence" (268).

The complaints about the goats extend to encompass criticisms of the Heraud family as well: villagers accuse the family of being dirty, turn up their noses at animal excrement in the streets, and complain that the Heraud children smell like goats. Residents and tourists alike in Chersogno thus betray their fear of "animalization," a significant part of the working of the "anthropological machine" that, according to Giorgio Agamben, governs contemporary philosophy and politics. As villagers grumble about the proximity of the Herauds to their companion species, they fret about the problem of "defining the border—at once the separation and proximity"—between animal and human natures (Agamben 59). As Kate Soper suggests, such exclusionary thinking—animals are dirty, and we are clean; animals are stupid, and we are smart—becomes a tool used by humans to affirm superiority (86). Such thinking supports a myth of human exceptionalism that marginalizes humans and nonhumans alike. Graziella Parati notes that Minister Claudio Martelli's immigration laws were known as *sanatoria*, laws intended to "heal" (*sanare*) the diseased body of multicultural Italy. Parati points out that "this terminology borrowed from the rhetoric of illness [. . .] is based on the assumption that becoming a country of immigration involves the contamination of its (almost) monocultural past and present" (170). For posthumanist philosophy, fear of contamination by the human other parallels and confirms the exclusion of the nonhuman other. Haraway argues forcefully that "[t]he discursive tie between the colonized, the enslaved, the noncitizen, and the animal [. . .] is at the heart of racism and flourishes, lethally, in the entrails of humanism" (*When Species* 18). Marchesini calls this humanism's "myth of purity," the extraction of human identity from its relationships to other beings (*Tramonto* 47). In the case of the Heraud family, goat herders and cheese makers accused of living too animal a life, this kind of binary thinking results in a forced estrangement from the rest of the town; eventually, they are left with no space to inhabit.

In a moment of despair, Philippe retreats to his stables and cries, surrounded by his animal companions. In a frank framing, the camera captures a dark, straight long shot of the stable. The scant light creates a moody chiaroscuro, but the human figure, albeit at the center of the frame, lacks the commanding stature of the protagonists in Caravaggio's canvases. Philippe, seated with his head bowed, instead exists on the same horizontal plane as most of the goats (one is above him). Positioned in the shadows, he takes up approximately the same amount of screen space as they do. The soundtrack features pouring rain, quiet human sobbing, and bells on the goats' collars. He, the film, and the goats thus momentarily participate in visual, auditory, and emotional terms in what Haraway sees as the "ramifying tapestry of shared being/becoming among critters (including humans) in which living well, flourishing, and being 'polite' (political/ethical/in right relation) mean staying inside shared semiotic materiality, including the suffering inherent in unequal and ontologically multiple instrumental relationships" (*When Species* 72).

Philippe's unwillingness to respect the logic of species boundaries, geographic boundaries, and cultural boundaries finds no corresponding openness in the town. Yet just as the goatherd-philosopher retreats to the animals for solace, so do the villagers lash out against the goats in an attempt to enact a retributive justice. In a first instance, they throw jars of maggots into hay in the goats' stalls. Later, they call a supposedly conciliatory meeting with Philippe. Yet in a visually dramatic juxtaposition, as a silent assembly waits for this appeasement, the film crosscuts to the Frenchman, roaming gray mountains in search of two missing goats. When he at last finds them, they have been slaughtered and suspended from an archway, a brutal act that strikes a mortal blow at the possibility of cohabitation. Perhaps intended as an admonitory symbol, the sacrificial goats are literally the death of what could have been a "significant otherness," the end of companionship. As Haraway insists regarding dogs, animals "are not surrogates for theory; they are not here just to think with. They are here to live with. Partners in the crime of human evolution, they are in the garden from the get-go" (*Companion* 5).

The circularity of the title "The Wind Blows Round" connects to cycles of life and also recalls the tradition of the *rueido*, which villagers proudly cite as a symbol of their willingness to help one another. This historical event-turned-collective-memory first occurred when the Chersognesi collaborated to hide hay from the Nazis. When a former resident of the town recalls the *rueido*, he underlines that the hay fed the animals that produced the milk and cheese that nourished the villagers. In theory, then, this circle implies mutual respect and cohabitation, and Chersogno in this vision becomes a location of natureculture, a zone in which, according to Haraway, intricate material intertwinings form a vital part of collective memory (*Companion* 1–10). In a discussion with a friend, Philippe posits that culture comes not from language, not from protecting borders, but quite simply from living together, day after day. This philosophy corresponds to Haraway's companion species philosophy, for which "all ethical relating, within or between species, is knit from the silk-strong thread of ongoing alertness to otherness-in-relation" (*Companion* 50).

Although part of collective memory, the *rueido*'s circle of inclusion is no longer part of collective *praxis*—though it exists in lexical and symbolic memory, its material reality in the community has been forgotten. When a religious procession, winding its way down a mountain path, encounters a cartload of hay blocking the way, the residents look around with alarm, hypothesizing that "the Frenchman did it." The scene immediately follows a shot of maggots writhing in hay in the goats' stall and thus rotates around the substance central to the *rueido*. As the camera alternately cuts and pans around the faces in the crowd, capturing residents in medium shots and medium close-ups, its restless fragmentation reproduces the isolationist attitude that makes the community into a space of exclusion. When at last the camera cuts to a shot of the entire group, their action, as a group of men moves the hay and the procession continues, constitutes a collective misrecognition, a failure to acknowledge in the golden grass the physical stuff of shared landscape, history, and community. Landscape, as Mortimer-Sandilands emphasizes, "is a site of forgetting as well as remembering," and in *The Wind*, when the residents push the hay aside, the act is "a physical break in memory, a step in the process of the erasure of presence from history" (281).

Late in the film, a tourist scout and a nostalgic former resident find that another member of the town has committed suicide under the same archway where the slaughtered goats were hung. This final tragedy, subsequent to the Herauds' departure, makes it clear that the fate of the animals and the humans were intimately linked. In short, the townspeople had a choice: "[D]ifferent types of memory combine to enable (or not) socially sanctioned and culturally meaningful interactions with the more-than-human world" (Mortimer-Sandilands 271). In Chersogno, the *rueido*'s circle takes another potential form: that of a fence or a trap that, like Agamben's anthropological machine, keeps things simultaneously in and out (37). Returning to the image of the welcoming dog at the beginning of the film, we recall that he was tied, and that behind him, the camera framed a cage. Although animals might have suggested the potential of companionable cohabitation, and although the residents of Chersogno proudly maintain their Occitan dialect, we discover that the Chersognesi have forgotten how to hear the messages communicated in a multitude of barking, bleating, crowing voices.

Transhumance and Transmigration

In *Le quattro volte*, the wind also blows round, in a manner of speaking, but here in terms of the Pythagorean philosophy of metempsychosis, or the transmigration of the soul, that inspired its form. The "four times" of the title refer to the passage of the soul through four different phases: human, animal, vegetable, and mineral. Four segments dedicated, respectively, to an elderly goatherd, a young goat, a tree, and the making of carbon constitute the film in its entirety. The film is set at the very southern tip of the Apennines in Calabria, where the practice of "horizontal transhumance," or herding from mountains to the sea at the same latitudes, has been practiced for centuries. This is also where the "Mediterranean scrub, which originates in that area [...] constituted the favorite habitat for goats" (Bevilacqua 858). Perhaps first domesticated in the Fertile Crescent, goats and sheep were probably brought to Calabria by Greeks, Romans, and Arabs (MacHugh 5382; Portolano 16), passengers on a voyage of geocultural hybridization that began many centuries ago. Like the Occitan Alps, Calabria is a place where relationships between men, dogs, and goats have written their histories in the soil. Haraway notes that the guardian dogs, sheep, goats, and herders that migrated into Africa, Europe, and Asia "have literally carved deep tracks into soil and rock," tracks comparable with the "carving of glaciers": companion relationships shape the animals who shape the landscapes that shape our human existence (*Companion* 66). Although in Calabria, the geological traces of transhumance are more faint than elsewhere in Italy (the paths of migration from mountains to the plains were so numerous that they were less deeply carved), the history of herding left and continues to leave cultural and historical traces across the region.[9]

The film's Pythagorean framework offers intriguing clues to its interpretation. Pythagoras lived in Magna Graecia, a part of ancient Greece that was centered in Southern Italy and included what is today Calabria; Pythagorean philosophy thus had its seat there. Although modern philosophy often associates Pythagoreanism with theories of mathematics, ancient writers understood it as "a belief in the immortality of the soul in that they held mortality to be ultimately a *topos* of transmigration, just as a snake does not die when it sheds its skin" (Luchte 14). Through the documentation left by Pythagoras's followers, we find evidence of the doctrine of transmigration "as a practice of recollection, as a conception of the migration of the soul, and as a notion of the kinship of all life, 'one great family,' this having practical, ethical implications, such as vegetarian abstinence" (Luchte 16). Drawing on a text by Diogenes Laertius, Luchte notes that Pythagoras believed his own soul to have been in a perpetual state of transmigration, and that it could pass "into *whatever plants or animals it pleased*" (17, emphasis in original). The Pythagorean "eschatology," he continues, sees the soul "in kinship with All, and is similar to All" (19).

Frammartino's *Le quattro volte* is based, visually and philosophically, on this notion of universal kinship, and more incisively on the recollection of such kinship. As such, it historicizes the human/animal question and emphasizes its rootedness in the Calabrian landscape. The mere fact that "human" can be juxtaposed to "animal" testifies to the improbable linguistic notion that beings as diverse as stingrays, elephants, and hummingbirds might fall into one category; it reflects a kind of "species provincialism," as Laurie Shannon defines it (477). In considering nonhuman animals in the plays of William Shakespeare, Shannon notes that, in English, "'the human/animal divide' and 'the question of the animal'" are "modern rhetorical propositions rather than universal or inevitable features of thought (philosophical or otherwise) on these subjects" (474). Before the Cartesian shift in the seventeenth century, Shannon observes, "there were creatures. There were brutes, and there were beasts. There were fish and fowl. There were living things. There were humans, who participated in animal nature and who shared the same bodily materials with animals" (474). In short, then, humans took their place "in a larger cosmography, constitution, or even 'world picture' than the more contracted post-Cartesian human/animal divide with which we customarily wrangle" (474). Although our short memory of kinship recounts our history of forgetting, Braidotti notes that "evolutionary theory acknowledges the cumulated and embodied memory of the species" (528). *Le quattro volte* reinscribes physical memories of this larger cosmography on celluloid, radically resituating the human as one of four (but potentially infinite) entangled protagonists.

Part of the project of recasting the roles in cinema also requires material and perceptual shifts. In *Le quattro volte*, it becomes evident that, as Braidotti argues, life "is far from being the exclusive right of one species—the human": "Becoming animal consequently is a process of redefining one's sense of attachment and connection to a shared world, a territorial space. It expresses multiple ecologies of belonging, while it transforms one's sensorial and perceptual coordinates, to acknowledge the collectiveness and outward direction of what we call the self. The nomadic subject is immersed in and immanent to a network of human and nonhuman (animal, vegetable, viral) relations" (530). For Frammartino, the human plays a decidedly supporting role, in a film that arguably has no place for leading actors. By almost entirely eliminating human dialogue, the film emphasizes other critical ways of being: gestures, gazes, and material presence.[10] Although the goatherd, goat, tree, and carbon occupy central spaces in the sections of the film dedicated to them, there are also ants, snails, dogs, dust, bells, trucks, chainsaws, villagers, and a church that have agentic significance in the film. Each section is interwoven with those before and after it: this goat in front of that tree, those carbon makers in front of that goatherd's door; this ant on that goatherd's face, and then those ants on that tree bark, and so on. Intermingled images in the cinematic frame show that, whichever way the soul passes, other beings continue to pass in, around, and through it.

As the first sequence proceeds, we learn that the goatherd treats a cough each night by mixing dirt, swept up and blessed by a woman in the village church, into a glass of water. When he enters the church to collect his "medicine" in one sequence, a shot of dust particles, floating against a dark backdrop, shows the mystic, and insistently material, omnipresence of the substance in the very air he already breathes. As the elderly man exchanges goat milk for holy dust, the economy of transcorporeal exchange—the movement of substances across and through bodies—takes cinematic shape, linking church, custodian, goatherd, goats, grass, trees, coal, smoke, and dust, as well as film, filmmakers, and cinematic subjects.[11] In proposing that ecocritics take up "dirt theory," Heather I. Sullivan reminds us that dirt particles surround us at every turn: "They are the stuff of geological structures, of the rocky Earth itself, and are mobile like our bodies" (515). Citing geomorphologist David R. Montgomery, Sullivan argues that dirt is a cyborg (in its mix of organic and inorganic materials) but also "almost mystical," the "motherly 'placenta'" that nourishes civilizations and whose health determines their rise and fall (517). On Frammartino's microregional scale, when one day the goatherd loses his packet of dust, the next morning he is unable to get out of bed. When he first discovers his loss, he makes a late-night run to the church, carrying a goat's bell that he found earlier. Our eyes show us the man, but our ears hear the bell's clanging; we already perceive that he is becoming-goat, his audio-visual presence half metamorphosed. The next morning, surrounded by goats who escaped their pen and entered his bedroom, he takes his last shaky breath. After his casket is closed into the wall of a cemetery, blackness fills the screen, accompanied by a rich soundscape. It is the black screen that for Gilles Deleuze has a genetic value, and "with its variations and tonalities, it acquires the power of a constitution of bodies" (200). The next scene opens to reveal the back end of a mother goat, out of which, miraculously, precipitously, and somewhat messily, there emerges a wet, bleating kid.

The birth of the baby goat announces another critical shift, as the protagonists of the film are no longer just the herd but also its individual members. In fact, the film upends humanist hierarchies and reenvisions a world in which human protagonists play only a supporting role. It actually *shows* how the cinematic frame might empty itself of a long-standing human occupation at the center. A key scene in this regard happens in the first section, when a steady shot captures a religious procession marching through an archway at the edge of town, as the villagers make their way into the countryside. In the same frame, a dog pulls a rock out from under the back wheel of a truck, and the vehicle, parked on an incline, rolls backward into a pen of goats, releasing them into the street. The camera pans back to the archway, as the barking dog herds the goats through the archway to occupy the town, now emptied of its human inhabitants.[12] The reversals continue as the camera cuts to a shot of the goatherd's kitchen, where a large goat stands on the table, bleating and knocking an aluminum pan full of snails off one edge. Thus through their positioning in cinematic, residential, and physical space (center frame, in town, in the house, on the table), and also by their active participation in the creation of the story, goats have fully overtaken the film, asserting their agentic power. For a significant portion of the film thereafter, goats will have a central position on screen, and shots of varying distances capture them gazing toward the sky, jockeying for position on an upended metal tub in their stable, and trotting down the road on the way to pasture.

In a further step toward posthumanizing cinema, *Le quattro volte* tells the story of one goat, a baby, who gets separated from the herd on its first day out to graze in the mountains. As the small white kid appears at the bottom of an embankment across which the rest of the herd successfully jumped, we are confronted with the individual specificity of *a* goat, no longer the generalities of the species. This is another radical move for cinema. Contemplating the conventions of Hollywood film credits, Akira Lippit points out that paratextual cinematic language reassures spectators that "no animals were harmed" in the making of a particular film, while humans instead can be comforted that "[a]ll resemblances to persons living or deceased is [sic] purely coincidental" (11). Through this language, two different taboos recognize different "modes of violation" of a human or an animal subject: "Copying the human figure amounts to a form of killing if it is seen as eliminating the singularity thought to establish human identity. Killing a particular animal suggests that animal's individuality, disturbing the frequent representation of animals as constituting packs or hordes" (Lippit 11).

Films, suggests Lippit, but even more incisively film credits, which project the spectator back into the "real" world beyond the film, play on irrational anxieties that, in the extreme extension of this logic, suggest that "to imitate another human being is to assail that individual's singularity and force it to become, like an animal, multiple; to kill an individual animal is to grant it singularity, allowing it to become unique, to become-human" (11). Frammartino's film grants the goats a nonhuman individuality without staging the ritual of death and in a simple narrative gesture undermines this supposed taboo. As the small kid rambles, bleating, around the mountainside, at last settling in front of a tree to sleep, the line of connection between goatherd and baby goat and tree is imprinted on the celluloid of the cinematic frame and etched into the material of the mountains.[13] In *Le quattro volte*, in the "neoliteral" terms that Braidotti suggests should accompany the "bioegalitarian turn," goats are not seen as a "signifying system that props up humans' self-projections and moral aspirations. Nor are they the keepers of the gates between species. They have, rather, started to be approached literally, as entities framed by code systems of their own" (528). And in keeping with this bioegalitarianism, the goat will cede its cinematic place to a tree, whose story will become that of coal, and the film will close with a wisp of smoke that, falling from the sky as particulate matter, will touch a whole cosmography of beings.

Mountain/Goats

The Wind Blows Round is a cautionary tale that seeks to correct utopian visions of agrarian pasts and multicultural agrarian presents. *Le quattro volte*, on the other hand, offers an unidealized alternative to the human/animal rupture. The landscapes in which the two films are set, mountain ranges that traverse all Italy, were always already deconstructing the myth of purity by challenging the boundaries of human and cinematic vision. Purity correlates to the humanist paradigm, Marchesini writes, because it aspires to trace the image of man emerging from an orderly context. In the cinematic frame, the Alps and the Apennines defy the possibility of completeness and of purity: though the camera pans around the mountains, the landscapes exceed the boundaries of the frame and give a sense of their immensity beyond it.[14]

Why, though, should we stare at goats as we contemplate the majestic mountains? Mountains risk transporting us with our nineteenth-century aesthetic imagination into the space of the sublime; goats, generally speaking, do not. As such, goats take us deeper into the unidealized reality of contemporary Italy, gently indicating the need to confront its material spaces visually, politically, philosophically, and environmentally. A revised understanding of Italian space, and the hybrid voices in which it speaks, has been called for on many occasions in a human political context. In her advocacy for a narrative space for African-Italian writers, Parati argues that Italy needs a context for "Italophone literature in which multinational and multiracial voices can become part of the discussion of the Italian cultural tradition," and that this space should be one of cultural hybridity (172, 187). Cinema's role in envisioning this hybrid has also been recognized, again especially in terms of human political ends. Turning his gaze to the landscape, Giorgio Bertellini emphasizes that cinema can help ensure a "constant civic engagement with our natural and cultural space—the most solid guarantor of our national civil patrimony" (49).

Taking one step further into the landscape, posthumanist theory gives Italian hybridity an ecological, more-than-human home and allows the notions of cohabitation and coevolution to enter the discussion as critique and as possibility. To return to Iovino's notion of the landscape, we must remember, in fact, that landscapes are always already "warehouses" storing centuries of geological, biological, narrative, and other evidence of the entanglement of the human and more-than-human world. Looking down from the mountaintops to see the goats eating tree bark, climbing on tables, liberating snails, and running out of the frame is arguably a compelling way these films think past a cinema of humanist purity. Staring at goats, far from the inane psychological exercise proposed in *The Men Who Stare at Goats* (2009, dir. Grant Heslov), becomes a way to (re)member a multispecies past, to perceive the layers of cohabitation written on the landscapes, and to reposition the human within this space.

Recalling the practices of transhumance and transmigration and their rootedness in the Calabrian mountains brings us to an etymologically complicated space: *trans* means "across or beyond"; *migration* comes from the Latin for "to move," "to change," or "to turn into"; and finally *humance* comes from *humus*, "earth," which recalls the potential root for *humans* themselves in the soil.[15] As Mortimer-Sandilands argues, memory is not simply a function of the brain but rather "involves a recognition of a relationship between the body/mind and the external world," and it is thus "always already social, technological, and physical" (274). The films, shot on location in direct collaboration with the environments they depict, help change our memories of a human/*humus* relationship, a relationship that has always had many companions. They both enact (as cinematic productions) and show (as cinematic spectacles) the potentials of cinema to participate in the transformation of these memories.

In a final cinematic act of memory, *Le quattro volte*'s closing credits list the following:

- The dog Vuk
- The silver fir of the Pollino
- The goats of Caulonia
- The coal of the Calabrian sierra

Closing credits provide final documentation of the extensive collaborative practice, the artistic and material cohabitation, that results in a film. *Le quattro volte* recalls that its presence on celluloid results from a collaboration that is transhuman:[16] both *beyond* the human and rooted in the *humus* that nourishes and gives shape to dogs, trees, goats, and coal, as well as Pythagoreans, goatherds, Alpine villagers, and French cheese makers. This short list inaugurates a possibly infinite list of closing credits, a list that recalls our responsibility to this multiform world. If we do not heed this call to (re)member our past, as *The Wind Blows Round* warns, our collective future—in all its entangled political, social, cultural, environmental iterations—will pay the price.

Notes

1. In the preface to his *Storia della natura d'Italia*, Fulco Pratesi insists that "in our country, there exists no place that can in some way be considered 'natural,' that is to say with the appearance and the components that it would have without the modifications made by man" (9). Unless otherwise indicated, all translations from the Italian are mine.
2. See, for example, pp. 27–28, in which Pratesi chronicles early records of transhumance, or seasonal herding from the mountains to the coasts, during the Neolithic period (in Italy, from 6500 to 2500 BC), and pp. 94–95, in which he cites uses of natural pastures above the tree line during the medieval period.
3. The original Italian is used in the Anglophone world, so I will refer to the film by the Italian title.
4. Citing Jane Bennett's notion of "vital materialism," Iovino argues that the "political consequences of this horizontalism are co-dependency, enlargement of the horizon of accountability beyond the linear visions of human intersubjectivity, and awareness of the complex landscape of actants in which human action is situated" ("Material" 58).
5. See, for example, the diverse essays on the collaborations that contribute to film "authorship" in Virginia Wright Wexman, *Film and Authorship*.
6. Such work is beginning to take root in film studies. See, for example, the foundational work on "ecocinema" proposed in the collection *Ecocinema Theory and Practice*, ed. Rust, Monani, and Cubitt.
7. Nine months is also the time it took to make the film, as Luca Caminati points out. Caminati argues that the film, deeply entangled in the material reality of the communities in which it was filmed, is a case of "participatory ethnography" or "shared anthropology" in the definition of filmmaker Jean Rouch (129).
8. See, for example, Pratesi 176–77; or Piero Bevilacqua, "La transumanza in Calabria." Goats can also be cyborg creatures, subjects of medical and transgenetic experiments like the "spider-goat" project in the field of synthetic biology. As reported in *The Guardian*, scientists splice spider DNA onto goat DNA, producing goats whose milk contains dragline silk, a fiber with exceptional properties (Rutherford).

9. In Abruzzo and in Puglia, for example, the traces are distinct (Bevilacqua 858). See Bevilacqua for the many traditions and products linked to the Calabrian practice of transhumance.
10. Language is thus demonstrated to be, as Massimo Filippi and Filippo Trasatti argue, "one of the possible means of communication between bodies, which is specialized in man, yes, but precedes and anticipates him in the form of breaths, gestures, postures, gazes, encounters" (15).
11. Scenes at the beginning and end of the film feature smoke rising from the mounds made by the coal makers, further evidence of the transitory nature of matter.
12. The extra materials included on the Italian version of the DVD chronicle the numerous takes required to capture the sequence, which demanded complicated acting on the part of the dog, Vuk, and ultimately the goats. The short documentary thus chronicles a film production that collaborates with but also relinquishes itself to the more-than-human world.
13. Although the goat's death is implied as the film fades to black and its cinematic soul passes into the story of the tree, it is not actually represented.
14. I thank Giovanna Faleschini Lerner for this insight.
15. See Sullivan on further connections between "humans" and "soil" (518).
16. Here I refer to the historical practice of "transhumance" and not to the transhumanism movement, whose complex relationship to posthumanism is beyond the scope of this essay.

Works Cited

Agamben, Giorgio. *The Open: Man and Animal*. Trans. Kevin Attell. Stanford: Stanford UP, 2004.

Ahuja, Neel. "Postcolonial Critique in a Multispecies World." *PMLA* 124.2 (2009): 556–63.

Berger, John. *About Looking*. New York: Pantheon, 1980.

Bertellini, Giorgio. "The Earth Still Trembles: On Landscape Views in Contemporary Italian Cinema." *Italian Culture* 30.1 (2012): 38–50.

Bevilacqua, Piero. "La transumanza in Calabria." *Mélanges de l'Ecole française de Rome. Moyen-Age, Temps modernes* 100.2 (1988): 857–69.

Braidotti, Rosi. "Animals, Anomalies, and Inorganic Others." *PMLA* 124.2 (2009): 526–32.

Caminati, Luca. "Narrative Non-Fictions in Contemporary Italian Cinema: Roberto Munzi's *Saimir* (2002), Giorgio Diritti's *Il vento fa il suo giro* (2005), and Pietro Marcello's *La bocca del lupo* (2009)." *Studies in Documentary Film* 5.2–3 (2011): 121–31.

Deleuze, Gilles. *Cinema 2: The Time-Image*. Trans. Hugh Tomlinson and Robert Galeta. Minneapolis: U of Minnesota P, 1989.
De Rancourt, M., et al. "Mediterranean Sheep and Goats Production: An Uncertain Future." *Small Ruminant Research* 62 (2006): 167–79.
Di Natale, Roberto, and Delia Solazzo. *La capra nell'allevamento famigliare*. Verona: Informatore Agrario, 1991.
Filippi, Massimo, and Filippo Trasatti. "Avviso agli Ospiti." In *Nell'albergo di Adamo: Gli animali, la questione animale e la filosofia*, ed. Massimo Filippi and Filippo Trasatti, 9–19. Milan: Mimesis, 2010.
Haraway, Donna J. *The Companion Species Manifesto: Dogs, People, and Significant Otherness*. Chicago: Prickly Paradigm, 1993.
———. *When Species Meet*. Minneapolis: U of Minnesota P, 2008.
Iovino, Serenella. "Ecocriticism and a Non-Anthropocentric Humanism." In *Local Natures, Global Responsibilities: Ecocritical Perspectives on the New English Literatures*, ed. Laurenz Volkmann, Nancy Grimm, and Ines Detmers, 29–53. Amsterdam: Rodopi, 2010.
———. "Material Ecocriticism: Matter, Text, and Posthuman Ethics." In *Literature, Ecology, Ethics*, ed. Michael Sauter and Timo Müller, 51–68. Heidelberg: Winter Verlag, 2012.
Krall, Florence R. *Ecotone: Wayfaring on the Margins*. Albany: Albany State U of New York P, 1994.
Lippit, Akira Mizuta. "The Death of an Animal." *Film Quarterly* 56.1 (2002): 9–22.
Luchte, James. *Continuum Studies in Ancient Philosophy: Pythagoras and the Doctrine of Transmigration: Wandering Souls*. New York: Continuum, 2009.
MacHugh, David E., and Daniel G. Bradley. "Livestock Genetic Origins: Goats Buck the Trend." *PNAS* 98.10 (2001): 5382–84.
Marchesini, Roberto. *Post-human: Verso nuovi modelli di esistenza*. Turin: Bollati Boringhieri, 2002.
———. *Il tramonto dell'uomo: La prospettiva post-umanista*. Bari: Dedalo, 2009.
Mortimer-Sandilands, Catriona. "Landscape, Memory, and Forgetting: Thinking Through (My Mother's) Body and Place." In *Material Feminisms*, ed. Stacy Alaimo and Susan Hekman, 265–87. Bloomington: Indiana UP, 2008.
"Natura." Valle Maira website. http://www.vallemaira.cn.it/pagina.asp?id=62.
Parati, Graziella. "Strangers in Paradise: Foreigners and Shadows in Italian Literature." In *Revisioning Italy: National Identity and Global Culture*, ed. Beverly Allen and Mary Russo, 169–90. Minneapolis: U of Minnesota P, 1997.
Portolano, Nicola. *Pecore e capre italiane*. Ed. Baldassare Portolano. Bologna: Edagricole, 1987.

Pratesi, Fulco. *Storia della natura d'Italia*. Soveria Mannelli: Rubbettino, 2010.

Rust, Stephen, Salma Monani, and Sean Cubitt, eds. *Ecocinema Theory and Practice*. New York: Routledge, 2012.

Rutherford, Adam. "Synthetic Biology and the Rise of 'Spider-Goats.'" *The Guardian*, January 14, 2012. http://www.guardian.co.uk/science/2012/jan/14/synthetic-biology-spider-goat-genetics.

Shannon, Laurie. "The Eight Animals in Shakespeare; or, Before the Human." *PMLA* 124.2 (2009): 472–79.

Soper, Kate. *What Is Nature? Culture, Politics and the Non-Human*. Cambridge, MA: Blackwell, 1995.

Sullivan, Heather I. "Dirt Theory and Material Ecocriticism." *Interdisciplinary Studies in Literature and Environment* 19.3 (2012): 515–31.

Wexman, Virginia Wright. *Film and Authorship*. New Brunswick: Rutgers UP, 2003.

Contributors

Deborah Amberson is Associate Professor of Italian at the University of Florida. Her research encompasses modern Italian literature and cinema, with a particular focus on literary modernism. She is the author of *Giraffes in the Garden of Italian Literature: Modernist Embodiment in Italo Svevo, Federigo Tozzi and Carlo Emilio Gadda* (2012), and she has published articles on Italo Svevo, Carlo Emilio Gadda, Pier Paolo Pasolini, and Roberto Rossellini.

Simone Castaldi is Associate Professor of Italian at Hofstra University. His research interests include Italian cinema, visual arts in the 1970s and 1980s, and the literary avant-garde. He has published a book titled *Drawn and Dangerous: Italian Comics of the 1970s and 1980s* (2010) and articles on authors, directors, and topics including Elio Petri, Pulp and the avant-garde, and Tommaso Landolfi.

David Del Principe is Associate Professor of Italian at Montclair State University. His research interests focus on the ecogothic, Monster Theory, and Feminist Vegetarian Theory. He is the author of *Rebellion, Death, and Aesthetic in Italy: The Demons of Scapigliatura* (1996) and of articles on authors including Ugo Tarchetti, Camillo Boito, Mary Shelley, Bram Stoker, Carlo Collodi, and Clara Sereni.

Giovanna Faleschini Lerner is Associate Professor at Franklin and Marshall College. Her research interests encompass representations of history in film and literature, interart criticism, women writers, and the literature and cinema of migration. She is the author of *Carlo Levi's Visual Poetics: The Painter as Writer* (2012), and she has published articles on Luchino Visconti, Carlo Levi, Francesco Rosi, hospitality in Italian migration cinema, and the contemporary Italian documentary.

Daniele Fioretti is Visiting Assistant Professor of Italian at the University of Miami, Ohio. He works on modern and contemporary Italian literature, with a particular interest in avant-garde and experimental literature.

He has edited a volume of Paolo Volponi's letters to Pasolini (2009) and coedited a volume on the Bildungsroman (2007). He has published articles on Volponi, Giuseppe Ungaretti, Luigi Capuana, Carlo Goldoni, Ennio Flaiano, and Cesare Pavese.

Valentina Fulginiti is completing a PhD in Italian Studies at the University of Toronto. Her research interests include contemporary Italian narrative and theater, with a particular focus on translation. She has published and presented on the work of Luigi Pirandello, Carlo Bernari, Italo Calvino, Umberto Eco, Ermanno Rea, and Wu Ming, among others.

Matteo Gilebbi is Senior Lecturing Fellow and Cultural Advisor in the Department of Romance Studies at Duke University. He is also the managing editor of the journal of modern Italian literature *L'Anello Che Non Tiene*. His primary area of research is the interaction between literature, philosophy, and mass media in modern and contemporary culture. His publications focus on the relationship between literature and digital technologies, and on the interaction between poetry and philosophy.

Alexandra Hills is completing a PhD in German at University College London. Her research explores representations of war, emotions, and gender in Austrian and Italian films of the 1970s. She considers how the concept of the "creaturely," as it is understood by Agamben and Santner, opens a critical space for examining issues of the inscription of power on the human body.

Serenella Iovino is Professor of Comparative Literature at the University of Turin and Research Fellow of the Alexander-von-Humboldt Foundation. President of the European Association for the Study of Literature, Culture and Environment from 2008 to 2010, she serves on the editorial boards of journals including *ISLE*, *Green Letters*, *Ecozon@*, and Roberto Marchesini's *Zooanthropology*. Author of four books and numerous essays, she specializes in ecocritical theory and environmental humanities. Recent works include *Ecologia letteraria* (2006; repr. 2014), *Material Ecocriticism* (coedited with Serpil Oppermann, 2014) and, as guest editor, *Ecozon@*'s issue on Mediterranean Ecocriticism.

Elizabeth Leake is Professor of Italian at Columbia University. Her research interests encompass twentieth-century Italian narrative and theater, fascist Italy, Italian cinema, and early Danish cinema. Her books include *The Reinvention of Ignazio Silone* (2003) and *After Words: Suicide and Authorship in Twentieth Century Italy* (2011), which deals with the thought of

Guido Morselli, Amelia Rosselli, Primo Levi, and Cesare Pavese. She has published articles on Clara Petacci, Amelia Rosselli, and Ignazio Silone.

Roberto Marchesini is an Italian philosopher active in the area of cognitive ethology and zooanthropology. His work in posthumanism focuses on the role of the heterospecific and of *technē* in identity formation. Marchesini directs the SIUA (http://www.siua.it), or School for Human Animal Interactions. His publications include *Post-human: verso nuovi modelli di esistenza* (2002), *Il tramonto dell'uomo* (2008), *Intelligenze plurime* (2008), and *Modelli cognitivi e comportamento animale* (2012).

Giuseppina Mecchia is Associate Professor of French and Italian and Director of the Program in Cultural Studies at the University of Pittsburgh. Her publications include a volume edited with Tim Murphy, *The Futures of Empire*, on Michael Hardt and Antonio Negri's *Empire* trilogy; a special issue of *Sites: The Journal of French and Francophone Contemporary Studies* (with Todd Reeser); a special issue of the journal *Sub-Stance* on Italian postworkerist thought; and articles on French and Italian cinema, philosophy, and politics.

Elena Past is Associate Professor of Italian at Wayne State University. Her research focuses on modern and contemporary Italian literature and film, in particular crime fiction, the eco-noir, and ecomedia studies. She is the author of *Methods of Murder: Beccarian Introspection and Lombrosian Vivisection in Italian Crime Fiction* (2012), and she has published articles on the toxic waste crisis in Naples, Mediterranean cinema, and crime fiction and film.

Gregory Pell is Associate Professor of Italian at Hofstra University, where he focuses primarily on cinema and poetry. His articles examine such poets as Dante, Paolo Ruffilli, Tommaso Lisa, and Mario Tobino, and such filmmakers as Kore-Eda, Sergio Rubini, Mohsen Melliti, and Matteo Garrone. His latest research deals with the novelists Vitaliano Trevisan and Angelo Cannavacciuolo. Additionally, he is working on a monograph on the relationship between art and poetry in the works of Davide Rondoni, Seamus Heaney, and Derek Walcott.

Index

Abram, David, 223–24, 230*n*
Adams, Carol J., 34*n*, 180, 184, 188–89
Adorno, Theodor W., 147
Agamben, Giorgio, xxxi*n*, 5, 10, 14*n*,
   27, 35*n*, 50–52, 62, 93, 100–106,
   106*n*, 120–21, 130, 132, 134–36,
   141–42, 144*n*, 145, 149, 154–55,
   161, 173*n*, 198, 203, 238
   Anthropological machine, xxxi*n*, 10,
      62, 101–6, 106*n*, 238
   Bare life, 5, 10, 100–101, 104, 120,
      134–35, 173*n*
   Bíos, 5, 35*n*, 100–101, 104–5, 135, 149
   Inoperativity, 5, 103–5
   Zoē, 5, 27, 35*n*, 100–101, 104, 135, 149
Ahuja, Neel, 234
Alaimo, Stacy, 217–18, 222, 229*n*, 249
Alberti, Leandro, 233
Alfano Miglietti, Francesca, xxvi
Almansi, Guido, 65
Amselle, Jean-Loup, xxix*n*
Andersen, Karin, xxvii, xxxi*n*, xxxiv*n*
Andreozzi, Giorgio, 76, 90*n*
Animetaphor, 10, 32, 94–95, 98
Anthropocentrism, 5, 8, 11–12, 26,
   53*n*, 58, 64, 67–68, 75, 84, 89, 93,
   95–96, 99, 103–4, 121, 145–46,
   149–51, 155*n*, 160, 162–63, 167,
   171–72, 173–74*n*, 180, 182, 185,
   187, 189, 192, 193*n*, 198–99, 206,
   210, 211–12*n*, 234
Anthropomorphization, xviii–xxiv,
   xxix*n*, 57–59, 61–64, 67–68, 71*n*,
   75–76, 82–86, 153, 160, 194*n*, 206,
   208, 226

Apocalypse/postapocalypse, 10, 135,
   147–48, 151, 160–61, 163, 165–67,
   170, 173*n*, 183, 187, 190
Arendt, Hannah, 125*n*, 134–36
Aristotle (Stagirite), xiii–xiv, xxii–xxiii,
   xxxiii*n*, 101
Atwood, Margaret, 111–12, 170, 172,
   174*n*
Augé, Marc, xxvi, xxxiii*n*

Bachelard, Gaston, xxxiii*n*, 80
Bacon, Francis, xvi, 79
Bakhtin, Mikhail, xxxiv*n*, 150, 162
Baldacci, Luigi, 33, 36*n*
Bandura, Albert, xv
Baracchi, Claudia, 48, 52*n*, 55*n*
Barad, Karen, 219, 226–27, 230*n*
Barthes, Roland, 117, 125*n*
Bataille, Georges, 7, 25, 31–32
Baudrillard, Jean, 168
Baumgarten, Alexander Gottlieb, xiii,
   xxi, xxviii*n*
Beard, George M., 180, 188, 193*n*
Benedetti, Carla, 160
Ben-Ghiat, Ruth, 205, 211*n*
Benjamin, Andrew, 112
Benjamin, Walter, 135, 201
Bennett, Jane, 216–18, 225, 229*n*, 247*n*
Bentham, Jeremy, 22, 26, 30
Berger, John, 236
Bertellini, Giorgio, 245–46
Bevilacqua, Piero, 247–48*n*
Biasin, Gian Paolo, 51, 54*n*
Bildungsroman, 154, 157*n*
Biocentrism, 10, 94, 99–100, 102–6

Biopolitics, 4–5, 10, 14n, 100–105, 115, 131–36, 142–43, 149
Borges, Jorge Luis, 69, 71n, 216–17
Bouchard, Norma, 6, 205
Bowlby, John, xv
Bradley, Daniel G., 237–38
Braidotti, Rosi, 3, 5, 40–43, 45, 47–48, 50, 52, 53n, 55n, 155n, 159, 162–63, 172, 219, 228, 234–35, 242–43, 245
Burke, Edmund, xviii, xxxin
Burke, Kenneth, 64
Bussolini, Jeffrey, 6–7
Butler, Judith, 44, 47

Calarco, Matthew, 199, 212n
Calvino, Italo, xxvi–xxvii, 12–13, 147, 173n, 206, 210, 215–32
　The Baron in the Trees [*Il barone rampante*], 220
　"Being Stone" [*Essere pietra*], 224
　The Cloven Viscount [*Il visconte dimezzato*], 220–21
　Cosmicomics [*Le cosmicomiche*], xxvi, 12, 173n, 217, 220–21, 225–28, 229n
　"Identity" [*Identità*], 226
　Marcovaldo, or the Seasons in the City [*Marcovaldo ovvero le stagioni in città*], 221
　Mr. Palomar [*Palomar*], 12–13, 206, 215–17, 220–25, 228, 230n
　The Nonexistent Knight [*Il cavaliere inesistente*], 221
　"The Petrol Pump" [*La pompa di benzina*], 218–19
　Six Memos for the Next Millennium [*Lezioni americane. Sei proposte per il nuovo millennio*], 222, 225
　t zero [*T con zero*], 220–21, 227
　The Watcher [*La giornata di uno scrutatore*], 220, 228
　Why Read the Classics? [*Perchè leggere i classici*], 218
Cambon, Glauco, 65
Caminati, Luca, 247n

Campbell, Timothy, 15n
Campbell Bertoletti, Susan, 192
Cannibalism, 11–12, 63, 161, 164–70, 172, 186–89, 191
Carnivorism, 11, 23, 148, 165, 172, 180, 182–83, 186–90
Carrera, Alessandro, xxxin, xxxiiin
Cartesian, 242. *See also* Descartes, René
Cassano, Franco, 5–8, 198, 204–7, 209–10
Cats, xxvi–xxvii, 13, 23, 27–28, 66, 77, 84, 87, 166–67, 182
Cavalieri, Paola, 14n
Cavani, Liliana, 10, 12, 111–13, 115–21, 123–25
　Night Porter [*Il portiere di notte*], 10, 111–13, 115–16, 118–21, 123–25, 126n
Cavarero, Adriana, 41, 45, 47–48, 51–52
Cavour, Camillo Benso di, 2
Celli, Giorgio, xxvi, 13
Chavasse, Pye Henry, 180
Chiesa, Lorenzo, 4, 14n
Chomsky, Noam, 70n
Coda, Elena, 194n
Cohen, Jeffrey Jerome, 194n, 195, 230n
Collodi, Carlo, 11, 179, 184–86, 191–92
　The Adventures of Pinocchio [*Le avventure di Pinocchio*], 11–12, 179–81, 184–86, 190, 192, 193n
　"Bread and Books" [*Pane e libri*], 191–92
Concentration camps, xxv, 5, 62, 100–101, 112, 115–16, 123–25, 148, 197
Copjec, Joan, 123–24
Cordelli, Franco, 159–60
Cortázar, Julio, 69, 71n

Darwin, Charles (Darwinism), xxvi, 8–9, 26–27, 33, 35n, 58, 101, 146, 180, 187, 215, 226

Deacon, Terrence William, xxiii*n*
Debenedetti, Giacomo, 24, 31, 34*n*, 36*n*
De Certeau, Michel, xxxiii*n*
Deganutti, Massimo, xxvii, xxxiv*n*
Dekoven, Marianne, 34*n*, 146
De Landa, Manuel, 224
Deleuze, Gilles, 10, 15*n*, 41, 79, 130–31, 137, 139, 141–42, 217, 225, 228, 243
   Becoming-animal, 79, 83, 86, 88–89, 131, 137, 139, 142, 228, 242–43
   See also Guattari, Félix
Della Seta, Roberto, 2
De Lucca, Robert, 32
De Matteis, Carlo, 54*n*
De Michele, Girolamo, 174*n*
Derrida, Jacques, 3, 7–8, 10, 14*n*, 23, 25–27, 32, 34, 41, 45, 70, 83, 86, 90*n*, 94–95, 145–46, 154, 171, 199–201, 206–8, 210, 212*n*
   Animots, 32, 76, 86–88, 94
   Carnophallogocentrism, 23, 45
   Phallogocentrism, 9, 23, 39–41, 45, 47–48, 52
Descartes, René, 4. *See also* Cartesian
Diamond, Cora, 33–34
Di Natale, Roberto, 238
Diritti, Giorgio, 12, 233–41
   The Winds Blow Round, 12, 233–41, 245
Di Spigno, Stelvio, 61
Dogs, xxx, 6, 13, 21–24, 29, 48, 52*n*, 60–61, 69, 76–79, 82, 84, 86–87, 89, 90*n*, 119, 132, 142, 156*n*, 166–68, 171, 182, 194*n*, 203, 206, 216, 234, 236–37, 239, 241, 243–44, 246, 248*n*
Dolar, Mladen, 31
Duggan, Christopher, 14*n*

Ecocriticism, 5, 12, 198–99, 211, 211*n*, 230*n*, 234, 243
Epistemology, xiv–xv, xxii–xxiii, xxxii*n*, 26, 30–31, 33, 36*n*, 40, 50, 79, 84, 95, 100, 145, 192, 216–17.
   See also Gnoseology
Erikson, Erik, 168
Esposito, Roberto, 3–4, 14*n*, 15*n*

Fabietti, Ugo, xiv, xxviii*n*
Faeti, Antonio, 59, 68
Famine, 190–92, 194*n*
Farley, Paul, 126*n*
Fascism, 8, 111–14, 116–17, 121, 123, 125*n*, 133, 202, 205, 211*n*
Fellini, Federico, xxiii, xxvi, xxviii
Feminism, 4, 39–41, 49–52, 130–31, 137–39, 162
Ferme, Valerio, 6, 205
Ferretti, Gian Carlo, 151
Fiddes, Nick, 34*n*
Filippi, Massimo, 248*n*
Fiorani, Eleonora, xxvi, xxxiv*n*
Fitch, W. Tecumseh, 70*n*
Foucault, Michel, 4, 10, 100, 130–35, 141, 143*n*, 145, 149, 156*n*, 216
Frammartino, Michelangelo, 12, 234–35, 242–44
   Le quattro volte, 12, 233–34, 241–42, 244–46
Freud, Sigmund, 29, 31, 78, 80, 85, 117, 119, 125*n*
   Organic repression, 29, 78, 85, 119
Fukuyama, Francis, xxviii

Gadda, Carlo Emilio, 225
Gallagher, Catherine, 191, 194*n*
Gallese, Vittorio, xxix
Garibaldi, Giuseppe, 2–3, 14*n*
Gender, 2, 8–9, 12, 23–24, 26, 34*n*, 40, 43, 47–48, 53–55*n*, 137, 139, 144*n*, 155*n*, 163, 167–68, 180, 182, 185, 188–89, 201, 206, 211*n*
Gentile, Giovanni, 4
Giardina, Andrea, 60
Giglioli, Daniele, 161
Ginzburg, Natalia, 125*n*, 131, 143*n*
Giorgio, Adalgisa, 131
Girard, René, xv–xvi

Gnoseology, xxviii, 30, 76, 145. *See also* Epistemology
Goats, 12–13, 43–47, 52–53n, 54n, 75, 85, 103, 170, 203, 233–41, 243–46, 247–48n
Godwin, William, 182
Gogol, Nikolai, 9, 75, 85
Gordon, Robert, 112, 125n
Goss, Sarah, 192
Gothic, 11, 162, 179–80, 192, 194n
Ecogothic, 11, 179, 193n
Gramsci, Antonio, 2, 4, 211n
Greene, Naomi, 121, 123
Grosz, Elizabeth, 47, 53n
Guattari, Félix, 10, 79, 130–32, 137, 139, 142, 143n, 228. *See also* Deleuze, Gilles

Haraway, Donna J., 57, 66–67, 70, 71n, 162, 166, 169, 171, 217–19, 225–26, 228, 235–37, 239–41
Companion species, 71n, 166–67, 169, 171, 240
Natureculture, 217, 219, 221, 240
Hauser, Marc, 70n
Hayles, N. Katherine, 52, 113
Hegel, Georg Wilhelm Friedrich (Hegelian), 50–51, 120
Heidegger, Martin, 4, 27, 30–31, 33, 62, 104, 106n, 135, 206, 212n
Henderson, Andrea, 185, 193n
Holocaust, 10, 100, 112, 116, 125n, 135, 147. *See also* Concentration camps
Horses, 24, 143, 182, 194n
Human-animal divide, 6, 10, 87, 93–95, 98, 101–5, 212n, 242
Humanism, xviii–xix, xxi, xxiii–xxvi, xxviii, 3, 5, 8–11, 14n, 26–27, 39–41, 47–48, 50, 111–12, 114–17, 124, 125n, 136, 145–46, 148, 155n, 160–61, 169, 198, 206, 211–12n, 215, 228, 234, 239, 244–46. *See also* Posthumanism
Hurley, Kelly, 192

Hybridization, xiv–xv, xvii–xix, xxi–xxiii, xxv, xxvii–xxviii, xxi–xxii, 6–8, 10–13, 32, 63–64, 94, 145–46, 148, 151, 155, 156n, 161–62, 164–65, 167, 169, 184–85, 194n, 215–21, 223, 225–26, 228–29, 241, 245–46

Iovino, Serenella, 5, 7–8, 12, 198–99, 211n, 215–32, 233–34, 246, 247n

James, William, 30–33
Janaczek, Helena, 172
Jay, Martin, 163
Jousse, Marcel, xvi–xviii

Kafka, Franz, 9, 15n, 75–76, 81, 85, 136, 140
Kerner, Aaron, 112
Ketterer, David, 160
Klossowski, Pierre, 117
Kojève, Alexandre, 50, 52
Kristeva, Julia, 45
Kúlka, Tomas, 116
Kundera, Milan, 116

Lacan, Jacques, 45
Lakhous, Amara, 13
Landolfi, Tommaso, xxvi, 9, 54n, 69, 71n, 75–91
"Agitated Words" [*Parole in agitazione*], 88
Cancroregina [*Cancerqueen*], 71n, 75, 86–87
"The Cockroach Sea" [*Il mar delle blatte*], 80–81, 85
"The Death of the King of France" [*La morte del re di Francia*], 80–81, 85–87, 89
"Fable" [*Favola*], 76, 82
"Fear" [*La paura*], 77, 79
"The Fisherman's Beer" / "The Sinner's Coffin" [*La Biere du Pecheur*], 79, 81
"Gogol's Wife" [*La moglie di Gogol*], 85

"Hands" [*Mani*], 77–79, 81, 89
"Kafka's Daddy" [*Il babbo di Kafka*], 81, 85, 89
"Maria Giuseppa," 76–77, 86, 89
The Moon Stone [*La pietra lunare*], 75, 85
"New Insights into the Human Psyche: The Man from Manheim" [*Nuove rivelazioni della psiche umana. L'uomo di Manheim*], 77, 82
Rien Va, 88
"The Storm" [*La tempesta*], 76–77, 82
"The Stroll" [*La passeggiata*], 88–89
"The Tale of the Werewolf" [*Il racconto del lupo mannaro*], 86
The Two Spinsters [*Le due zittelle*], 81–85, 87
"Violet Tone of Death" [*Viola di morte*], 89
"The Wax Tooth" [*Il dente di cera*], 86–87
"Week of Sunshine" [*Settimana di sole*], 76, 87, 89
Latour, Bruno, 217–19
Lautréamont, Comte de, 9, 76, 80, 82
Lee, Paula Young, 181, 193n
Leopardi, Giacomo, xxiii–xxv, xxxi$n$, xxxiii$n$, 76, 208
Levi, Carlo, 11–12, 197–214
  Christ Stopped at Eboli [*Cristo si è fermato a Eboli*], 198–99, 201–7, 210, 211n
  A Face that Resembles Us [*Un volto che ci somiglia*], 210
  Fear of Freedom [*Paura della libertà*], 198–200, 205, 211n
  Fear of Painting [*Paura della pittura*], 205
  Fleeting Rome [*Roma fuggitiva*], 208
  The Peasant and the Watch [*Il contadino e l'orologio*], 200
  The Reasons of the Mice [*Le ragioni dei topi*], 207–10, 212n
  The Watch [*L'orologio*], 197, 200, 207, 211n
Levinas, Emmanuel, 27–28, 125n
Lippit, Akira Mizuta, 32, 94, 244
Lizards, 27, 30, 33, 146, 148, 208
Lollini, Massimo, 14n
Lombroso, Cesare, xxxiii$n$, 194n
Lorenz, Konrad, xv, xxix$n$
Luchte, James, 242
Lundblad, Michael, 13n
Luperini, Romano, 24, 34n, 36n, 71n
Luzi, Mario, 9–10, 93, 95–100, 102–6, 106n
  "And the Wolf" [*E il lupo*], 97, 104
  "Between Night and Day" [*Tra notte e giorno*], 98
  "Fog" [*Nebbia*], 98
  "Fragility" [*Fragilità*], 96
  "In One Point" [*In un punto*], 98
  "Invocation" [*Invocazione*], 97
  "Man—or Shadow," 95–96
  "Me Abjure? Who Can Say" [*Abiura io? Chi può dirlo*], 98
  "Serenade in Azeglio Square" [*Serenata in Piazza d'Azeglio*], 97
  "Terrace" [*Terrazza*], 97–98
  "Where Are You? I Can't Find You" [*Dove sei? Non ti trovo*], 99
Lyotard, Jean-François, 22, 79, 90n

MacHugh, David E., 237–38, 241
Macpherson, C. V., 113
Maggi, Armando, 119, 122–23
Malthus, Thomas (Malthusian), 11, 180, 190–92, 194n
Manganelli, Giorgio, 60
Manghetti, Gloria, 96
Maran, Timo, 229n
Marchesini, Roberto, xiii–xxxvi, 6–8, 57, 59, 70, 94–95, 105, 106n, 146, 149, 151, 155, 155–57n, 219, 236, 239, 245
  Anthropopoiesis, xiv, xvii–xviii, xxviii$n$, 57–58, 94

Marchesini, Roberto (*continued*)
  Eccentration, xv, xvii–xx, xxii–xxiv, xxxiv$n$
  Mestizoization, xiv, xxix$n$
  Mimesis, xiii–xxvi, xxviii$n$, xxx$n$, xxxii$n$
  Ontopoiesis, xv, xvii–xix, xxiii
  Zoomimesis, xxvii, 94–95
Marcus, Millicent, 126n
Marrone, Gaetana, 125, 126n
Marx, Karl, 123
Maternity, 9, 39–41, 44–45, 47–48, 52, 54n, 55n, 122, 131, 134, 136–38, 144n, 163–64, 182–85, 187–89, 243
Matricide, 9, 39, 47–49, 163
Maurizi, Marco, 105
Maxia, Sandro, 24, 30–31, 36n
Mazzini, Giuseppe, 2, 13n
Mazzoni, Cristina, 188, 194n
McLane, Maureen Noelle, 183
Meat. *See* Carnivorism
Mediterranean, 6–7, 16, 204–6, 241
Meeker, Joseph, 167–68, 174n
Mehlman, Maxwell J., 165
Menechella, Grazia, 188
Merry, Bruce, 65
Metempsychosis, 9, 62, 65, 67–68, 241
Mice, 29, 59, 77–79, 89, 207–10
Modernism, 22, 26, 33, 42, 85, 163, 197, 205
Monkeys, xxix$n$, 11, 81–85, 87, 152–54
Monstrosity, 11, 32, 41, 65, 80–81, 155n, 160–65, 172, 179–84, 187–92, 193–94n, 203, 207
Montale, Eugenio, 9, 57–73, 76, 173n
  "The Animals" [*Gli animali*], 58–59
  "Annetta," 66
  "*L'arca*," 60
  "The Badger" [*Schiappino*], 62, 70n, 71n
  "The Bat" [*Il pipistrello*], 62, 65–67
  "*La belle dame sans merci II*," 62
  "*La busacca*," 69
  "The Capercaillie" [*Il gallo cedrone*], 65, 71n
  "Clizia in Foggia" [*Clizia a Foggia*], 62, 67–69
  "The Condemned" [*Il condannato*], 66–68
  "The Eel" [*L'Anguilla*], 64
  "The Hope of Even Seeing You Again" [*La speranza di pure rivederti*], 63
  "I Have Never Understood Whether I Was" [*Non ho mai capito se io fossi*], 60
  "Kingfisher," 61–62
  "The Ligurian Beach" [*Una spiaggia in Liguria*], 69–70, 71n
  "One Must Prefer" [*Si deve preferire*], 62
  "The Prisoner's Dream" [*Il sogno del prigioniero*], 62–63
Montanari, Massimo, 193n
Morante, Elsa, 10, 12, 129–44
  Aracoeli, 12, 132, 137–42
  Arturo's Island [*L'isola di Arturo*], 132, 134
  History [*La Storia*], 132–33, 135–37, 139–43
  House of Liars [*Menzogna e sortilegio*], 132
  The World Saved by Children [*Il mondo salvato dai ragazzini*], 132–33
Moravia, Alberto, 59, 125n, 143n, 173n
Morelli, Giorgio C., 97
Moretti, Franco, 157n
Mori, Masahiro, 174n
Mortimer-Sandilands, Catriona, 238, 240–41, 246
Muraro, Luisa, 4, 8, 14n, 41, 47–48, 55n
Murray, Les, 59

Nazism, 5, 10, 100, 111–12, 116–17, 124, 125–26n, 135–36, 168, 197, 240
Negri, Antonio, 4, 14n, 15n
Neocapitalism, 113, 157n

Neorealism, 115
Nietzsche, Friedrich, 117–18
Nussbaum, Martha, 28

Oppermann, Serpil, 216
Ortese, Anna Maria, xxviii, 1, 13
Orwell, George, 170–71, 174*n*
Otter, Chris, 193*n*

Palazzeschi, Aldo, 82
Papini, Maria Carla, 152, 154
Parati, Graziella, 238–39, 245
Pasolini, Pier Paolo, xxvi–xxvii, 10, 111–13, 115, 117–24, 125*n*, 131–32, 134, 143–44*n*, 156*n*, 209, 212*n*
   Salò, or the 120 Days of Sodom [*Salò o le 120 giornate di Sodoma*], 10, 111–13, 115–25
   Trilogy of Life (*Decameron, Canterbury Tales, Arabian Nights*), 113, 119
Pavese, Cesare, 9, 12, 39–56
   Dialogues with Leucò [*Dialoghi con Leucò*], 40
   The Harvesters [*Paesi tuoi*], 39, 42–48, 53*n*, 54*n*
   The House on the Hill [*La casa in collina*], 39, 44, 47–49, 55*n*
   The Moon and the Bonfires [*La lunà e i falò*], 39, 44, 47–49, 51, 53–54*n*
Payne, Mark, 59
Perec, Georges, 216–17
Perniola, Mario, 166
Petroni, Franco, 22, 35*n*, 26*n*
Piaget, Jean, xiv
Picasso, Pablo, 205
Pick, Anat, 113
Pickering, Andrew, 215, 219
Pico della Mirandola, Giovanni, 155, 157*n*
Pincio, Tommaso, 159
Plato (Platonic), xiii, xxxiii*n*, 14*n*, 60, 136, 228
Pliny the Elder, 218

Poe, Edgar Allan, 83, 85
Posthistory, 39–41, 48–52, 121, 124
Posthumanism, xxiv–xxviii, xxxiv*n*, 6, 8–12, 39–41, 51–52, 57, 64–65, 103–5, 111, 113, 118–21, 125, 145–47, 154–55, 155*n*, 160–61, 164–66, 169–70, 172, 206, 215–21, 223–29, 230*n*, 234–35, 239, 244–46
Pratesi, Fulco, 233, 238, 247*n*
Prehistory, xxvii, 9, 15*n*, 40–41, 51, 54*n*
Preti, Giulio, xxxiii*n*
Proietti, Salvatore, 159
Pseudo-Longinus, xxxi*n*
Pugno, Laura, 11–12, 159–61, 163–71, 174*n*
   Sirens [*Sirene*], 11, 160–65, 167–70, 172, 174*n*
Pulcini, Elena, xvi
Pythagoras (Pythagorean), 68–69, 241–42, 246

Rabelais, François, 150
Racism (Race), 26, 40, 53*n*, 100, 152, 162, 168, 239
Ravetto, Kriss, 111, 115, 117
Re, Lucia, 144*n*
Remotti, Francesco, xiv, xxviii*n*, xxxi*n*
Rich, Adrienne, 41
Richardson, Ruth, 181
Rinaldi, Rinaldo, 122
Risorgimento, 2
Rizzolatti, Giacomo, xxix
Rizzoli, Lisa, 97
Rohman, Carrie, 26, 215–16
Rowe, Stephanie, 182
Rushing, Robert, 165, 169, 173*n*

Saccone, Eduardo, 35*n*
Sade, Marquis du, 117
Saint Girons, Baldine, xxi, xxiii
Santner, Eric L., 114–15, 118–20, 124
   Creatureliness, 10, 111–15, 118–20, 122, 124
Savinio, Alberto, 76, 85

Schmitt, Karl, 101, 136
Schoonover, Karl, 115
Science fiction, 152, 159–60, 172, 173*n*
Scotellaro, Rocco, 210, 211*n*
Seaman, Myra J., 112–13, 118
Senhal, 59–60, 63–64
Severino, Emanuele, 55*n*
Shannon, Laurie, 242
Shelley, Mary, 179, 182–84, 190–91, 193*n*, 194*n*
    Frankenstein; or, The Modern Prometheus, 11, 179–87, 190, 192, 193*n*
Shepard, Paul, 57
Showalter, Elaine, 188
Sica, Paola, 63
Simons, John, 57, 61, 67
Singer, Peter, 14*n*
Slaughterhouse, 11, 23, 167, 181–82, 193*n*
Sloterdijk, Peter, xxviii
Solazzo, Delia, 238
Soper, Kate, 238
Southern Italy, 11, 198–205, 207, 210, 211*n*
Speciesism, xxvii, 9–10, 40, 43–44, 50, 53*n*, 58, 93–94, 98–99, 101–2, 104–6, 184, 189, 192
Spiders, xix, 7, 9, 67–69, 80–82, 85–87, 89, 247*n*
Spinoza, Baruch, 141–42, 227
Stavick, J. E. D., 188
Steiner, Wendy, 201, 211*n*
Stiglegger, Marcus, 125*n*
Stoker, Bram, 179–80, 183, 187, 191–92, 193*n*, 194*n*
    Dracula, 11, 179–80, 183, 186–87, 189–92, 194*n*
    "The Dualitists, or, The Death Doom of the Double Born," 187
Sullivan, Heather I., 243, 248*n*
Swift, Jonathan, 191, 194*n*
Symmons, Michael, 126*n*

Tarchetti, Igino Ugo, 11, 179, 187–88, 191, 194–95*n*
    Fosca, 11–12, 179–80, 186, 186–92, 194*n*
    "Hunger" [*La fame*], 191
Teratology, 162
Theriomorphosis, xxvii, xxxii*n*, 9, 59, 64–65, 71*n*, 75–76, 82–83, 85–86, 88–89, 95, 98–99, 106, 152
Thoreau, Henry David, 229
Todorov, Tzvetan, xxvi, xxxiv*n*
Tonutti, Sabrina, xxx–xxxi*n*, 57
Toscano, Alberto, 4, 14*n*
Tozzi, Federigo, 8–9, 12, 21–38
    Adele, 21–23, 34–36*n*
    The Farm [*Il podere*], 23–25, 34–36*n*
    Memories of an Employee [*Ricordi di un impiegato*], 28–29
    Three Crosses [*Tre croci*], 24, 29, 34–35*n*
    With Eyes Closed [*Con gli occhi chiusi*], 23–24, 31–33, 34–36*n*
Trama, Paolo, 82, 84
Transhumance, 241, 246, 247–48*n*
Trasatti, Filippo, 248*n*
Tronti, Mario, 4
Turtles, 13, 208, 217

Uncanny, 21–22, 31–32, 118–20, 167, 174*n*

Vampirism, 65, 71*n*, 186–91
Vegetarianism, 179, 181–84, 190–91, 193*n*, 242
Vico, Giambattista, 15*n*
Virilio, Paul, xxvi, xxxiv*n*
Volponi, Paolo, xxvii, 10–12, 145–58, 173*n*
    Corporeal [*Corporale*], 11, 146–52, 154, 157*n*
    The Green Lizard [*Il ramarro*], 146
    The Irritable Planet [*Il pianeta irritabile*], xxvii, 11, 146, 152–55, 173*n*
    My Troubles Began [*Memoriale*], 147
    The Old Coin [*L'antica moneta*], 146
    The World-Wide Machine [*La macchina mondiale*], 147

Von Hofmannsthal, Hugo, 79, 82, 84–85
Vrettos, Athena, 180, 193n
Vygotsky, Lev Semyonovich, xv

Wallace, Jeff, 113
Waller, Marguerite, 124
Wheeler, Wendy, 219–20, 228, 229n
Wittgenstein, Ludwig, 129
Wittig, Joseph, 114, 117, 125n
Wolfe, Cary, 1–3, 8, 13, 14n, 113, 154, 219
Wolpert, Lewis, xxxiin
World War II, 8, 10, 62, 111, 135, 140, 147. *See also* Nazism
Wulf, Christoph, xxxiin
Wu Ming 1, 160, 173n, 174n
Wu Ming 5, 11, 159–61, 166–71
   Free Karma Food, 11, 160, 162, 165–70, 172, 174n
Wu Ming collective, 159, 174n

Zambon, Franco, 65
Zapf, Hubert, 198
Žižek, Slavoj, 121–22

GPSR Compliance

The European Union's (EU) General Product Safety Regulation (GPSR) is a set of rules that requires consumer products to be safe and our obligations to ensure this.

If you have any concerns about our products, you can contact us on

ProductSafety@springernature.com

In case Publisher is established outside the EU, the EU authorized representative is:

Springer Nature Customer Service Center GmbH
Europaplatz 3
69115 Heidelberg, Germany

www.ingramcontent.com/pod-product-compliance
Lightning Source LLC
LaVergne TN
LVHW012059070526
838200LV00074BA/3667